THE KIND OF WESTERN I'D LIKE TO READ-PART THREE

DESIRE REALIZED

BUC KEENE

THE KIND OF WESTERN I'D LIKE TO READ-PART THREE
DESIRE REALIZED
by BUC KEENE

Printed in the United States of America

ISBN 9781628711523

www.xulonpress.com

Hope deferred maketh the heart sick:
but when the desire cometh,
it is a tree of life.

PROVERBS. 13:12

To all the great folks who like to read *the kind of western I like to read*.

Special thanks to Martha Ireland for her help in preparing this manuscript for publication and to my wife Janis, for her patience, inspiration, and enthusiastic interest in this yarn.

Author's Introduction To Part Three

There are loves and even dalliances in most stories and songs, but once in a while a great love story or song comes along. . . one that lifts our hearts to sing, draws us up into the magic and wonder of that kind of loving, and releases us with a knowing smile as to what at least part of that kind of loving is all about. I hope you know love like that.

Buc Keene

Other Xulon Books by Buc Keene

The Kind of Western I'd Like to Read
East of the Pecos
Part One

The Kind of Western I'd Like to Read
Hope Deferred
Part Two

CONTENTS

Chapter One

Across the River

Spring, 1869

Malo Cactus cocked his head to one side and listened. The half-breed had slid from his horse and paused near a wild plum thicket to relieve himself. There it was again—a low groan. Warily he slid an arrow from his quiver and nocked it, then moved stealthily toward the sound.

Malo Cactus was the son of a Comanche warrior and a kidnapped Mexican girl, and although he had grown up Comanche, he commanded the respect of neither his father's people nor of his mother's. Now in his declining years, he had been relegated to the role of an arbitrator, a go-between with the Indians and the Mexican Comancheros; the traders from south of the border who bartered with the Comanche. He had been riding to meet one of these traders near the mouth of the Pecos. He was to arrange a rendezvous with a band of Comanche who held three white captives, up on the Llano Estacado, and was to try to set up a trade for the new repeating rifles of the white man.

The breed stood staring at the naked man lying in the bushes. The man appeared to be dead, apparently robbed and then dumped here; perhaps the sound he had heard had been his dying breath. Malo Cactus crept closer and prodded the man in the back with his arrow. There came another low moan; he was alive. The half-breed looked him over, appraising the strong and well muscled form and an idea struck him. The Comancheros paid well for strong young men to work in the mines of the Sierra Madre in Old Mexico.

Quickly, he put the arrow in his quiver and hurried to his horse for the water skin that hung there. He might make a good trade with this one, maybe for a fine horse and gun and one of the Long Knives' blue coats with the shiny brass buttons. Then he would command respect in the village, he might even be given a woman. . . a pretty, young one, to warm his blanket on long winter nights.

He pulled the unconscious man from the brush. There was a knot on his head, and dried blood had dribbled from his left ear. The man groaned again when Malo Cactus lifted him, with an arm under his shoulders, and then gave him some water from the skin. The white-eyes choked and groaned, turning his head away. The half-breed dropped him back to the grass. Finding a leather thong, he bound the man's hands in front of him. Bringing up his horse, he grunted and pushed until he hefted the dead weight of the younger man up and draped him over his pony, face down. Passing a rawhide rope under the horse, he secured his captive's hands and feet, then taking the lead, he walked the pony from the glade in a south-easterly direction. The unshod pony left little impression in the grassy turf of that place.

Two days latter, he was sitting besides a small fire and heating water in a bowl he had fashioned from green leaves and set carefully on the hot stones next to the flames. He was shaving bark from a willow into the water, and watching his captive. The white man sat leaning against a tree, the Indian's blanket hanging loosely from his shoulders and a white band torn from the breed's shirt, wrapped about his head. His eyes were dull and listless, staring at the ground, unseeing. For two days the man had moaned and tried to reach his head with both hands, whenever they stopped.

Malo Cactus had managed to get a mixture of willow water and mescal down him, which seemed to have a calming effect, but now the breed was concerned for his captive's strength. The man had not eaten anything, and if he lost weight and was too weak, the Comancheros would pay next to nothing for him.

The half-breed slipped out of camp with his bow and arrow and returned with a rabbit. He ripped off its fir and gutted it, then spitted the fresh meat over the coals of his small fire. He had dug a couple agave plants and roasted the roots the day before, these he pounded into a meal and mixing that with water, he placed the flat dough on a hot stone to bake. Within thirty minutes he had the willow tea poured down the gringo's throat. Unresisting, the man drank methodically of the liquid, after Malo Cactus pinched his nose and pulled his head back. Now he was mechanically munching a tortilla and some roast rabbit. The half-breed grunted in satisfaction and returned to eating his own meager meal. The white-eyes was giving him no problem. "Bueno," he said, "bueno."

By the third day, the man had improved noticeably and Malo Cactus traded places with him on the horse. With his feet unbound, the younger man, trotted along behind, his hands still tied to a lead rope held by the rider. He offered little resistance, except for when he stepped on a thorn or sand burr with his bare feet, and then he would yowl, fall down, and attempt to dislodge it from his foot. This usually resulting in his being drug until Malo Cactus could get his pony stopped. He would stop the horse and wait while the man pulled the thorns from his feet. He began to call him "Wakaree-ty" for he was as slow as a turtle.

That evening Malo Cactus presented Wakaree-ty with a new pair of fur lined moccasins made from rabbit skins, in hopes of making better time. Wakaree-ty put them on without saying a word and seemed oblivious of the change. Malo Cactus thought he must be one of the crazy ones and that was why the white-eyes had thrown him away. This was all the better, no one would be looking for him, and he did not need a good head to work in the mines.

The afternoon of the fifth day, having avoided the small settlement of Del Rio, Malo Cactus and Wakaree-ty were sitting on a sandbar at the mouth of the Pecos River at it's juncture with the Rio Grand. The half-breed watched a mule train and two wagons making its way along the Mexican side, to a point opposite him, where it then stopped. A fat Mexican with a big mustache that drooped down around the corners of his mouth, waved a hand to him, and he waved back. He motioned for Wakaree-ty to mount, then getting up behind him; he kicked his horse out into the current and crossed over to the waiting caravan.

"Senor Bad Cactees," the Mexican said, "wha' du ju hab heer?"

"Wakaree-ty, him heap crazy. Me find, me trade for bueno caballo, new gun, long knife and blue shirt with brass button."

"Ai caramba! Ju expect me to traï' all dees for wan crassie gringo? Ju maus be crassie jorself."

"Huh! Wakaree-ty no probleemo—heap good work—strong lak el toro—you bet."

Malo Cactus pushed the white man off the back of his horse to land in a cloud of dust. For an instant, fire flashed in Wakaree-ty's eyes, then his dull manner returned and he got slowly to his feet.

"He ees no good—he has no espíritu—no wan weel waun heem, I geeb ju wan caballo, that ees all."

"Huh! No need espíritu to work mine. Heap good no one want. Him throw away gringo—no one look. Him strong, him young—work lak hell long time in mine, you bet. Give bueno caballo, bueno boom-boom, bueno blue shirt, make Malo Cactus important chief."

The Comanchero looked the youth over. He was indeed young and strong and would be worth any two of the other, pathetic captives he had. He haggled with the half-breed for over an hour but in the end Malo Cactus was given a fifteen year old gelding, an old single-shot breech load rifle with ten cartridges, and a staff sergeant's blue shirt from the 4th Cavalry. The owners of Tayopa, Guaynopa and Guaynopita mines would pay well for this young man. . . if no one was looking for him, so much the better. After making arrangements to meet again in the new moon and take the Comanchero to the Comanche camp, Malo Cactus mounted his new horse and leading the other, rode back across the river, leaving the crazy white-eyes with the trader.

Domingo Diaz stood pulling his mustache and watched Malo Cactus ride across the river, and then turned to the naked youth.

"Ju maus geet some breeches on, there are senoritas on thee wagons." He walked to one of the wagons covered with canvas stretched over hoops, and rummaged around in the back. He returned with a thin pair of peasant pants, shirt and thonged sandals. "Poot dees on," he said and tossed them to where the white man sat. "Wha deed ju say jor name was, Waka-ty? Dees ees too hart, I jus call ju Tye." Diaz stepped in front of him and cut loose the rope binding his hands.

The man he called Tye, just stared at the clothing lying on the sand, but at the Mexican's urging, he bent and slowly pulled on the pants and the shirt, buttoning it up. With the sandals on his sore feet, he was led over to one of the wagons and told to get inside. Vacantly, he looked at the fat Mexican, who lost patience and rudely pushed him into the back of the wagon.

"Ju ride een dare and leab the senoritas alone," Domingo growled.

Tye tumbled into the darkened interior amongst the feet and bodies of other prisoners. It took several minutes for his eyes to adjust from the glare of the bright sunlight outside. Two boys around ten years of age and three girls in their early teens, all Mexican, were huddled together on one side of the wagon. On the other side, was a white girl about sixteen. She sat with a forlorn look on her face, but brightened momentarily on seeing that Tye was a white man. She then lost hope again, when he failed to respond to her questions. He found a spot and rode in silence as the caravan started out, the wagon jouncing over the rough trail.

The caravan Domingo Diaz was leading followed in a westerly direction along the Rio Grande. They traveled for several days when a hail storm caused them to pull up in the shelter of some oak and cottonwood trees, to wait out the punishing weather. In this rough country, farms and villages were few and far between, and these they avoided. When a settlement was encountered, Diaz would leave his Mexican drovers in charge, and ride in for a night of tequila and senoritas. He would return from these bouts in a surly mood and strike out with a leather quirt at any of his captives who were not quick to respond to his orders.

Once, when he lashed the youth called Tye, the white lad caught the quirt and jerked it from the Mexican's grasp, but he had it thonged about his wrists. When Domingo grabbed the handle and hauled back, his captive, who had been blankly staring at the whip in his hand, let go, and Diaz stumbled backwards to land on his fat rump in the dirt. There was a chorus of laughter from the other drovers, until he turned a menacing eye in their directions. Hurriedly they turned to other tasks.

Diaz got laboriously to his feet and walked over to Tye and raised his arm to strike him a vicious blow, when the white girl screamed and rushed in between them. Tye stood mildly by and watched as the big Mexican grabbed the girl by her hair to fling her aside, and then went after her with the whip.

"Ju leetle speet-fire, I teech ju na to eenterfeer."

The girl was scooting backwards on the ground trying to avoid him, then turned, to rise to her feet and run away, but not before Diaz lashed her across her legs and bottom a couple of times.

The days wore on and whenever there was a steep hill to climb, the captives were made to get out and walk with their feet unbound, although their hands were kept tied. Noon and afternoon siestas brought stops and meager meals; mostly of rice, beans and tortillas. Night times were spent huddled together in the wagon against the cold, the white girl seeking the comfort and warmth of Tye's body, under a scant Indian blanket and the Mexican girls and boys, likewise, bundled together.

The girl's name was Sarah. She talked to Tye, but got no response from him other than his acceptance of her. She decided he must be an imbecile and couldn't speak, but it was comforting to talk to him just the same. She proceeded to tell how she had been taken by the Comanche from her home along the Trinity River, after she had wandered too far into the woods picking blackberries. The Indians had immediately taken her across the border and traded her off to Domingo Diaz, and she had been traveling west with him ever since.

"I know mama and poppa must be worried about me and may even think I'm dead. Oh, how I wish you could understand, you could help me escape and get back home. I think Domingo Diaz intends to sell us to work in some mines down in Mexico. I heard we were to go to El Paso Del Norte first."

They skirted south of the Big Bend country, keeping on the Mexican side to avoid any chance encounter with what Diaz called the "Yankee soldados," who patrolled the Old Military Route north of the river.

Once Diaz saw that he passively accepted and followed orders, Tye was allowed more freedom. Diaz assigned him camp chores of cutting wood, hauling water, and helping with the stock. It was obvious to the trader that the youth was not in his right mind, but seemed to know how to do things. He wondered that he never spoke and considered him a mute.

Sarah took Tye into her confidence and spent long hours talking to him and explaining her gathering fears as to what might become of them.

"I don't like the way Diaz and the others look at me," she said one day. "I think they prowl about to spy on me whenever I go off into the brush or bathe in the river. Tye, would you please stand watch the next time I take a bath?"

Tye just looked at her. She saw just the hint of a frown crease his brow for an instant, before the blank stare returned. They were sitting with their backs against a shade tree while the rest of the camp was in siesta. Sarah's hands were bound but her feet were untied and Tye had not been bound up for several days. An ant crawled up Sarah's bare leg to disappear under her thin dress.

"Oh," she said, startled, "Tye, there's a bug on me." She jumped up and, turning away, pulled up her dress to reveal her body underneath.

"Get it off of me," she said.

For a moment he stood staring at her, then looked up into her face, puzzled. The ant was crawling along the backside of her thigh towards her bottom when Tye reached out a finger, cocked it against his thumb and snipped the ant off of her leg. Sarah, blushing in embarrassment, dropped her skirt and stood looking down at him.

"Bug!" he said and for a brief moment, he smiled.

"You can talk?" Sarah forgot her embarrassment in the excitement of this discovery. She sat back down and took Tye's hand. Touching his finger, she said, "finger." He stared at her uncomprehending.

"Finger," she repeated.

Finally he said, "Finger."

The girl giggled happily. "Nose," she touched his nose.

"Nose," he repeated, and then felt of his nose. He seemed surprised to find it there. "Nose," he said again, and reached a hand to touch Sarah's nose.

She giggled and touched his eye. "Eye," she said.

"Eye," he copied her and touched her eye. Somewhere a curtain was pulled back from over his clouded mind and for the next several minutes, the girl touched and named things and Tye responded, naming each item perfectly. After that, like a small child at his lessons, Sarah tutored him, teaching him to say short sentences.

The incongruity of it all was amusing to watch, the small white girl leading the bigger white boy about, naming things. Domingo Diaz and the rest of the drivers laughed at the pair of them over the next few days.

"Bueno, ees goot, the leetle senorita teech thee turtle to talk. Maybee he weel be worth more dinero," Diaz muttered to himself, "jus as lonk as he doan geet no brigh' ideas."

Tye's recall of things gradually came back to him, but he seemed to have little understanding of who he was, where they were, or what was going on. Once when Sarah had been talking to him about the need to escape, he told Domingo to help Sarah escape.

Diaz flew into a rage and jerked the poor girl about by her hair and slapped her with his big hands.

"Ju no eescape," he yelled. "I feex ju so ju canna go back."

Like an innocent child, Tye stood by watching in confusion, as the Mexican pushed and shoved the girl into the back of one of the wagons, then clumsily crawled his great bulk in after her. Tye could hear the girl screaming and crying while the wagon rocked back and forth, then her cries were reduced to sobs. The other drovers gave each other knowing looks and grinned.

Troubled, Tye walked slowly to the wagon and peered inside. He saw Sarah lying spread-eagled on the floor of the wagon, her hands and legs tied to the sides and her dress gone. Diaz was on his knees, unbuckling his pants.

Puzzled, Tye spoke. "What are you doing?"

"Beat it imbecil," the Mexican growled.

"Tye, help," Sarah cried.

Tye climbed inside the front of the wagon and suddenly Diaz tumbled out of the back end with his pants below his knees. He landed flat on his back out cold. Tye had kicked him in the face.

"You don't hurt Suzanne," he said. He turned to untie the crying girl and hand her the torn dress.

For a week, Tye lay in the back of the wagon, his back a mass of inflamed welts from where the whip had cut him. Sarah bathed his feverish brow and attended to the cuts on his back with the soothing juice of the aloe vera plant.

Domingo Diaz's nose was broken and one eye was still swollen nearly shut. When he had regained consciousness, he had his men take the child-like gringo and strip him of his shirt, then tie him to a wagon wheel. Staggering to his feet, he had proceeded to whip him with his leather quirt until he collapsed in exhaustion, even though Tye did not cry out. Tye was eventually untied and shoved into the back of a wagon where the other captives sat huddled in fear. Sarah was left to tend to him, unhindered by Diaz, while the caravan moved on.

They were less than a day's journey from El Paso Del Norte, when Diaz called a halt by the river. This was the place he was to meet up with his contacts from the Sierra Madre. The lost mines of Tayopa were somewhere west of the Sonora-Chihuahua border. Lost in the rugged peaks of Espinoza Del Diablo—the Devil's Backbone—was the hidden canyon of the Rio Aros and the legendary lost gold and silver mines of the Conquistadors.

In 1742, an Indian associated with Cristobel Rodriguez, a Spanish explorer who was searching for the Perdió mines, rediscovered the mines and reopened them. By 1762, the mines and settlement were abandoned due to the hostilities of the Indians, and now, it being a favorite haunt of Geronimo, the area, for the most part, remained lost in antiquity, for neither Mexican nor whites dared enter these wild canyons without a large, armed escort.Diaz knew all of this and was only too happy to turn his captives and supplies over to others. Let someone else worry about the location and the malo Indians, "Ah jus want mío dinero and to geet on back for thee next load," he muttered. He would exchange his loaded mules for the unloaded string the "Silenciosos," the silent ones, would be bringing and then he would get the hell out of there.

"Eef the gringos like thees captives, especially the leetle white senorita and thee imbecil, I make mucho dinero," he said to himself.

"Before supper, I waun thee senoritas to geet washed up and dressed een thee fine clothes we brought. Juse soap and wash jor hair and comb out thee nits. We maus make ju preseentable for the caballeros who come for ju tomorrow. Imbecil, ju help dem."

The captives were all marched down to the shallows of the Rio Grand, stripped of their clothing, and ordered to bathe. A bar of soap was thrust into Tye's hand and he was pushed out into the water. Domingo Diaz sat on a log on the shore, holding a shotgun and ogling the girls as they self-consciously washed and suds their hair.

Tye was oblivious of his immodest state or that of Sarah and the others, but the white girl was not. Covering her bosom and front as best she could with her hands, she hurriedly waded out into deeper water, looking for a place to duck down away from the prying eyes of her captors.

"Senorita Sarah, doan wade out too far. Ju stay close where I can keep thee eye on ju," Domingo called. Sarah paid no attention to him and continued to wade on out until the water was nearly at her waist.

"Imbecil, go and breeng her back to chor."

With his hands shading his eyes, Tye stood knee deep in the water holding the soap and looked questioningly back at Domingo, not comprehending.

"Go estupido," Diaz waved his hands towards the girl, "breeng her back."

Tye began to wade after the girl. The river flowed fairly shallow at this point, although quite wide, and Sarah was not far from the middle when she reached waist-high water and ducked down under the surface. When her head popped back up, she began soaping her hair.

Tye stopped a few yards from the girl and seeing her washing, began to soap his own head, while Domingo Diaz hollered, "Come back before I choot ju." Suddenly, a contingent of U.S. Cavalry rode into sight on the opposite side of the river.

"Tye, look!" Sarah stood up, and was pointing to the line of blue-coats that had pulled up their horses at the water's edge and sat watching the strange sight.

"It's the Yankees," she cried. "If we can make it to the middle of the river we will be back in Texas and can escape. Hurry!" She began a wading, half swimming, struggle towards the middle of the river, screaming and waving her arms. Tye just stood there confused, watching her go.

Diaz was going crazy. "Moof ju crassie gringo, ju are in thee way. Stop or I choot," he yelled at the fleeing girl. He began to run out into the shallows towards the standing white youth who watched with detachment, as the line of troops turned and rode into the water, heading for the wading girl.

"Ju crassie bastardo," Diaz said as he puffed up. "Ju let thee leetle puta escape."

The Mexican leveled the shotgun at the bobbing figure of the girl and fired. The distance was too great to be of any effect, but at the sound of the report, Sarah dove under the water and swam towards the lunging mounts of the U.S. Calvary. Diaz fired a second time, then broke open the action, while fishing in his shirt pocket for fresh shells. There were puffs of white smoke and then bullets were kicking up the water around the fat Mexican and his captive, followed by the report of the rifles.

"Ji-yi-yi," Diaz cursed. "Those damn soldados are trying to keel us. Come on, Tortuga, we maus geet back to our own side." Domingo grabbed Tye's arm and hurried him back, while the blue-coats let loose another volley. Tye stopped to look and saw Sarah reach the soldiers. One of them leaned down and pulled the girl up onto the back of his horse, then handed her a jacket.

Diaz hit the youth between the shoulder blades with the butt of the shotgun. "Muyo pronto," he yelled, "geet jor asno to chor."

They stumbled through the water towards the Mexican side of the river where the other captives waited wide-eyed. The Mexican muleskinners were lined up on the bank and were returning rifle fire at the American patrol, but were too far out of range to do any harm. The soldiers finally turned and rode back to the Texas shore, the rescued girl safe in their company.

"Son-of-a-beetch," Diaz raved. "Thee senorita cos' me tweny pieces of oro and she was steel de virgin." He fixed angry eyes on Tye as the young man walked from the water and calmly put on his clothing. "I ought to keel ju, she was almos' as valuable as ju, now ju weel have to breeng me twice as mucho dinero to make up for thee loss." The Comanchero turned and stormed off to the wagon to retrieve a bottle of tequila.

Shortly before noon the next day, an armed band of white men rode in leading a string of pack mules with empty panniers. The leader, a big man with a craggy jaw and a patch over one eye, looked over the Mexican captives and, haggling over the price, began to argue with Diaz. Finally a bargain was struck and the two boys and three girls were blindfolded, their hands tied in front, and set astride behind the other horsemen.

The big man fixed his eye on Tye and then walked around him, sizing him up. "Where'd you come up with this pumpkin roller?" he asked Diaz.

"Heem Comanche captivo, he bueno strong, good to work een thee minas. Heem hab vacar head, he no remeembers nautheeng. Ees bueno—no wan look for heem. I waun forty, ob thee tweny dollar, oro piece.

"Forty pieces of gold, why you dumb Mex, that's eight hundred dollars. You can go to hell and I might just send you there." The one-eyed man pulled his pistol and cocking it, pointed it at the fat Mexican.

"Awrigh', doan be so hasty, Senor Hutch," Diaz held up his hands. "Ju geeb me four hunert dollar and ju can hab heem."

"Ha! Fifty bucks is all he's worth, why just look at him. He can't even talk—he's dumber than a stump and doesn't know if he's afoot or horseback. I probably shouldn't even give you that—more like twenty five."

"Feefty bucks? Ji-yi-yi! He cos' me more dan dees. I pay wan good rifle, wan good caballo and wan good chert for heem. I feed heem, I clothe heem, I take care of heem when he ees seeck all dees time. I maus make thee profito or eet ees no juse to bother weeth thee captivos. I need aleese two hunert dollar."

The big man pulled out five twenty dollar gold pieces and threw them at Domingo Diaz's feet.

"That's all you're going to get out of me ya thieving greaser—take it or leave it. If you don't wanna deal with me fair n' square you can just take this dummy back to the Comanch and good riddance." Hutch turned on his heel and strode away.

Diaz knelt and picked up the gold pieces. Rising, he looked after the retreating form of the white man, a scowl on his fat face. Finally he shrugged, put the coins in his pocket and turned to Tye. Giving him a shove he said, "Go wuan, Tortuga, he weel cho ju wha' to do."

Domingo Diaz turned and climbed aboard the lead wagon and started his caravan toward the settlement.

Twenty men, each armed with two pistols, a Winchester repeating rifle and twin bandoleers of ammunition crisscrossing his chest, kept vigilant watch, as the string of mules made its way south into a broken and wild land of volcanic rock, covered with mesquite, sage and chaparral.

After a day's travel, the prisoners' blindfolds were removed and Tye sat his horse staring around at the unfamiliar terrain with no sense of comprehension. The trail they were following led upward into sparse pine trees and crossed high plateaus, intersected with ravines and washes. On the distant horizon was a serrated mountain range that the big man leading them called the *Espinazo Del Diablo*, The Devil's Backbone. Somewhere near its base was Huaynopa.

Reese Hutchins scowled as he studied the old Spanish trail that would lead them to Guaynopa Canyon and the Rio Guaynopa. Downstream of that river, and two miles south of the fabled lost city with its fabulously rich silver and gold mines, at the base of high cliffs, was the junction with the Rio Aros flowing in from the north. It was rumored that upstream somewhere were the remnants of the Guaynopita or the Little Guaynopa mine, and Reese suspected the Company had already located them for future exploitation. The Tayopa mine, with its huge vault and locked steel doors, was just a few miles from Guaynopa, and was also under development. Rumor had it that the vault contained vast amounts of gold and silver bullion kept under close guard.

Two white miners and explorers had only recently discovered the exact location of Huaynopa and had sold their discovery to New York investor J. Paul Crouse. They had reportedly been killed by the Apache after revealing its whereabouts. Now, the secret of the location was closely guarded and made known to only a few of the closest confidantes. Reese Hutchins was one of these and had been hired to lead hand-picked fighting men, to guard the supply caravans from the hostile Indians.

"If it weren't for those damned Apaches and the chickenhearted Mexicans at San Pedro, these hellish treks through this God-forsaken wilderness could be eliminated," Reese grumbled. Hutch, as he was sometimes called, was a hard-fisted, violent man who lived to conquer and dominate other men. He liked nothing better than to beat a man down with his fists and had killed several, reveling in the feel of power it gave him.

There was talk of a railroad spur to run from Chihuahua to San Pedro once the Mexican Federales and the Juaristas quit fighting and the Apaches were corralled, he mused. Then supplies could easily be brought in overland from San Pedro or even Madera, a little more than a day's journey away. The frightened villagers of Bacadehuachi and Nacori could once again work the mines, which would eliminate the need of a slave labor force. But for now, supplies had to be freighted in under armed guard and slave workers had to be bought, fed, housed and clothed all under guard, and all that cut into the profitability of the operation.

"If I could just bust into the vault some night," he mused silently, "me and the boys could overpower the guards, load up the mules with the gold and quit this miserable business once and for all. Trouble is, where would I go with all that loot? I'll have to think on it."

For now, the job was a love-hate one, for he enjoyed the authority and power he wielded over the others, but hated the long, grueling hours on the trail. He almost looked forward to skirmishes with the elusive Apache, for it at least broke up the monotony of the ride. He chuckled to himself when he thought of the trade he had made with ol' Fat's Diaz for the white guy. He had bullied the so-called Comanchero pretty good. Personally, he thought they were all way overrated.

Hutch looked with disdain at the white kid riding passively along with the others. He realized the kid showed potential for hard work and strength and wondered just how tough he might be. Too bad he was so stupid; it might be fun to take him on in a fight. As it was, the kid did what he was told and caused no trouble, and short of deliberately picking a fight with him, he could see no way to make it happen. Still, he didn't like the guy. Something didn't quite add up. He sat a horse too easily and looked to be way more capable than what he was letting on. "I'll have to let Swatch know to keep an eye on him, once he's turned over to that thick-skulled, slave driver," he said.

After three more days of travel they reached the eastern base of the Sierra Madre Mountains and began to encounter ruins in several places, evidence of the Spanish occupation and its attendant mining operations, some two-hundred years earlier. These had been more than just mines—whole towns had been built, complete with fortresses, homes, and churches. The influence of the Jesuit priests was in evidence everywhere.

They climbed Mount Toni-Vali with its concentric walls of native stone. In the distant past, the Opatas, a peaceful, settled tribe, had built these defenses against their enemies. From the peak, there was a splendid view to the west, north and southeast. Northeast of this position, Geronimo was rumored to have his Apache stronghold.

For several more days, the caravan continued south toward Guaynopa Canyon which eventually became visible below them, its vast, riven sides scarred with draws and coulees. It descended at sloping angles, to the river below. Here the ground was covered with manzanita interspersed by native grasses, the occasional agave, aloe, and yucca plants, and the ever-present prickly pear, mesquite, and chaparral. Here and there a gnarled pine lifted its twisted branches and windblown crown to the sky.

An easy descent was made down a switchback trail with scant cover. Here the guards became even warier, for it was a likely spot for ambush. To the north, a mile or so away, rose a rocky promontory that served as an Apache lookout, and even now, as they took the trail downward, puffs of white smoke floated lazily into the still air.

"Everybody look alive," Hutch called from the head of the column. "The 'Paches have spotted us, we may have to make a run for cover."

They rode with rounds chambered and hammers cocked on their rifles, but no hostiles appeared, just answering smokes off across the distant hills.

They continued down a faint trail until they reached the bottom of the switchback, and then proceeded farther down the canyon that was strewn with brush and boulders, alongside a rushing stream. Several miles farther down, the canyon widened and deepened with high, perpendicular, palisaded cliffs rising from the canyon floor to a flat-topped mesa, a thousand feet high and dark with timber. Rounding a bend of the river, they saw the first of the workings. They had reached Huaynopa—the Guaynopa mining camp.

Scattered amongst crumbling and decaying buildings of stone and adobe brick were several new adobe structures. In the center of what might be called a street, a hundred yards from the river's edge, was a long, low, wood-framed structure with a canvas roof. A tin smokestack trickled blue smoke into the air.

Mexicans and Indians worked everywhere, some tending gardens, others hauling crushed ore to twenty, working arastas, powered by mule. Many other arastas lay idle and in disrepair. The gold concentrates were run through cut stone troughs, or sluices, that carried water brought from the river through a system of canals and ditches. A series of removable, wooden lattices over burlap, served as riffles to trap values. Other workers hauled in ore and carted away tailings and slag to huge piles of the stuff in a dump at the base of the near cliff. Several clay furnaces, or ovens, belched smoke, and were being fired from piles of wood. Here the values were brought from the sluices under armed guard, into an adobe hut, where they were prepared for smelting. For every dozen or so workers—men, women and children—there stood a boss or supervisor armed with a whip, encouraging production.

From all appearances, Guaynopa was a thriving, bustling community, complete with houses, gardens, outbuildings, barns, stables and barracks. Horses and mules grazed in newly fenced fields or stood lazily switching flies in one of several corrals. Goats, pigs, and sheep were in pens behind the adobe huts, and chickens clucked about almost everywhere but the gardens, where the smaller children kept them shooed away.

A road led up through a gully, past a crumbling mission church that stood a silent sentinel of the past. It then wound its way on up around a conical mountain to end near the top at the open adit—the famed mine's portal. Mule-drawn carts, carrying ore from the mine and timbers back up, traversed the road cut out of the living rock by human hands. Workers were busy lifting the heavy chunks of ore from the wagon and breaking them up with sledgehammers into smaller pieces, to be fed to the arastas.

A new hacienda, surrounded by a covered veranda, stood on a low lying knoll in back of the pasture land overlooking the village and there were trees flourishing about the manicured grounds. A Mexican lad busied himself watering plants from a nearby irrigation ditch. Grape arbors and rose gardens garnished the exterior of the place and it had the appearance of a woman's touch, a place of cool and quite solitude in the otherwise hot, noisy, and dusty village.

The caravan stopped in front of the clapboard building while several dogs ran up to bark at the mules. The captives were hauled from the horses and led inside the dark confines of the building, where the children were handed over to an old squaw who led them away.

Tye stood gazing around the room, piled high with goods, more like a general store than anything. A Mexican stood behind a long counter and waited on two Indian women who were buying cornmeal. From a cubical office in the rear, a white man, wearing a green visor and sleeve garters, appeared to talk with Reese Hutchins.

"How'd it go Hutch?" he asked. Reese had been reaching across the counter to snag a pouch of smoking tobacco off the shelf and turned mildly to the other man.

"Pretty much without incident, L.T.," he said. "Brought your supplies and this *malo hombre*," he turned to indicate the white youth with hands tied, looking vacantly around.

The mine boss, who's name was Louis Tom Jones, said skeptically, "Where'd you pick him up? He 'pears to be a might addled."

"He is. I think somebody brained him, probably the Comanche. I bought him off'n ol' Fats Diaz for a couple hundred bucks which, I might add, I need to be reimbursed for. He claimed to have bought him from the Comanch. I think there was a white gal, too, but the dumb bean-pot let her get away."

Jones pulled out a thick wallet and handed the big drover several bills. "You think anyone's looking for him?"

"Naw, I doubt it. Seems he's got what they call amnesia or something—doesn't seem to know anything and hardly even talks. The greaser called him Wy—Tye—something. I think it was Comanch for turtle. Wouldn't matter anyways, no one's going to ever find him in this hell-hole."

"Well, turn him over to Swatch and put him to work," Jones said. "Let's get the mules unloaded."

Chapter Two

Hope dashed and the Guaynopita Mines

Late Spring, 1869

The weeks following Colt's funeral were a sad and difficult time for Suzanne. The girl constantly affirmed her conviction that Colt was alive and sought out Sonny every chance she had, to question him as to whether or not he had heard anything. His answer was always a no, and soon the cowboy began to avoid the hollow-eyed girl. Suzanne lost weight, spending long hours in her room, in prayer and fasting, when not teaching. It was only here that she found a modicum of peace and solace for her anxious heart, enabling her to continue with her teaching duties. Her students, for the most part, were a comfort to her, often bringing her a flower or apple or some other token of their simple concern and sympathy. She would smile and thank them and reassure them that Colt was alive somewhere and that all would turn out alright. These times of avowal, if nothing else, seemed to reassure her own heart.

In time folks, even the Sabers and her own parents, came to see her as one who just could not accept the awful truth of Colt's death. Heavyhearted, they merely abided her declarations of his survival, and then changed the subject. It did not take Suzanne long to realize she was being looked upon as some sort of oddity, and she ceased to voice her opinions to others. Only Kathreen remained her close confident. She kept up a regular correspondence with her friend in Saint Louis, a friend who proved to be a friend indeed. Often, at her lowest moment it seemed, a letter would arrive from the fiery redhead telling her, "Trust God and do not give up hope."

One day, during recess, Suzanne was sitting at her desk looking over some papers and since it was a warm spring day she had the window open. She overheard a couple of her students talking about people who had been captured by Indians, when one spoke of a white girl who had been rescued from the Comancheros by soldiers from Fort Bliss in El Paso. The student said there had been a white man, too, but he had not escaped.

Suzanne called the boys in, and on further questioning, learned that one boy's father had returned from Saint Gaul the day before, and had picked up the story down there. Apparently the girl was to be on the next stage coming through from the west, on her way to return to her parents on the Trinity River.

Hurriedly, Suzanne dismissed the children and went with the boy to speak to his parents. The father had little to add, but suggested she write the post commander at Fort Bliss if she needed to know more. That evening, for the first time since Colt had gone missing, she rode Checkers out to the Crossed Sabers.

"Sonny," Suzanne said, "I need you to go with me to Saint Gaul to meet the eastbound stage tomorrow. Will you?"

Sonny stood with his hat in hand, fidgeting in his mom's kitchen looking at the schoolteacher. "What for?" he said guardedly.

Suzanne set her coffee cup down on the table. "I know you all think I'm a little crazy, but I have just received word that the soldiers rescued a white girl from the Comancheros. She had waded across the Rio Grand to get away from her kidnapers and there was a white man, a captive, who did not escape, I want to go to speak with her when she comes through tomorrow on her way back to her parents. I intend to be on the morning stage to Saint Gaul. Will you go with me?" There was a pleading look in her sad eyes.

Sonny looked at his mother; there was a brief flicker of hope in her eyes. He heaved a big sigh, "Okay, I'll pick you up at your place at daylight."

The next morning Suzanne sat restlessly on the seat of the stage as it rumbled south. Sonny sat back watching the nervous girl, but saying nothing. His heart ached for her, despite the sense of loss he felt in his own heart, the loss that she must be feeling seemed overwhelming. Oh, if it were only true. . . if somehow Colt had survived, but he clenched his teeth. He had seen first hand the gruesome proof of Colt's senseless death and now, this too, all seemed so pointless.

The Wade's Landing Stage arrived at the depot in Saint Gaul about an hour before the east bound was to arrive. Suzanne and Sonny took a short stroll to look at Comanche Springs and the new irrigation canal under construction.

When the stage drew up in a cloud of dust, they watched as a slender girl with brown hair emerged from the coach and stood looking questioningly at them. They introduced themselves and learned her name was Sarah Lambert. Hurriedly, Suzanne told the girl about Colt's disappearance and asked her about the white captive she had been with.

"You mean Tye? I don't think his name was Colton, I only heard him called Tye or sometimes Turtle by Diaz, the Mexican who held us captive. He called him imbecile or estupido sometimes, too, which was totally rude—just because he didn't talk much—that wasn't right."

"What did he look like?" Suzanne asked.

"He was nice looking; blonde hair, good build, you know—strong. I think he was a little older than me but it was hard to tell; didn't have much in the way of clothes except for the peasant pajamas that mean Mexican gave him."

"What color were his eyes?"

"His eyes. . . they seemed a little bit funny—they seemed to be dark, I think."

Suzanne was crestfallen. "Did he say anything to you?"

"No, not at first, he couldn't even talk until the day the ant crawled up my dress," she chuckled, "then I heard him say, 'bug,' after that I was able to teach him a few words. He seemed to be a little tetched in the head."

"Did you see anything unusual about him—any scars or birthmarks maybe. . . like a little brown spot on the back of his neck just below his left ear?"

"Sarah shook her head. "Nope, no scars—nothing on his neck either. I saw most of him pretty well. . ." The girl hesitated and lowered her voice, looking at Sonny. "We didn't have any clothes on when I was rescued. We had been made to bathe in the river, and when I waded out so old Diaz couldn't look at me—well, Tye, he was made to bathe, too, and he just stood there in the way, between me and that horrible Mexican so he couldn't shoot without hitting him. That's how I got away. When I saw those Yankee solders, I lit out for the other side of the river. I called to Tye to come on, but he just stood there like a little lost boy, not understanding. He just didn't seem to know what to do or where he even was.

"Oh my! I must hurry to the privy before the stage leaves, will you excuse me?" The girl rushed off.

Suzanne turned to Sonny, a pleading look in her eyes. He gave her a slight smile and shook his head once.

Sarah returned and said, "Oh, one more thing. That wasn't the first time Tye helped me out. Once when Diaz was about to"—she cleared her throat—"uh, work his will on me—had me all trussed up in the wagon and all. . .well, Tye came over when I called out to him for help. Do you know, he climbed into that wagon and kicked that Mex in the face and knocked him clean out of the wagon with his pants below his knees. 'Don't hurt her.' That's what he said: 'Don't hurt her.' I wish you could have seen it. I think it surprised everybody. I was scared half to death, but it sure surprised me, and saved me from being ruined, too, although I doubt he knew it. It cost him a beating with the whip that nearly killed him, but Diaz never tried that again.

"Oh, look! They are boarding the coach, I gotta go. It was nice talking to you, and I hope you find Colton. I'm afraid Tye was not him. Goodbye." She ran for the stagecoach and disappeared inside.

On the return trip, Suzanne sat silently next to Sonny, staring out the window. They were the only passengers bound for Wade's Landing. Presently, she turned to Sonny and said, "It sounds like Colt—rescuing that girl like that." She paused. "That's the kind of thing he would do—don't you think?"

Sonny looked at the poor, distraught girl, whose soulful eyes met his, pleading. He knew she was grasping at straws, that she was drowning in a river of sorrow and was casting about for anything to hang on to that might bring her hope, but it was no kindness to not be truthful with her.

"Suzie," he said gently, "It was not him. Colt's eyes were as blue as that ring on your finger. It was not him."

His words fell like a final death knell, bringing a curtain down on the tiny flicker of hope she had clung to so desperately. His use of the familiar name caused a shadow to pass across her eyes; Colt had called her that. She stared at the ring on her finger and her eyes filled with tears, then the floodgates of her grief burst open. Suzanne Kluesman began to weep inconsolably. Collapsing into Sonny's arms, she sobbed and sobbed and sobbed. Sonny held her gently until she cried herself to sleep, and then for the rest of the way back to Wade's Landing.

Two days later, he rode out at the head of two thousand Texas longhorns, bound for Denver, in Colorado Territory.

The whip popped and raised a welt on the back of the Mexican lad working alongside the white youth. "Bend your back to it, you lazy pepper belly. Turtle's doing all the work." Swatch Cardiston stood scowling at the two as they wrestled a pine log from off the wagon and stumbled towards the yawning mouth of the mine adit. Cardiston was a big man with a thick, bull neck and small eyes that looked out at the world from under heavy, beetling brows. Several days' growth of beard covered his hard face, and an angry leer of contempt followed the two workers as he coiled the bullwhip and slung it over his shoulder. "I oughta flay the hide off'n both of ye. This wagon shoulda been empty a half hour ago."

Turtle had been working about the mine for several weeks. Some of the other workers called him Tye, but Cardiston liked the name Turtle; besides belittling him, it seemed to fit better, even though he wasn't all that slow, except for his mind. Once, while he was laying on the lash just to watch the dummy jump, the kid made a lightning-like grab and caught the whip unexpectedly, then jerked it out of his hand. Without any expression at all, he coiled it up and walked over and handed it back to the astonished taskmaster and said, "Don't," then went back to work. The amusement of the other laborers was short-lived when Swatch had vented his fury on whomever he could reach with the blacksnake.

Initially, the white boy had been a slow learner and was only just now catching on. Cardiston scowled his dissatisfaction, for even though the Turtle had taken a lot of drubbings, Swatch never quite gleaned the satisfaction of seeing the kid cower in fear like the rest of those under his charge and Swatch had a reputation to maintain as the toughest boss in the camp. After the whip incident, he went out of his way to provoke the kid but got no response. The jackass was just too dumb to get mad. He did think twice about whipping him, though. He could not afford to be laughed at again, and somehow Swatch could not escape the feeling that the white kid was in some sort of sleepwalk and that one of these days he was going to wake up. He wondered what kind of hell-to-pay there'd be then.

Cardiston had taken charge of the "Turtle" since the first day and set him to holding drills, while a black man named Ezekiel, drove the steel with an eight-pound single jack. Fortunately, the white youth totally trusted the black man not to miss and soon a bond formed between Zeke and Tye that gained them a reputation of being faster than any other drilling team.

They were following a free milling gold seam that led horizontally back into the mountain as they drilled and blasted away the rock. The chunks of ore were then busted up into smaller pieces with single jacks and loaded by hand on ore carts, then pushed out of the tunnel, where the ore was transferred to wagons to be hauled to the furnaces below. Tye held the steel steady and paid little mind to the golden light reflected back from the seam of pure gold in the quartz vein they worked.

"Does yo wanna swing dis hamma, son?' Zeke asked Tye one day. "Alls yo has to do is thump dis steel in de middle whilst I holtz it."

Tye traded places with the black man then picked up the single jack and took a mighty swing, but unaccustomed to the flickering candle light from the headlamps they were wearing, his aim was off and the hammer struck the steel a glancing blow and bounded off to hit poor Zeke's hands, smashing and breaking several of his fingers.

Swatch came running at the black man's cries and sizing up the situation, jerked the sledge from the confused youth and struck him a backhanded blow which felled the boy and knocked out his candle.

"Get your ass to the front of the mine, you mindless dim-wit. You've ruined my best driller, this nigger's gonna be laid up for months. You two Mexes help him out to the wagon; he can go down with the next load."

The two Mexicans dropped their shovels and helped the groaning Zeke to his feet, both his hands dangling useless at his side.

Tye was put to busting up rock, loading it onto the ore carts, and hauling it out of the mine to dump in the waiting wagons. It was backbreaking work and he was sorry for Zeke. The black man had treated him kindly.

Tye grew lean and strong on the hard work and meager fare. Even though there seemed to be an abundance of food in the camp, portions were miserly for the enslaved workers. They were housed in a prison vault that had been hollowed out of the mountain and secured with a heavy iron door that was locked at night. A stream of water trickled through from seeps in the cavern and sleeping arrangements consisted of piles of straw along the walls. There were numerous prisoners and the men and boys were kept separate from the women and girls who shared quarters in a barracks in the camp below. Frequently, they could hear screaming and yelling at night from that quarter whenever a guard came to select a woman or girl. Tye did not understand what that was all about although he was told "the boss's using them." Most of the captives were Mexican or Indians with a few foreigners and some white folks and most tended to be young, around his own age. The men were kept busy in the mine and with the heavier work, while the women, girls and boys worked at the rest of the camp chores and lighter duties; tending livestock, the fields, gardens and orchards or on wood-gathering or irrigation duties.

During the hot summer months, the coolness of the cavern was a welcome relief, but as the days turned from summer to fall, then winter, it became bitterly cold. Finally they were each issued a heavy jacket and an extra blanket. A fire was kept burning near the entrance of the cavern and this helped some although the smoke from it came close to off-setting any advantage gained.

Eventually, Tye was assigned to the timber crew and was pleased to be out in the sunlight again. He worked with three Mexican lads cutting and hauling timbers for shoring up the mines. They drove two wagons across the river and up the long, winding grade that led to the top of the mesa, here they spent long hours felling and sawing pine and fir trees, loading the logs onto the wagons, and hauling them back to the mine where they were piled for later use.

Up on the plateau an old orchard was being restored; trees of peaches, pear, apple, pomegranate, and figs, had been cultivated in the distant past, and most showed serious neglect. Work was underway to prune, irrigate and restore the orchards. Water from a crystal clear spring bubbled up on top of this mesa and had been dammed to run into the fields and orchards. By springtime, wheat, corn and oats were being cultivated and old stone fences were being repaired to keep out the wild cattle that wandered the top of the plateau.

In spite of the harsh treatment he received from Swatch and the other overlords, Tye eventually gained the respect and admiration of the other workers; largely because he did not complain or shirk his duties and often went out of his way to do more, once he understood what was required of him. He would occasionally help others, coming to their aid if a task was more than they could seem to handle. Often it earned him a lash from the whip or a rebuke from some surly boss.

Some of the slaves bullied the others, taking food or anything of value from the weaker ones, particularly the younger or new slaves. To them the "Turtle" was an object of ridicule and laughter, until one day Blacky, a Mexican ringleader of this element, tried to take a melon away from the young white man and was promptly knocked unconscious by a lightening, one-two punch, the kid threw. It eventually came to the mine superintendent's attention that he could box and thereafter he was featured in a boxing match on Saturday nights, which he usually won, though sometimes he was beaten about the head and shoulders quite badly.

Most of the mine bosses took him on and, when defeated, badgered the tougher ones into seeing if they could beat the kid. Tye fought with an abandon that belied any animosity he might feel, other than when he was in the ring. After taking a few punishing blows, it seemed that a rage would consume him until his opponent was defeated. Even then, he would have to be restrained until he calmed down. Afterward, he seemed perfectly inclined to follow the vanquished overlord's orders as though he had never even fought him.

L.T. Jones sat looking across his desk at the tall, muscular white boy. "How come they call you Turtle?" he asked.

"Don't know," Tye said.

"Well, from all accounts, you're anything but slow. Do you like working in the mine?"

"Like being out in the fields better," the young man said. "I like seeing the cows."

"You do, aye? Well, maybe we've been wasting your talents underground. Do you think you might be able to work some of those wild cows up on the mesa?"

"I think so."

"I think so, too," Jones said. "You have the look of a horseman. You ever cowboy?"

"I don't know—I like horses."

"I'm going to take a chance on you and set you to ridin' herd on them cows up top of the mesa, you think you can handle that?"

"I reckon," Tye said.

"We'll get you a horse and saddle and you can work with Rodriguez. We'll try you out for a couple a weeks and see how it goes. I can't keep calling you 'Turtle'—do you have any other name?"

"Sometime they call me Tye," he said.

"Well, okay, Tye it is. Incidentally, I won a pretty good poke off you on that bout you had with Swatch last Saturday night. He swears to get even with you. Are you interested in a grudge-match with him sometime down the line?"

"I suppose that'd be okay," Tye said. He still didn't understand what it was all about but it sure hurt when somebody hit him in the head.

Felipe Rodriguez was a vaquero from Sonora and was quite handy with a rope. From the first time he placed the lasso in Tye's hands and watched him sit his pony and automatically build a loop, he knew that this guy had worked cattle before, even if he couldn't remember. When Tye expertly spurred his horse through the thick brush and snagged a wild calf on a short loop, Felipe saw there was no room for any doubt.

"Ju juse thee ríata before, eh, Senor Tye, we weel geet along jus fine."

From then on, it took only a little nudging in the right direction for the white caballero to do the things they had to do. Tye took to cowboying like a goat to a garbage dump. The two riders spent the late winter and early spring months doctoring cows, delivering calves and, in general, looking after the herd. Eventually, from being driven from grass to grass when graze grew short, the stock grew used to their presence.

By new grass, Tye was comfortably at home in the saddle and enjoyed Jasper, the quick footed little sorrel mustang he rode. The cow pony was good in the brush and savvy once he had a critter on the end of his rope. Jones had dug up a pair of boots, spurs, chaps and a decent sombrero for the rider.

It was the habit of the two riders to return to the mining camp each evening, after closing a large pole gate at the top of the mesa where the road started down, effectively barricading any escape route for the cattle, although the cows had never shown any inclination of leaving the good grass and timber for the precarious wagon road. The cowboys were eventually assigned a place in the bunkhouse, shared with other field workers.

One evening when Tye rode in, L.T. Jones hailed him and told him to come up to the ranch house for supper. Seated around his table were several of the overseers along with Swatch Cardiston and Reese Hutchinson. Hutch had just arrived that afternoon with another mule train load of supplies. Among the captives he had brought was a freckled faced, white girl in her teens, named Penelope.

When the meal was finished, L.T. sat back in his chair and lit a long, black cheroot, blew smoke towards the ceiling, and said, “This Saturday night we’re going to have that grudge match between Cardiston and the ‘Turtle’ here.” He looked in Tye’s direction and gave an amused laugh. Tye felt his face flush and his ears turn red at Jones’ belittling remark.

L.T. went on, “So Swatch, you been wanting another chance to pin the kid’s ears back, ya givin’ any kinda odds on who’s gonna win?”

“Ten to one, on me,” growled Cardiston, glaring at the cowboy. “He caught me off guard last time but it ain’t a-gonna happen again.”

"Ten to one it is then and just to sweeten the pot for the winner, I'm gonna throw in this fine little filly that Hutch has fetched in from San Antone. Hutch, where's that freckle-faced kid you brought us?"

There was a shuffling in the kitchen area and then the girl was led in between two stout Mexican women and all eyes turned to stare at her.

"Gent's, meet Miss Penelope Stauffer," Jones said, "and to the victor go the spoils."

The girl's face blanched white and tears began to trickle down her cheeks.

"Hot-damn," Swatch said. "For sure I'm a-gonna clean that cocky kid's plow now. 'Turtle' this little honey-pot's all mine." He turned to leer at the girl who fastened horrified eyes on the big slave-driver before she was led away.

Tye sat passively watching the girl depart with no sign of interest. L.T. noticed, and wondered if he had made a mistake. If he won't fight for the girl, what would he fight for? Ten to one was pretty good odds. Somehow, he had to light a fire under this kid.

Later, Jones caught Tye at the door as he was leaving. "I want you to move into that little adobe shack next to the old church. We'll see about getting some Mexicans over there to clean it out and get you settled in all comfortable like. If you play your cards right, come this Saturday night, you might have a little house guest to take care of the place on a permanent basis—someone to come home to and keep you company, if you know what I mean." He gave the cowboy a nudge and shut the door with a knowing laugh.

"Kid don't talk much, does he?" Reese Hutchinson said to Jones as the door clicked shut.

L.T. turned to look at the one-eyed man. "No, but don't let that fool you none, he's hell on wheels once he's in the ring and has had his ears boxed a couple of times. Ten to one's good odds and Cardiston's way overconfident, my money's on the kid."

Hutch looked coldly at the mine boss. "If he whips Swatch, I want a piece of him." There was a malevolent glint in his good eye.

Chapter Three

Tye and Penny

Summer, 1869, Rio Guaynopa, Mexico

Tye sat his horse looking across the canyon from the top of the mesa. About halfway up on the eastern wall was a three-hundred-foot-long gash riven in the solid rock. Back behind the overhanging cliff ceiling he could see the remains of old cliff dwellings—houses of adobe and rooms cut from the living rock and there were several huge clay pots standing on the floor, twice as high as a man's head. Absently he wondered who had lived there, then turned Jasper to ride through the tall fir and pine trees, searching for strays. He rode out onto a promontory of the butte, once again pausing to stare at the cliff dwellings from this vantage point. Across from him, he noted movement on top of the opposing canyon wall. Then he saw a white puff of smoke rising into the air. Far to the northeast came an answering puff of smoke. Tye sat watching, completely unaware of the smoke's significance, when Rodriguez rode out of the trees and pulled up alongside of him. The vaquero sat looking at the signals for a moment.

"Apache making thee smoke-talk, wan of thees days they weal attack thee gringos' minas and keel everyone, thees ees a good place to be—only wan way up. Too bad we don' hab thee rifle, perhaps Senor Jones geeb ju wan eef ju ask heem. We could choot thee cougar and coyote and maybe thee Indios eef they come."

Tye unsaddled the sorrel, put his rigging over the corral rail, and stood watching the hearty mustang roll over four times. The horse stood to his feet and shook himself, then went to water. Tye enjoyed watching the horse. "Any horse that can roll over four times is a horse to ride the river with," he mused. He was leaning against the top rail, absently wondering where he had heard that when L.T. Jones walked up and placed a foot on the lower rail, then stood studying the horses in the enclosure.

"Rodriguez says you need a rifle for cougar and coyotes up on the mesa, you seen any of those varmints up there?"

Tye shook his head, "I've seen smokes though. Felipe says they are Apache talk."

"Them sneakin' Injuns is always lurkin' about, where 'bouts were they?"

He pointed towards the eastern wall. "On top of that cliff, just above those cliff dwellings."

"Huh," Jones scoffed. "The old pueblos—I should take you up there sometime. There's over fifty spooky rooms, all empty except for the ghosts of long-dead Indians that haunt them. It's no place I'd want to spend a night."

"What were those huge pots up there for, water?"

"Yeah, maybe, no—wait, there's water from a seep if I remember right. I think those pots were used for granaries."

They stood looking at the horses stirring up dust as they milled around some hay being tossed to them by a Mexican lad. "You ready to take on Swatch tomorrow night?" Jones asked.

"I guess," Tye said.

"I got a lot of money ridin' on you boy, you don't sound very enthusiastic," he stepped away then said, "Don't let me down," and walked off.

The youth watched him go, then turned and walked back to his adobe shack. He picked up a bucket and went out to a nearby irrigation ditch for water, then he filled a washbasin that sat on a stand by the door and washed his hands and face. A gunnysack filled with dried corn silk lay at the head of his little bunk, covered with a towel. When he picked up the towel to dry his face, the pillow fell on the floor. Picking it up, he punched it a few time before he tossed it back on his bed when an idea hit him. Tying a rope about the end, he hung the sack from a rafter and began to practice his punches. For the next hour, he danced around the punching bag working out, only vaguely aware of what he was doing and acting more out of instinct on something from his distant past.

His little hut was a single room with a flattop clay oven built into an alcove on one wall. There were shelves and a counter-top along that wall as well. A table and two chairs, the bed and a couple boxes stood on end to hold candles for light around the other walls. One window let in the daylight. His few clothes hung from the wall on nails, but it was quarters far superior to the prison vault he had stayed in previously. A Mexican woman cooked his meals and this evening had left him some rice and a couple of chicken tacos on the table. These he ate, then lay on his bunk, the punching bag pillow under his head. "I wonder why they want me to fight with Swatch," he thought. "He's mean and awfully big. I better not let him get a hold of me." He drifted off to sleep and had a disturbing dream of a smiling, blond-haired girl shooting a buffalo from off a windswept hill.

Jones had one of the ancient, stonewalled, corrals restored and a boxing ring set up in the center. Spectators, consisting mostly of the bosses and company personal and those Mexicans and Indians who made up the trusted, household labor force, lined the walls or sat on top of the small enclosure. The Mexican storekeeper was holding the stakes and there was much good-natured betting going on.

L.T. Jones stepped to the center of the makeshift ring, a single rope supported by posts driven into the ground, and rapped on a tin pan with a heavy wooden spoon.

"This is to be a fight to the finish—grudge match, with no holds barred. The last man standing will be declared the winner. When an opponent is knocked or thrown from the ring, that round is over and a two minute rest shall be allowed before the next round begins."

Cardiston stood, stripped to his waist and flexed his muscular arms, while glaring past the mine superintendent to where Tye stood. The young man wore a pair of cut-down long-johns with the back flap sewn shut by one of the Mexican women.

The big mine boss licked his lips and snarled, "You're hash, boy."

"Return to your corners and at the sound of the gong, come out fighting," Jones said. Both men retreated to their respective corners.

Felipe Rodriguez waited for Tye with a slight smile, "Stay out of hees reech and wear heem down."

L.T. rapped on the pan and the fight began. Tye, surprised at the racket the pan made, stared over at the superintendent, momentarily distracted. A heavy blow landed on the back of his neck, knocking the cowboy to the ground, followed by a vicious kick to the ribs. Stunned, he lay there as Cardiston raised a heavy boot to stomp on the downed man.

Tye twisted to the side, grabbed the upraised foot and heaved upwards, knocking the big slave driver over backwards. Slowly the kid got to his feet, a ringing in his ears. A cold, deadly anger welled up inside him at the cowardly attack. Crouching, he waited, his eyes on the big man who struggled to regain his feet. As Swatch rose from the ground, Tye leaped towards him and in rapid succession threw a left, then a right, another left, and right, at the mine boss's nose, smashing it and starting it to bleed. With a roar of pain, Cardiston came at the youth, trying to catch him in a bear hug.

Tye danced on nimble feet and sidestepped his opponent's rush, then landed a powerful right into the heavy belly of the taskmaster. The air rushed out of Swatch's lungs and he bent double, stumbling towards the ropes. Quickly, Tye rushed from behind, placed a foot against the big man's rump and gave a hard push, propelling him violently from the ring to land in a pile of dust. The pan rattled and the round came to an end amidst a chorus of laughter from the crowd.

"Ju awrigh?" Rodriguez asked. He began bathing Tye's face with a cold, wet towel.

"Yeah, I think so, my ribs hurt."

"Ju mus na let heem catch ju, jus keep doin' wha' ju are doeeng and ju weel wear heem down and ween."

The pan rattled again and Tye stepped out, his eyes on Swatch Cardiston. There was an angry sneer on the burly man's face.

"You're buzzard bait," he hissed and made a rush at Tye.

The youth side-stepped the charge, grabbed an outstretched arm by the wrist and using the big man's momentum, he pivoted on his heels and swung Cardiston around in a half circle, then propelled him into one of the corner posts, fetching him a resounding smack across his face and chest.

Swatch yowled in pain and went down. Quick as a cat, he whirled for the youth in his hazy vision and made a grab for him, but came up with nothing but air. Tye eluded his grasp and landed another punishing blow to Cardiston's throbbing nose. Swatch staggered at the explosion of light and choked, gasping for air as blood ran down his throat. He stopped and pivoted slowly, watching the young man who danced around him in a circle. His rage at a boiling point, he closed on the kid, trying to pin him in the corner, but Tye ducked under his arms and thudded two more heavy blows to Cardiston's mid-section.

Bellowing like a bull and grinding his teeth together in furry, Swatch charged after the elusive youth, but the kid was just too fast. If he could only get his hands on him, he would crush him like a bug.

Tye could see the big man was tiring and picked up the pace, darting in and out and aiming repeatedly for his adversary's nose. Then it happened. He was following a left jab with a right cross and Cardiston, ignoring the pain to his face, managed to grab Tye's right wrist. He yanked Tye into his embrace and wrapped gorilla-like arms about him, fully intending to crush out his life.

The young man could not break his hold and felt the wind squeezed out of him. In desperation, he kicked his feet upwards, bending nearly double, and using his opponent's hold as a fulcrum, he bridged his body up and over Cardiston's head. The slave driver staggered under the top-heavy weight, stumbling towards the edge of the ring, and there he shook the youth off over the ropes and out onto the dust of the corral. Tye dropped nimbly to his feet as the pan banged the end of the second round.

Two minutes later they were back at it again. Tye was actually enjoying the fight now, toying with the bigger man who was cursing him and breathing out threats, while those who had backed him yelled at him, "Murder the tricky bastard."

Tye saw in Cardiston's smashed nose a weakening chink in his armor and continued to jab mercilessly at it. Swatch bawled in pain like a wounded buffalo each time Tye landed a punch. Finally, the fight virtually stopped, with Cardiston standing still, helplessly trying to breathe and staunch the flow of blood from his battered nose. His hands opened and closed in helpless rage and his tearing eyes lost sight of his opponent, while the crowd roared their disappointment.

Tye stepped up behind him and said, "Why don't you just sit down and I will quit hitting your nose?"

"Huh?" Cardiston said, "where you at?" He turned in a daze and then seeing Tye dimly through bleary eyes and spinning vision, he suddenly struck out with both hands and seized the young man by the throat. A roar went up from the watching crowd in their thirst for blood. An evil laugh gurgled from Swatch's blood-flecked lips.

Tye felt his wind cut off and knew the big man intended to strangle him. With a supreme effort, he drove his arms up between those about his throat and broke Cardiston's grip long enough to smash his forehead into what was left of Swatch's nose. There was a loud pop and Cardiston staggered back a step, then another and fell like tall timber, over backwards, to land out cold on the ground, oblivious to the shouting and cheers of the crowd. Tye stood rubbing his throat and looked down at the big man lying prone on the ground. Satisfied that he wasn't getting up, he turned and walked towards the grinning Felipe.

Tye sat on the edge of his bunk gingerly feeling the tight wrappings about his ribs. It hurt to breath and his neck and throat ached from the death grip of Swatch Cardiston's fingers. He heard riders approaching and then L.T. Jones hollered out. "Here she is, boy, you won her fair and square." Then he spoke to someone. "Go on in there, girl, he ain't a gonna bite ya—well, not hard anyway, ha, ha, ha." The door creaked open slowly and Tye saw the freckle-faced girl from the hacienda, look cautiously inside.

"That was great fighting kid," L.T. called, "I won a pile of gold. I'll just leave you two to get better acquainted. If you need anything, holler." Tye heard him ride away chuckling.

His head aching, Tye looked at the frightened girl and waved her inside, then turned to lie back on his bunk and close his eyes. He was vaguely aware of the girl moving about before he fell asleep.

Sunlight was streaming in the single window when he awoke and sat up with a groan holding his ribs. Sitting in a chair, her head slumped over on the table, was the girl, Penelope, fast asleep. He vaguely remembered Jones bringing her by the evening before. Quietly, he got up, pulled on his boots and taking up the water bucket, went out to wash his face. He carried the bucket to the ditch for a fresh pail. It was Sunday and the Mexican woman who usually cooked his meals had the day off. He would have to fend for himself. Walking back into his hut, he found the girl sitting up, awake, her big eyes following him in fear.

"You get on the bed," Tye said.

The girl jumped up, her frightened eyes darting to the door.

"Go on," Tye waved her to the bed. "You finish your sleep while I fix breakfast, you can't have slept well, sitting on that chair." He turned and began to mix up some biscuits.

The girl gave him a dubious look and slowly walked over to the bed and lay down. Soon she was fast asleep. An hour later she was sitting across the table from him, yawning and rubbing sleep from her eyes. Picking at the eggs in front of her, she looked guardedly at the cowboy.

Tye buttered a hot biscuit and dribbled some honey onto it, then looked at the girl's plate. "Ain't you hungry?" he asked.

"Not very," the girl said. "How come I'm here?"

"I don't know. . . what did they tell you?"

"That I was to come and stay with you," she said.

Tye took a sip of the hot coffee.

"I think they thought. . ." she broke off. . . "I guess I'm supposed to stay here and—and well, help you," she finished lamely.

"Help me? Help me do what? I don't need any help."

"I don't know—help you. . . keep house, cook—ah—make the bed. . . I don't know, they didn't say."

"Ain't much housekeeping to this place and the Mexican woman does the cooking. Can you cook?"

"Yes, my mother taught me that much."

"Your mother," Tye seemed puzzled. "Where is she?'

"She's back in San Antone with the rest of the family."

"San Antone?" Tye was trying to recall the name. "Where's that?"

"You don't know where San Antonio, Texas is?' she asked incredulously.

He chewed thoughtfully. “I think I’ve heard of it. Is it very far from here?”

“Yes, very far and they blindfolded me so I don’t even know where I am or which direction it is.”

“I was blindfolded once.” He went on eating but said no more. The girl waited for him to go on and thought it strange when it became apparent he had no more to say.

“What is your name?” she finally said.

“They call me different things. I like Tye the best but. . .” he paused, looking reflective. “I don’t think that’s it.”

The girl smiled for the first time showing pretty, even, white teeth. “Is this a guessing game?”

“No.” He took a swallow of coffee.

“So, what is it?”

“What’s what?” He looked over at the girl and chewed slowly.

“Your name, dummy,” she looked exasperated and shook her head. “What is your real name?”

“Well, it’s not that. Some of them call me that, but that’s not it. Some call me turtle but that’s not it either. You can call me Tye, I like that best. What’s your name?”

Penny sat with a peculiar look on her face and wondered why she had been given to this young man who obviously did not know why she was here and did not seem to know much else either.

“Penelope,” she said, “Penelope Stauffer, but everyone I know calls me Penny.”

“Hum, Penny? No, that’s not right. I know this name from somewhere, but I don’t think it was a girl’s name. Penny—Penny,” he repeated and shook his head.

“You may call me Penelope if you prefer,” she said, and smiling again, she relaxed a little, her curiosity aroused at his obvious confusion over her name.

"Huh!" he went on, "It just doesn't fit. Penny—Penny." He shook his head again. "How old are you?"

"I'll be eighteen in June, why do you ask?" She felt a little annoyed at the question. Didn't he know that a girl was considered a woman at eighteen? In ways, it seemed that she was being treated like a kid by a guy who was more like a kid than a man himself, at least in his understanding.

He said, "No reason, I just wondered."

"Well, it's not considered polite to ask a lady her age," she said. "Not that I've seen all that much of polite company since I was taken."

"Oh, sorry. . . taken, where were you taken?"

"Here," she said, a little irritated. "I was taken here. Weren't you kidnapped and brought here against your will?"

"I don't know, I guess. I don't seem to remember much. What did they take you for, to work in the gold mine?"

"You really don't know, do you?"

"Nope."

Dryly she said, "I think the kind of work they have in mind for me is not in the gold mines."

"Well, what kind of work is it then? Are you going to eat those eggs?"

"No," she said. "That bed over there probably has more to do with the kind of work they had in mind for me to do and it scares me half to death."

"Aw, it's just a crummy old bed—it ain't going to hurt you," Tye reached for her plate and slid the eggs off onto his own. "It's sure better 'n tryin' to sleep in a chair."

Penelope gave a bitter chuckle and looked half amused at the innocent face of the cowboy. "I'm beginning to believe that you really don't know. How'd you get this far along in life without knowing about the birds and the bees and—and beds and all?"

"I know about birds and bees and beds," he said tolerantly, "what do you take me for?" Then he added, "of course I don't see what one has to do with the other."

Penny looked at him and actually giggled. "Tye, if you're for real, no one is going to believe it and if you are not. . . well, I have to admit this approach to the whole subject is. . . ah, shall we say, very unique? Can I ask you something?"

"Sure," he said. He pushed back his empty plate, looking expectantly at her.

"What do you think about getting into that bed over there, with me?"

Tye stared blankly at her for a minute and then a smile broke out on his face. "I see what you mean, it would be pretty crowded, wouldn't it? I doubt we'd get much sleeping done," he chuckled, "one or the other of us would be spending half the night picking ourselves up off the floor."

"This dress is the only thing I have on and I don't sleep in my clothes," she said meaningfully, watching his face.

"I don't either," he said nonchalantly. "I sleep in my long-johns. You're liable to get pretty cold without anything on. I bet you could find a pair of long-johns at the store, you want I should ask?"

She shook her head, an amused look on her face. "That won't be necessary."

"Well, I'll tell the boss we could use another bed and some more blankets down here. He must have forgotten there was only one bed."

"What are you going to do today?" Penny asked, changing the subject.

"Thought I'd try'n climb up to those old cliff dwellings on the canyon wall," he said. "You wanna come along?"

The girl brightened, "Yes, I think I would like that, will it take very long?"

"Probably most of the day, it won't be an easy climb; we'll have to scale up the rock face."

"I don't mind. Do you want me to make us a lunch?"

Tye rode up to the hacienda on the hill and knocked on the door. A pleasant-faced, white woman in her mid-forties answered it and L.T. Jones hollered from within the house, "Who is it, Evita?"

The woman answered, "It's the young man from the fight last night—the one you gave the girl to." There was iciness in her voice that went unnoticed by Tye.

"Well, tell him to come on in, don't leave him standing on the veranda."

Tye followed the lady, unaware of her attractiveness. Her full figure and dark hair and eyes gave mute testimony to Spanish blood. She was wearing a colorful dress with a flaring, pleated skirt, and had a gardenia in her hair. They went into a large room tastefully decorated with Navaho rugs and a stuffed couch and chairs. A huge fireplace filled one end of the room, and spacious windows looked down on the fields and camp below. Jones sat in one of the chairs, his booted feet up on a coffee table, and he was peeling an orange from a bowl of fruit.

"What do you need, son?" Jones said patronizingly. "Evee, perhaps you could find us something cool to drink?" The woman frowned and left the room.

"Sorry to barge in on ya like this," Tye said. "That girl you sent down there last night is going to need some things and I think we could use another bed. The two of us ain't a-gonna fit in the one I got."

"Ho, ho," Jones laughed. "I never thought about that. Guess you would need another bed with all that nocturnal activity, wouldn't you?" He chuckled some more and popped a section of orange into his mouth, giving Tye a knowing wink.

Tye said, "With all the what, sir?"

Evita walked back in with a couple glasses and a pitcher of cold tea. Jones grinned and said, "Never mind, son. Tell Juan to give you whatever you need down at the store. How's the calf crop coming along?'

Tye visited with the mine superintendent for another twenty minutes and then got up to leave; unaware of the scrutiny Evita had been giving him from where she sat across the room, sewing.

"About that rifle," Jones said. "Do you know how to use one?"

"I think so."

"Tell Juan to give you one of those Winchesters and a couple boxes of shells. You practice up, if them damned Apaches attack us we'll need every gun we got. Evita, show the Tu—Tye to the door."

The door clicked behind the young cowboy and Evita turned to L.T. "Are you crazy?" she said. "Giving that prisoner a gun? What if he murders us in our bed?"

L.T. Jones gave her a wry look and then scoffed, "I doubt you've got to worry about anybody murdering you in bed. . . or anyplace else either, for that matter."

Tye and Penny hiked up river to the base of the escarpment below the cliff dwellings. He carried a coil of rope and the Winchester slung over his shoulder and turned to reach a hand out to the girl scrambling over the rocks behind him. A faint trail led upwards through a jumble of boulders and shale that screed out from the rock wall a third of the way up. Carefully, they found their way to where the bare rock rose straight up, and then stopped.

Tye looked at the sandals Penny wore.

"I don't think you can climb this cliff with those on your feet."

Penny glanced down at her feet and then nodded. "I'll take them off."

"You're going to try and climb this rock barefooted?" Tye looked surprised.

"Why not? I've been barefoot most of my life." She slipped the sandals off, lashed them together with a piece of twine, and hung them about her neck.

It was a warm spring day and already the stone was heating up. "Won't the rock be too hot for your feet?" Tye asked.

"I'll get used to it," she said simply. "C'mon, let's go."

Tye removed the rope and, tying one end around his waist, he passed the other end to the girl. "Better tie this around you," he said, "we don't want you to slip and fall."

They started up a narrow chimney of fluted rock where foot-holds had been cut into the granite on either side. The passageway extended up for about fifty feet to a necked down spot, barely wide enough for a man to squirm through. When they reached this spot, it became apparent they would have to bridge their feet against one wall and their back against the other and work their way up another ten feet or so. There was a series of handholds chiseled out to aid their progress, and a small shelving of rock enabled them to stand and catch their breath before continuing on.

"You ready?" Tye asked the girl.

Penny licked her lips and looked up nervously. "Let me go first," she said.

"I better try it first, that way if you slip I can catch you with the rope. Here, hold the rifle until I get past that narrow spot, then send it and the sack up to me."

He squirmed and wriggled through the tight place and, once past it, found that the trail opened to a sloping upward angle from there, that they could walk. He lowered the rope down for the sack and rifle that Penny tied up, and pulled them up. Setting them on a shelving of stone, he then turned to help the girl.

"I don't know if I can get through there," she said.

"I'll keep the rope taut and help you, c'mon."

Penny retied the lowered rope about her middle and struggled to traverse the throat of the rock chimney, but seemed to have trouble knowing where to place her feet and hands. Twice she slipped and would have fallen if the cowboy hadn't been holding the rope. The second time she scrapped her backside painfully on the rough stone.

"Oh, that hurt," she cried. "I've chafed myself."

Tye stared down at her. He had seen her painful slip before the rope pulled tight and stopped her.

"Where are you hurt?" he asked.

Penny glared up at him, "None of your business. If you'd hold that rope tight like you're supposed to, I wouldn't be polishing these rocks with my fanny."

"Sorry," he mumbled and held the rope tighter.

Penny scrambled the rest of the way up without further mishap to stand beside him on the slope, and then turning away from him, she pulled up her dress to stare at the angry, red scratches on her white bottom.

"Darn it. That scraped me pretty good; look what you did." She turned her bottom towards him, holding the skirt out of the way and studied his reaction.

Tye saw a couple of angry, red marks on the white, rounded cheeks of her derriere before looking away and again mumbled an apology.

"I'm sorry, maybe you could put some mud on that and take the sting away."

Penny was puzzled. Why didn't he seem to notice her? It was something of a paradox. She had been frightened and terrified when she was first given to him, fearing the worst after what she had experienced at the hands of her other captors. She had been cruelly taken from her home by thugs who had hustled her across the river and then turned her over to the Comancheros, who had in turn, sold her to the armed caravan that brought her to Guaynopa. They had manhandled her, abused her with many indignities and harsh treatment, including stripping her, and exposing her to the lewd gazes of those ruffians who had pinched and poked her with cruel fingers. But she was spared the ultimate design of their lust only because their lust for gold was stronger. They knew she would command a higher price if she was not a "soiled dove" as they put it. By the time L.T. Jones and that sham of a wife, or whatever she was, got through with her though, there was not much left intact of her virtue, honor or anything else. Since then she had become somewhat inured to the raw life of the mining camp, determining to make the best of a bad situation and watch for her chance to escape.

Her being brought to Tye had completely disarmed her, for she found that, not only did he not pose a threat to her person or womanhood, he seemed totally unaware of the latter and this indifference was disturbing. . . even challenging. She thought the least he could do was acknowledge she was one.

She was stumped; their conversation about the bed this morning and now, his seeming indifference to the bold display of her posterior, was confusing. She began to wonder just what it would take to light a fire in him.

Dropping her dress, she said, "Well, let's go see if we can find some mud then," and walked carelessly over the stones barefoot, following the trail on upward.

Panting and sweating, they finally emerged out upon the pueblo floor of the huge cavern in the cliff face that housed the ancient cliff dwellings, and sat down to rest. In the distance was the tinkle of water falling into a pool.

"I hear water," Penny said. "Let's go see if we can find it."

They traversed the front of the ancient ruin, pausing to stare in wonder at the huge clay granaries, not unlike a clay pot but about fifteen feet high, with square cut holes in the sides, the first about eye level with the rest extending upward. Tye peered inside first one and then walking around it, he looked into a second one. They were both empty, the remnants of a couple of old ladders lay rotting on the ground nearby.

"They must have loaded these through the top," he said. I wonder how they got the grain up here."

They walked over to the houses built from adobe brick that fronted rooms carved into the rock. These were structures with vacant windows and doors, long since abandoned by their inhabitants. All that they looked into were but single rooms and all appeared to be empty. The sighing of the wind through these buildings echoed a low mournful sound from the overhanging ceiling of the cavern and Tye felt some uneasiness at its moan. No wonder Jones said this was no place to be at night. A strong wind would set up quite a wail.

Penny had walked to the far end of the natural amphitheater and cried, "Come, look, Tye, I found the water." He walked over to where she stood looking into a pool of water that filled a tank cut from the living stone, about forty feet across and about four feet deep. Water was trickling from fissures in the stone walls behind and above it and drained through a shallow trough at the outlet to disappear into cracks in the cavern floor. Steps led down into what had obviously been the community water supply.

"This is great," Penny said, "I am going to take a bath." She walked down the steps, her light dress billowing up around her waist as she entered the water. Tye saw the flash of her white legs beneath the surface as she launched into a shallow dive and swam to the other side. She surfaced and turned to grin at the watching cowboy.

"C'mon in, the water's great, I'm going to take off my dress and wash it. Why don't you come in?"

"I don't want to get my clothes wet," he said.

"Then take them off," she called, "I don't mind."

Tye sat down and took off his boots and then watched curiously as Penny unbuttoned the front of her dress and pulled it off over her head. The water half covered her breasts and he stared at the bobbling, youthful orbs as the water gently rocked them up and down.

He felt something stir in him at the sight of her, but with it came a sense of uneasiness, as if he should not be looking at her like this, and he wondered why. There was a strange recollection, a distant memory that he could not quite recall. . . something about girls. . . women, that set them apart and it was more than the obvious and fascinating differences between Penny and himself. It felt forbidden, as if he was trespassing and he did not know how—against whom? Was it Penny? It might be, but from the way she was watching him while slowly swishing her dress back and forth in the water, he was led to believe it was not her.

There was someone else in the back of his memory, knocking on a door he could not quite open. There seemed to be someone calling; it was sad, beautiful, mysterious, a distant voice almost like a song, but so very far away. He strained to hear it, to remember, but it seemed to fade and die off, the harder he tried to recall.

Visibly shaken, Tye stood. With ashen face, his eyes locked onto those of the girl in the water. She stood smiling, beckoning to him, but there was something in her eyes that alarmed him; a needful—almost desperate—look, and he wanted to run, to get away. Turning he stumbled barefoot on the stone floor of the place and walked off to stand at the edge of the cavern and look below.

"Oh, Tye," he heard the girl call with something akin to desperation in her voice. "Don't go. . . I won't do. . ." her voice trailed off. "Come back," then in a quieter voice, "the water's fine." All was silent for a moment except for the trickle of the water. Far below the river roared and then he heard Penny begin to cry. He stood absently watching the rushing river and the activities of the camp in the distance through unseeing eyes.

The sighing of the wind in the cavern behind him carried to his ears the echo of the girl's sobs. They seemed to be amplified, bringing a haunting cry in answer to a place inside of him, a cry his heart knew but his head did not. Why was this girl crying? What was the other cry calling to him on the wind of this place? Jones said this place was haunted—was it?

"Penny," Tye called, "Put your clothes back on."

The crying stopped and he could hear gentle rustling in the waters behind him.

"Alright," Penny called, there was a catch in her voice. "They're on, you can come back now."

He turned and walked back to where he had left his boots. Penny slowly walked up the steps from the tank, her light dress clinging wetly to her body. She found a place in the sunlight and lay down on her stomach to dry. She rested her head on crossed arms and turned away from him, her eyes closed, but he could see the long dark lashes against her cheek were wet with tears.

The inner turmoil he felt had brought a rush of feelings and desires he could not identify and with it there was a longing. Then, too, there was a strange tenderness for the feelings of this young girl beside him. It all seemed so foreign—so new to him, yet somehow familiar, too, like he had done this or something like it before. God, why couldn't he remember?

Why had he said that? God. . . Jesus? He seemed to know who they were but it was also like he had suddenly made a new discovery or maybe it was more like they had been gone and just now got back. Lord—he remembered that too—Lord, help me to remember. Who am I?

"You all right?" he said to the girl.

She shivered in the sunlight and repositioned her head. "No," she said, her eyes still shut.

Timidly he asked, "What's wrong?"

She did not answer right away, finally she said, "I feel so hurt—so rejected and alone. . . I'm worthless and ruined." She gave a little sob. "Why wouldn't you look at me?

"I don't know—it didn't feel right."

"Every other man around this awful place has been trying to see me like that ever since I got here—don't you find me pretty?"

"Yes. . . of course I do."

"Well, what's wrong then. . . do you already have a girl?"

"Yes. . . No. I don't know—I just can't remember. I haven't even thought about it. . . you know. . . what used to be before I came here, but now. . . here in this place, I feel things that I haven't been feeling, things that I am feeling now. Things that maybe I've felt before but can't remember where or when."

"Do you have amnesia?" Penny asked. She turned her head to look at him sitting there, his hands resting on his knees.

"I don't know, what's that?"

"It's a condition where people loose their memory."

"Maybe," he said. "Do they ever get it back?"

"Sometimes, I guess. I don't know much about it. I think, though, that is what you've got. You've got amnesia."

"I can't remember much before I came to the mines. It's all sort of hazy and mixed up, but I do remember my head hurting a lot—sometimes it still does."

"You must have had a head injury, let me see." Penny rose to her knees and lifted his hat off his head and began to feel about his scalp, parting his hair. Her finger paused at a little, brown spot behind his left ear.

"You have a cute little spot here, just at the hair line, but I think it's a birthmark." Feeling higher, she found a ragged scar that was barely healed. "You've been hit in the head here."

Tye lifted his fingers and gingerly felt of the spot. "Yeah, I've noticed this, what do you think happened?"

"I don't know, you've received a nasty blow, is all I can tell you."

The cowboy stood and walked anxiously back and forth. "I need to know. I need to find out what happened and who I am. How can I find out?" He turned an imploring look on the girl.

"Well, if anybody would know around here, it would be that wretched superintendent, Jones. I suppose you could ask him, but I doubt he would tell you much."

Tye stopped. "Why wouldn't he?"

"Because, as long as you don't know anything, you're no trouble to him, and no threat to what he is doing here."

"What's he doing here?"

"You don't want to know," she said cynically. "You are probably better off like you are, believe me, I wish I didn't remember who I was and what's gone on here."

Tye reached down and grabbed the girl's arm. "C'mon," he said, "I've got to go talk to him and find out what he knows."

"Okay, but my advice to you is, do not let them know you know if you find out."

"Huh?" he looked confused.

She scoffed, "Never mind—you'll find out." They started across the pueblo floor towards the trail back down.

Chapter Four

Schoolhouse Dancin'

Fall, 1869, West Texas

On a golden day in September, Sonny returned from his trail drive to Denver. He'd had a good trip for the most part and was pleased to turn over nearly eighty-thousand, Yankee dollars to Grant. It was a happy day on the Crossed Sabers, in what had otherwise been a rather gloomy summer.

"You going to go see Suzanne?" his mother asked. She had come out to where he stood on the porch looking up the road towards town.

"You think I should?" he said.

Jessica shook the tablecloth in the breeze and then began to fold it. "It's been a difficult time for her—maybe you could cheer her up some, Son—she doesn't smile any more and I know she's dying by inches inside. I think if anyone can pull her out of this, it's you." She touched his cheek, blinked back a tear, and went back inside.

Sonny knocked on the door of the Kluesmans and Suzanne's mother answered. "I've come to see Suzanne, is she in?"

"Sonny," Mabel Kluesman cried, "When did you get back? Suzanne is on that trail that goes down to the river from over by the church. She seems to spend a lot of time over there."

"Thanks," Sonny said. "I just got in yesterday, I'll go see if I can find her." He turned back to his horse.

"I am glad you came to call, she's been so melancholy since". . . she broke off. . . "well, for a long time now. I think she will be glad to see you."

Sonny left his horse switching flies in the shade of a big chinaberry tree, and took the path along the river. He saw Suzanne before she was aware of his presence. She was sitting on a log with her arms clasped about her knees and her chin resting on her hands, and was staring at a washed out hole in the trail. He had to look twice to be certain it was she. Suzanne was so frail and thin that the dark dress she wore scarcely fit her.

"Hi, Suzie," he said.

"*Colton!*" Suzanne gave a desperate cry and started up from the log at the sight of him and then crumpled to the ground in a faint.

Sonny rushed to her side, knelt and gathered the stricken girl into his arms and then sat down on the log holding her on his lap. He patted her cheek.

"Suzie—Suzanne, wake up, I'm sorry, I didn't mean to frighten you so—there now, it's alright, it's alright."

Suzanne's eyes fluttered open and she looked about, confused. Finally, her eyes focused on Sonny's face and she slowly sat up.

"Oh, Sonny, it's you. What happened?"

"You passed out for a moment or two."

"You startled me so. I thought you were Colton—you sound just like him and when you called me Suzie". . . she broke off. "He was the only one who said my name like that."

Sonny helped her to a place beside him on the log, a supporting arm about her shoulder. "You alright?" he asked.

"I think so. When did you get back?"

"I rode in yesterday; we had a pretty good trip."

"I am glad. You didn't hear anything abut your brother while you were gone, did you?"

Sonny shook his head and watched her eyes cloud with disappointment.

"What's been going on with you Suzanne, I reckon it ain't nice to say but you don't look so good."

"I'm not good, Sonny," she said quietly and looked down at her hands fidgeting in her lap.

"You've lost a lot of weight haven't you, aren't you eating right?"

"No, daddy says he is going to spank me if I don't start eating."

"Well, has he?"

"No, I'm just not hungry, I don't want to eat."

"If you don't eat you will die, do you want to die?" Pulling away from him, Suzanne once again resumed the position he first saw her in. Her hands clasped her knees and she rested her chin on them while staring at the hole in the ground.

"Yes," she sighed.

"Well, I am not going to let you die," Sonny said emphatically. "You are too precious, too lovely and too important to me, and to all of us, for me to sit idly by and let that happen. If I'd known you were wasting away to nothing, pining for my lost brother and all, I'd a rode back here and given you that spanking myself and made you eat. Do you hear?" Sonny took her by the shoulders and forced her to turn her face to him. "You are going to start eating and you are going to be happy and feel good again, do you hear me?"

Suzanne gave him a pathetic look and then shook her head no and closed her eyes.

"Yes you do and yes you are. Colt would never have wanted you to be like this. He would have wanted you to go on with your life—be the person God intends you to be—the princess, the queen that Colt knew."

At these words, Suzanne's eyes filled with tears and she hid her face against Sonny's shoulder and began to weep.

"Oh Sonny," she sobbed, "I miss him so—he just can't be dead. I couldn't go on if I thought him dead. I've prayed and I've prayed for God to bring him back—to give me some sign, some hope that he's still alive somewhere and trying to come back to me, but it all seems so hopeless." Suzanne broke down in a flood of fresh tears. A lump rose in Sonny's throat as his own eyes moistened.

"I know, hon, I know," he squeezed her shoulder and held her tight. "It tore the heart out of me, too, at first—sometimes it still does," he said huskily, swallowing hard. "Sometimes I get so mad at God I could cuss, but you know, it wasn't until I gave my pain and grief over to the Lord that I began to see life was still worth the living and. . . you will too—you'll see, you will too. I am back now and I'm here to help you."

Suzanne pulled back and withdrew a hanky from her pocket and blew her nose. Wiping her eyes with just the hint of a smile, she said, "I did, you know—cussed and yelled at God. It's probably why he hasn't answered my prayers."

Sonny chuckled, "Yeah, if he was like us that would probably be so, but he ain't."

"Don't say ain't in front of the schoolteacher," she gave him a feeble smile and sniffled.

Sonny laughed again and said, "That's better, c'mon; let's go find you a big, juicy, beef steak, we've got to get you feeling better."

"Ugh," Suzanne said, "That sounds perfectly awful, it's my heart that needs to get well."

"I know, and I'm here to remind you that your broken heart can be mended. The season for your grief is over now. Colt would have wanted that, and if perchance he is alive somewhere, he will find you again and in the meantime you'd better be ready if he does."

"Sonny, do you think there's a chance?" she asked wistfully. "That really wasn't him in that coffin was it? He might be alive."

Sonny stood and pulled the girl to her feet. "Suzanne, I have to be honest with you. I am afraid I have reconciled to the fact that Colt's dead, but I'm not God and I don't know what's ahead. I know it must be confusing for you now, but I urge you to put Colt to rest in your thoughts. Give him over to God and concentrate on what you need to do now. Can you do that?"

Suzanne slowly nodded and allowed Sonny to take her hand and lead her back up the path. "Will you help me?" she asked timidly.

Suzanne found some solace in Sonny's encouragement and constant attention. It seemed he went out of his way to insure she was eating properly and with her parents help, little by little, she began to regain both her appetite and weight. She had some sense that he might be neglecting his work at the ranch, but when she saw the Sabers at church, both Grant and Jessica seemed genuinely concerned about her welfare and assured her that they could spare Sonny if it would help her get back on her feet.

For a time, she had stopped going to church altogether, partly because she could not bear to see the look in everyone's eyes when they looked at her, but mostly because of a profound sense of betrayal by God. Why had He let her down and taken Colton? Then hope would kick in and she would imagine Colt to be alive somewhere, and would repent of her hard thoughts towards God and earnestly begin praying for his safe return again.

After his return in the fall, Sonny soon had her back in church, telling her that she should curry God's favor by doing the things she knew to do.

"Neglect of your inner spirit is just as lethal as neglect of your body, if not more so," he had said, and he was right. Once she began going to church and attending to the "Word of God" as it was preached, she began to experience an inner strength to face each new day. A breakthrough really came for her on the day she sat back down at the piano and played for the song service. A power and anointing swept over her and flowed down through her fingers and out into the music that swelled in rhythm and melody until the whole congregation began to sing with one voice and one heart.

Suzanne played with the tears streaming down her face and a healing—a kind of cleansing, seemed to wash her free of the hurt, loneliness and loss. It was as if she was playing her music for Colt—that somewhere in the darkness of his lostness he would hear it and be drawn back to her. That was a Sunday that Reverend Cummings did not preach. As long as the girl played, the people kept asking for another song, and there wasn't a dry eye in the house. Smiling, Pastor

Cummings just folded his hands, sat back in his chair, closed his eyes and let the music wash over him in what he knew was a sovereign act of God.

By Christmastime, she had renewed her activities at both school and church. She turned down a number of invitations to local parties and dances, but when she did attend, it was at Sonny's insistence and in his company. At first she found it produced a great melancholy to attend these functions for she was always reminded of Colt, but Sonny was a force that would not be denied and she eventually began to experience a good time with the sanguine cowboy.

She no longer spoke of her belief that Colt was alive, but rather kept those thoughts to herself, pondering them in her heart. She drew strength from a determination to be herself, to be the girl Colt remembered when he came back, and was grateful that Sonny had awakened that idea in her on the day he found her by the river.

Before springtime, Sonny's attentions became obviously more than just the concerns of a brother for his sister's well-being and on Valentines Day, he boldly presented her with a box of chocolates, and a request to escort her as his date to the Community Sweethearts Dance.

Suzanne stood in the open doorway gazing at the tall cowboy with his slicked-down hair, holding his hat and grinning as he handed her the heart-shaped box of candy.

"What's this for?" she asked.

"It's for you, sweets for the sweet."

"Well, thank you, you didn't have to do that, in fact, I'm confused, why did you?"

"I figured it was time for me to stop looking after my brother's interest and declare my own and besides that, there is a Biblical precedent."

"A Biblical precedent, what do you mean?"

Sonny looked a little uncomfortable and fidgeted with his hat. "You know—the part where if a man dies without leaving any kids, his brother is to take his wife and raise up children for him."

Suzanne's mouth dropped open. "I wasn't his wife yet," she said sadly.

"In the Biblical economy of things you were. You were engaged and that was the same thing."

Suzanne looked past Sonny to white clouds drifting in a blue sky. "I haven't given up on Colt," she said. "What would he say if he came back and found you paying court to me?"

Sonny shifted uncomfortably from one foot to the other. "Well, I have thought about that and to be honest with you, if I thought he'd be back, I wouldn't even be here, I'd bow out as gracefully as I could and let you two resume your love affair, but I don't think that is going to happen and if it hadn't of been for him I would have declared my suit for you long before this."

Suzanne shivered uncomfortably. "I'm cooling off the house, what time do you want to pick me up?"

"You mean you'll go?" Sonny asked excitedly.

"Well, of course I'll go with you. I certainly would not go with anyone else, but not as your date—you may escort me as you have done previously. My heart is forever and always in your brother's safe keeping."

"Aw Suzanne," the cowboy was crestfallen. "I can't compete with his ghost. You've got to give me a chance at your heart, too."

"Colt has it," she said simply. "You want it, go and get it from him. I will be ready at six o'clock," with that, she turned and went inside, closing the door.

The desks had all been pushed to the sides and the school was gaily lit with lanterns and decorated with red and white crepe paper, cutout hearts and little cupids. A string band was tuning up by the stove, and folks were arriving in horse and buggy, carrying covered dishes to the school cloakroom, now serving as a temporary pantry.

Sonny, looking handsome in a dark new suit, string tie and a soft gray Stetson, helped Suzanne step down from the buggy. Entering the crowded school house, he removed his slicker and helped Miss Kluesman remove her coat. She was resplendent in a pink dress, her hair done up in a stylish curl and supported by the turquoise and rhinestone combs that Colt had given her so long ago. The beautiful sapphire necklace and earrings that had once belonged to the Empress Carlotta, were in brilliant display, matching the engagement ring on her finger. She appeared positively radiant. Sonny made the comment on how lovely she looked for the second time that evening, making a mental note that Suzanne was making a statement to him with the Spanish combs and jewelry.

It was a lovely evening, the opening dance, a waltz and Sonny swung Suzanne out onto the dance floor and held her in impeccable fashion while he danced with all the charm and grace he could muster, a fact that did not go unnoticed by Suzanne as she twirled and lilted about.

"You are certainly dancing well," she said. "What's gotten into you?"

"Me?" he acted surprised. "Perhaps I am on a quest for a missing heart."

"What about Kathreen?" she asked. He momentarily broke rhythm but soon corrected his step.

"What about her?"

"I thought she was your sweetheart." Suzanne gave him a penetrating look with those blue eyes of hers.

Sonny thought the look could cut through cold steel when she looked like that. "I haven't heard from her for awhile," he said.

"Well, I have, she writes to me often. Maybe it's because you stopped writing to her."

"Pretty hard to send letters from the Goodnight Trail."

"Do you want me to tell her you asked me out?"

Sonny miss-stepped again and his neck flamed red above his starched collar. "I reckon not." He clipped off his answer.

"Why not?" Suzanne feigned surprise. "Don't you think she ought to know, or are you moving on from her just like you did from Margarita?"

Sonny chuckled in spite of his embarrassment. "Who can explain the affairs of the heart?"

"So, Kate isn't going to get any more of an explanation than Margarita did?" Suzanne said cryptically, "It makes one wonder what kind—if any, might be in store for someone else down the line."

"Come on, Suzanne, Margarita wasn't Kate and Kate's not you."

"What's the difference, we all have feelings?"

Sonny pursed his lips and studied on the question as they moved about the room, then he said, "Some water runs on top of the ground and some's found in a good well and some's subterranean rivers that gush up like an artesian spring. Guess which one you are?"

"So, it's alright to go around trifling with a girl's affections then, is that it?"

Sonny smiled indulgently and shook his head. "Naw," he said, "you gotta remember most of us cowboys ain't as smart as Colt was. We have to sorta test the waters first; find the one that suits us. Some water's good for wading in, and some's good for swimming in, and some's way over your head—you can sink in that kinda water and never be seen again."

Suzanne's face blanched white. "Do you think that's what happened to Colt?"

Sonny blinked and looked puzzled for a moment. "I though this was about me, how'd he get into this conversation?"

Suzanne was pensive. She patted his shoulder and said, "He never left, Sonny—he never left."

Sonny scowled, then gave a big sigh. "Suzanne, you saw him in that casket, or what was left of him. I don't wish to be cruel, but when are you going to come to terms with that?"

In slow, measured tones, Suzanne answered him. "I am never going to come to terms with that because that was not him. He did not have the spot on his neck."

Sonny was incredulous. "Suzanne, I lived with him since he was a baby. We did everything together and I knew him like the back of my hand. We bathed together; slept together, even compared notes on how we were put together, when we was little kids. I never ever saw any brown spot on his neck. Now you explain that?"

Suzanne bowed her head for a moment and then lifted her eyes to a spot behind Sonny's ear. "You never danced with him with your head on his shoulder like I did. He had a spot right there," she lifted a finger and touched his neck, "a cute, little, brown spot, that I used to adore when we were close. That poor soul in the box was not Colton." Suzanne broke away from him and walked from the dance floor, just as the music ended.

Glumly, Sonny followed and saw Clay Anderson, the big cowboy from the Box 7, step up and ask Suzanne to dance. He felt nettled at Suzanne's last remark and slumped to the bench in a dark mood, watching the dancers.

"I suspect he's pretty deeply entrenched," a voice said beside him. Sonny looked up to see Gunner Kluesman holding a cup of coffee and watching his daughter, as Anderson whirled her about the floor.

"Howdy, Mr. Kluesman, didn't see you there for a minute," Sonny said.

"I was watchin' you two," he said. "Son, if you're going to pitch your hat into the ring, you better be prepared for the long haul 'cause, in no way, has she given up on your brother."

"I know," Sonny said dejectedly. "I halfway hope she's right and I halfway hope she ain't, and I think the back half is about to overtake the front half."

Gunner chuckled. "Life's like that—it goes on for the living. Mabel and I wanna thank you for all the help you've been to our gal and for what it's worth, we're in your corner. Just take it slow and give it time and you'll do okay."

Sonny espied Margarita talking with a couple of other girls who were sitting on the benches alongside the wall. She gave him a dark look as he strolled over and said with an easy smile, "Evening ladies, Margarita, would you like to dance with me?"

The Mexican girl flashed dark eyes at him then with a sigh, rose to her feet and took his arm and allowed him to lead her out onto the floor.

"How caum ju wan to dance weeth me now?" she asked.

"Why, Margie," he drawled, "I've always enjoyed dancing with you."

She scowled, "Doan call me dat, I am Margarita, Consuela, Delgado, Esteban, Nuevo. Ju know I doan like dees name ju call me."

"Sorry, Margie," Sonny chuckled, "I just can't seem to remember all that other stuff, how you been?" He looked over her head and caught Suzanne watching them as she and Clay danced past.

The girl frowned again. "Wha du ju care? Ju doan talk to me no moor."

"Yeah," he said looking back at her. "I have been kinda busy, you seeing anyone now?"

"Ju been busy weeth thee Senorita Susanna, I know, I see ju. Wha' would jor broder say eef he could see dees, wha' ju do?"

Sonny looked a little annoyed with her, what was wrong with everybody? Colt was gone. . . dead. "Well, Margarita, he can't and that's the end of it. Now, do you want to dance with me or not?"

"Jes," she said, chastised. She allowed Sonny to pull her close while they swayed to the music.

The evening wore on, and Suzanne danced with the Trinidads, both Al, and Ron, and even once with James. Clay Anderson asked her to dance twice more and some of the other cowboys as well, but Sonny made no further effort to dance with her. He seemed to be having a good time with Margarita and some of the other girls and did not approach her again until the last dance was announced.

Clay Anderson had just stepped up to Suzanne, and was awkwardly attempting to request the dance with her, when Sonny shoved in front of him and said, "Saved the last dance for me, didn't you?" He took her arm and led her towards the floor as the band started a slow waltz.

"That was rude," Suzanne chided, "I shouldn't even dance with you now, after you ignored me all evening."

Sonny held her at arms length and danced stiffly. "I'm surprised you noticed, what with you being in the arms of that big gorilla from the Box 7 the whole time."

Suzanne's voice was steady and low and in slow, measured tones she said, "Mr. Saber, you brought me here as my escort, not as my date, and I was under the impression you wished for me to have a good time. If you plan to take me home as my escort, I suggest you go find your manners, wherever you left them. Clay Anderson has been a perfect gentleman and I might have enjoyed this last dance with him, if you hadn't barged in."

Sonny stopped and let go of her. Red faced, he bowed stiffly from the waist and said, "Well, excuse me, Miss Kluesman. I will speak to your father to insure you get home safely—good night!" With that declaration, he left her standing there and walked off the dance floor.

Flabbergasted, Suzanne watched as he went over to where her father was standing, spoke briefly, then strode out the door of the school into the night.

Clay tapped her on the shoulder and said, "Alright if I cut in?" She turned to look at the smiling cowboy and nodded. They finished the dance together and then applauded the band with the rest of the dancers.

Clay said, "I see Saber left, do you need escortin' home?"

"No thank you, Clay, my folks are here and I can go home with them, but thanks for asking, that was thoughtful of you."

"Anytime, ma'am, anytime," he tipped his hat and left the building.

They got their coats and she walked out with her parents. "What went on between you and Sonny?" her dad asked. "He left here with a burr under his blanket, if I'm any judge."

"I'm not sure," Suzanne said. "I think he has ideas of trying to take Colt's place in my affections."

"He brought you here in your buggy, didn't he?"

"Yes."

"I 'spect he's walking back to the place to pick up his horse then. You drive on and we'll follow you in our rig. If you see him 'long-side the road, be careful not to run him down."

Suzanne looked startled at her father, and then relaxed when she saw the twinkle in his eye.

"Oh, daddy, you're teasing me."

They drove out of the schoolyard onto the road towards town, but did not travel more than half the distance before they saw Sonny striding resolutely along. Suzanne pulled up alongside of him and held the pinto in, to match his steps.

"You want a ride?" She asked sweetly.

"Nope," Sonny said.

"I thought you cowboys didn't like to walk if you could ride."

"Sorry, ma'am," he drawled, "I can't ride with ya, I lost my manners and I'm too busy lookin' for 'em."

Suzanne placed a hand over her mouth and stifled a chuckle. How alike these Saber boys were. That was exactly the way Colton would have acted.

"I'll drive alongside you here for a little—in case you find them," she said. "Wouldn't want you having to walk all the way to your horse and ruin those fancy dancing boots of yours."

Sonny stopped and looked down at the toes of his boots. He wiped the dust off first one and then the other on the back of his pants leg and said, "Well, I'll be doggoned, ma'am, here's my manners. Somehow they got shoved down into my boot tops alongside a my heart. Just let me haul 'em up out o' there and dust 'em off a mite. . . there, now that's better." Sonny swallowed hard. Cleared his throat, and went on, "A-hum. . . I beg your pardon, Miss Kluesman, for my rudeness earlier this evening and if you would be so kind as to accept my apology, I believe I would be ever so grateful, and could take you up on your generous offer of a ride."

Her folk's buggy rumbled past them as she pulled Checkers to a stop. "See you young people at home," her father called out.

"Get in," Suzanne laughed, and then shook the reins against the pinto's rump once Sonny gained his seat. They rode in silence for awhile then Suzanne said, "You thinking about going wading again?"

"Huh?" Sonny said. "Oh, you mean Margarita?" He chuckled, "Naw, I already got my feet wet once—I think I'll head for deeper waters, if you don't mind."

"Suit yourself," she said, "but you're wasting your time if you're talking about me. I already told you where my heart is."

The spring roundup marked the anniversary of Colt's disappearance and Suzanne had just rolled up the buffalo robe and put it away for the year. She sat on her bed looking longingly out of her window, scarcely noticing the singing of the robins calling to each other or the warm breeze that ruffled her curtain and brought the scent of apple blossoms. Her thoughts were on what might have been. With a heavy heart, she looked to the unfinished wedding dress on the stand in the corner.

"Lord," she said, "how long? I should be happy at home with my husband and maybe a little one on my knee by this time. What went wrong? Why have things happened the way they have? Where is Colton and will I ever really be happy again?" She lay down on her bed and let the grief envelope her once again, her tears soaking her pillow. Finally she fell asleep.

Chapter Five

Playin' House

Tye knocked at the door of the hacienda but there was no answer. He had left Penny at the adobe making up a double bed someone had brought while they were on the hike. Trouble was they had taken away the single bed when they left. That made two things he needed to talk to the mine boss about.

He knocked again and the door swung ajar. "Hello," he called. "Is anybody home?" He thought he heard voices in the back, so pushed the door open and stepped inside, calling again. From somewhere in one of the back rooms he heard a man's voice and then the sounds of a woman groaning. He walked down a long hallway with several doors on either side, towards the noise. The sounds seemed to be coming from the end where one door was open.

Cautiously, he approached, his heart beating faster. It sounded as though someone might be hurting Mrs. Jones. Stepping over articles of clothing strewn on the floor, he stopped in the open doorway and stood riveted to the spot at the spectacle that met his eyes. Reese

Hutchinson and Evita Jones were on the bed in intimate embrace, and neither of them had any clothes on.

"What are you doing to her?" Tye burst out, then his face flamed in embarrassment as realization struck him.

The couple paused, shocked at the unexpected interruption, then Hutch dove off the other side of the bed and grappled for a six-gun hanging in its holster on the back of a chair. Evita gave a short scream and struggled to cover herself with a crumpled sheet.

"What the hell are you dong here?" Hutchinson snarled and cocked the gun, pointing it at Tye.

"I—I was looking for Jones," Tye stammered.

His voice deadly, Reese said, "Well, it ought to be plain enough to even a dummy like you, he ain't here, so get and keep your trap shut too, if you know what's good for ya."

Tye hurried back down the hallway and out the front door. He heard Evita say, "Do you think he'll tell?" He did not hear Hutch's response.

"Now what are we going to do?" Tye said. He sat on one of the chairs looking at the bed against the wall. "I couldn't find Jones at home. I asked around, but no one seemed to know what happened to my bed."

"I don't have fleas, you know," Penny said sarcastically.

Tye was confused. "What do you mean?"

"I've slept in a bed with a man, ya know, even if it was against my will. There's plenty of room for two people—'sides; there is not room in this little place for another bed anyway. We can barely turn around in here as it is."

Tye looked dubious, "Do you think? What about not sleeping in your clothes? I already saw that today."

"You what, who did you see like that?"

"Up at the ranch house," he said. "I walked in on Evita and the big guy with the patch over his eye a half hour ago. They were in bed. . . like that."

"Good Lord, Hutchinson and Mrs. Jones? Tye, you'd better be careful, that man is a killer. He'll come looking for you if Jones finds out—not that it'd matter all that much to him."

"You think the mine boss wouldn't care?" Tye was surprised.

"I know he wouldn't—except for his pride. Do you know where he probably was?"

Tye shook his head.

"He was probably down in one of the Mexican adobe huts breaking in a new girl."

He looked at her puzzled. "Breaking in a new girl? Do you mean he takes it upon himself to train each new girl that is brought in here?"

Penny's eyes opened wide and her jaw dropped. Suddenly she burst out laughing. Tye sat looking at her, the unanswered question still on his face. He gave a slight grin, watching until her laughter subsided.

"Tye, you are priceless," she said, "and yes—that's exactly what I mean, but not like you think. He did me, the beast, and I'd wager he's treated every other girl or woman in this place to his Sunday afternoon training, too, at least those he took an interest in."

"Huh! He's busier than I thought; working on Sundays like that while everybody else is taking it easy. Too bad he doesn't stay at home, I think his wife could use a little of that training herself."

Again his comments took Penny by surprise. For a brief moment she thought she saw a slight twinkle in his eyes but when she looked again, it was gone and that same blankness had returned.

"I'll keep my dress on," she said.

"Hum?" The lad turned to look at her.

"I washed it today, remember? I can sleep in my dress tonight, it's clean. There's no need for anyone spending the night on a chair."

"Oh, yeah, that's good. I probably should have washed my long-johns too."

"You got another pair?"

"Yes," he said.

"Well go jump in the irrigation ditch with a bar of soap and then put them on. I don't want any stinky man in bed with me."

A little while later Felipe Rodriguez stopped his horse in the twilight and sat looking at the cowboy sitting naked in the irrigation ditch holding a bar of soap.

"Wha are ju doeeng, compañero?" he said.

"Huh? Oh, Penny wanted me to sit out here with the bar of soap. She doesn't want any stinky man in her bed."

Rodriguez chuckled, "Senor Tye, she wans ju to juse thee soapa. Ju are dat steenkeeng hombre."

When he finally finished washing, Tye sat on the edge of the bed clad in his clean long-johns with his eyes following Penny's movements as she finished wiping the supper dishes and placed them on the shelf. She folded the dish towel and draped it over the back of the chair, her eyes catching his.

"What are you looking at?" she asked.

"You, I'm looking at you."

"Do you like what you see?"

"Yes, it's nice," he said simply.

"What's so nice?" she had a questioning look in her eye. "What exactly is it that you think is nice?"

Tye's face turned red in embarrassment. "I can't tell you," he said.

Penny looked askance, "You can't tell me? What on God's green earth would prevent you from telling me. . ." she paused, "unless it was something naughty. Was it?"

Tye turned and crawled into the bed, pulling the covers over him and facing the wall. "I think it's time for me to get to sleep.

Penny laughed, "Ho-ho—it was something naughty—what was it?" She came over and knelt on one knee, on the bed and began to pull on the blanket, trying to roll him over.

"Nothing," he yelled. "It was nothing, c'mon let go, I gotta get some sleep."

"Oh no you don't, you've got to tell me what it was that was so nice." She yanked the blanket down and began tickling him.

Tye squirmed against her tormenting fingers and tried to keep from laughing but to no avail. "Stop it Penny—it was nothing," he chuckled, "leave me alone."

"Not until you tell me, Mr. Tye—whatever-your-name-is. Tell me."

"Alright—alright, quit tickling me," he laughed and rolled over and grabbed her wrists and pressed her down on the bed, holding her hands spread out on the pillow.

Penny said, "You're going to tell me or you're going to have to hold me like this all night long, otherwise I'm going to keep pestering you until you do."

In resignation, Tye sighed and let go of her and lay back down. "I was just thinking how nice you jiggled when you moved," he said.

"How nice I what—jiggled? Where was I jiggling?"

Lamely he said, "You know."

Penny rose up on one elbow to study the red faced cowboy. She laughed, "Can't say it can you? Well, it's nice to know someone around this God-forsaken place can appreciate my femininity and still treat me with a little respect, even if I am about to crawl into bed with them. Tye, I think I like you." She sat up and re-arranged the blankets over them, blew out the candle and lay back down beside him in the dark.

"Goodnight Tye," she said, "and thanks for that."

Sometime later, Tye came awake with Penny climbing on top of him under the covers. "What are you doing?" he gasped. He was vaguely aware of her pressed over him.

"I'm trying to get on the other side of you," she whispered.

"How come?" He whispered back and wondered why they were whispering.

"Because, I have to sleep on the inside—next to the wall, I can't sleep on the outside, now scoot over."

He squirmed over while the girl on top of him wriggled and slid off to drop in the niche he had vacated next to the wall. It seemed to Tye that Penny's exaggerated movements on top of him, left little room for doubt regarding their close proximity and that she was in no particular hurry to get off of him, either.

They both lay on their backs panting in the dark from their struggles. Finally Tye swallowed hard, his mouth dry, and his heartbeat slowly subsiding in his chest.

"Why in the world do you have to sleep next to the wall?"

"Because," she said.

"Because is no reason."

"It is for me."

"Okay, because it is, good night." He turned on his side and made to go back to sleep.

After a few moments he heard her whisper timidly in the dark, "It's silly, I know but, ever since I was a little girl, I have had to sleep on the inside of the bed. . . in case something tries to come out from under it and get me while I'm sleeping."

Tye scooted over some more. "Get you huh?" he chuckled. "Why are we whispering?"

"Shh," she said, "I don't want it to hear me, then it won't know where I am."

"Oh, that's nice—just as long as it doesn't know where you're at, it doesn't matter if it knows where I'm at—is that it?"

"Shh, not so loud," she giggled. "Of course it doesn't matter. By the time it's finished eating you, it will be too full to wanna bother with me."

"So, that's the way of it then, is it?" he said out loud. Then, leaning over out of the bed, he poked his face down underneath it and hollered, "Hey! Down there, she's on the inside—over next to the wall. . . there's a nice tender girl named Penny and she's a lot sweeter than the stinky man on the outside. I thought you ought 'a know."

Penny squealed in fright and ducked down, pulling the covers over her head, then grabbed her arms about his waist and lay there trembling and giggling nervously. She was up next to him so tight he was having trouble laying back down. Of course the fact that he was laughing uproariously didn't help either. He finally managed to get comfortable while the clinging girl's giggles subsided and they both regained their composure.

"That was mean," she said. "Just for that you are going to have to protect me from the boogie-man all night long."

"From the boogie-man?" he said dryly, "Who's going to protect me. . . from you?"

All through the next week, Tye looked for an opportunity to speak with Jones to no avail. He was growing anxious to hear what the boss might have to say about his identity and origin. He and Penny had acquired the things they needed from the store and Tye had found the Winchester to his liking. After firing a few shots it was apparent he could hit what he was aiming at and obviously had experience as a shooter. He wondered about handling a six-gun and felt a vague affinity to the ones he saw some of the men wearing.

Penny had managed to secure some woman's undergarments and an extra pair of long-johns that were too baggy, but a modicum of modesty was set up between them, with Tye waiting outside while she got ready for bed. They still slept together in the same bed with Tye, for the most part, oblivious as to the impropriety of such an arrangement and Penny no longer caring. Instead she was actually enjoying the closeness that was developing between her and the cowboy in a brotherly-sisterly sort of way that had remained platonic even though the sensual aspects of their togetherness, from time to time, were not lost on the girl. Penny found it a welcome relief to the horror and abuse to which she had previously been subjected, and mostly feared that something might happen to bring their domestic situation to an end.

At times she even felt almost like her virtue and chastity had been restored, consequently she was careful to do nothing that might upset the precarious balance that existed between them, though more and more, she realized she was wishing it could be otherwise. She sensed, if not knew, that once Tye found out who he was. . . remembered, things would decidedly go one way or the other between them, and she held out little hope that it would be to her benefit.

Ever since that first night in bed when she had deliberately tried to see if he would respond to her and had gained sufficient proof, even though he had remained ignorant of it, she was satisfied that other than his mind, he was fully functional. She thought it best to keep things between them as they were for now. It wasn't as though she did not desire his attention that way, it was more like she felt responsible not to take advantage of him and possess something he was not able to knowingly give. For the girl, those quiet moments of sharing in the dark before they went to sleep became the highpoint of her day and she found herself looking forwards to bedtime for that reason, along with the delight of snuggling up to him.

Penny threw herself into the work of taking care of their little adobe hut. She fashioned curtains for the window from some print flour sacks, and kept the floor swept, and flowers on the table. She planted a vegetable garden, tended it, obtained a few chickens, and had Tye knock together a coop for them. She made daily trips to the market to shop for the food stuffs needed to fix nice meals and have supper ready for him at the end of the day. She began to pay particular attention to her appearance, having obtained a pretty white dress and spent time sewing on a red one. Often she wore a wild flower fixed in her hair which seemed to enhance her homespun beauty to the point that some of the men about the camp began to take note of her, often making remarks as she passed by, not all of them necessarily uncomplimentary.

Tye soon became accustomed to having Penny waiting for him when he rode in from the mesa and except for a vague disquieting feeling he could not identify, he too enjoyed the time of closeness in their bed. He decided to drop the subject of a second bed as there was, indeed, no room for another one anyway, but he still watched for an opportunity to talk to L.T.

Jones. It wasn't until the next Sunday afternoon that Tye found a chance to head up to the big house on the hill. He met Jones coming down the path that led to the village and stopped to talk with the mine boss.

"Hello, Tye," Jones said. "How are things going?"

"Fine sir, I was coming up to talk to you."

"What's on your mind, son?"

"I want to know what you can tell me about where I came from."

The mine superintendent looked skeptical at the youth. "Who you been talking to, that big-mouthed girl I sent down there?"

"Not really," Tye said. "She just asked me some questions that I realized I didn't know the answers to and she said I should ask you."

Jones looked nonplussed, "I'll just bet she did." He studied the cowboy, one hand clasping an elbow, the other stroking his chin whiskers. "I don't know much really. Hutch and the boys brought you here and they got you from the Comancheros who got you from the Comanche out of Texas. Don't you remember anything?"

"No sir, hardly anything. Where is Texas?"

"Oh, its north of here a ways," he dismissively waved his hand. "You don't need to know, you're doing a fine job here. Isn't everything to your liking?"

"Well, yes. . . he paused, "I just don't know who I am, is all."

Jones forced a laugh. "You're Tye, my prize-fighter. How'd you like to take on Reese Hutchinson?"

"Who?'

"Hutch, he wants to go a few rounds with you."

"You mean the one-eyed guy, don't you? I don't know, I don't think he likes me."

"Aw, hell, son, he don't like anybody, I'd like to see you beat his ears back. By the way, Mrs. Jones needs some help arranging the furniture and asked me to send up someone for the afternoon. You think you could go up and give her a hand? I got things to attend to down in the village for the rest of the day."

Innocently Tye said, "Got some more girls to train huh? Guess a boss's work is never done."

Jones frowned, then said, "Just go up and help Evita." He turned and stomped off down the trail.

Tye walked up onto the porch of the hacienda and hearing voices, he went around back to see Evita Jones berating the Mexican lad who did the watering.

"Manuel, you have let my roses die at the end of the hacienda, why did you not water them?"

"I deed, Senora," the boy protested. He was standing there with no shirt on, his mistress holding him by one arm.

"Then why did they?" she said angrily and shook him.

"They no geets enough of thee sun, I theenk," Manuel said

"I am going to have to chastise you again, Manuel, come into the house with me." She turned, with cheeks flushed, and Tye thought there was a strange light in her eye.

Evita Jones stopped suddenly, the color rising in her face even more, and let go of the boy's arm, when she saw the cowboy standing there with hat in hand.

"What are you doing here?" she demanded.

"The boss said you needed help moving some things and sent me up here," Tye said. He watched as the boy fidgeted and moved away from the woman while rubbing his arm.

Evita regained her composure and turned an aloof look on the lad standing behind her. "Run along now,

Manuel, I will deal with you later. Come into the house Mr.—ah—it's Tye isn't it? I will show you what I want you to do."

Tye followed her into the spacious living room. He noticed that although she was wearing a light housecoat, her legs and feet were bare except for a pair of thonged sandals.

Indicating Jones' chair in front of the fireplace she said, "I want this chair, and then mine, slid over near the patio doors where we can catch the evening breeze."

Tye grasped the chair from behind while the boss's wife bent over from the waist to pick up one of the Navajo throw rugs from the floor. He was startled to see her short housecoat ride up in the back revealing her undergarment beneath. He caught his breath and looked away, wondering if she knew how much of herself, she had just exposed to his view.

Straitening, she led the way to the spot where she wanted the chair and directed him to place it at the desired angle. She squatted in front of him, to spread the rug, her housecoat parting over her thighs. With a mischievous look she said, "Well, don't just stand there, help me straighten this rug."

Red faced, Tye squatted down and reached for the end of the crumpled rug.

"Does that look about right?" she said.

Something in the tone of her voice caused him to look up at her, while nodding affirmation, only to have his gaze arrested. Mrs. Jones, seemingly unaware of the visual image her immodest posture was presenting to the young man, was staring at him with a strange look on her face.

Tye started up, lost his balance and tumbled over backwards. Embarrassed, he hurriedly got to his feet, with a wild beating in his heart, and a quickening of his pulse. He vaguely recollected seeing girls without their clothes on before; there had been Sarah at the river and Penny up at the cliff dwellings, but that had all seemed so indistinct. It had been nothing compared to this. Nervously, he averted his eyes and wondered if he should leave.

Evita stood to her feet, her robe falling back into place. "My, you are clumsy aren't you?" she said. "We need to move my chair now." She turned and walked across the room, loosening the belt at her waist. Tye followed to the chair and this time watched in fascination as the older woman bent over to collect another rug, an action which caused her housecoat to part and free her large, pendulous breasts, allowing them to bobble into view.

Tye stared open-mouthed. *"So this was what a woman's breasts looked like"*. He was mesmerized at the whiteness of her bosom, while something stirred in the back of his mind and seemed to check those thoughts stirring in the front of it. Either he had imagined it, had dreamed it, or he had been in close proximity to someone else like this before. Who, he wondered?

"This darned robe," Mrs. Jones said, "I can't seem to keep it tied. Slowly, deliberately, while watching the cowboy's reaction, she lifted each breast and tucked it back inside.

"You naughty boy," she said, "were you looking at my bubbies?" She cast a side-long glance at him and then smiling, led the way back across the room.

Tye awkwardly slid the chair after her until she stopped. "Put it here," she said, indicating the spot. Once again, she squatted to unroll the rug in front of her chair and again the gown parted, this time to catch in front, revealing her full cleavage.

"Help me," she commanded.

He knelt, staring, knowing he shouldn't, but somehow transfixed by the display of her feminine charms moving about under the light housecoat.

She saw his look and said, "This damn thing is just in the way," and so saying, she let the housecoat drop from her shoulders and kicked it away, an action that again exposed her to his astonished gaze. She remained in this salacious posture with the comment, "Besides, it's too hot to wear anything, anyway. . . do you like what you see?"

Tye broke as if from a trance and turned away. "I—I better leave." He started to scramble up but Evita grasped the front of his shirt and pushed him over backwards.

"You did like that, didn't you?" she said. "Would you like to see more of me?" She began unbuttoning his shirt. "Who'd ever thought such a good looking fellow was so bashful, come on get these clothes off, I'm not going to hurt you."

He felt helpless, almost detached, as Evita Jones straddled him, her large breasts pressing into his face while she worked the shirt up off his back. With his face pushed into the warmth of her cleavage, the feel and smell of her awoke an image somewhere deep inside him.

He was on a perfect hill, the sun shining down on a lovely girl with golden hair and his face was pressed to her bosom, and then suddenly there was this huge green snake. He was terrified.

"No!" he shouted, "I can't do this." He started up and scrambled to his feet, knocking Evita Jones sprawling across the floor. "You're Jones' wife—he's been good to me, I can't do this to him—to you, besides, there is someone else. Let go of my shirt, I'm getting out of here."

"Why, you ungrateful pup," Evita Jones hissed. "I offer myself to you and you turn me down? If you run out now, I'll tell Jones you came in here and tried to rape me." She gave a mighty yank on Tye's shirt and pulled it the rest of the way off of him. "Then you'll see how good he is."

"You're crazy," Tye said. "Let me out of here." He darted out of the patio door without his shirt, past a gaping Manuel and the surprised cook who had just emerged from the kitchen at the sounds of Mrs. Jones yelling.

The boss's wife began to holler for help and scream "rape, rape," as Tye raced away down the hill towards the village; her screams still ringing in his ears.

Penny looked up as he burst through the door. "What happened?" she asked. "Where's your shirt?"

"I left it," Tye panted, "Jones' crazy wife pulled her clothes off and then started on mine—she got my shirt."

"You mean that vixen tried to seduce you?" Penny asked incredulously.

"Yeah, something like that." Slowly his breathing began to return to normal.

"Well, that conniving harlot, I am not surprised."

"I gotta get away from here, they'll be coming after me. She started yelling rape—Jones'll be coming for me as soon as he gets back."

"I doubt it," Penny said. "She'll rant and rave and they'll have a big fight and then go off into the bedroom and makeup. I've seen it all before."

Penny was right. Tye spent an anxious evening until bedtime but no one showed up at the door. Eventually, he went to bed and fell into a fitful sleep filled with troubling dreams. He dreamt he was lying on a hill top and kissing a beautiful girl. There were white, fluffy clouds overhead in a brilliantly blue sky and then she was naked and he was feeling her. *"Don't,"* she said, and turned away, moving off. He reached for her, calling to her but she seemed to fade away. He then saw her standing, naked in the river beckoning to him. He started towards her but the water got too deep and was running so swiftly he could not get to where she was. She called and called to him, beckoning, until the water swept him away. He called back, but she did not answer. All at once he was at the pueblos and the beautiful girl was again standing in the pool, smiling and beckoning to him and calling his name.

He was sitting on the ground, hurriedly pulling off his boots to join her, but then it was no longer the girl, but Mrs. Jones without her clothes, laughing at him and screaming "rape, rape," her voice echoing off the cavern cliffs.

"Tye, Tye! Wake up—wake up, you're dreaming." Penny was shaking him and he came awake with a start in the darkness. His body was damp with sweat and his heart was thudding in his chest.

"Goodness," Penny said to him, "that must have been some dream. What was going on?"

He didn't answer for a moment but lay there in the dark, his mind a whirl of jumbled, mixed up thoughts. "I don't know," he said finally. "There was this girl and she was in some sort of trouble. We were together on this river and she was standing in the water without any clothes on and calling to me. I tried to get to her, but couldn't because the current swept me away. After that I was at the pueblos, the cliff dwellings, sitting on the ground pulling my boots off and she was there in the pool—in the water, you know, like you were. She was smiling and waving to me to come in and when I tried, it wasn't her anymore but Mrs. Jones just laughing and then screaming 'rape' at me." He swallowed hard. "It was just plain crazy."

"You woke me up, you know. Do you have any idea what you were doing to me?"

"No," he said, "to you?"

"Yes, me, your hands were all over me." Penny was quiet for a moment and he said nothing.

"At first I was dreaming that it was Jones molesting me and I said, 'don't', but then I woke up and it was you. You—were. . . I was pulled back against you and it was kinda nice, but then you started groaning and trying to call out some other girl's name. That's when I woke you up."

Tye lay on his back, staring up at the dark ceiling with unseeing eyes as his pulse slowly subsided. A haunting sense of the past seemed to lurk just out of reach of his recall. It felt that, if he could just somehow turn the corner, he would know who she was—the girl in his dream, and knowing that would bring the rest of the story. He struggled to remember, but the harder he tried, the more the memory seemed to slip away. Besides, there was something else, this girl here in bed with him. What had he done to her? It was obvious she had been caught up in his wild dreaming and not without effect, if her sighing was any indication. He felt chastened and ashamed somehow, although he was not sure why.

"Penny, I'm sorry," he said.

"For what?"

"For—for whatever I did to you—I—I didn't know I was doing that stuff to you—I'm sorry."

She didn't respond right away. Finally, she sighed and turned over on her side away from him. "I'm sorry, too, not for what you did, but that you didn't know it was me. Who's Suzanne?"

Like a bolt of lightning Suzanne's image appeared in his mind's eye, and like the tide rolling in, his memory came flooding back.

"*Oh! Dear God*," he cried. He sprang from the bed and fumbled for matches to light the lamp. *"I know who I am."* Stumbling to a chair, he sat trembling while his memory catapulted back into place with a flood of recognition. He saw Suzanne clearly in his memory; her smile, her eyes, her golden hair, and sweet form, and with an ache tantamount to the stab of a knife, he remembered the long and hard-fought battle he had gone through to win that girl's heart. What had happened to them that he had now lost her? Where was she and was she still his? Frantically his mind groped for the answers he could not know, as the past months of their separation fell into place.

Penny stared back at him wide eyed. "You do?" she said, "Who?"

"My name is Colt—Colton Saber. My folks own the Crossed Sabers Ranch on the Pecos River and Suzanne is my sweetheart, my fiancée, we were about to be married when something happened."

Penelope sat up in the bed and pulled the blanket up around her shoulders. "What?" she asked. "What happened?"

Colt thought about it for a moment, "I'm not sure; it was in the spring. . . spring roundup. Suzanne was getting her wedding dress ready and—um—I remember working down south of the place on the river, when something happened. . . . oh, I remember, I saw smoke and went over to investigate. Somebody had trussed up one of our yearlings and it was laying there by a fire. I got down to turn it loose and that was the last I remember. Somebody must have hit me in the head and knocked me out—probably took my horse and rigging, too. How long have I been here? It's spring now isn't it?"

"I don't know," Penny said, "you were here when I came and that's been two or three months now. I got the impression you had been here a long time, at least a year or more."

"Yeah, I know I spent a winter here and it was so cold in the cavern. I've got to get out of here and back to Suzanne. She's got to be worried sick."

"How? They've got guards watching everybody. Do you know the way out?"

Colt studied on that for a moment. "I can find my way once I get shut of this place," he said.

"What about the Indians?"

"The 'Paches—I'll just have to dodge 'em; travel at night."

"Take me with you." Penny jumped from the bed and rushed to grab his arm. "Take me with you—promise?" She looked at him with imploring eyes.

Colt paused, "I guess, it's not going to be easy—we'll have to plan our escape carefully."

"Tell me about Suzanne," Penny said. "What is she like?"

"Okay, but I'll have to quit your bed. Give me a blanket and I'll roll up here by the stove. Tomorrow, you'll have to start squirreling stuff away for our trip out of here."

For the next several hours, Colton related to Penny the story of his courtship of the blacksmith's lovely daughter. He told of the weeks of struggle to get her a Christmas tree from the Davis Mountains, and the interruption of returning the Kiowa girl, Seeaugway, to her people; of the hardships of that journey which seemed to keep him from his beloved and of the hope that was generated upon his return when he presented her the Christmas tree. Penny wanted to know the details of that first kiss in the moonlight and how they had spooned, and she expressed amazement, as he told of the rebuff he received in St. Louis, and of his incredible rescue of Kathreen McClusky. By the time he had shared the disruption of taking the Empress Carlotta to Yuma, and of his falling into the hands of the Apache, and then of the wonder of their reunion and his capture of Suzanne's heart, along with the delightful but frightening trip to the Sweetgrass, the sky was lightening in the east.

Penny was drowsing and no longer listening. Still, Colt lay pondering all that had happened and wondering about what had gone on since his capture. The all too familiar ache in his heart for his sweet Suzanne returned with a vengeance and he vowed to get back to her as soon as possible. Roosters were crowing when he finally fell into a fitful sleep on the hard floor by the stove.

Chapter Six

Comanche Moon and Roman Candles

Spring, 1870, West Texas

After his return from the drive to Colorado, Sonny settled into the routine of ranch life. The influx of cash to the Crossed Sabers enabled them to make some much-needed improvements about the place including replacing some of the worn out machinery.

For a time he chaffed under the rebuff Suzanne had given him at the dance. How was he to regain her heart from his dead brother? Did he even want to? Mostly, his concern had been to see her restored to her former, vivacious self, although he did admit he was drawn to her. He wondered if the attraction was only because of the challenge she presented by being unavailable to him. When Colt was alive he had never allowed himself to pursue an interest in the blacksmith's daughter. It was much simpler to play the field and fill his desire for companionship of the fair sex with girls like Kathreen and Margarita. Suzanne was Colt's girl. But now that he was gone and she was left so desperately undone by it all, his heart just naturally went out to her. He had made up his mind to do all he could for her, for the sake of his brother's memory, if nothing else; only to find his own fickle heart becoming entwined and drawn to her; so that what he did for her now took on new meaning for him as well.

Spring brought with it the hope of new life and although Sonny felt some regret at the way he had allowed time, distance, and punching cattle to dull his interest for Kathreen McClusky, he was not too concerned about the redhead in Saint Louis. The cattle drive had pretty much put an end to their correspondence and he felt certain that, by this time, she had moved on to other interests. As for Margarita. . . well, she remained a friend, but as he had pointed out to Suzanne the night of the dance, Margarita was not her. Margarita definitely wanted to take him to places he did not want to go, although she was not above using her wiles to get him there. How many times on their rides out into the countryside had she allowed him liberties, only to decline her ultimate favors in lieu of marriage? He knew she was right about that and wouldn't have gone there anyway, but couldn't help feeling somewhat manipulated by her. With that came a certain level of resentment—he did not like the feeling of being used. Coupled with that was the knowledge that he himself was being less than gallant, so it was not difficult for him to allow the newness of spring that was sweeping away the gray of winter, to also sweep away his past romantic involvements, and look, instead, with fresh interest and hope at Suzanne Kluesman.

"Dad, are we going to make another drive to Colorado this year?" Grant Saber was bent over the weir down by the pond when Sonny asked the question.

The rancher pulled free the top board and watched as the water spilled out into the ditch to race away and flood the alfalfa field. Standing, he replied, "No, I don't think so. We sent all our prime stuff last time." He dropped the dripping board next to the gurgling weir and then added, "We need to give it a year, let the herd build back up so we can ship only two-year-olds to the Army, they bring the best price. Meanwhile, we can be beating the brush for strays and mavericks and should be in pretty good shape to push a big herd north next spring."

"Some of the neighboring ranchers have been asking—the Box 7 and the Rocking S in particular were interested in adding cattle, if we were going to make the drive," Sonny said.

His father studied his son with clear, gray eyes. "You feel like making that trip right now?"

"Not really," Sonny said.

"I didn't think so. Let's give it a year, we came out pretty good on that last trip and I'd like to concentrate on fixing things up around here, and it might be a good idea for us to stick close to home for awhile."

"That suits me," his son replied. He thought it uncanny that his father knew he did not want to leave again. He wondered if he knew it was because of Suzanne.

"Things are kind of up in the air right now," Grant went on, "Custer's shenanigans up on the Washita last November have the plains tribes in an uproar and it pushed a lot of them out onto the Llano and in our direction. Some of the bands have been raiding east of here, and we are not without exposure. I've been thinking we should give an eye to our fortifications."

Sonny nodded his head. News had come of Lieutenant Colonial George Armstrong Custer's attack on Black Kettle, the peace-loving head of the Cheyenne nation. Washita Creek was a small stream that flowed from the panhandle of Texas into the Indian Nations. The story from Fort Stockton had it that this past November Custer had led an early morning attack against Black Kettle's sleeping camp in a heavy fog. Just at dawn, he divided his forces into three groups and had the 7th Cavalry attack the defenseless camp while the brass band Custer always traveled with, played his favorite tune, *"Gary Owen."* The troops marched in and went to work slaughtering the astonished Cheyenne. When the battle was over there were one hundred and three Indians dead, but only eleven of them were full-grown fighting men. Casualties to the 7th were minimal as most of the unwary Indian warriors choose to flee rather than stay and fight.

Sonny could only wonder at the callousness of the man. Much goods were captured as the camp was prepared to winter on the Washita. Fifty-three women were taken back to Fort Riley in Kansas, among them was the beautiful Cheyenne Princess, Mo-nah-se-ta, the daughter of Little Rock, second to Black Kettle as chieftain. Her father was killed in the attack along with Black Kettle and his wife, as they fled from the camp. Riding double on a pony, both Black Kettle and his wife had been shot in the back as they were crossing the stream. They lay ignobly in the water for several hours after the battle was finished.

What was even more appalling to Sonny, was that Custer took Mo-nah-se-ta with him, along with a couple of other Cheyenne women, to lead a peace negotiating mission to these same Indians shortly after the attack. Once the government learned that Black Kettle was, indeed, on the reservation assigned to him by the Army, they sent the Lt. Colonial to patch things up.

Apparently they thought the Cheyenne Princess would give the unlikely ambassador an audience with the disenfranchised chiefs.

He had boldly faced the Chiefs of the southern bands, suing for peace. Rock Forehead and Little Robe, both formidable chiefs of the Cheyenne, sat down with the Long Hair and, although Custer did not smoke, he allowed a peace pipe to be shoved upon him and was warned, "Should he ever go against the pipe again, he would be killed," it was reported.

Custer was supposedly, somehow, married to the Indian Princess, Mo-nah-se-ta, after he had unwittingly put his hands on her in the Cheyenne camp. This was according to some custom of the Cheyenne of which he was ignorant, but was not above capitalizing on, for after the Cheyenne, along with the Kiowa and Comanche, had fled to the relative safety of the vast Llano Estacado, and out of reach of the *long-knives* for a time, Custer, it was rumored, had taken up with the lovely Mo-nah-se-ta, living all the past winter with her, while he made forays out on the Staked Plains in search of her departed kinsmen.

Meanwhile, his wife, Libby, was left unattended at Fort Riley in Kansas where she, ever his champion, suffered the enduring enmity for Armstrong of the entire U.S. Army Officer Corps, along with that of most of the men of his command. Her husband had earned their disdain a few years before, when, with callous disregard, he had left his command to go in search of the self-same Elizabeth, after he had previously left her behind. While he was gone, a Major Joel Elliot and eighteen of his men were killed and mutilated by the Indians just a couple of miles from where the 7th was encamped, and no one attempted to recover their bodies even though they were in plain sight. This stunt had cost "Yellow Hair" a court martial, with eight counts against him, the worst being the desertion of his command. He was convicted on all eight counts and sat out one year as a civilian without pay. It was only due to the efforts of General Sheridan, or "Little Phil" as he was known on the range, that Custer got his commission back, albeit as a Lt. Colonial and not as a General.

The upshot of all this was that the Indians were extremely hostile towards the white-eyes in general and to the "Forked-Tongued Soldiers," in particular, and were bent on taking it out on the isolated settlers and ranches of the frontier.

"I think it best we ride out by twos and threes," Grant said. "You take those two Brazos River boys under your wing, son, I'd hate to have to send word back to their folks that they'd lost their hair to some Comanche."

Sonny nodded and walked soberly back to the barn.

Two Dogs stared at the full moon, its white light even brighter here in the Gap where the old stage station stood. He waited in silence as his warriors filed quietly through. Snake-Who-Talks led the war party, his war bonnet glistening in the moonlight. Thirty braves followed the younger chieftain towards the river, and Two Dogs was anxious that their medicine be good this night. The people were angry with the encroachment of the long-knives and the way their brothers, the *Sha-hi-ye-la,* had been treated. He was intent on counting coup and carrying away much goods and many ponies on this raid. Perhaps then he would have enough ponies to obtain a second wife. His first wife, Little Calf, was complaining of the way the cold crept into her bones and was no longer interested in sharing his blankets, except to keep warm. She had urged him to take a second wife, to make her job easier.

The war chief smiled when he thought of the women of the *Sha-hi-ye-la*, the Cheyenne. Many of them were quite comely and he had even seen the Cheyenne Princess, Mo-nah-se-ta, one time. Her beauty and form were legendary on the plains. He had heard that her father was offered eleven ponies as a bridal gift for her hand—an unheard of price to pay for a wife—but the hapless brave who purchased her did not gain the approval of the young maid, and after several days of attempting to woo her to his blankets, he lost patience and tried to force his attentions upon her and claim the just due of a husband. *Spring Grass*, for such was her name, would have none of it and withdrew a pistol from beneath a blanket and shot him in the knee, then haughtily removed herself from the crippled warrior's lodge and returned to her father.

Two Dogs shook his head and kneed his pony forward. With a crippled knee, the *Sha-hi-ye-la* brave had paid a much greater price than eleven ponies, and still the chief's daughter remained unmarried, although she had been with child when taken by the "Yellow Hair" on the Washita. Perhaps she had not entirely refused the young brave after all.

In spite of her beauty and charm, Two Dogs would certainly think twice about entertaining any thoughts of being with her under a courting blanket, but there were many other young maids with the Cheyenne that he would have no such qualms about.

A stab of anger coursed through the Comanche Chief's heart when he thought of the shameful treatment of the Cheyenne by the Long Knives and their cowardly attack on the sleeping village. Black Kettle had been a fool to trust the whites and the Great White

Father in Washington, and allow his people to be herded onto the reservation. Never would the Comanche give place to such nonsense. It was obviously a ploy to group everyone together in order to slaughter them more easily. The idea of a raid on one of the outlying rancheros of the Tejanos, swift and unexpected, should net plenty of horses and supplies to bring back to the encampments of the people, as well as much glory. Then it would be easy to pick a pretty maid to share a courting blanket.

Smooth Stone, one of his young scouts had reported that there was just such a place, an isolated ranchero some miles downstream of the white men's settlement. Slowly, Two Dogs followed the others down the road to the crossing where Snake-Who-Talks sat waiting for him by the water.

"What is keeping you?" the younger chief asked, "The men are anxious for battle."

Two Dogs smiled grimly, "They will have chance to bloody their lances soon enough. For now, we must pass silently to below the settlement of the white-eyes without being seen. Tell the men to keep in the shadows until the moon is down. There will be time for haste later, now is the time for stealth."

Snake-Who-Talks scoffed silently, then turned his pony to pass along the string of warriors and relay the command. It irked Two Dogs that the young war chief did not give him more honor nor respect the medicine. Ever since the time they had burned the two Tejanos and he had heard the stone sing, Snake-Who-Talks had seemed skeptical of his ability to lead. He minimized the importance of good medicine, not just his, but all of the elders as well, and had mocked the dream. Two Dogs feared one day he would live to regret it.

His thoughts were intruded upon as he approached the river crossing. The bleached skulls of long-dead horses gleamed white in the moonlight, their hollow eyes staring vacantly at the procession of warriors as they waded their mounts across the river. He pulled in his pony, remembering a time thirty springs ago when he was a mere youth. He had finally been allowed to accompany his father and the older braves on a raid, his first. They had traveled many days down into the land of the Mejicano and had successfully captured many horses, which they had driven across the Grand River and fled north, with the angry Mejicanos in hot pursuit. They had easily outdistanced them by riding day and night and repeatedly changing mounts on the run. They then traveled leisurely until they had to cross the dry dessert. For two days they went without water and then the horses smelled the waters of this crossing and bolted headlong until they reached the river's edge. Unfortunately many of the overheated ponies died from drinking too much water or miring in the quicksand. Later, their skulls were stuck on willows to mark the safe places to cross. Two Dogs shook his head sadly, he had lost a fine spotted pony that day. He glanced backward over his shoulder, then urged his pony into the water to cross.

An hour later, the Indians rode past the sleeping settlement. From across the river, a lone dog announced their passing, but no one in the town paid any attention. Distant music from a tinny piano came softly on the night air as the war-party on the far shore made its way past the ferry landing and disappeared along the cattle trails amongst the willows.

Two Dogs had never seen the place before and was surprised at the number of buildings in the town. He wondered now at the wisdom of this foray, for it was obvious that many of the white-eyes lived here. If their presence should become known to the settlers, strong pursuit could be mounted against them for their incursion here. But his decision was made and he would not give Snake-Who-Talks the satisfaction of seeing him abandon their quest. He trusted that his band of warriors was enough of a force to meet whatever resistance they might encounter, even though most of them were untried youths who were more inclined to follow the bravado and posturing of Snake-Who-Talks, than himself. Eager for battle and with little experience in actual fighting, the younger braves would bear watching when it came time to fight, Two Dogs knew. The closest most of them had come to battle had been during the recent flight from the long-knives onto the staked plains, and although there was great resentment among the people, these braves, mostly young, were yet unproven in any real battle.

The people had been lied to and betrayed when the Chiefs of the Great White Father in Washington had gone against the pipe at the Medicine Lodge Council. Promises had been broken and the treaty papers ignored. Just four moons ago, the long-knife with the yellow hair, had cowardly attacked the Cheyenne camp of Black Kettle. Even though the Cheyenne Chief had no backbone to resist and had impassively moved onto the white man's reservation, still, he and his wife did not deserve to die as they did. The whites continued to pour onto the plains in the great, smoking iron horses, and wantonly kill the buffalo. What would the people do if they killed them all? They must fight for their lodges and their lands and their way of life.

Strong medicine was available to the warrior who eradicated the white plague, and Two Dogs had sat four days with just the medicine pipe and without food or drink, waiting on the old ones for guidance before starting this raid. Finally on the fifth day, a dream came to him. He had seen one of the tall lodges of the whites with windows like eyes, weeping, and knew that this was a sign they would vanquish the Tejanos who lived there. It was only after this vision of the weeping lodge that he gained the approval of the band's elders for the raid.

The Comanche chief grimly shook his head and rode after the others. They followed the river to a point several miles downstream, when Smooth Stone held up a hand and stopped. The moon was slipping beyond the horizon, when the young brave rode to where Two Dogs sat his horse.

"We can cross here, there is no quicksand."

Two Dogs nodded and waved the young warrior forward. He took his place at the head of the Indian file and entered the water. Slowly, with just the ripple of water against the horses' flanks, the band of Comanche rode across the river. At their approach, the frogs stopped their early morning croaking.

"Soon it is time," Two Dogs said when they reached the other side. "Prepare for battle." He slid from his pony and laying aside his war bonnet, he removed a tin of paint from the pouch at his side, then proceeded to apply war paint to his face, chest, arms and legs. The rest of the Indians did likewise, some helping others with the fierce markings on face and back. The horses were decked out with battle paint and other paraphernalia and then the war party remounted and moved silently up the bank, to head north on the other side of the river.

Grant had sent Sonny to town to buy up a case of ammunition. In the event there should be trouble with the Indians, he did not want to run short. When Sonny had returned that evening, the rancher distributed several boxes to the hands in the bunkhouse.

"In case we come under attack, I want you boys well armed," he said. "We will be a formidable force with a crossfire from the house and bunkhouse."

Beans Murdoch said, "Is it true that the Yankees sent that long-haired dandy, that kilt all the Cheyenne up in the panhandle, on out on the Llano to make peace with them now?"

The lanky Murdoch had teamed up with Swede Jorgenson, and the pair of them had just returned the day before from manning the line-shack north of the Gap.

Grant studied the sober faced cowboy before he spoke. "If you mean Custer, then yes, that is what I understand. Why do you ask?"

"Well, it beats me how they can send him out to kill the Injuns one day and back the next to make peace with the same bunch. Seems kinda loco to me."

The rancher turned towards the door to leave. "It is bewildering, the way the Army does things," he said. "In any case, it has stirred up a hornets' nest with the plains tribes and we best be ready, so see to your guns."

The door clicked behind him and the men in the bunkhouse looked soberly at each other. Their job was hard enough without having to look behind every bush for some marauding savage.

"You seem to think Custer had no business battling those Injuns," Mickey Brown said to Beans.

"Ridin' into camp before daylight and killin' women and babies in their blankets hardly constitutes a battle," Beans replied, "more like slaughter if you ask me."

"You got snakes, the best thing you can do is find the nest and destroy it," Brown said. He opened the door of the stove and spit a stream of tobacco juice into the fire.

"Women and babies, too? It was the same kind of thing that part-time soldier boy, full-time politician did up near Denver in '64—snuck in on the Cheyenne where they were camped on Sand Creek after they'd been told to camp there by the Army, then they massacred them. The Yankees don't fight fair."

"Well, they sure whipped our tails in the late unpleasantries," Pop Cranston put in with a sour grin. He was peering over the spectacles perched on the end of his nose, having put down the newspaper he was pretending to read, while listening to the cowboys' palaver. "The government is going to resolve the Injun problem one way or another and we might's well get used to it. Whether we like how they do it or not is another thing."

Lance and Rusty had been listening to the older cowboys when Lance finally said, "A bunch of marauding savages stole Ruthie Hollister from her home just up the river from ours, last year. They murdered her ma and pa and two little brothers and left their scalped and mutilated bodies for all of us to see. She was eighteen and just about to marry James Easley when it happened. She was carried off and hasn't been seen since. Somebody's got to stop all the killin'."

"I know," Beans said. "The Injuns cause a lot of trouble on the plains, but killin' kids and babies. . . it just don't seem quite right for us to be doin' that."

The rest of the cowboys looked uncomfortably at Murdoch. This was injecting an uncertain note into the oneness of the ranch, and some of them were wondering if Beans could be counted on in a fight.

Apparently, he had never experienced Indian depredation, first hand. The silence fell heavily in the room.

Pop Cranston cleared his throat, "I saved a news article that you fellers might find interesting, it appeared a few years back in a Denver paper. Would you like me to read it?"

The cowboys settled down with some nodding. Beans Murdoch kicked his boots off and lay back on his bunk. "What's it about?" he said.

"There's two sides to every coin and I think this brings some perspective to our position out here on the frontier. Listen to this—it's a letter to the editor of the *Rocky Mountain News* entitled, *The Fort Lyon affair*:

> The issue of yesterday's News, containing the following despatch, created considerable of a sensation in this city, particularly among the Thirdsters and others who participated in the recent campaign and the battle on Sand creek.
>
> > *Washington, December 20, 1864*
> >
> > *"The affair at Fort Lyon, Colorado, in which Colonel Chivington destroyed a large Indian village, and all its inhabitants, is to be made the subject of congressional investigation. Letter received from high officials in Colorado say that the Indians were killed after surrendering, and that a large proportion of them were women and children."*
>
> Indignation was loudly and unequivocally expressed, and some less considerate of the boys were very persistent in their inquiries as to who those "high officials" were, with a mild intimation that they had half a mind to "go for them." This talk about "friendly Indians" and a "surrendered" village will do to "tell to marines," but to us out here it is all bosh.

The confessed murderers of the Hungate family—a man and wife and their two little babes, whose scalped and mutilated remains were seen by all our citizens—were "friendly Indians," we suppose, in the eyes of these "high officials." They fell in the Sand creek battle.

The confessed participants in a score of other murders of peaceful settlers and inoffensive travelers upon our borders and along our roads in the past six months must have been friendly, or else the "high officials" wouldn't say so.

The band of marauders in whose possession were found scores of horses and mules stolen from government and from individuals; wagon-loads of flour, coffee, sugar and tea, and rolls of broad cloth, calico, books, and such, robbed from freighters and emigrants on the plains; underclothes of white women and children, stripped from their murdered victims, were probably peaceably disposed toward some of those "high officials," but the mass of our people "can't see it."

Probably those scalps of white men, women and children, one of them fresh, not three days taken, found drying in their lodges, were taken in a friendly, playful manner; or possibly those Indian saddle-blankets trimmed with the scalps of white women, and with braids and fringes of their hair, were kept simply as mementos of their owners' high affection for the pale face. At any rate, these delicate and tasteful ornaments could not have been taken from the heads of the wives, sisters or daughters of these "high officials."

That "surrendering" must have been the happy thought of an exceedingly vivid imagination, for we can hear of nothing of the kind from any of those who were engaged in the battle. On the contrary, the savages fought like devils to the end, and one of our pickets was killed and scalped by them the next day after the battle, and a number of others were fired upon. In one instance a party of the vidette pickets were compelled to beat a

> hasty retreat to save their lives, full twenty-four hours after the battle closed. This does not look much like the Indians had surrendered.
>
> But we are not sure that an investigation may not be a good thing. It should go back of the "affair at Fort Lyon," as they are pleased to term it down east, however, and let the world know who was making money by keeping those Indians under the sheltering protection of Fort Lyon; learn who was interested in systematically representing that the Indians were friendly and wanted peace. It is unquestioned and undenied that the site of the Sand Creek battle was the rendezvous of the thieving and marauding bands of savages who roamed over this country last summer and fall, and it is shrewdly suspected that somebody was all the time making a very good thing out of it. By all means let there be an investigation, but we advise the honorable congressional committee, who may be appointed to conduct it, to get their scalps insured before they pass Plum Creek on their way out.[1]

When Pops finished reading, all eyes were turned on Murdoch who shifted uncomfortably on his bunk. "Well, shoot, that's sorta my point," he said defensively. "I ain't sayin' we don't have to fight the Injuns, it's just that we got big-wigs in Washington callin' the shots, and they have no earthly idea of what's goin' on out here. They send some dandy who's buckin' for rank like this Custer, and he spends more time in front of the mirror curlin' his hair, than he does leadin' his men and he goes marchin' in with a brass band and sends all the real warriors skedaddlin' and then cleans house on the defenseless."

"Ja," Swede Jorgenson put in, coming to his partner's defense, "and dot pisses off da Injuns and den dey come after us for sure now."

Beans Murdoch made a sheepish grin and shrugged his shoulders. "That's all I meant."

The charged atmosphere in the bunkhouse relaxed and the other cowboys began to harangue Murdoch.

Mickey Brown fired a boot at him and said, "Criminy, Murdoch, for a minute there I thought you'd turned into a copper-headed Injun lover."

Sonny climbed the stairs and walked into the room he shared with his youngest brother, Tommy. The twelve-year-old was on the floor by the window, busy tying something onto some rocks he had piled up, and the boy looked up at his brother with a big grin as Sonny came through the door.

"What you doing?" Sonny asked.

"Gettin' ready for Injuns," the kid replied.

"Huh, what's that you got there?"

"Look at this, it's my sure-fire Injun whomper," Tommy said and held up a sling-shot in one hand and a bunch of rocks he had tied firecrackers to in the other.

"That'll never work. . . where'd you get those firecrackers?"

"Will too," Tommy vowed with certainty. "Watch this."

With amusement, Sonny watched as his little brother took a match and lit the stub of a candle he had stuck to the floor. Next he slid up the bottom half of one of the double windows, took a firecracker-loaded rock and placed it in the pouch of his *"Injun whomper."* He then rose cautiously to his knees to peer over the window sill. He waited a few moments, searching in the full moonlight for a good target. Opposite him, across the yard, he spied his mother's big, yellow tomcat walking along the top of the woodpile that was stacked against the fence. The cat was nonchalantly walking along with its tail straight up in the air as if it owned the whole world, and had no idea of the impending doom that was about to descend upon it from the upstairs window.

Tommy held the fuse of the firecracker to the candle flame and when it sputtered to life, he took practiced aim and shot the smoking missile out the window at the insolent feline's rear-end. The results were spectacular, if not amusing, in anybody's book. The timing was perfect, for the stone bounced off a stick of wood and hit the tomcat squarely under the tail, at the same moment the firecracker exploded. In the blink of an eye, the startled cat leaped straight up in the air with a terrified yowl, seemed to gain traction on nothing but air, and streaked for the barn, to disappear from sight.

Tommy turned to his brother with a look of triumph in his eyes. "Pretty neat, huh? I singed his fanny good and proper."

Sonny pretended that he had not seen the cat. "Wha'd you do?"

"I hit that dar. . . dumb cat, right square in the hind-end, that's what. . . didn't you see it?"

Laughing, Sonny slowly shook his head, "Better not let mom find out you dinged that cat, she'll singe your butt."

As if on cue, they heard their mother holler up the stairs, "Tommy, what on earth are you doing? You better not hurt that poor cat."

Tommy's eyes grew round with uncertainty, afraid Sonny might give him away, but his older brother just laughed again and shoved his younger brother onto the bed.

"Where'd you get the fireworks?"

Tommy sat back up. "From the peddler that came through town a while back, see, I got a whole bunch of them." He pulled out a cigar box from under his bed to reveal several packets of firecrackers and some roman candles.

"That ain't likely to do much harm. If the Comanche hit us, you'd better use that .22 Colt bought for ya, where's it at?"

Tommy pulled out the rifle from behind his bed and leaned it up against the sill. "I'll use this once I finish with my artillery," he said with confidence. "I'll blow 'em up first, then I'll shoot 'em."

"Huh," Sonny scoffed, "you'd better keep your noggin down, otherwise that tow-head of yours is likely to end up decorating some Injun's saddle blanket. I'm going to bed—blow that candle out before you burn the house down."

"I will, just as soon as I finish tying up these bombs."

———

In the predawn, Two Dogs rode to the front of the band. Smooth Stone had stopped near the crest of a low hill and held up a hand

"The paleface ranchero is just over this hill," he said to the chief.

The war-chief dismounted and handed the pony's jaw rope to one of the braves, then moved cautiously to look over the ridge at the buildings spread out below. He could just make out a large barn with what looked like several horses in a corral next to it. Beyond that was a fenced in field with what he took for more horses cropping the dew-covered grass. His eyes took in a pig pen where the foul-smelling *muviporo* were rooting about. There were several other smaller buildings spread between the house and barn. A long low building to the right of the corral with a smoke pipe on the roof and several dark windows, gave Two Dogs the idea that the occupants, if any, were still a sleep, a fact he found reassuring. A larger two-story lodge, with a smokeless chimney and dark windows left him with the same impression. With a start he realized this was the lodge of the white-eyes that he had seen in the dream. Two windows on the upper end looked out like dark eyes in a sad face.

Snake-Who-Talks sidled up to squat beside him and stare down at the peaceful scene. "Why do you wait?" he said, "It is good, the paleface still sleep, this is a rich prize, look at those ponies. We will kill the Tejanos in their beds, take the women, and count much coup against these intruders."

Two Dogs did not look at Snake-Who-Talks when he answered, "Our medicine is good—this is the lodge with the weeping eye I saw in my dream. The attack will be just before the sun rises, when the lodge's eye weeps, there will be enough light to see then. Many mistakes are made by being too hasty."

"Huh," the younger chief scoffed, "We will lose all the advantage. We must move now while the opportunity is here."

"We will circle around and come in from the other side of the white-man's lodge where the ground is level. Tell the braves to work their way into position of the lodge and that long low building. There may be many guns there. . . and keep to cover. No one is to start the attack before the eye of the lodge weeps and there is light enough to see all the buildings well. I will give the signal once everyone is in place, then we will rush the big lodge and the long-house when the signs are right."

Snake-Who-Talks scowled, "I say we gallop down this slope, fire the weeping lodge and the long-house and kill anyone who comes out, and that we do it now.

There is no sense in waiting longer, the darkness is our best medicine."

"You speak as one of the foolish ones, we do not know this place. Go tell the others what I have said, and follow my orders, or prepare to meet me in the knife-dance when we return to the village."

The younger chief spat disdainfully, but rose to his feet and went back to speak to the others. Perhaps he should meet this *tamu*[3] in the knife-dance—the young warriors were tired of being led by such a nervous rabbit.

Two Dogs sprang lightly onto the back of his pony and led the band of Indians a half-mile to the north, where they eventually gained the level of the valley floor. Slowly, they turned and rode towards the white-eyes' lodge. For now, he turned a deaf ear to the whispering of the braves behind him, but he knew that Snake-Who-Talks was fomenting rebellion among the younger braves of the war party. He would have to bring him before the war council when they returned. If the boastful braggart turned their medicine against them and caused this attack to fail, he would take the raw-hide in his teeth against him, in the circle of the knife.

Holding up a hand, the chief stopped and surveyed the situation. He saw that near the front, the Tejano's lodge had a fenced in yard with a long row of wood stacked against it. The wood pile extended nearly to some smaller outbuildings which, in turn, reached to where the pen of the *muviporo*[4] were rooting their *mubi*[5] in the mud. Beyond that stood the barn and Two Dogs determined that they could proceed without discovery by moving quietly behind the woodpile to take up positions next to the small buildings and the barn. If he divided his force, they could effectively launch their attack on both the long-house and the tall lodge and maybe even divert some of the warriors to capturing the horses. He turned to give the order to his warriors when a rooster crowed.

"I will go first," Snake-Who-Talks said. It was his intention to ride to the end of the woodpile and then sneak, under the cover of darkness, to the white man's lodge with a few chosen braves and attack the white-eyes in their beds, taking their scalps. He had already spoken to several, but did not trust Two Dogs with his plan, for the older chief was paying far too much attention to his superstitions and medicine. The younger chief knew the rest of the band would follow his lead, once he had started the fight. He must hurry though, already the sky grew light in the east and he was counting on the darkness, once he reached the end of the woodpile, so that Two Dogs would not see what he was about.

Two Dogs looked uncertainly at the young chief. "You must follow my plan of attack. Once you gain the shelter of the barn safely, give a sign and I will send others to your position, then watch for my signal, we will charge and circle both the long-house and the tall lodge and kill any who come out, but not before the eye weeps." He turned to the others, "Be watchful for any *sarii*[2], the white man's dog, and shoot them with arrows, should any bark and warn of our presence. Today is a good day to avenge our people on the arrogant white man and cover ourselves with glory. Fight bravely and well and you shall carry away much goods."

No one saw the upstairs window go up, but suddenly a silvery stream of water poured down from one of the lodge's eyes. All the warriors turned to look at Two Dogs and the Chief smiled, the dream had been straight talk. He nodded to Snake-Who-Talks while the rest of the Indians looked to their weapons, and then sat, intently watching the young chieftain kick his heels into his pony's ribs and ride towards the woodpile.

———

The sun had not yet peeked over the eastern hills when Tommy came awake with the crowing of the rooster. Feeling an urgent need to pee and having forgotten to bring a coffee can upstairs, he looked at his snoring, older brother, being careful not to awaken him. Quietly he slipped out of bed and noiselessly slid up the bottom half of the nearest window. His parents didn't like him peeing from the upstairs windows. His mother complained that, not only was it improper and smelly, but it also killed her flowers. He didn't trust Sonny to keep his big mouth shut should he awake and catch him doing his business, but he had to go too bad to try to make it downstairs and out back. Besides, peeing out the window would not make him wake all the way up. When he was finished he could just go back to bed and get some more sleep.

He stood there, a solitary figure in the window against a brightening sky outside and was making water when he caught movement out of the corner of his eye. Thinking it was the "dumb ol' tomcat" again, and that it would be a good joke on the rest of the household to wake them up with a bang, he abandoned his plan of going back to bed. After finishing his toilet, he knelt and scratched a match to light the candle. Selecting one of his bombs, he placed it in his slingshot and then rose to look out the window again.

But Tommy did not see the tomcat. Instead, he saw the war bonnet of a Comanche riding his pony stealthily along behind the woodpile. Without a second thought, he touched the wick of the firecracker to the candle, drew back on his slingshot, and let fly. The rock arched out of the window and struck the unsuspecting war chief in the back of the head with a resounding whack at the same moment that the firecracker detonated with a thunderous bang. Once again, his timing was faultless and when the firecracker exploded, it caught the decorative fringes of hair on the war bonnet on fire, which in turn caused the eagle feathers to ignite and burst into flame.

In a panic, the Indian let out a startled scream of pain and fright, while his arms beat frantically at his flaming headdress. His rifle went flying one way and his pony catapulted forward like he'd been shot out of a cannon, carrying his tormented rider across the yard, directly under Jessica Saber's clothesline, which was still concealed in the morning darkness. The line caught the young chief under the chin. For a moment, the line stretched with the redskin's forward motion, then it snapped taut and, with an angry twang, swept the hapless Indian off the back of his charging horse to dump him in a smoldering heap on the ground. Here he lay, choking and coughing, struggling to catch his breath, his hands grappling at his throat to ward off the unseen fingers clutching him there.

Tommy knelt for a moment, watching the spectacle with his mouth wide open, then in the growing light, he saw some twenty or thirty Indians, all in war paint, sitting their horses like stone. Transfixed, they were watching the fantastic spectacle of the young chieftain's war bonnet bursting into flame and his erratic antics from being swept off his pony by some unseen hand, and dumped on the ground.

"Indians!" Tommy yelled, sounding the alarm. With his slingshot, he began rapid-firing exploding projectiles into the stunned band of warriors below. Next, he grabbed up a roman candle and held it to the flame, and began to discharge colored balls of fire into the Indians' midst. For the next several minutes, pandemonium reigned supreme, while the twelve-year-old alternated his barrage of exploding rocks, with the awesome display of the roman candles.

Sonny leaped out of bed and grabbed his rifle. Working the action, he began shooting into the milling savages below.

"What in blue-blazes did you do?" he asked.

"Whomped 'em," the lad replied and took aim at another warrior in the cluster of startled savages.

The Comanche were fighting to keep their seats and stay on their crow-hopping horses. The whole bunch had turned into a wild melee of kicking, bucking ponies and discombobulated warriors, all seeking to escape the bombardment of exploding, stinging rocks, shooting fireballs, and whistling bullets. The entire scene more closely resembled the mayhem of a raiding skunk in a hen house than it did the noble Redman on the warpath.

Soon they could hear Grant firing from downstairs, and shouting and shooting coming from the bunkhouse. The cowboys there lay down a withering fire at those Indians who had managed to get their horses started in hasty retreat. One brave, a mere youth, galloped his pony around the woodpile to where the fallen chief with the smoking headdress sat, bewilderedly holding his throat. Reaching a hand for him, he swept him up onto the back of his pony and raced after his fleeing companions, but not before one final, well-aimed rock exploded against the back of the frantic chieftain being rescued.

Chapter Seven

On the Run

Summer, 1870

"Felipe, how did you come to this place?" Colt sat his horse alongside of the Mexican vaquero on top of the mesa, they were staring north out across the canyon to the rugged badlands beyond.

"Senor Jones, he hire me to herd thee vacas," he replied.

"He hired you?" Colt was amazed. "I thought everyone here was slave labor."

"Oh, no, most of thee Mejicanos work for thee monies."

"How did you get here then?"

"We come heer from thee villages of Nacori and Bacadehuachi. I come from Madera—een Sonora."

"I thought this place was supposed to be a secret."

"Si, eet ees," Rodriguez said. "We doan know dees way heer, we were brought weeth thee blindfolds on."

"So, you are not held prisoner here, you could leave?"

"No, Senor Tye, we have signed thee paper that say we stay until thee mine, she plays out—then we get thee wages and go."

"Are you getting paid now?"

"The Mexican rider looked sheepish and shrugged, "We geet thee credit at thee store and sign for thee goods we juse now—dees is, how do ju say—deduct from de monies we have earn. We geet thee rest ween thee minas close."

"Then you can't leave, you don't know the way out of here?"

"No, no—eet ees mucho deefeecult—somewhere down thee Rio Guaynopa." The vaquero waved his sombrero to the south. "Perhaps many day, or no so many days, only thee boss, he knows."

"Has anyone ever tried to leave?" Colt asked.

"Jus a few, they doan geet so far. Senor Reese, he track them down and breeng them back, sometimes they dead, tied over thee caballo. Heem mucho malo hombre."

"What about up the river to the north, has anyone ever tried to go out that way?"

"Some, he try, but mucho bad Indio that way. They captura and torture, then keel and mutilar thee bodies and throw them from thee cleef tops into thee camp below. Why do ju ask?" Felipe looked at him questioningly. "Ju are not theenking of goeeng away, are ju?"

"I was just wondering is all," Colt said. "They brought me here when I could not remember the trail."

"Doan theenk about eet, wan day thee minas weel be emptee of de oro and we weel all go home."

For the next two weeks, Penny and Colton accumulated food stuffs and supplies and hid them in gunny sacks under the bed in the hut. Colt worked with a restlessness, eager to be on his way back to Suzanne and home. How he missed her, nights were long as he recalled all the sweet memories he had made with the blacksmith's daughter. His heart broke as he realized she must think him lost to her—even dead. He must hurry back, as soon as he could.

Cooler minds prevailed, however, for it was Penny who convinced him to take it slow and not arouse suspicion.

"Which way do you intend for us to go?" she asked him one night after the light was blown out.

He shifted uncomfortably in his place on the floor. "They'll expect us to return over the trail we were brought in here on, but I think if we follow the river south, we can make our way into Mexico and then head east and eventually cut back north to the Rio Grande.

"Isn't that dangerous? The Mexicans have no love for us Tejanos."

"I know—at least that's true for the Federales and the Juaristas, but most of the people are not hostile to Americans. I think if we disguise ourselves as Mexican peasants, we should be able to travel unnoticed through the county. See if you can roundup some Mexican clothes in the next few days—large sombreros. . . stuff like that."

Penny was able to get a Mexican dress and shawl from the store, and the day before the new moon, they gathered all their supplies together in preparation of leaving. Colt was to bring a saddle horse and mule from the corral when he rode in from the mesa, and had contrived to get a pack saddle on the pretext of hauling salt up to the stock. It was just before dark and they were packing the last of their supplies into the panniers, when there was a knock on the door. Colt quickly shoved the remaining gear under the bed and shut the lids on the pannier boxes, then sat down on one and rested his feet on the other, while Penny answered the door.

"Who is it?" she called.

"Jones," the mine superintendent said. "Is Tye there, I need to talk to him."

"Come in boss," Colt called. He picked up a cup of cold coffee and leaned back against the wall.

L.T. Jones walked into the dim lit hut and glanced at the pack boxes. "What you doing with those?" he questioned. Colt could see Penny's face turn white from where she stood behind the man.

"Oh, I got these to do some packing tomorrow. I need to haul some salt up on the mesa and wanted to keep the dew off 'em. What's on your mind?"

Jones turned to look at the cowboy. "Ever since you beat Cardiston that night, Reese Hutchinson has been wanting a match with you. Are you up for one this Saturday night?"

Colt shrugged, "Don't see why not, but you might wanna think twice about where you put your money, I have been beaten a time or two."

The superintendent chuckled, "I think you're still the best bet, and you've got the hands and speed of some of the best I've ever seen, even in New York. I'm counting on that come Saturday.

"Okay," Colt said, "it's your funeral."

Jones gave him a peculiar look at his answer, then laughed again and turned to leave. Penny opened the door. "Saturday then, I'll get it set up. It'll be good to see Hutchinson get what he's got coming to him for a change." He walked out of the door after bidding them goodnight, and left.

Penny stood shaking and then collapsed onto the bed. "I thought for sure he had found us out," she said. "My, aren't you the cool one?"

Colt grinned sheepishly, "Don't kid yourself, he scared the dickens out of me."

Colt waited until after dark, then slipped out the door and brought his sorrel and a little bay mare from the corral and tied them behind the hut. A mule, already tethered, stood munching an armload of hay. He quickly loaded the panniers on the pack mule and then Penny and he stole away, leading the animals in the dark. The mule made out with a disgruntled braying at being pulled away from the hay and Colt had to walk back and put a hand over its muzzle to quiet it down. He was reminded of Jake, a jug-headed mule of his father's, that had no sense of timing but was likable in spite of it, and he felt a wave of homesickness envelope him.

Finally, the mule settled down and followed the horses as they stole down to the river's edge to head downstream, skirting the shoreline. Where the road from the village joined the trail heading downriver, a guard was barely visible, sitting on a rock and smoking a cigarette.

"We're going to have to cross to the other side and try to swim the animals past, without him seeing us," Colt whispered. "If you don't want to spend the rest of the night riding in wet clothes, I suggest you pull them off and tie them on top your saddle."

Penny looked doubtful, "You mean you want me to get naked?' she whispered back.

Colt felt the heat rise up his neck to his ears and was thankful for the darkness hiding his embarrassment.

"It's up to you, I reckon you're near invisible in the dark anyway. . . I'm going to."

They sat in the dark, one-hundred yards upstream from where the guard was posted and removed their clothing. Colt had secured a couple pairs of Indian moccasins and handed a pair to the girl who stood shivering in the dark with her arms folded across her breasts.

Averting his gaze, he handed her a pair of moccasins. "Put these on, they'll protect your feet from the rocks some."

They tied their clothing and boots to their saddle horns, then Colt began to strip brush off the bushes along the bank and affix branches to the bridles and saddles of the animals.

"What are you doing?" Penny asked.

"These will breakup the outline and silhouette of the animals. With a little luck, if the guard does look our way, he'll just imagine its brush and driftwood going by."

Carefully, Colt led them out into the current and across to the far side. The water was deeper here and the current swifter next to the sheer rock wall of the cliff. The horses snorted once as they lost footing and began to swim, following the bobbing cowboy and girl. The animals quickly overtook them in the swift water and Colt whispered hoarsely to the shadowy, white form of the girl, "Grab the saddle horn and hang on."

He saw the guard jump up and stare across the river, he paused for a moment, then sat back down, the glow of his cigarette, a red coal in the dark until they were swept out of sight around the bend.

The water was cool but not uncomfortable and Colt let the current carry them along for about two miles, when he heard the roar of rapids up ahead. Striking out for the eastern shoreline, they made their way until they regained footing in the shallows near the edge.

"Aren't we going to get out and get our clothes back on?" Penny's teeth chattered as she spoke.

Colt looked at her, then turned his eyes away, "Not yet, put your coat on. As long as we stay in the water, we leave no tracks." Penny shrugged into her coat covering the faint outline of her white figure, as Colt led the way splashing through the shallows around the rapids, until once again the river narrowed down between the canyon walls and turned into swift, deep water.

"We can keep swimming or climb on out here and take a chance on them not finding our trail," he said.

"Can we swim that fast water in the dark?" Penny asked.

"Probably, but I am a little worried that our grub will get wet if the mule bobs under. Maybe we should pull out here and try to find the trail."

"Okay," Penny said, "I am kind of tired."

They made their way up the sloping bank and stopped on a level spot to get back into their clothes. He boosted the tired girl up onto her horse and swung into his own saddle and urged his pony along in the dark, trusting the surefooted little gelding to find the way. Eventually they came upon the trail. Riding up an ascending pathway that led away from the roar of the river, they surmounted the steep cliff it was passing through. Presently they came out on top, some two hundred feet above the water and Colt pulled the sorrel to a stop on a rocky ledge and dismounted.

Visibility from starlight was a little better once they got out of the canyon and Penny said, "What are we stopping for?"

"Wait here," he said, "I am going back to try to brush out the tracks we left when we came out of the river." He handed the reins of his horse to the girl, "I'll be back in a few minutes." Colt disappeared into the dark along their back trail while Penny dismounted and, holding the reins, took advantage of the delay and dark to get private. She was just finishing up when the mule lifted his tale and strewed a steaming pile of road-apples on the rocky ledge.

She heard Colt approaching, swishing a clump of brush over the ground and was standing by her horse when he reached her side.

"You alright," he asked.

"Yeah, you were gone quite awhile."

"We traveled farther than I thought; I hope I covered our tracks well enough, phew! What's that smell; don't tell me one of these nags did their thing."

"I'm afraid so," Penny chuckled, "that ol' lop-eared mule left some dumplings over there so I don't know how much good brushing out the tracks is going to do."

"That's just great," Colt said. "Why'd I even bring that chuckle-head anyway?" He found an empty gunnysack in the pack and went to the pile of pungent, manure. Taking a stick he lay the sack down and carefully brushed the droppings onto it, then gathering up the four corners, he carried the smelly load to the edge of the cliff and tossed the contents over the edge. Far below they could hear a splash. Folding the sack with the soiled side in, he rolled it up and tucked it under one of the girths of the pack mule. "There, you can just carry that until I can wash it out. Penny, hand me your canteen." Colt emptied the contents of both canteens over the spot in hopes of washing away any residual stain, but knew that the practiced eye of a good tracker would probably not miss what happened here. If they could just gain a few days on any pursuit, the sign would be less noticeable, if at all.

Sunrise found them several miles downstream. At one point they had passed a fork where another river flowed in from the west and now the trail followed a much wider stream. Colt did not know if it was the Rio Aros or not, he had not been able to learn much about the country as Rodriguez had not known and he dared not ask anyone else lest he arouse suspicion. Felipe had mentioned another river, but did not recall its name.

"How you doing?" Colt asked the girl.

Penny said, "Okay, I guess, do you think they are after us?"

"I am sure they will be—probably send that wolf, Hutch, after us once they discover we're gone. He loves a blood-trail, so I hear. We better put as much distance between them and us as we can."

The girl sighed, "Okay, I'm game, let's go."

They rode all morning through a jumbled maze of canyons, coulees, rocks and brush, in what seemed a never-ending wilderness of wild water and inhospitable land. Nowhere was there sign of civilization, either past or present, and there was very little evidence of even wild game. Only a few birds and lizards were seen.

A little after noon, Colt turned his horse up a small stream that flowed from a narrow side canyon, and they wound their way through brush, scrub oak and willows, until he found a grassy spot not much more than a half acre in size. Here he pulled up and made a stop. They dismounted and loosened the cinches on their saddles, allowing the horses and mule to graze, then they sat in the shade of a tree and munched on some jerky and biscuits.

Penny retrieved her jacket from behind her saddle and rolled it up for a pillow, then curled up on the grass in the shade and was soon fast asleep. Colt looked at the girl and thought of Suzanne. Here he was again, miles from his sweetheart, even in a foreign country now, with somebody else—another girl, but not the right one. He studied the sleeping girl and shook his head in resigned frustration, before it began to nod. He'd close his eyes for just a few seconds. His chin dropped to his chest and he slowly slid over onto his side.

Something cold, round, and hard was poking him in the back of his head and he came awake with a start. Sitting up, his eyes fell upon a dead stick that had been poking him. Looking quickly about, he saw that the sun was already below the mountain top. Beyond the sleeping girl, the animals were quietly grazing at the end of their tethers.

"Penny, wake up," he shook her by the shoulder. "I overslept, we've got to get going." He jumped to his feet and walked out to get the horses while Penny disappeared into the bushes for a few minutes. Colt swung into the saddle and studied the horizon for signs of pursuit until the girl reappeared and mounted the bay mare. Kicking the sorrel in the ribs, he led the way back down to the main trail.

"Do you think they will catch us?" Penny looked fearfully over her shoulder.

"Not if I can help it, I shouldn't have fallen asleep." They rode in silence, Colt mentally berating himself for the lost time. He was uncertain as to how long it would take Hutchinson to figure out their back-trail, for they wouldn't even be missed until he failed to show up on the mesa. If Rodriquez didn't say anything until he rode in this evening, they may not have even be missed until now. There was the possibility that the bay mare and saddle would be missed from the coral, and that could mean somebody may already be tracking them. He hoped Hutch would not have an Indian tracker, and that they would be looking east on the inbound trail from Texas and not on this one, but he could not be sure.

He hated having to ride this unknown country in the dark, for it made for slow progress through the broken and rough terrain, but he had to try to make up for lost time. Darkness overtook them several miles downstream, but they continued on, riding with caution, until finally Colt had to rely on his horse to keep to the trail. The hearty little mustang seemed to find its way with no problem.

Colt dozed in the saddle, but came suddenly awake when he realized his horse had come to a stop. It was pitch black and he could see nothing, the sky being overcast with no moon or stars to shed even a little bit of light. A stiff wind was blowing and there was the smell of rain in the air.

Lightly, he touched his spurs to the pony's flank, but the animal only sidestepped once, stood still, then snorted and shook its head, rattling the bridle and reins against its neck. He could barely hear the river over the rising wind, it seemed a long way off in the distance and then he realized they must have climbed to considerable height in the dark.

Colt swung down from the saddle and stepped backwards into space. Had he not been holding the horn and cantle of his saddle he would have fallen into the blackness. It was the only thing that saved him, for his feet went out from underneath of him; while rocks and gravel rattled off the cliff face to disappear somewhere far below. With all his might he managed to drag himself back up into his saddle while the horse stood trembling in one spot. Finally his boot found the stirrup and he regained his seat, breathing heavily.

"What's going on?" Penny asked sleepily.

"Dead end," Colt said. "See if you can back your horse up and get it to turn around but whatever you do, don't get off."

With great difficulty, the animals were made to back-step in the dark, the mule being the most contrary. Finally, they found a wide enough spot to get turned around and Penny's horse led the way back down. They seemed to be on a steep hillside and were picking their way slowly back the way they had come, when it began to rain.

"We need to hole up," Colt called to Penny. "Watch for an arroyo or some sort of shelter, it's too wet and dangerous to go on in the dark."

"Okay," Penny called back. "I think there's a spot up ahead, it looks to be an overhang in the rock, we can get under that, I don't know about the horses."

"Good, hole up there."

They dismounted and, pulling their jackets and bedrolls from behind their saddles, they crawled up to sit under the overhanging rock out of the rain and wait for daylight. The horses and mule were left standing in the rain with backs humped, their heads down and tails to the wind. Colt tied off the reins of his horse to a root then dallied the reins of Penny's horse about his saddle horn. The mule's lead rope was already tied to the sorrel's tail.

Penny shrugged into her jacket and buttoned it up, then shook out a blanket to wrap about her shoulders before settling down in a spot with her back against the stone. Colton soon joined her.

"We're going to have to wait out this storm and for daylight before we can get off this mountain," he said."

"What do you think happened?" the girl asked.

"Lost the trail somehow, I just about went over the edge and would have if I hadn't of held onto my saddle."

"That's scary, what would I do if something happened to you?"

Colt was silent for a moment. "According to Felipe Rodriguez, there's supposed to be a village within a day or so of the mines— Nacori or maybe Bacadehuachi. You keep to the river and try to reach there."

"What then,? They aren't going to take too kindly to a white girl."

"Dress in the Mexican clothes and keep a hat on your head and try to blend in, try to get to San Pedro in Chihuahua and maybe onto the railroad and go east."

"The farther east I go, the more Mexicans I will run into," she said.

"I know, it won't be easy, but we'll just have to figure out a way."

"Just don't leave me," she said in a frightened voice. Colt patted her shoulder and she scooted up next to him for warmth.

"Tell me about your girl—Suzanne, wasn't it?" Penny said.

Colt sighed and settled back against the rock, staring out into the black night as the rain poured down. "Oh, Suzanne," he sighed. "She's five foot two with eyes of blue and if Helen had a face that launched a thousand ships, Suzanne's would easily launch a million."

"Helen, who's Helen?"

"Helen of Troy, you know. . . in the story of the Greeks."

"Oh," she said and rested her head against his shoulder.

"Suzanne is the most beautiful girl in the whole, wide world and what's amazing is that she doesn't even know it. She is sweet and innocent and pure and good and has a figure that would send Eve looking for more fig leaves. She is charming and witty and trusting, without guile; and is loving and kind and generous. She embodies all of the feminine virtues and is completely devoid of any of the vices. She's smart and intelligent and is only lacking in one thing as far as I can see."

"What's that?" Penny asked.

"She's just naive enough to be in love with me."

Penny turned to look up at him in the dark.

"You think that's naive?" she said.

Colt chuckled, "Yeah, but don't tell her, I'd just as soon she not find that out."

"Where is she now?"

"Home with her folks, I imagine, probably trying to figure out what happened to me."

"Maybe she thinks you're dead."

"No, she'll know I'm not."

"How can you be so sure?"

"'Cause I'm not dead."

"How can she know that?"

"We are connected."

"Connected, how?" Penny sounded confused.

"It's a little hard to explain. You ever heard the expression, 'it's better felt than telt'?"

"I think so," Penny seemed to sit up and take notice of what he was saying. "Can you try?"

"Um. . . let me see," he said. "The people we are—you—me, Suzanne—in fact everybody, we're more than just a body that's walking around. We know this because whenever we see a dead person, the body of someone we knew, we immediately recognize that the person is no longer there. The person-hood or personality—the spirit is gone."

"Are you talking about our soul?"

"Yes, your spirit and soul is the real you, and the real you has the wonderful ability not only to be known but to know others. What is even more amazing, it is enduring—we last forever with an on-going awareness—not just self-awareness, but the consciousness of others and of the world. . . or other-worldly, as in the case of heaven or hell."

"I still don't understand what this has to do with you and Suzanne, and how she would know you are alive."

"Love, it's through our love that we know. I have come to love her and she me in such a way, that we each know who the other is. She shows me who she is by the things she says and does, by the way she looks and acts and by the way she thinks. The more of herself she reveals to me, the better I know her. The more we open up and share our hearts, the closer we become. When we marry, the final merging will take place, and that's where she and I are at—we are at that marrying point. You see, she knows me and I know her and, just as I know she's waiting on the threshold to be made complete with me, she knows that somewhere I am waiting to be made complete with her. That connection is so strong between us that it goes beyond the mind. It is an affair of the heart."

"Yeah, but how can she be sure you are not dead? That happens to a lot of people who are in love."

"She would know if I were dead, just as I would know if she were."

"How?"

Colt smiled into the dark, "We'd just know—the broken connection would tell us."

"Huh," Penny scoffed, "that doesn't sound very rational."

"I told you it was hard to explain. There are some things that go beyond reason, ya know."

"Like what? Name something else."

"Oh, love, feelings, desire, even thoughts. If a scientist were to dissect the brain or heart of a dead man, he would find flesh and blood and maybe some other tissue. Maybe he would learn something about how the human body works and might even be able to tell what the guy did and didn't eat, but he'd learn nothing about who the man was, how he thought and felt, if he loved or hated, if he was smart or dumb, cowardly or brave, caring or selfish, stingy or generous. He would have to go talk to someone who knew the man and had spent time with him, to find that out. That information would remain long after the body had turned to dust."

Penny was surprised, "How would it remain?"

"In the collective memory of all who ever knew him, and in his own on-going, eternal, self-awareness, and most of all, in the all-knowing mind of God."

"I still don't see how that can necessarily tell you that Suzanne is alive, or that she knows you are, and that you are coming for her."

"It's in our knowers," he said simply.

"Your knowers? Colt are you sure you know what you are talking about?"

"Yep, I know what I know about her and she knows what she knows about me and that's because we've kept nothing from each other."

"Nothing?" she voiced surprise.

"Well, almost nothing—there's still the promise of marriage in front of us, something we both long for, and the very reason I am heading back to her now, so we can be complete."

They lapsed into silence for so long that Colt thought Penny had fallen asleep. He was just about to doze off when she said," What color is her hair?"

"Blond—beautiful, long, blond tresses and curls. She's fair skinned, although she may have one flaw."

Eagerly Penny sat up, "What?" she said.

"She doesn't have any freckles."

"Oh, you!" Penny poked an elbow into his ribs. "That's not nice—I hate them, everybody always teases me." She began to pound on his shoulder, while Colt chuckled in the dark. Finally the girl settled back in the blanket and said, "I wonder if I will ever know somebody like that?"

"You will," Colt said.

"How do you know?"

"Because you are the kind of girl who will readily give her heart to the one who is deserving of it, once you know that you are wanted—warmly, passionately, wanted."

"Oh, I hope so, I hope so," she said. Penny yawned and laid her head back on his shoulder, soon she was fast asleep.

Colt came awake to a gray dawn, and was startled to find they were sitting on a ledge under an overhanging rock, high up on a steep slope that dropped hundreds of feet below them. Their tracks of the night before had followed a faint trail—not much more than a goat or deer path—that led upwards. Silently, without waking the girl, he stepped out onto the trail and followed it up to where it ended abruptly at a precipitous outcropping of rock. In the light, he could see that the path extended on over the edge, to drop some ten feet and then meander across a narrow hogback ridge and out of sight around a bend of up-thrust granite. The trail was impassible for a horse and, had it not been for the alertness of the cowpony, they could have fallen to their deaths on the rocks far below. As it was, Cold had barely escaped a nasty, if not crippling, fall when he had dismounted in the dark.

"The Devil's Backbone," he muttered, "we sure got off the beaten path on this one." He turned and hurried back to where he had left Penny and the horses.

Penny was standing next to the horses and mule, looking worried. "Where were you? I was about to come looking."

"Just checking out the trail ahead, there's no going any farther that way. We need to head back down—and no more traveling in the dark."

Carefully they made their way back down the slippery, muddy trail. Colt and Penny were on foot leading their animals and by late morning they arrived at the bottom of the false track. It was easy to see how the horses had chosen the wrong trail in the dark, for the main trail had been partially covered by a slide of dirt and gravel and deer and mountain goats or sheep had made several passes over it since. Mounting the horses, they rode around the slide and back onto the main trail that followed through the brushy river bottom. Finding a glade of cottonwood trees some distance from the path, Colt led the way to a secluded spot near the river itself and called a halt.

"I think we can risk a small fire here and boil some coffee, maybe make a little breakfast. The horses and mule need some graze too."

"Are you going to unsaddle them?" Penny asked.

"No, I'll just loosen the cinches a little, they'll be alright."

"The poor things, they've been saddled for two days."

Colt grinned, "Make that two nights and one day—they're good."

Soon a small fire was blazing with the coffee pot bubbling on a hot rock next to it. Penny had gone to the river to wash-up, and Colt was broiling some strips of bacon on a willow stick over the hot coals. A couple of dry biscuits were warming next to the flames and the collective smells of the food had his mouth watering and his stomach growling.

Penny returned clad in a pretty Mexican skirt and white blouse that accentuated her figure to advantage. She looked refreshed and Colt decided to go wash up too, as soon as they finished their breakfast.

He greeted the girl as she approached the fire. "Good morning Senorita, you look lovely today." Penny blushed and smoothed her hands over the skirt.

"Do you think so? These were the only other clothes I brought."

Colt handed her a biscuit and some bacon. "You look great. It's a good idea to dress that way, as long as you don't attract too many of the local Don Juans. We should reach one of the villages today, and after I eat, I'll get into some Mex-clothes too."

"Do you think anyone followed us?" she said.

"I'm hoping they are looking on the western trail. That rain last night should have done a good job of wiping out our back trail in spite of the time we lost climbing that deer track. By the time they figure out that we went this way, we should have sufficient lead to make good our escape."

"I hope so. It is such a relief to be shut of that dreadful mining camp."

Colt nodded and rose to his feet. He retrieved the Mexican clothing and a sombrero, dropped his Stetson into the pannier box, then pulled the Winchester from the saddle boot and walked back to where Penny was sitting by the fire.

"Do you know how to shoot?" he asked.

She nodded, "My father taught me how."

"Good," he said. He chambered a round, eased the hammer off cock, and handed the weapon to her. "I'll leave this with you while I go down and clean up. If you spot any trouble, fire a shot."

Penny took the gun, looking wide-eyed at him. "Do you think they'll come?"

"No, I don't, this is just in case—it's still Indian country, too, don't forget."

"Well, hurry back," she ran her fingers through her hair in an effort to remove some tangles.

He went to the river, removed his clothing and waded in. The water was cold but revitalizing and he hurriedly washed up and climbed out onto the grassy bank. Shaking his head to free his hair of water, he dressed in the Mexican garb. It was while he was pulling on his last boot that he heard Penny scream.

Rushing back to the campsite, he was horrified to see Penny spread prostrate on the ground, while Reese Hutchinson straddled her body, obviously intent on working his will on the struggling girl. He was tearing off her blouse while two of his henchman, a Tobias Roland and a man called Lute Berry, held her helpless by the arms. Their horses were cropping grass nearby.

Casting about for a weapon, Colt seized up a stout stick and charged towards the struggling, screaming girl, with a roar of rage. Suddenly a rope sang out and settled around him, pinning his arms, hauling him up short and jerking him off his feet. An Indian rider, who had been hiding in the trees, kneed his horse into view, keeping the rope taut. Turning his mount, he trotted him towards the scene at the campfire, dragging Colt behind.

"Ha, ha," Hutchinson laughed as Colt skidded to a stop, his mouth full of dirt. "You fell right into my trap just like I figured you would, didn't you, dummy?" The one-eyed man moved off of the crying girl and got to his feet. There was a malicious look in his eye. Penny jerked her arms free of her captors and clutched at her torn clothing trying to cover herself.

Panting, Colt sat up, spitting dirt from his mouth. "Let her alone."

Hutch walked towards him, "You thought you could get away, didn't you? Let me show you what we do to runaways around these diggings." He swung his leg in a vicious kick, catching Colton in the chest with a heavy boot, and knocked him over backwards, while his men roared with laughter.

Penny screamed, "Stop it, you beast," but was quickly silenced when Lute grabbed a handful of her hair and jerked her head backwards.

"Shut up, you little tramp, your boyfriend is only getting what he's got coming to him."

Colt tried to scramble to his feet and free his arms from the rope, only to be yanked down again and kicked in the ribs by Hutchinson. Hutch went into a rage, kicking and stomping at the hapless cowboy, until Colt finally took a blow to the side of his head and slumped into unconsciousness.

"Better let up, Hutch," Tobias shouted as the big man stomped on the inert form. "Jones wants them back alive and in one piece."

"I'm gonna kill the smart aleck, son-of-a-bitch," Hutchinson panted, and swung another wicked kick to Colton's back.

The Indian rider turned his horse and spurred away, dragging Colt's limp body from under the murderous boots of the deranged guard, keeping him just out of his reach, even as Reese chased after and made several attempts to catch the unconscious cowboy and continue his assault.

Finally, Hutchinson gave up and turned back to the watching riders in disgust. "Tie the bastard onto his horse," he puffed, his eye falling on the fainting girl. "The freckle-puss, too, and let's get the hell out of here."

Colt faded in and out of consciousness as they jogged along the trail back towards Guaynopa Canyon. His feet were tied into his stirrups and his hands behind his back and the trotting of his horse sent jolts of shooting pain throughout his bruised and battered body. He was scarcely aware when they made camp for the evening, and spent a fitful night that seemed to be punctuated by Penny's screaming and crying, and a burning thirst, the later being finally alleviated somewhat when one of the men held a canteen to his lips. He drank thirstily, then lapsed back into unconsciousness.

By noon of the following day they reined up in front of the company store and L.T. Jones came out to glower angrily at the young man. Penny was drug from her horse and turned over to two large Mexican women, then led, limping, away. She cast an anxious look back at Colt.

"I'm so sorry, Colton," she cried.

Jones' jaw clenched. "What did she call you, Colton—is that your name? Well, fat lot of good it'll do you now. I am extremely disappointed in you, *Colton,"* he said witheringly, "I treated you like a son, gave you the run of the camp, even gave you your own horse, place and gal," he gestured towards the retreating form of the girl, "and you treat me like this. Not only have you spurned my generosity but you had the audacity to affront my wife." He held up the shirt Colt had left in the clutches of Evita, "I know why you left."

His head aching, Colt stared down at the mine boss in confusion. "I never did anything to your wife, it was she. . ." his words were interrupted by a sharp blow to the mouth from the back of Reese Hutchinson's hand.

"Shad up!" the one-eyed man snarled. The blow knocked Colt backwards and he would have fallen had his feet not been tied fast in the stirrups.

"Take him back to the mines," Jones said. Turning, he waved them away in disgust and went back into the store.

Colt's captors led him on up the road to the mine portal with the steel doors. Rough hands untied him and hauled him out of the saddle, then drug him over to dump him in a pile on the ground in front of a grizzled Mexican guard, who held a Winchester and had double bandoliers of ammunition crisscrossing his chest.

"Jones says to lock 'em up and throw away the key," Lute Berry laughed coarsely, then turned to mount up and ride off with Tobias Rolland, who led away the sorrel Colt had ridden.

"Geet on jor feet ju estupido caca," the Guard growled and jerked him roughly to his feet, then shoved him through the iron doors. Colt fell onto the dirty floor of the vault as the heavy steel doors clanged shut behind him.

Chapter Eight

Suzanne Grieves, Sonny Comforts—The Deputy, Sheriff, and The Judge

Early summer, 1870

The hot, dusty, days of summer settled in on the Pecos River Country. For a time, after the attempted attack of the Comanche, the ranch was on high alert, as was the surrounding countryside, but after Tommy's spectacular ambush of the pillaging savages, there had been no further incursions by hostiles, and eventually the crisis passed. So did Tommy's momentary renown, much to his chagrin.

The green grasses of spring were curing and fading to the gray and yellow of nourishing prairie hay, and on the Crossed Sabers, they were finishing a second cutting in the meadow of irrigated, alfalfa. Lance and Rusty helped out willingly enough, as long as Becky was handling the reins on the hay wagon. The two youths openly vied for the teenage girl's affection. Becky was blossoming into a lovely young lady of near marriageable age, a fact not lost on her two, would-be suitors, or on a number of other local boys as well. They were fervent in declaring their suit every chance they got, much to the delight of the girl, and the annoyance of her father.

"Those two boys are only half a boy whenever Becky's around," he grumbled. He couldn't help smiling at some of their antics, for he was often reminded of the way Sonny and Colt had competed with each other, but not without a pang of regret for his lost son.

Suzanne Kluesman was a frequent visitor to the ranch. Once the Indian scare died down, she was often found driving out in her buggy on weekends, accompanied by Sonny, who tried to monopolize her time. Grant and Jessica would give each other knowing looks as they observed Sonny's eyes following the girl about, and it was apparent to them that it was just a matter of time before the one-sided suit of their sanguine son would find and capture the heart of this sweet girl.

As for the young schoolteacher, whenever she was not preoccupied with her school duties, Suzanne would find a solace and comfort in visiting the ranch with all its activities. She found it easy to be caught up in the busyness of the place, working with Colt's mother and sister, and enjoying the sense of permanence she found there. It was almost like being close to Colt somehow, for she would imagine him off working on the range somewhere and that he would come riding in soon, to find her helping his mother and sister. It helped keep her hopes alive. It almost worked, too, if it weren't for the haunting memory of the fading white cross in the family's cemetery plot up on top of the hill.

Suzanne had not returned to the graveside since the day of the burial more than a year before, refusing to believe that it was Colton's body buried there, but then one night she had a troubling dream. She dreamed of seeing Colt, white-faced, in a dark place. He was lying on the floor of a tunnel or cave calling to her, his arms reaching out to her, imploring. She saw he was in pain, but she was unable to get to him and then he seemed to be fading, vaporizing, becoming wraith-like, until he dissolved into nothingness and disappeared.

She awoke with a great sense of dread and fear. *What did it mean? Was Colt dead, calling to her from the grave?* She cried out into the night, "Oh God, please help me understand, let me know. . . is Colt alive?" She lay there with tears streaming from her eyes, listening, but the only sounds she heard were the crickets chirping and a dog barking a long way off.

"I see Suzanne's rig here," Sonny said as he walked through the kitchen door. "Is she here? I hope she didn't drive out here by herself."

Jessica paused from peeling potatoes and looked at her oldest son. "Yes, she's up at the graveside on the hill." The look on his mother's face alarmed him.

"The graveside?" he said, "She never goes up there. I wonder what's going on."

"I don't know," Jessica replied, "Perhaps you should go and find out."

Sonny walked out the front door and stood on the porch, shading his eyes and looked up the hill where he could see the girl's form sitting, huddled on the ground, her arms clasped about her knees in that posture he had come to associate with her grief.

"Oh, Lord," he whispered and stepped off the porch to hurry up the hill. Silently he approached her, his hat in his hand.

"Suzanne," he said softly, "What's going on?"

Suzanne slowly lifted her head and turned to look at the tall cowboy.

"Oh, Sonny. . . it's you."

Sonny moved to squat down on his heels beside her, his hat in his hand twisting round and round. He studied the white cross she was looking at. Never had he seen Suzanne look as pathetic and sad as she did right now.

"It's been so long," she said with a tremor in her voice. "Oh, Sonny. . ." her voice caught and she turned to clutch his arm, "Tell me he's not in there—that it was somebody else you buried here." She began to weep inconsolably.

Sonny shifted his weight, wrapped an arm around her shoulder, and pulled her close, letting her cry. He said nothing, not trusting his voice while struggling with his own emotions. He almost wished she were right, that he could tell her it was someone else in that grave, for his heart went out to this heartbroken girl, and he, too, missed Colt. . . but he didn't believe it. He had known that this day would come; the day Suzanne reconciled to Colt's death and put him to rest, but knowing did nothing to lessen the pathos and sadness she was now going through.

"I dreamed of him last night," she said through her tears. "We were in some place, but separated, and I saw him—all white and in pain, calling and reaching to me. It was all dark and foreboding, like in a cave or tunnel, and then he seemed to fade and dissolve away—like—like a ghost—or something." She broke into fresh sobbing and leaned her head on Sonny's shoulder.

His legs began to cramp and he sat down heavily on the ground beside her until the crying subsided.

"I thought people went to heaven when they died, if they knew the Lord. Why did I see him in that place?"

Sonny was speechless, he did not know. He hoped it didn't mean Colt ended up in the other place, but he had enough presence of mind not to voice this fear to the distraught girl.

"It was just a dream, hon," he said without conviction. "I don't think we should make too much of it, Colt had a genuine faith."

"If he's dead, he would be in heaven, wouldn't he?"

Sonny felt an inward sense of relief. This was the first time Suzanne had entertained the possibility of his death.

"I'm sure he and Ringo are riding the ranges of heaven," he said with a slight smile.

"So, do you think I saw him in the grave. . . what I saw in my dream, was that his grave?"

Sonny didn't know how to answer her and while he was trying to formulate an appropriate response, she went on: "Maybe that was God's way of letting me know that—that this is Colt buried here." She gave a huge sigh, her breath catching in a little hiccup. "I was so sure he was still alive. I could feel it, like he was. . . that his spirit was somehow letting me know." Suzanne turned questioning, tear-filled eyes to Sonny. "Is that possible?" she sniffed.

Sonny was skeptical, "I don't know. . . communication with the dead is forbidden and dangerous territory."

"I am not talking about that," Suzanne said annoyed, "of course I wouldn't do anything like that. I am talking about the thing that was between us. . . he and I. . . the way our souls were intertwined as one. He was closer to me than—than," she seemed at a loss for words, "than my very skin," she finished lamely. "We were so connected we knew each others' thoughts, we took the same breaths, our hearts beat to the same beat. If he were alive, his thoughts would be to me, and lately it seemed they were, more so than ever before, but now, I don't know, they seem to be closed off. I feel so confused." Suzanne lapsed into a pensive silence, her eyes staring at the grave marker, unseeing, while her thoughts drifted miles away.

Sonny shifted uncomfortably, his position awkward, but nothing compared to the awkwardness he felt inside. One thing was clear; if he was ever going to head off these feeling she had for his brother and corral them for himself, his work was cut out for him. It was a little scary—a love like that—and a daunting task, but if Colton could win her, then he could, too. . . no matter how long it took.

"That's not really Colton in there," Sonny nodded towards the grave marker, "only what's left of his earthly body, he is fully alive in Paradise."

"How can it be paradise for him if I'm not there?" Suzanne made the comment in the utmost sincerity and innocence without a hint of guile, but the significance of her remark was not lost on Sonny.

With a gentle smile, he gave a low chuckle, "I guess it wouldn't be, would it?"

Suddenly, the implication of her remark dawned on her.

"Oh—I didn't mean. . ." she fumbled for words—"of course heaven is heaven, I know I have nothing to do with making heaven, heaven, it's just that we had talked about being there together. . . um, at least when we were married and all . . how it would be like Adam and Eve you know. . . in paradise. . . that's what I meant."

Sonny squeezed the troubled girl's shoulder, pulling her close. "I know what you meant, Suzanne,' he smiled and nodded his head.

"You must think me terribly vain for making a statement like that."

"Not at all," he said. "I understand perfectly. Heaven wouldn't be heaven without you there. I am sure Colt felt that way and I know that's the way I feel."

"You do?" The sad eyed girl turned to look at him in surprise.

"Yes Ma'am, indeed I do. I love you. If you ain't going to be there, then I don't want to go either."

Suzanne pulled away from Sonny and stared up at his face, her mouth open in dismay, only to discover the twinkle in his eye. "Oh, Sonny, you're joking. . . don't joke with me now, what a preposterous thing to say. I am not going to make it heaven for anyone."

"Maybe not in heaven," he said, "but you could sure make it heaven-on-earth for me, if you only would."

Suzanne gave a deep sigh and turned away. "Sonny, would you mind very much if I sat here alone for a while? I need a little space to try to sort things out."

Sonny forced a smile, nodded his head in assent, and got to his feet. "Okay," he said and strode off back down the hill, feeling her eyes on his back, watching him go. He resisted the urge to turn around and look at her until he reached the front porch. Only after he had stepped up into its shade did he turn to look back up at her. Suzanne had resumed that same position, seated on the ground with arms clasped about her knees, her chin resting on them, staring at the little white cross.

Something changed for Sonny after that day. He felt a deep humiliation at the way Suzanne had brushed aside his declaration of love and he made a conscious decision to be his own person and quit pursuing her, at least on her terms. He knew that winning her as a substitute Colton was futile—he could not compete with his brother's ghost, which had now taken on legendary proportions, at least in her mind. This left him with a sense of hopelessness and just a little bit angry. That, in turn, made him decide to distance himself from the blacksmith's daughter.

"Dad, there's a bunch of mustangs running wild up on the Sweetgrass," Sonny said to his father a few days later. "I'd like to take Rusty and Lance as soon as you are done haying, go catch a bunch of 'em, break 'em out and sell them to the Army."

"You sure?" Grant gave his oldest son a quizzical look. He had noticed a cooling in the relationship between his son and the pretty schoolteacher. "Might take you some time and there's still Indian trouble up that way."

"Yeah," Sonny said, "I'd like to get away from the ranch for awhile—can you spare those boys?"

"I reckon, we'll be done haying next week. What about Suzanne?"

"What about her?" Sonny acted as if he did not know what his dad meant.

"You'll be gone several weeks—you think she'll be alright?"

"I'm quite certain Miss Kluesman is all right in her own way and doesn't need me," Sonny could not help the tinge of bitterness he allowed to creep into his voice.

Grant studied his son's face, "Son, that girl depends on you far more than either one of you realize right now. She's coming out here and spending time up on that hill because she is still combing your brother out of her hair and putting him to rest. You've got to show just a little bit more kindness and understanding."

"Dad, I've done all I know to do. She couldn't see me with a magnifying glass and if she does look at me, all she sees is him. I have to clear out for a while. She asked me to give her a little space and that's just what I am a-gonna do."

"Okay son, I'll leave it up to you. If you fellas want, you could finish off that line camp we built on the upper Concho, maybe finish up the corral and break the horses out there. It wouldn't be too far to drive them to Fort Concho and San Angelo from there."

"You mean Colt and Suzanne's honeymoon cabin? I wouldn't stay there if it were the last place in Texas."

Grant shook his head and shrugged. "Suit yourself, better pack a wagon load of stuff then." He turned and went into the barn.

———

Suzanne missed seeing Sonny at church the next Sunday and after the service, asked Becky where he was.

"Oh, he's busy getting ready to go to the Sweetgrass," Becky said.

"The Sweetgrass, what's he going to do there?" She felt a pang, remembering her trip with Colton to the high prairie.

"Mustangin'," the girl replied, "Lance and Rusty are going too—they are going to try to sell wild horses to the Army."

"Huh? I wonder why he never mentioned it to me," Suzanne remarked.

"I don't think you two have talked since he decided to go," Becky said.

"No, I haven't talked to him for awhile, it seems as though he was off somewhere else the last few times I came out."

"Yep, he sees you coming and takes off."

"You mean he is purposely avoiding me?" Suzanne said in surprise.

"Yes, I think he is."

Suzanne's heart sunk, "What on earth for?"

"It's beyond me," Becky said, "I thought maybe you could tell."

Suzanne sighed, "I suppose it's because he told me he loved me and I passed it off and asked him to leave."

"You think?" Becky said, "I wish a certain someone would tell me he loved me."

"Becky," Suzanne said, her eyes opening wide, "Which one?" She smiled at the girl whose face had colored.

Becky regained her composure, "Never mind that, why did you tell Sonny to leave you alone?"

"Becky, you know how I love Colton, how I could not resign myself to accept his death, but now it has been so long without any word, I fear that it might be true. I pray and I pray and ask God, and the harder I pray, the more it seems like it is so. Do you have any idea how despairing that makes me feel? Sonny's been such a support to me for these past, horrid months, and now you tell me he is going away—what shall I do?"

"If it was me, I'd go tell Sonny I didn't want him to go."

"Well, I don't want him to go, he's been a good friend, but I just wish I could know about Colt, whether he's alive or dead. I don't think I can juggle another declaration of love, even if I believed it was true."

"It's true," Rebecca said. "Sonny's had a lot of girl-friends, but I doubt he's told any of them he loved them. If he said that to you, it would be a first." Becky walked off to join her parents, leaving Suzanne standing there to ponder what she had said.

Suzanne drove home in a reflective mood. She had thought just the opposite. Sonny had played fast and loose with Margarita and Kathreen and the Lord only knew how many others. Suzanne figured his stock-in-trade was his, "I love you." She had never once considered that his saying that to her had come from any deeper part of him than his usual, good-natured, surface emotions. Had she missed something here, taken for granted Sonny's confession of love as trivial, when in fact he was telling her something more? Even if it were so, did she really want Sonny to love her? She did not love him—at least not like that, not as she had loved Colt. She liked him well enough, in fact, he was fun to be with and comfortable to be around, but she had never thought of him in terms as a lover—had never thought of anyone but Colt in those terms.

"Oh, God," she whispered, "I do not want to think of anyone but Colt as my lover, what can I do? I am sure that's exactly the terms Sonny's thinking of me in, maybe the terms he thinks of all women in. He certainly thought of Margarita and Kathreen in those terms, if his behavior towards them was any indication. How could I love a man whose affection I could never be sure of?"

Overwhelmed best described the way Suzanne felt by the time she arrived home. Overwhelmed to the point that all she wanted to do was go up to her room and get into bed and pull the covers over her head. Wearily she put up her horse and buggy and walked up onto the back porch. From out of a wicker basket, she heard whining, and looked in to see a cute, spotted puppy.

The pup was jumping up against the sides of the basket, eager to greet her and finally managed to topple the basket over, which enabled him to come wriggling out.

"Well, look at you," Suzanne said, squatting down to chuckle the little guy under his chin. The little fur-ball stood on his hind legs, licking her hands, whining, and squeaking, making an occasional happy, little yap.

"What makes you so happy—don't you know how sad and confusing this day is?" She scooped the wriggling pup up and squeezed him while he licked her ear and face.

There was a note tied with a ribbon to the handle of the basket, she opened it and read:

> Dear Miss Kluesman, this is Nuisance. I am going away to give you the space you requested and since I won't be around to be one, I thought my friend here could fill in for me while I am gone—careful, he likes to kiss—a lot, Sonny.

Suzanne began to laugh and cry and then hugged her puppy until he yelped and scrambled from her arms to tumble onto the porch. He stood, barking his little bark at her as if to say, "That was too hard a hug."

Summer wore on and with school out, Suzanne found more time on her hands than she liked. Her visits to the Crossed Sabers had become less frequent, for the time she spent at the family cemetery plot became fraught with loneliness and despair. With Sonny gone, she found less and less reason to make the long drive out there. It was surprising to realize just how much she did miss the happy-go-lucky, good natured, cowboy. She wondered out loud a couple of times, when out at the place, as to just when he would be back, but no one seemed to know. On her last visit to the lonely grave on the hill, she had looked at the space next to the white cross and smiled bitterly, recalling Colton's words of proposal: *"Would you like to be buried with my people?"* She had nodded her head slowly and said, "The way I feel right now, yes, I would."

The puppy, Nuisance, was a joy and comfort to her. The little mutt was a mixed-breed mongrel, if appearances were any indication. He showed signs of intelligence and loyalty and was fun to watch, especially when attacking and shaking vigorously an old boot of her father's. He was not without a streak of naughtiness, especially when it came to chickens, and often sent Mabel's flock squawking and cackling to the roost, in spite of the scolding he got. Soon folks came to associate the little guy with Suzanne and would enjoy seeing the pup perched on the seat beside her whenever she drove up in her buggy. Suzanne had started taking long walks around town in the cool of the evening with the puppy, but, after a few rude remarks from the sheriff or one of his deputies, she switched to walking up the road that went north along the river, just a few blocks from her parent's house.

One evening, she was watching Nuisance barking after a jackrabbit and failed to notice, as she was facing the other way, the rider approaching her from town.

"Howdy, ma'am," a voice said behind her."

"Oh, Mr. Anderson, you gave me a start, I did not hear you ride up. Where did you come from?"

"Town ma'am," the big rider said, "had to pick up a few things. Are you going far?"

"No, just taking a walk with my pup—he's off over there chasing rabbits."

"Mind if I step down and walk with you awhile?"

Suzanne looked up at him, shading her eyes from the westering sun.

"No, please do." She watched as he swung a leg over the saddle and stepped easily down. It was like seeing him for the first time. Tall, muscular, with thick neck and broad shoulders, yet he moved effortlessly without awkwardness, which she took note of, for he had always left her with the impression that he was somewhat clumsy.

Her eyes followed his hands as they swept off his hat and caught up the reins to lead his horse. She could not help but notice their size and how big they were. His fingers, thick and strong, his one hand, spread out, would cover my entire face, she thought and a strange little shiver ran down her back. She kept stealing glances at his hands as they walked along, saying nothing. The idea that his two hands could entirely encircle her waist, came unbidden, and caused her to blush in shame. "*What is the matter with me?*" She silently chided herself, "*I've never paid attention to anybody's hands before.*" Then she remembered Colt's hands, big, strong, and capable, but oh so gentle and soft when embracing her. With a pang, she realized how much she missed that, too, and it made her breath catch in an involuntarily little gasp. Clay Anderson stopped to look at her.

"You alright, ma'am?" he said.

Feeling foolish and a little bit blue, she nodded. "Never mind me, tell me about yourself, you work out at the Box 7, don't you? How long have you been there?" She realized he was a man of few words and he reminded her of one of her students.

"I've been ridin' for the brand for the past three years now, ever since the war."

"Did you fight in the war?"

"I did ma'am. I was conscripted when Texas seceded."

"What was that like?" Suzanne felt she may be over-stepping her bounds but wanted to encourage him to talk.

"Not good, ma'am, I don't much like talking about it."

Suzanne swallowed hard and changed the subject. "You don't have to keep calling me 'ma'am,' my name's Suzanne."

"Yes, ma'am, I know it is, ma'am."

She felt a little frustrated with him and amused at the same time. How could such a big and powerful man, capable in his work, be such a child when it came to being around folk. . . women and girls in particular? She had seen it with other cowboys as well. Take the two young riders off with Sonny chasing wild horses, Lance and Rusty, for instance. They could argue and jabber all day long about horses and cows and Indians and such, but just let a girl or a woman come around and they'd clam right up and become totally tongue–tied, incapable of more than one syllable answers, and Clay Anderson was like that. She guessed it was part of their charm, as well as their frustration.

They walked in silence then, finally Clay spoke, "How far you going, ma'am?"

Suzanne was a little startled at the question and more so, when she realized just how far they had come from town, and that the sun was already set. She could hear Nuisance barking off in the distance behind them.

"Oh, my goodness, I better turn around and hurry back," she said.

"I'll see you back safe, ma'am," Clay said.

"No, you don't have to, it's a long way out to the Box 7, and you'll be riding in the dark."

"I've ridden in the dark before, ma'am, it don't much bother me."

"No, you go on, I'll be just fine, I will start back and you ride on. Now where is that puppy?"

"Goodnight then, ma'am," Clay Anderson stepped up into the saddle, "and ma'am. . . I'm glad we had this talk, can we do it again?"

"Perhaps we shall, Mr. Anderson." She peered up at him in the gathering twilight and watched him place his hat on his head. Again she noted the size of his hands. "Perhaps we shall, and goodnight to you." Suzanne started back up the road toward town, calling for her puppy.

As she walked, she pondered the question of why Clay Anderson's hands had made such an impression. She could scarcely recall what his face looked like, although it was pleasant enough, but the way his hands looked was indelibly stamped on her mind's eye. She began to have all manner of imaginings of his hands doing things—strong and capable on the end of a rope while holding a plunging bronco; powerful and deadly in a fight or using a weapon; gentle yet firm on the rein of a green-broke cowpony and safe and protective with a newborn calf. She could just see him holding a little chick in his palm or petting a furry little kitten, all gentle and careful like. How would he be with children, a baby or a little boy or girl? How would he be with a woman? "Careful I bet," she said and smiled.

Nuisance finally came bounding out of the brush and trotted happily up to her, his tongue lolling out, a mute testimony to his dominance of the rabbit population. With a start, Suzanne was pulled from her reverie and realized that her reflection of Clay Anderson's hands had somehow been transferred to Colt and Sonny, as though it were their hands she was thinking about, and what was even more disturbing to her, was that somehow, Sonny had gotten into the mix, as though her subconscious had already come to terms with the loss of Colton, but recognized that the brother was alive and well and had even declared his love for her.

Suzanne sighed, she hated it. . . what was happening. She did not want to loose the loving feeling Colt had inspired in her, but could not deny an increasing awareness and interest in Sonny's whereabouts, and what he was doing.

"Nuisance, remind me to take a look at Sonny's hands when he gets back," she said. The dog tucked his ears and looked up at her, wagged his tail and increased his pace for a few steps.

She had not traveled half the distance back to town, when Nuisance stopped and growled a warning at a dark figure huddled next to a boulder just off the right hand side of the road.

"Who's there?" Suzanne called, frightened. She was mentally berating herself for not having brought the little .38 pistol Colt had given her.

The figure rose up in the dwindling light to reveal the toothless, leering grin of Claude Bollinger, Sheriff Wiggins' poor excuse for a deputy.

"It's just me, girlie," he said. "Ain't you out kinda late and kinda far from home?"

Suzanne felt the first signs of fear rise up in her throat. This fellow, who always seemed the buffoon, now posed a real threat to her safety, should he be bent on causing her trouble. She endeavored to calm her nerves and try to talk him out of any mischief he might be contemplating.

"Oh, it's you Deputy Bollinger, yes, I was just walking the dog and the little rascal got off chasing rabbits. I am afraid I am a little bit late, but I am sure papa is coming out to meet me."

"Your pa's asleep on the living room settee," he said gleefully, "and that no-account Saber bunch ain't nowheres to be found. Guess you'll just have to give me your arm and let me escort you back to town."

Suzanne forced a grin as the deputy stepped to her side, his eyes fastening on her bosom. She nearly choked as the wind carried the smell of his unwashed body and foul breath to her.

"Why, Deputy Bollinger, how thoughtful of you to be concerned about my safety. . . Oh, did I ever thank you for the part you all played when the Sheriff's nephew assaulted me? I was so grateful for the way the towns-people pitched in and took care of that knave—did you see him on that rail—and all that tar and those feathers? I wonder how he ever got all that stuff off."

"He didn't," Bollinger growled, "It killt him."

Suzanne could see Claude looking nervously about while she continued walking back towards town.

"It did?" she said, "Well, it's too bad, although I suppose he had it coming. Do you think he went to hell or did he have time to repent?"

"The hell if I know and what's more, I don't give a damn! Why don't you shut your pretty yap and open up the front of that dress and show me your knockers?"

The deputy made a grab for her dress front and yanked at the material causing buttons to go flying and Suzanne to scream.

Suzanne stumbled backwards and lost her footing while Bollinger pressed his advantage, causing the two of them to fall over backwards onto the dirt road. Nuisance set up a frenzied yapping and was leaping onto the back of her assailant, who had managed to get astride the struggling girl and tear at her clothing.

"You little temptress," he panted, "you're going to show me these beauties if it's the last thing you ever do."

Suzanne screamed and struggled under the foul smelling brute. He had thrust his face into hers, his breath reeking of cheap whiskey and rotten teeth.

"Get off me," she cried, breaking her hands free of his grip when he fumbled at her skirt. Clutching his hair, she yanking his head backwards, but Claude doubled up a fist and struck a blow to her cheek. Suzanne lost her grip in his hair and sought to cover her face, when out of the dark she heard a clatter of hooves, than a loud, *Thwack!* Uncovering her eyes, she saw a spur-mounted boot kick Claude Bollinger in the face and send him somersaulting over backwards off of her.

She sat up, clutching her torn garments about her shoulders and watched as Clay Anderson vaulted from his running horse and, without breaking stride, ran to where the unconscious Bollinger lay, and picked him up. Hefting him high over his head in mute rage, Clay shook him so violently, that the horrified girl could hear his neck as well as his back crack and break. Clay continued to shake the deputy like a rag doll, with arms and legs flailing about helplessly at impossible angles. Finally, in disgust, he flung him aside and came over to kneel by the distraught schoolteacher.

"You all right, ma'am?" he said in that same cool voice. Suzanne nodded in a daze. Clay put his coat around her shoulders and placing his hands about her waist, he lifted her as easily as if she were a child, up onto his horse, then swung up behind her and started for town. Nuisance took one final sniff at Bollinger's inert body, then lifted his leg and peed on the lifeless form, before trotting after the horse and riders.

When they reached her home, Clay slid from the back of his horse and reached for Suzanne. She slid wearily into his arms and allowed him to carry her up the path and onto the porch. He gently set her on her feet and knocked on the door.

Gunner Kluesman answered his knock, Mabel not far behind him, and Clay handed the trembling girl to her father, then he briefly told him what happened. Suzanne began to weep and was led off by her mother while Gunner stepped out onto the porch and closed the door.

"Where is that scurvy skunk?" the blacksmith asked, his tone deadly.

"I reckon he's dead," Anderson said.

"Dead?" Kluesman looked puzzled.

"I killed 'im," Clay said calmly.

"Where's he at?"

"Out of town a-ways—side the road. I 'spect I better go and get 'im and haul him over to the sheriff."

"I'll go hitch up a wagon and give you a hand," Gunner said.

A half hour later they pulled up in front of the sheriff's office and Gunner hollered, "Sheriff, you better come on out here."

Wiggins came to the door pulling up a suspender over the top of his long johns and said, "What's going on out here?"

"We got your deputy here in the back of the wagon," Gunner said loudly.

"Deputy—which one, Lem or Claude?"

"The one you call Claude."

"Well, dump him on the porch and let him sleep it off," the Sheriff groused and turned back to the office.

"He's dead," Gunner said.

That hauled the sheriff up like he'd been clotheslined off a fast horse.

"Dead?" he said with mouth agape, "Who killed 'im?'

"His neck's broke," Kluesman started to say when Clay broke in.

"I did," the big man said.

"What the hell for?" the Sheriff shouted and stepped off the porch to peer into the back of the wagon at the body of his deputy. His anger rising, he turned on Anderson, "How come you killed him?"

"Your deputy assaulted my girl," Kluesman said bitterly. "If Clay hadn't killed him, I would have."

"How do you know Claude done that?" the sheriff demanded, "were you there?"

"No, but Clay was, thank God, he saw the whole thing and luckily got to her in time."

"I don't believe it," Wiggins said. "Deputy Bollinger was on his rounds and doin' his duty, I am afraid I'm going to have to ask you for your gun, Anderson," He turned to the big cowboy and held out a hand.

"Doin' his duty," Gunner expostulated. "You mean going around peeking into bedroom windows after dark, don't you? My gal's all beat up and her clothes half torn off, and if Clay here hadn't come along when he did she'd be in a whole lot worse shape. That slimy weasel deserves all he got and a hell of a lot more."

"You only have his word on that," Wiggins whined and drew his gun. Cocking it, he pointed it at Clay's head and nervously reached for the Colt at the big rider's side. Clay reached a big ham-fisted hand up and caught the sheriff's hand, revolver and all in one huge grasp, and closed his fingers tightly around the whole affair.

Wiggins cursed and tried to pull the trigger but the huge hand prevented the hammer from falling and the gun was slowly bent and twisted out of the sheriff's hand, while that worthy yowled with pain. The gun finally fell to the ground and Anderson calmly kicked it under the porch.

"I'll be at the Box 7, if you need me, Mr. Kluesman. I reckon there'll be some sort of coroner's inquest and I'll ride in and confirm your daughter's testimony, if you-all let me know when."

"You're under arrest," Bertram Wiggins cried and then began screaming for his deputy. "Lem, get your sorry ass out here and bring me that scatter gun."

Anderson ignored the sheriff and stepped aboard his horse, then with a nod towards Gunner, he turned his mount and started to ride away.

Meeker appeared in the doorway scratching his rump, a double barrel shotgun under his arm. "What's going on?" he yawned sleepily.

Sheriff Wiggins jerked the gun from his grip and would have gunned Clay Anderson down if Kluesman hadn't knocked the barrel up with his buggy whip. The scatter gun exploded harmlessly upwards through the roof of the porch.

Wiggins turned on the blacksmith in fury, "You are interfering with an officer of the law in the performance of his duties," he bellowed. "I am placing you under arrest." He broke open the shotgun, his fat fingers digging to extract the spent shells, and then began to fumble at his pocket for fresh ones. Gunner leaned from his wagon seat and jerked the shotgun from his hands and struck the weapon over the porch rail, bending the barrel and splintering the stock. He glowered at the red-faced lawman.

"Sheriff, your days are numbered here," he warned. "I'd be almighty careful how I handled this case if I were you. Folks around here are just about fed up with your kind of law and I needn't remind you there's a new man in Austin. He's sent that carpetbaggin' Yankee

Governor high-tailing out of Texas, and you'll be next, if you ain't careful. Now you get that trash out of the back of my wagon before I haul his worthless carcass home and feed it to the hogs and maybe have you join 'im."

A coroner's inquest was held two weeks later when Judge Roy Bean came through on the stage. He was on his way from Saint Gaul to his trading post and saloon, off west of the Pecos, up the Comanche River. Before recovering his rig from the livery barn, he was downing a whiskey at the Branchwater Saloon, when Sheriff Wiggins came in and dropped a nickel on the counter, ordered a mug of beer, and began to help himself to the free lunch. He piled a plate with bread, boiled eggs, pickles and slices of ham and cheese. After being told the infamous judge was seated in the back, he brought his overloaded plate and mug of beer over and set them down with a clatter on Roy Bean's table.

"You're just the man I'm lookin' for," Wiggins said.

The judge looked up at the paunchy sheriff and scowled, "What the hell do you want?"

Nervously, the sheriff sat down and said, "I'm Sheriff Bertram Wiggins and two weeks ago one of my deputies was murdered by a big lummox from one of the local ranches. He killed him with his bare hands. He has resisted arrest, refusing to sit in jail until we could hold a hearing, and said he'd be available to testify at the time, if we'd send word out to the Box 7. I need you to hold court and hang the son-of-a-bitch."

Roy Bean eyed the balding, red-faced lawman, his eyes lingering on the red veins of his flushed cheeks. They bespoke of a man long used to the inside view of a whiskey glass. Wiggins pulled his hat off and wiped sweat from his brow with a dirty, red bandana.

Bean reached over and took a slice of bread from the Sheriff's plate and began to build a sandwich.

"Ain't got no jurisdiction on this side of the Pecos, but I might be able to render a legal judgment if certain fees and official papers are filed by your office. You'll need to request a special waiver to existing statutory law, in view of the urgency of the matter, and the absence of the regular circuit riding judge."

"Huh?" Wiggins looked confused and then he mumbled with his mouth full of food, "What's that mean?"

"It means," the judge took another slice of ham, following it with cheese and pickle, "that I can hold court here on this side of the river, if you are willing to alleviate the sovereign State of Texas of all court costs, including my honorarium and expenses, and pay them yourself."

Bertram paused in his chewing, his eyes following the last hard boiled egg, as Bean popped it into his mouth.

"What sort of expenses?" he asked doubtfully.

"Oh, you know," the judge waved his hand, "the usual—court room set up, advanced notices in the paper, fliers posted in public places, room and board for officiating judge, things like that. . . don't worry, I'm sure we can come to terms, once the matter's been settled in court. I'll need a room over at the hotel and word out to the community immediately, fifty bucks ought to be enough to get the ball rolling." The judge took a huge bite out of his mammoth sandwich while Wiggins sat staring at his empty plate.

"Now, tell me what happened," he said with his mouth full.

For the next few days the town was abuzz with the news of the upcoming hearing. Folks about town were eager to ply the good judge with their own version of the story, a privilege allowed by the self-styled arbiter as long as they were buying the drinks over at the Branchwater—a situation Bean was more than happy to encourage. Many grievances, not necessarily bearing on the case in question, were aired to the famous adjudicator.

Bertram Wiggins was becoming less and less certain of his chances for justice as he watched the townspeople ply the judge with liquid refreshment and capture his ear. All he had was the judge's increasing expense tab.

At twelve o'clock noon on Friday, Judge Roy Bean rapped on the bar of the Branchwater Saloon with the butt of his Colt .44 and announced to the crowd, "The bar is now closed and court is officially open." He went on to say, "This is a formal inquest into the death of one. . ." here the judge paused to put on a pair of square lens, wire-rimmed spectacles and peer at a sheet of paper. . . "Deputy Claude Bollinger who died. . ." he paused again to squint at the paper. . ."of a broken neck on the evening of June 20th, last. This is not a trial but a formal hearing into the circumstances surrounding the deputy's demise. Draw near and be heard, all ye who have ought to say regarding this case." The judge removed his spectacles, blew an open-mouthed breath on them, and rubbed the glass against his shirt. He then put them back in his pocket and looked up. "Are all the witnesses present?"

Everyone was looking about for Suzanne Kluesman, who was conspicuous for her absence, although her father stood near the door against the back wall.

"Sheriff, wasn't there to be a young lady involved in these proceedings?" Roy Bean asked.

Wiggins shifted uncomfortably in his chair and mopped at his brow, "Uh—yes, Judge she's. . ."

"You will address me as 'Your Honor' while court is in session," the judge interrupted. "That'll be ten dollars for contempt of court." He rapped the butt of his colt on the bar and held out his hand to the startled sheriff, as the room erupted into laughter. Judge Bean turned a menacing eye upon the rest of the crowd while the red-faced Wiggins shuffled up and placed a twenty dollar gold piece on the bar in front of the magistrate. Then he just stood there waiting for his change.

"If there are any more outbursts of laughter in this court, I'll fine you all ten dollars apiece for contempt," Bean said, then turned back to the sheriff. Scowling, he said, "You may take your seat, Sheriff."

"What about my ten dollars change?" Wiggins whined.

"The judge picked up the gold coin and turned it over and over across the back of his fingers like a Mississippi riverboat gambler, then dropped it into his vest pocket. "You're out of order," he announced, "Take your seat before I fine you another ten bucks. I'll just keep the other ten till then."

A low ripple of laughter was heard throughout the room, but immediately stopped as the judge lifted his craggy head, looking like a hawk about to strike a pocket gopher. In the silence that followed, Roy Bean said, "Now, where is the young lady in question?"

"She's outside on the porch," someone from the crowd yelled.

"Out on the porch?" Bean said, "What's she doing out there?"

"She won't come into a saloon, Your Honor," someone else said.

Judge Roy Bean was nonplussed, he picked up his gun by the barrel, rapped it on the bar once, and walked to the bat-wing doors of the saloon to peer out. All eyes were upon him.

Suzanne stood up nervously, her hand clutching her mother's, when she saw the granite face of Judge Roy Bean staring at her from within the saloon.

"Miss Kluesman?" the judge addressed her kindly, "Why have you declined to grace my courtroom with your presence? Don't you know you would be a decided improvement over its present occupants?"

Suzanne was taken aback. She had not expected this, nor the twinkle she saw in Judge Bean's eye.

"With all due respect, Your Honor, I have never entered a saloon in my entire life."

The judge smiled like a cat at a canary convention. "I would never have supposed you had, my dear, now that I see you are a God-fearing young lady. But, since this is no longer a saloon, while I am officiating in my duly appointed capacity as magistrate for the sovereign State of Texas, you will be glad to know it has now become an officially legitimate courtroom. Will you please take your place inside?"

Suzanne looked at her mother, but Mabel Kluesman had a troubled look on her face.

"Forgive me, Your Honor, I would like to understand this. Are you saying that whenever you are sitting in judgment of a case, no matter where you are, that that place becomes an official courtroom of the State of Texas?"

"I believe, in effect, that is what I said," the judge said dryly.

"No matter where you are?" Suzanne persisted.

The judge nodded, a tolerant smile on his face.

"It's open to all the people in Texas?" she went on, "No matter what kind of place it is?"

"Every citizen has a right to step forward and be heard in a duly appointed court of law, yes, now can we get on with this hearing?"

"Well, Judge—ah, Your Honor, sir, since there are a considerable number of us, 'God-fearing' citizens in this great state, who hold convictions about passing through those swinging doors, don't you think it would be more fitting to hold your court in, say, a church or at least a public schoolhouse, instead of a saloon, when there's no courthouse available? I would be happy to lend you the use of my classroom over at the school."

The judge scowled and said, "Young lady, where is your father?"

"Here, Your Honor," Gunner Kluesman said, and stepped forward from where he had been leaning against the outside wall.

Judge Roy Bean turned an impatient eye on the blacksmith. "Sir," he said, "I order you to order your daughter into this saloon so we can get on with business."

Gunner shrugged and turned to his daughter, "Suzanne, I order you to enter this sal—ah—er, this courtroom so we can tend to business and go home."

Suzanne was indignant at the pompous audacity of the judge, throwing his weight around, and stood where she was, looking from her father's face to Roy Bean's and back again. Her father was pleading her indulgence and the judge was becoming more irritated by the moment.

"Okay, Daddy," she said, assuming a submissive stance while inwardly chafing at the circumstances. "Ask the judge if we could set a chair in the doorway and I could hear and testify during the proceedings from there."

"How about it, Your Honor, will that satisfy the State of Texas?" Kluesman asked.

The Judge's eyes flashed anger for a moment and then they softened and the wrinkles in their corners crinkled, as a smile broke over him. He began to chuckle.

"Far be it for the State of Texas to be the cause of one so fair to stray into the paths of sin." With that pronouncement, he turned on his heels, strode into the saloon and grabbed up a chair from the closest table, dumping the patron sitting on it onto the floor. Then he strode back over to the entrance of the saloon, set the chair aside just long enough to reach up and grab the bat-wing doors and jerk them from their hinges and toss them with a clatter, out on the porch, an action that sent a number of those standing about scurrying out of the way. Next he set the chair down over the sill with a loud thud, to the amazement of all the onlookers.

Holding out a hand to Suzanne, he cocked his head sideways, indicating the seat he had thus provided, and waited for her to come slowly over.

Suzanne took the proffered seat, but not before bending over and sliding the chair outside the threshold a few inches, fully onto the porch.

Judge Roy Bean stood staring down at the demure girl sitting primly with her hands in her lap, her eyebrows arched, and smiling back up at him.

"Thank you, Your Honor, I am ready to tell the State of Texas what happened."

The judge snorted appreciatively and bent at the waist to lift Suzanne's right hand to his lips, "You are just like the Jersey Lily herself, ain't you, young lady?" he whispered and then kissed the back of her hand a second time. Standing abruptly, he walked back to his place by the bar, fished the Colt .44 out of his waistband and hammered it on the bar for silence. "Court's now back in session," he bellowed.

Suzanne described in detail the circumstances of Claude Bollinger's attack and how Clay Anderson had rescued her. Her testimony was followed by Clay who gave his version and added that he had followed at a distance to insure her safe return to town. When he saw her being attacked, he intervened. The judge asked for any other relevant testimony and several stood to testify to the ineptness of the Sheriff's department and of the many affronts and indignities they had put up with since Sheriff Wiggins and his deputies had come to town.

The Sheriff objected loudly that none of that had to do with the case. He was called out of order and fined another ten dollars, which the Judge allowed he had already appropriated and then reminded the disgruntled lawman that this was a hearing and all had a right to express their opinions. The Sheriff sat down, seething with anger, while Deputy Lemuel Meeker started sidling towards the open door.

In his final summation, Judge Roy Bean ruled that the death of Deputy Claude Bollinger was justifiable homicide and, "what any decent, red-blooded Texan would have done." Bean added, "If I'd a' been there, I'd probably have strung up his corpse with a few parts missing, and let the buzzards pick it clean." He then fined Sheriff Wiggins one hundred dollars for dereliction of duty in appointing such a scoundrel in the first place, and suspended him from office, ordering him to turn over his badge to Clay Anderson, who he appointed acting sheriff until a new one could be elected. He abruptly broke off his oration, smacked the bar with the butt of his pistol and hollered loud enough for all to hear, "Bar's open!"

Sometime during the night, Bertram Wiggins and Lem Meeker packed a few belongings and left town for parts unknown. The next morning, Judge Roy Bean rumbled his buggy down onto Silas Wade's ferry and took his brand of law back west of the Pecos.

Within a week, folks noticed Suzanne with Nuisance, out for their evening stroll through town again, the new Sheriff often by the schoolteacher's side.

Chapter Nine

Wild Horses

Summer, 1870, Upton Sweetgrass Range

Sonny raised his head to peer over the binoculars at the wild horses below, "I ought a just shoot the rascal," he said.

Lance Gilles and Mathew Chambers lay spread-eagled on their stomachs on either side of the older cowboy, following his gaze to a herd of about fifty head of wild mustangs grazing in the valley below.

"Why would you shoot him?" Lance asked. "That don't make no sense, here we drag our tails all the way out here to catch horses and sell 'em to the Army and now you want to start shootin' 'em?"

"That stallion down there," Sonny said tersely, "is going to be more trouble than he's worth and 'sides, he ain't nothing to write home about anyway, look at that big jug-head and the long Roman nose."

"Aw, heck, Gilles, he ain't a gonna shoot 'im," Rusty said, "he's too much of a horse lover to do that. We'll just have to ride on down there and teach that ol' stud what a couple of Texas boys know how."

Sonny snorted, "Horse lover my fam-danny," he scoffed, "I'd shoot 'em sure 'nuff 'ceptin' he just ain't worth the price of a bullet, now dummy up while I figure out where they're waterin' and where the bachelor herd is hidin' out."

"Bachelor herd?" Lance said, "what's that?"

"That's the bunch of younger stallions this old rascal's run off," Sonny said. "They're the ones we want."

From his vantage point on the hill, he could view a wide valley near five miles long, and about a mile across. It was flanked on the far side by steep, eroded cliffs and on the near side by the long, rolling hill they were on. At the far end of the valley, they had left the wagon by a seep and buffalo wallow, where there were numerous unshod horse tracks, as well as longhorn and buffalo sign, indicating it was a favorite watering hole for the area. Sonny deliberately chose this as a campsite for their base of operation and thus deprived the wild herd of its access. The valley held good graze and most of the horse herd was calmly feeding. Only the grulla-colored stallion stood nervously watching on a low promontory. He made quite a spectacle, frequently testing the wind or pawing the ground with a front hoof while bobbing his head up and down. Not a handsome animal, with head too big and neck thick and short, but still, he showed strength and stamina and presented a picture of power and beauty in a wild, rugged sort of way. The stud tested the wind again, as if sensing their presence, even though the wind was against him.

"Look at that old brush popper," Rusty grumbled, "He knows we're here."

"The black mare's the one to watch," Sonny said. "If she stops grazing and starts moving, you can kiss this bunch goodbye."

"I see some pretty good looking animals down there," Lance said. "A couple of them, like that blaze faced red and that palomino with the white socks, I think I'd keep."

"You gotta catch 'em first," Rusty said. "So what's the plan, boss, do we just ride on down there and dab a loop on 'em?"

"Relay," Sonny said. He pulled back from the brink of the hill and put the glasses away. "Looks to be an entrance to a side canyon over on the far wall, maybe there's water in there. If we can run them in there and it happens to be a box canyon, we could build a fence across the entrance and catch them at our leisure. Let's go check it out."

"What about relay?" Lance said.

"Once we have them contained, we'll position ourselves up and down the valley and take turns runnin' 'em until they're tired, then we can get a loop on any of the ones we want and anchor 'em to a drag log."

"Drag log, what the heck is that?" Rusty said.

"It's a log we tie 'em off to that lets 'em fight the rope until they learn not to. After a couple of days, they can be led around, and in the meantime they can still get to feed and water."

That afternoon the three riders rode toward the side canyon and watched the wild bunch flee at full gallop up the valley. They found it was indeed a narrow box canyon, about three-quarters of a mile long and maybe a quarter mile wide. It had steep sides that nothing but a mountain goat or deer could scale and the valley floor was covered with good grass. What was even more to their liking, they found the bachelor herd. Some twenty-five to thirty young studs lifted their heads as one at the sudden appearance of the cowboys, then with shrill squeals of fright, the bunch thundered along the far side, skirting the riders, and fled from the box canyon to mingle with the others.

The riders watched them go then turned to ride on up the canyon. At the upper end was a grove of pecan, post oak, cedar and cottonwoods. They bordered a shallow pool, about an acre wide, into which a small stream cascaded down in a picturesque waterfall from off the cliffs above. The pond had bulrushes at one end and drained off about twenty yards before disappearing into the sand. A thread of willows and brush marked its underground course for another hundred yards or so. There were numerous horse tracks showing it to be a primary waterhole for the wild mustangs.

"This is perfect," Sonny said, "We can run some rails from the cliff sides in a sort of funnel shape by nailing them to the trees, and fashion a gate that can be closed once they come in to drink. Then we will have them in a ready-made corral. I have some ideas about using that pond to break 'em out, too."

They returned to the wagon and began to set up their base camp. An abundance of grease wood, and dead or dying cottonwood would provide ample camp fuel, and a half-day's work on the seep would turn it into a decent waterhole. They worked until dark with pick and shovel, cleaning out and rocking up the seep, until they had a clear running spring. They built a rickety fence with some of the dead logs and branches lying about, to keep the stock out of the spring, with a lower pool dug out to water them. Sonny fashioned a canvas tarp from the back wagon bows to a tree and some willows to serve as a rain fly and shade for their fire pit. A portable table was set up under here along with the wagon tailgate, which was dropped down to serve as both a workbench and kitchen table. A Dutch oven was unloaded along with a big coffee pot and a cast iron spider and roasting spit combination. This was placed over the fire pit. Soon a fire was burning and all hands pitched in to fix supper. They finished up their day with fried spuds and onions, thick slabs of ham, and sourdough biscuits, all washed down with cowboy coffee.

For the next two weeks, Sonny, Lance, and Rusty cut poles of cedar and post oak, leaving the branches on as much as possible, and fashioned a natural-looking fence that tapered down towards the spring to enclose close to an acre of ground, not including the pond. Whenever possible, they routed the rails to trees and the foliage they left on the poles camouflaged it somewhat. At last, the fence was complete and they concealed a brush-covered gate near its opening.

The wild horses had cleared out of the valley when they first started working and it was well into the second week before they returned, tolerating the presence of the cowboys, but keeping to the upper end. The cowboys noted that the grulla had once again driven the bachelor herd off, but only a short distance. Once the fence was complete, the riders spent several more days cutting eight foot logs and dragging them to points along the boxed canyon wall, for later use. Finally their work was done and they returned to camp to wait, leaving the valley to the wild horses. It took three more days before the horses started venturing back into the boxed canyon for water.

"Why didn't we build a fence across the end of that boxed canyon?" Lance said, "They all just went in there, and it would cut down on a whole lot of ridin' after them broomtails."

"We shoulda," Sonny said. "Ride on back to camp for some rope, shovels and anything else you thing we'll need. I never figured it'd be this easy to catch 'em in there. Rusty and I will ride down and block the entrance until you get back."

Sonny and Rusty wheeled their horses and galloped down to the mouth of the canyon while Lance headed back to camp for the tools.

About twenty feet inside the mouth of the boxed canyon, the entrance narrowed down to around forty feet in width and another fifty feet beyond that, the view up the canyon was blocked by a bend in the valley wall.

"Rusty, see if you can drag up some of those posts we left out in the main canyon, we can set them as soon as Lance returns with the shovel."

A cloud of dust marked his line of travel as Lance came racing back down the valley with tools and rope bouncing behind his saddle. He pulled up his snorting horse a little behind Rusty who had just dropped a five post turn of the drag-logs.

"Here they come," Sonny yelled, "Help me block the entrance and drive 'em back."

The lead mare rounded the bend at the head of the herd at full gallop with the grulla stud nipping at the lagers. The cowboys rushed their horses towards them, shouting and waving coiled ropes, causing the herd to break and split in confusion. Some tried climbing up the sides of the canyon, but the bulk of the herd turned tail and fled back the other way, while the stallion neighed his defiance at the intruders, then trotted off after his errant brood with a final whistle of rage.

"Well done, fellers," Sonny called, "that turned them. Let's get a fence across this opening."

The rest of that afternoon was spent digging post holes and setting posts and stringing rope from post to post with tumbleweeds hung on them. Sonny told the younger riders, "That ought a hold them until we can cut some poles for rails and spike together a gate, I reckon thirty or forty poles will do it."

Rusty said, "Where you going to find them? There ain't enough around the spring."

"We'll have to ride back up to the grove by the falls, there's plenty of post oak and cedars to do the job," Sonny replied.

"What about the wild ones? Won't we spook 'em out of there?" Lance asked.

"We'll squeeze easy and disturb them as little as possible—give them a wide birth and hope they settle down," Sonny answered.

"That jug head of a stud ain't gonna like it," Rusty Chambers said. "I think you were right in the first place, we shoulda just shot him and been done with it. He's just going to give us a lot of grief."

"Aw, he'll be to busy keeping that bachelor bunch from his ladies to be worrying about us," Sonny said. "I kinda like the ugly rascal, he's got sand."

The two younger cowboys looked at each other and grinned. "Enough sand to sandpaper all our fannies," Rusty laughed.

Sonny left the boys to guard the entrance while he rode back to camp for their bedrolls and some tools for cutting poles on the morrow. He was intending for them to spend the night guarding the opening, until they could get a secured fence in place. He selected some bacon, jerky, hardtack biscuits, their canteens full of water and at the last moment grabbed the coffee pot and some tin cups, before he rode back to the box canyon. The boys had a small fire blazing and had uprooted several dead bunches of grease wood to keep a fire going all night, figuring a blaze would discourage the horses from trying to run past them in the dark.

Later, they sat around the fire, occasionally feeding sticks into it and watching the stars come out, while the sparks ascended upwards to meet them. Over cups of coffee, they talked about their homes and families on the Brazos and questioned Sonny about girls.

"How do you get a girl to like you, anyway?" Lance asked.

"Beats me," Sonny said and shrugged his shoulders hopelessly. "I been trying to get the schoolteacher to acknowledge I'm even alive, but all's she can think about is my dead brother."

"Boy, that's tough," Lance sympathized. "She must have been really attached to him."

"She said their hearts beat together to the same drum," Sonny said, the dejection apparent in his voice. "How do you compete with something like that?"

"She sure is beautiful for an older woman," Lance said.

"What happened to the Saint Louie girl with all that fancy red hair you was sparkin'?" Rusty put in. "I thought you was pretty thick with her."

Sonny shifted uncomfortably, "I think we better hit the hay, daylight comes early this time of year."

"Aw, come on Son', we want to know," Lance interrupted, "you've had good success with lots of girls—that little Conchita from along the river for instance—how do you get 'em to like you?"

Sonny took a swallow of coffee, hiding a smile in his cup. He took a long breath and held it, letting it bulge out his cheeks; slowly he released it in a long gust of air.

"Conchita, huh," he chuckled. "Well, first of all you've got to consider that girls don't look at things the way guys do—in fact, looks don't seem to have a whole lot to do with it at all as far as I can tell."

"Huh!" Rusty scoffed, "Looks got everything to do with it as far as I'm concerned."

Sonny grinned at the redheaded cowboy who was poking a stick intently into the coals. "That's my point exactly," he went on. "Have you ever noticed how some times you will see the prettiest girl keeping company with the goofiest looking clod-hopper around?"

"Yeah," Lance spoke up. "What's with that?"

"It's because girls don't pay as much attention to the way a guy looks as to what he says."

Both younger cowboys looked at Sonny with skepticism, "What he says?" they both said at once.

"Yep," Sonny nodded, "What he says. I found out, quite by accident, being the accomplished, wordsmith that I am, that gals see a feller with their ears better'n with their eyes, so if'n you two milksops ever expect to really get Becky's attention, you better learn how to sweet-talk her or you're never going to get anywhere."

Rusty sat up and stared at him. "You mean we gotta talk all that maudlin stuff?"

Lance interrupted his friend, "What'll we say?" He seemed more interested in how this worked than Rusty. "What do you say to a girl?"

Sonny chuckled again, "Aw, you juveniles are too young for my secret, sure-fire, fool-proof, can't-lose, methods of roomancin' a gal, let's just go to bed."

"If it's so all-fired foolproof then how come you ain't been able to corral that schoolteacher—Miss Kluesman?" Rusty shot back

"What is it?" Lance was almost desperate. "Shut up, Rusty! C'mon, Sonny, you gotta tell us. There is no way I'm going to get any sleep now. . .tell me what to say to my girl?"

Sonny burst out laughing, in spite of the barb he felt at Rusty's comment. He wished he knew the answer to that question.

"It's really very simple and I'm surprised you young roosters ain't already figured it out, you just simply tell them what they want to hear."

"What they want to hear?" both boys said in chorus again. "What do they want to hear?"

Sonny gave them both a superior grin and said, "That's where the men are separated from the boys—you figure it out." He got up, poured out the coffee grounds from the bottom of his cup, set it upside down on a rock and walked off towards his blankets.

"I'm turning in, don't you two sit up jawing all night." He rolled up in his blankets and closed his eyes. The last he heard before sleep claimed him was Lance and Rusty arguing.

Lance was saying, "She wants to hear how pretty she is."

And Rusty said, "Naw, you knot head, she wants to hear how much dough you got and if you can take care of her."

Sonny came awake, with the ground vibrating to the rumble of horses running. "Wake up," he yelled at the two sleeping youths. "Here they come again." He grabbed a couple of tumbleweeds and stuck them into the dying embers of the campfire, while Lance and Rusty pulled on their boots. They followed his lead and caught up a couple of tumbleweeds, too, and held them to the flames. The ground was shaking as the herd rounded the bend, only to be met by the three men, each holding a blazing ball of fire.

"Run at them," Sonny yelled, and sprinted towards the lead mare, holding the burning tumbleweeds out to his sides. He then hurled them towards the mass of horses. His two companions did the same, and the leaders again shied violently and turned back into the frightened, plunging melee of animals. Pandemonium broke out as the flames landed amongst them, and with shrill cries of terror, they wheeled about and fled, plunging and bucking in all directions away from the fireballs. Two or three of the leaders broke past them, only to come up against the rope and shy away from it, then they turned and fled back after their retreating companions.

Suddenly, in the poor light, the stallion came charging, walleyed, at the men, his ears laid back on his head, and teeth bared.

"Look out," Rusty yelled, "he's gone plumb loco." The cowboys jumped out of the way of the charging stud at the last moment, and turned to watch him sail easily over the rope of their make-shift fence and gallop off into the night, his shrill whistle of defiance and rage drifting back on the wind.

"Well, that son-of-a-gun," Lance drawled, "ain't gonna be no catchin' him."

"Yeah," Sonny said, out of breath, "Least we saved the rest of the bunch for now. That stallion ain't going to quit though, listen." They could hear him whistling and calling off in the distance and from the boxed canyon behind them came an answering call. "That'll be the lead mare," Sonny commented. "Let's set a row of tumble weeds across the opening and keep a couple of torches handy. We'll have to take turns standing guard until daylight. He peered up at the stars, it can't be more'n a couple hours off, judging by the big dipper. If they rush us again we'll just torch off the weeds and meet 'em with a wall of fire."

Standing one-hour shifts each, they kept watch through the night and Sonny, who took the last shift, had coffee boiling when he roused the others at daybreak. A meager breakfast of bacon wrapped around a stick and broiled over the coals and some more hardtack biscuits was soon out of the way as the sun came up. Sonny and Lance rode up the boxed canyon with tools, leaving Rusty to stand guard until they could return with some poles to put up as rails.

The horse herd lifted their heads from grazing and fled up the valley before them until they came to the makeshift fence which funneled down to the opening near the water. For a moment it looked like the whole bunch would run right on through the opening and they'd have them, but then the wise old lead mare slowed and stopped. She trotted a few steps forwards to sniff at the brush-covered gate and shying suddenly, she snorted, wheeled with a loud squeal and charged away, leading the bunch back towards the riders.

Holding up his hand, Sonny and Lance pulled up and sat their mounts, watching the wild horses thunder past them on the far side of the canyon floor. "Darn, we almost had them," Lance said.

"Guess it's not going to be that easy," Sonny replied, "Let's go cut some poles."

The morning was spent falling small cedars, trimming them, and cutting them into twelve foot lengths. As soon as a half dozen poles were ready, Sonny sent Lance dragging them down the valley to Rusty, who busied himself spiking them to the posts they had set the night before. By late afternoon, the herd had settled down some, no longer running at the cowboys' approach. They stood on the far side next to the canyon wall, watching with ears pricked forwards and nostrils flared, ready to bolt at any moment, when the cowboys rode by dragging their strange-looking burden behind them. At last they had the fence and a pole gate up with the latter secured by short lengths of rope.

"There, that ought to hold 'em," Sonny said, "Let's ride to camp and clean up." As they rode up the valley, they heard a wild whistle and turned to see the grulla stallion, high on the hillside, watching their departure, while the wind rippled his mane and tale.

"Not to worry," Sonny said, "We got your family all safe and sound."

They spent the afternoon with camp chores and fixed a nice supper of spuds, onion, fried ham steak and finished it up with a jar of applesauce from Jessica's larder. One of the advantages of having brought the wagon was that they had been able to bring more grub.

"Boy, this is the life," Rusty said. He was leaning back against his saddle, his hands folded behind his head and staring at the fire. "We got good food, a good fire, good horses and good company. Who needs girls anyway?"

Lance and Sonny turned to look at each other and smiled. Lance caught Sonny's wink.

"That's right, Red," the older cowboy said with obvious sarcasm. "Who needs 'em? Live wild and free like that Texas stud out there, 'n if you want a mare just go find you one and add her to your harem."

Rusty frowned at the irritating moniker. "I ain't sayin' anything like that," he said. "What's wrong with ridin' in once in a while, if you feel like some female company, and then ridin' on again?"

"Aw, heck, Rusty," Lance put in, "You go around doin' stuff like that and pretty soon all the best gals are taken and there won't be any left for you, and the ones that's left won't even wantcha."

"So," Rusty said, "A man can't live wild and free if he's saddled down with a woman and a passel of kids—why just take a look at our folks 'n you'll see what I mean. I wanna see what's over the next rise and around the next bend, ain't that right, Son'?" He looked expectantly for corroboration at the older cowboy, who sat nursing a cup of coffee and staring into the fire.

"Hum. . . yeah, I guess so," Sonny said absently, then stood and walked off, leaving the two youth staring after him.

"What's eatin' him?" Rusty said.

"I don't know, maybe he's looked over one to many hilltops and around one to many bends."

"Yeah," Rusty said glumly, "I think the schoolmarm has ruined another good man."

"Ruined him?" Lance Gillis said in surprise, "You think being in love ruins a man?"

"Wal, look at 'im," he drawled. "Is that the Sonny Saber we used to know?"

"Mathew Aloysius Chambers," Lance said in mock severity, "Am I to understand that you have no interest in developing any lasting or permanent relationship with a certain young lady we both know?"

"Don't you dare call me that name," the redheaded cowboy flared up, throwing a smoking stick he had been poking in the fire at Lance. "If anybody finds out that's my name I'll nut you with a dull knife." He looked anxiously in the direction Sonny had gone.

Lance chuckled at his friend's temper, "Well," he said, "what about it. . .you giving me a clear field with Becky?"

Rusty settled back against his saddle and picked up his coffee cup. He took a swig and then looked at his grinning friend.

"Hell no," he said, "she don't even like you."

"Whadaya mean?" Lance said in annoyance. "It's you she don't like, she only puts up with you because she's a sweet girl and we can't seem to get rid of you so's we can be alone."

"Why, you conceited, puffed up toad, she'd rather be with me than the likes of you any day and you know it. . .that's why you're runnin' scared."

"Runnin' scared. . . you're nuts, scared of what?"

"Scared of what you know would happen if you left the two of us alone for more'n half a second, that's what."

"That's bull and you know it, Aloysius," Gilles fired the taunt at his friend like a red-hot dart.

"That cut's it," Rusty said, throwing his hat down. He sprang up from the ground, leaped across the fire and caught his friend, who was just getting to his feet, a solid blow on the nose. Lance yowled with pain and rolled over backwards, then scrambled up to stare at the insolently, grinning redhead standing with fists cocked, waiting.

"So, ya wanna fight, huh?" Lance said, wiping blood away and rubbing it on his pants. "Well, you been asking for it for a long time, you egg-sucking, carrot-topped coyote, and I'm just the one to give it to you." He lowered his head and charged, catching Rusty flatfooted. Throwing his arms about his friend's waist, he pinned the redhead's arms and bowled him over.

The two boys rolled backwards to land in the mud of the buffalo wallow next to the spring and knock down the make-shift barricade. Slipping and sliding, they grunted and puffed while throwing punches, most of which landed harmlessly, until they collapsed in the mud out of breath, but still glaring at each other.

At that precise moment Sonny returned and walked past the two mud-bespattered boys lying there. He scarcely paused, shook his head and passed on to the coffee pot without comment, as if seeing them in that condition was perfectly normal. Puzzled, Lance and Rusty starred after him, and then back at each other.

"He's a strange duck," Lance said.

"Yeah," Rusty replied, "that's what girls can do to ya."

"Not me," Lance scoffed, "gimme a hand up out of here."

"Me neither," Rusty said in denial, and reached out a hand to his friend. Together they helped each other to their feet and climbed out of the mud.

The next morning, the three rode through the makeshift gate and when Sonny dismounted to close it, he suddenly dropped to his knee and studied a set of hoof prints on the ground.

"Did either of you fellers see that stud this morning?" he said. Both boys shook their head. "I didn't either. I think he's back with the herd, looks like he's jumped back in."

They trotted their horses up the box canyon. Rounding the bend, they were met by the challenging whistle of the stallion. He was trotting nervously behind the bunch of wild horses, nipping and gathering them together. The cowboys spread out, their ropes at the ready.

"He's gonna run 'em," Rusty hollered, just as the lead mare neighed a command and broke into a lope, her head held to one side watching back at the following horses. The stallion whistled again and the bunch broke into a full gallop, thundering down the valley floor towards the riders.

Shouting and waving their ropes, Sonny and the other two tried to turn the charge, but the stallion was too much of a presence behind his panicked brood. Most of the herd bolted on past or between the riders, except for a few horses, whinnying to their departing comrades, which the cowboys did manage to turn back.

Once past the cowboys, the stallion quickly raced by his mares and took the lead, and Sonny, Lance, and Rusty turned to chase after them. They rounded the bend in hot pursuit just in time to see the stallion and a half dozen mustangs sail over the fence and race away up the larger valley. The rest of the herd slammed into the pole fence, the leaders screaming in fright with some going to their knees. The poles strained and some cracked, but the fence held and the horses turned to trot nervously back and forth, whistling to the ones that got away

"Doggone it," Lance hollered, "the red and palomino colts went with the stallion."

"So did the lead mare," Sonny said, "that should make the rest of this bunch a little more manageable. Let's see if we can drive 'em back up into our trap."

Riding to the side of the milling horses, they cleared the way for the wild ones to flee back up the canyon and when they bolted for the opening the riders gave chase, hazing them to the trap at the upper end. It went better than expected, for without the lead mare or the stud, the horses ran through the camouflaged gate to come up against the cliff walls and mill about inside the enclosure. Sonny and Lance dragged the hidden gate into place and secured it.

"Whooee," Rusty hollered, "we got 'em now."

"Now our work really begins," Sonny said, looking satisfied, "We've got to cull out the mares and young stuff, catch and geld all the colts and the bachelor herd. Boys, let's unlimber our ropes and start breaking horses." They led their mounts through the gate and shook out short loops. "Each of you rope a horse and drag it out of the enclosure, I'll man the gate."

Soon, Lance and Rusty each had a wild mustang on the end of a rope and rode back to the gate where

Sonny stood. Opening it, the tall rider stepped back while the other two dragged the pitching and bawling wild horses on through. While the colt he had roped stood panting, Rusty handed off his rope to Sonny who quickly tied the end to an eight-foot log, and then let it go.

The mustang came to life and galloped off, until the rope came taught and jerked the heavy log about ten feet through the air to land with a thud. The sudden impact brought the horse to his knees, his wind choked off, but as soon as the rope slackened, he was up and off again, only to be jerked up short once more.

Lance was holding a two-year-old colt that was slowly pivoting his cowpony while trotting in a circle around him. He kneed his mount over to the log pile and he and Rusty held the balky mustang while Sonny tied off the rope to another log and let it go. The two-year-old did a repeat performance of the first one's antics and tried to follow him as he slowly dragged off his log.

"After a day or two, they'll learn not to fight the rope and we can start breaking them out," Sonny said. "Let's go catch some more."

"What about the mares," Lance said.

"Leave 'em for now," Sonny said. "If you fellers want to catch those two that got away, we'll need 'em for bait. I'd kinda like to dab a loop on that feisty grulla stud as well."

By the end of the day they had half the bachelor herd back out in the box canyon, dragging logs behind them on short choke ropes. Hot, tired and dusty, with hands raw from ropes burning through, in spite of their gloves, Sonny, Lance and Rusty rode out for their base camp past the wild captives, admiring their own handiwork. Some of the earlier caught horses were already calmly grazing, but lifted their heads and chewed nervously as the riders passed them by.

"We done a good day's work here," Lance beamed; his nose swollen red and obviously stuffed up. Rusty's left eye was black and blue but there was no denying the exuberance of the pair.

Sonny chuckled to himself, these boys would do to ride the river with, their fight of the day before, long forgotten. He wondered what that was all about, but had a pretty good idea his youngest sister may have been at the bottom of it.

"You boys going to take another mud bath when we get back," Sonny asked. "They say it does wonders for the complexion."

"Aw, shut up," they both said together and, spurring their horses into a run, they raced off to camp. Sonny watched them go and shook his head. In his mind's eye he saw himself and Colt just a few years ago, trying to outdo each other.

By the end of the second day, all but the youngest foals were learning the hard, but permanent lesson of the rope. It took some of them longer than the others to realize that the treacherous, snake-like thing about their neck, choked off their wind from time to time, in direct proportion to how much they pulled against it. Already the bay and the two-year-old roan they had first caught had ceased to pull against the logs and were calmly grazing a circle about them.

"How they going to get to water?" Lance asked. They were sitting next to the pond letting their mounts drink.

"We're going to break these hosses the Injun way," Sonny drawled. Lance looked curiously at Sonny, and Rusty said nothing, but Sonny could see he was hanging on his answer as well.

"Injun way, what's the Injun way?" Lance said.

"If we keep 'em from drinkin' for a couple of days, these broomtails will be a whole lot more agreeable about being led to water. We start with the first bunch in the morning. In fact, what do you say we break camp by the spring and move the wagon on up here by this pound tomorrow? It will give you two children more water to play in."

Rusty gave Lance one of those looks and Lance looked back at his friend and nodded his head although neither boy spoke. Sonny had a momentary premonition that he better watch his back, he wouldn't put it past these two to be plotting some skullduggery against him. He wondered if maybe he should let up a little on egging them on, but. . . naw, they were just too easy, kinda like ripe plums just waiting to fall. "Let's ride," he said and pulling his horse's head around he spurred down the canyon.

"Would you look at that?" Rusty said. They had just ridden through the gate at the mouth of the box canyon out into the bigger valley and pulled up in time to see the stallion and the six others wheel and race away.

"It looked like they were nosin' around tryin' to get back to the rest of the herd," Lance said, "Maybe we should leave the gate open, I sure am partial to that palomino and the red horse with the flaxen mane and tail."

Sonny said, "There ain't much chance of the rest of the bunch getting away, anchored like they are to that firewood, and we got his mares shut up in the trap. . .we'll leave it open."

"I wonder if they were trying to get to water," Rusty said, "We got 'em spooked from comin' into the spring where our camp is."

"Now that's a thought," Sonny said, "maybe we ought to leave our camp where it is for a few more days and see if we can't coax 'em up into the box canyon."

"It's alright by me," Lance said, feeling mighty important at being included in the decision making process and not realizing Sonny was only thinking out loud.

Sonny turned to look at the exuberant towhead and scoffed, "You think so, eh?"

"You're such a piece of work," Rusty chided. "He wasn't asking for your qualified opinion."

Lance's face fell, "Wha'd I say now?" he asked in confusion, then muttered, "Some people's kids." He spurred his horse back to open the gate.

Sonny and Rusty laughed as they watched him go, "You could ease up on him occasionally," Sonny said.

"Him?" Rusty scoffed, "Aw, he's good for it, he needs somebody hazin' 'im, otherwise he'd get too big fer his britches and no one could live within a mile of 'im." The two rode for camp with Lance riding to catch up.

Chapter Ten

Escape from Guaynopa

Summer, 1870

Colt lay on the cold floor of the cavern in a semi-conscious state for over an hour. Finally his head began to clear, the throbbing behind his eyes reduced to a dull ache and he endeavored to sit up. The movement brought a sharp gasp as pain knifed through his right side and he knew some ribs were broken from the cruel stomping he had received. Gingerly he felt along his rib cage then, with great effort, he struggled out of his shirt, tore off strips from the bottom of it, and bound up his sore ribs as best he could. He put the remainder of the shirt back on and crawled to where the water was kept and managed to slake his thirst. Then crawling to the rear of the cavern, he collapsed on the straw tick that was somebody's bed, and passed out again.

It was dark and torches had been lit in the cavern by the time he awoke. The enslaved men had returned from the mine and were lining up, amidst much cursing and grumbling, for the evening meal. This was served from kettles on the back of two wagons just outside the steel doors, under the watchful eyes of the guards. Colt had no appetite and turned over to drift off to sleep again. Sometime later, he was awakened by a kick in the rear.

"Hey, hombre, thees ees my bed, wha ju doeeng heer?" The voice was not unfriendly and Colt rolled over to see a short, heavily built Mexican with a mouth full of white teeth, staring down at him.

"Uhm," he groaned, "Sorry, I needed a place to lie down. I'll move." He tried to get up and nearly passed out from the pain in his ribs.

"Heer now," the Mexican said, "Ju are hurt, ju stay down, and Ramondo weel fine another bed." The Mexican moved off to return presently dragging a straw filled tick with a couple of Indian blankets. These he spread along the cave wall near where Colt lay. "I like to sleep back heer away from the noise and steenk of thee others," he said, "there ees a leetle breeze that blows back heer."

Long after the others had quieted down and gone to sleep, Colt lay in the dark. His mind played over the events of the past few days, and he bemoaned the luck that had allowed Hutch and his men to catch them so quickly. He wondered about poor Penny and the fate that awaited her in this place. Somehow he would have to find a way to escape again. He made up his mind to try to take the girl with him when he did. He fell asleep with a cooling breeze, smelling faintly of a pack rat, blowing softly across his face.

He was awakened the next morning amidst angry shouts, as the inmates attended to their morning toiletries and lined up for a breakfast of cornmeal mush.

"Ju stay heer 'n I breeng ju some foods," Ramondo said. "There ees a new boss who comes on thees morning. I do not theenk he knows ju are heer. I weel cubber ju op weeth de blankeet, ju need to geet well before ju work de minas, else ju die."

Ramondo brought a bowl of mush and a canvas bottle of water and handed them to Colt. "Ju lay quiet unteel thee others leave, I weel cubber ju op." Colt made no argument and laid still as the Mexican spread the blankets over him.

He must have dozed, for the next thing he knew the cavern was quiet. Sunlight was streaming in through the cracks around the iron door and dimly lighting the compartment. He sat up, the pain in his side having subsided somewhat. Slowly he got up and walked to the door and peered through the crack. No one was in sight. He pushed against the door and it creaked and gave about an inch or two, then stopped short. He could see the heavy chain and padlock securing it and knew he was locked in.

He began to look around at the sleeping mats piled about, each holding the sparse goods of the individuals who slept on it. He took a drink of water and, feeling hungry, he walked back to where Ramondo had left the bowl of mush. As he approached, he was surprised to see a pack rat sniffing about and when he reached to throw a stone from the floor at it, he recalled having smelled one the night before.

He looked at the rodent with its cute little face and bushy tail. "The things may be cute, but they're a dang nuisance," he muttered and picked up his bowl of gruel. He was sitting there finishing the last of the mush when he saw the pack rat scamper across the end of his sleeping mat and disappear behind a rock at the back of the cavern. "He's got a nest in there," Colt thought, "I wonder what he's got stashed away." He knew the varmints were famous for squirreling away bright and shiny objects and decided to investigate.

Colt had seen candles at various points along the cavern wall and went over and collected a few along with a box of matches, then he walked back to where he had seen the pack rat disappear. Lighting a candle, he held it up to peer behind the stone and nearly had the flame blown out. A gentle breeze was blowing from behind the rock, bringing the slightly skunky smell of the pack rat.

"This air is coming from somewhere outside," Colt said. "Mr. Pack Rat, you just might be the answer to my prayer." He grasped the edge of the stone that was wide at the bottom but tapered up towards the top where it lay against the stone wall of the cave. It moved, grating loudly across the floor as he tugged on it, revealing a small space behind hung with cobwebs, and opening into an obvious continuation of the cavern he was in. A steady breeze was causing the candle to flicker.

Painfully, he knelt on hands and knees and squirmed through the opening holding his candle ahead of him, and came out into a wider and longer part of the passageway. It seemed to angle slightly upward. In the dancing light, he could see stringers of white quartz running parallel with this chute, all loaded with free-milling gold, dazzling yellow, back at him. "Huh," he said, "This is a richer vein than what they are working on over at the other place." He turned to look back at the hole he had just climbed through and spied the pack rat's nest.

A bundle of sticks, moss, pine cones and grasses was tucked into a corner and the rat was sitting up in the middle, his beady black eyes unblinking in the candlelight. Colt made a move for the nest and the rat took off, fleeing up the chute. Picking up a stick, Colt began to poke through the nest, to discover several articles stolen from the men within the cavern. He found an old pocket watch, a pearl handled clasp knife, a money clip with a few chewed up pesos in it and several buttons and empty brass rifle and pistol shells. He was about to turn away when the glint of gold caught his eye.

He moved a flap of cloth and saw a pile of twenty-dollar gold pieces along with several fair-sized nuggets. He picked up one of the coins and discovered they were minted from this mine. "So, Mr. Pack Rat, looks like you've collected my wages for me. I'm going to collect for working in this hellhole after all, thank you very much."

Colt squirmed back through the hole into the prison cavern. Hurriedly he collected a couple water bags and filled them, then found a leather pouch on someone's bunk, and dumping out a pack of greasy playing cards and some dice, he took it with him. He headed back towards the hole behind the rock, and with his side aching, and sweating profusely, he backed his way through the hole in order to pull the big rock back into place. Backing to where the pack rat's nest was, he stopped to set the candle into a melted pool of wax, while he put the rest of the treasure in the pouch. There were twenty-six twenty-dollar gold pieces, along with a handful of good-sized nuggets. Taking the pocket knife and silver money clip, he put them in, as well. When he had caught his breath, he took the candle and started up the chute, his head bent under the low ceiling, following the direction he had seen the pack rat take.

The passage seemed to angle upward and was irregular, which made him think it was an old steam or lava vent from an ancient volcano. It had followed the seam and blown-out the fissures in the rock, while laying down the minerals as the water cooled and dissipated. He still felt a light breeze in his face that guttered the candle and hoped it would lead him to the outside. He came to narrowed down places, some of which he had to crawl through, and once he thought he had come to a dead end when the passage ceiling nearly met the floor in a space too tight for him to pass. But after some patent removal of slab rock and boulders, he opened up a hole wide enough to wriggle through on his belly.

He lay for a moment on the cavern floor resting and catching his breath, watching the candle light flicker on the ceiling a few feet above him. He was thankful for the candles and absently felt in the pouch for the other two, satisfied they were still there. "I hope I get out of here before these candles are all gone," he said, his voice a low echo in the chute he was in.

Colt recalled the last time he had been trapped in the cave of Victorio and shuddered. He was developing a distinct dislike for spelunking—was that what Pops had called it? He remembered the term because it sounded so funny and seemed to have more to do with chunking a rock into a pond than cave exploration. Well, like it or not, he was going to have to explore this one on out.

When the pain in his side eased, he continued on, and found the passage widening and the ceiling rising so that he was able to stand upright and eventually he came out into a huge open space. Holding the candle aloft, he was able to see a cavern in which the ceiling was twenty to thirty feet above the floor. To the left was a well-defined passageway and farther to his right was a second tunnel, both which appeared to be workings from the past. Cautiously, he moved to the one on the right and watching his candle, he saw no movement of air coming from here to cause the flame to tremble. Whatever the source of the breeze, it was not along this passageway, although there were signs of chiseling in the stone, in what seemed to be a well-formed tunnel through the host rock.

Colt moved to the passage opposite, which appeared to be a continuation of the other, and indeed there was evidence of tailings and chipped rock lying about in the larger intervening amphitheater. It followed a fairly level plain into the mountain and he noticed once again the flame of his candle flickering and blowing away from him in a prevailing breeze. Here was an obvious draft that led him to believe there had to be an outlet along this tunnel as well as the one he had just traversed.

He was uncertain as to whether or not he should go down this passageway, concerned about his candle, which was burning low, and he wondered if he shouldn't have brought along a few more. Who knew how long it would take him to get out of here? "Lord," he prayed, "Show me the way to go." Should he explore to where the air was venting or try to track its source, somewhere ahead in the larger cavern? He made the decision to pursue the route to the left, although he hated the thought of it coming to a dead end. He could always retrace his steps to the prison cave and pilfer a few more candles if he had to.

He moved along a well made, but long abandoned tunnel in which the breeze was barely noticeable. Each step he took sent up little puffs of dust that settled slowly back to the floor, leaving strange ghost-like footprints in the dim light, like steps in snow behind him. Rounding a bend, he was startled to hear a scurrying sound on the floor to his left and turned in time to catch a glimpse of the gray, bushy tail of the pack rat as it ran out of sight ahead of him. Swallowing hard, Colt stopped to catch his breath and calm his heartbeat. It was surprising how tense he had become. "It's only a pack rat for crying out loud, wha'd you think it was, *Billy Goat Gruff*?" Time seemed irrelevant in the darkness and he wondered how far he should follow the passage. "I will retrace my steps when I reach the halfway point of my light," he decided.

He had about two inches left on the first candle when the passage abruptly ended; blocked by an apparent collapse or cave-in of the ceiling. A low, blowing sound could be heard in one corner and he saw a well worn path in the dust where the pack rat had gone through a hole, the same hole the air was whispering through. Colt knelt and pulled at a large boulder, causing dirt and gravel to tinkle away but the rock did not move. Making a place for the candle, he moved to where he could get both hands on the rock and succeeded in rolling back the large stone and increase the opening. The sound of the draft changed to an almost imperceptible sigh, and Colt sensed there was a lager portal or cavern just on the other side of the tunnel blockage.

Feverishly he began to pull rocks and gravel back, when suddenly he heard the clang of heavy steel doors being opened and saw light appear in the hole he had been enlarging. Quickly he blew out the candle and lay still, listening. There were angry voices and the crack of a whip and then the sounds of running feet, and the clank of heavy metal being set down.

Quietly Colt squirmed down through the hole until he could poke his head up, and after his eyes adjusted to the half-light, he saw a large cavern, not unlike the one the prisoners were held in, complete with steel doors. Two armed Mexican guards watched as half a dozen slave workers carried silver and gold ingots from outside the doors into the cavern. Here they were stacked in neat rows, four feet high. He counted at least a dozen rows of gold ingots and twice that many of silver, extending back into the cave. This must be the treasure trove where the mines' wealth was being stored. He had heard about this place but had never seen it. He understood it was somewhere on the same mountain, near the other workings, and was kept under close guard until such time as the New York office deemed it safe to move, once the Apache trouble was put down. Now here it was—"there must be millions of dollars worth of gold and silver stashed in this cave," he calculated.

As he lay counting the piles, he heard a harsh command of, "Vamoose," and then all went dark as the heavy steel doors clanged shut. There was a rattle of chain, then a lock snapped shut, followed by the sounds of a wagon moving away.

For a moment, he contemplated enlarging the hole and entering the vault but abandoned that idea, for there was no exit through those locked doors and past the guards. Carefully, he struck a match and re-lit the candle. He replaced the large stone he had dislodged, and piled up the rest of the rock to where the wind whispered through as before, concealing the hole. He began to retrace his steps in hopes that one of the other passages offered an escape.

His candle was burning his fingers by the time he reached the vaulted chamber and he quickly set it on a rock and lit another. "One down, two to go," he said. "Lord, I could use some help here."

Colt moved across the uneven floor to the far end of the amphitheater, looking until he found a low portal of another passage that resembled the original vent he had followed at first. Once again he detected a draft of air moving down it ever so slightly. He judged from the direction the flame flickered that it had to be coming from somewhere up the chute, hopefully from outside. He started up and found it a difficult assent, inclining steeply upward in places and often requiring him to set his candle down ahead of himself and use both hands to navigate through a tight spot. It was apparent no effort had been made to improve this passage and he began to wonder if he should not have chosen the other one.

Colt labored through the chute for another half hour or so. It inclined upward in stages with few level places, and often he was required to inch through narrow spots on his belly while passing the light ahead of himself as he struggled on through. He had just broken through one of these places when a strong breeze nearly blew out the candle. Shielding it with his hand, he found he was in a tunnel large enough to stand erect. Regaining his feet, he paused. Hot and sweaty and covered with dirt and cobwebs, he wiped off his face and took a long drink from one of the water bottles. With the candle held high, he proceeded across the irregular floor of the tube, on up a gentle incline until, rounding a bend in the chute, he suddenly stopped.

A faint glint of light illuminated the darkness some one hundred yards distant, and Colt gave a huge sigh of relief. His heart thudded in his chest as he scrambled up the passageway, his eyes fastened on the life-giving circle of light growing brighter and brighter. He felt like he was being delivered out of a tomb. Before him was what appeared to be an obvious cave-in of the ground outside into the chamber where he was now standing. Sunlight was streaming though a small, wash-tub sized hole, with a blue patch of sky beyond it. Never did the sunlight and sky appear as welcome to him as it did at that moment.

In his eagerness to escape, he failed to notice that the hole slanted down into a pit about twenty feet across and six to eight feet deep. This marked the end of the passage and he nearly stumbled into it while looking up. To his horror, the bottom of it was a squirming, slithering mass of rattlesnakes. There must have been a hundred of them in there, and an immediate rattling and buzzing started up as his boots kicked rocks and gravel down, while he struggled to regain his balance and step backward. When his eyes adjusted to the light, he saw amongst the coiling and crawling serpents, the remains of several human skeletons, the grinning skulls of some poor unfortunate souls who had either fallen or, more likely, been thrown into this den.

Colt recoiled from the sight, then began to study on how to cross to the opposite side, when a shadow passed across the overhead opening. He looked up into the black, staring eyes of an Apache warrior. At first, the Indian did not appear to see him, but when Colt involuntarily gasped his surprise and fright, the Indian in turn shouted a startled, "Hoo-hah!" and disappeared.

A sudden thought gripped Colt's imagination, and he realized that the brave had been as startled as he was, if not more so. He was again reminded of the superstitions that had chased away the Comanche that time in the Jeff Davis Mountains and wondered if it might not work to his advantage here. Colt began a low moaning call, raising it to the high pitched wail he had used so effectively on those other fierce guardians of the plains. The sound was amplified off the surrounding rock and echoed back from the depths of the tunnel below to rise to a crescendo, an eerie, ghostly cry that set every rattlesnake in the pit buzzing in evil accompaniment.

His heart thudding in his chest, Colt stepped back into the shadows and waited, listening. At first he heard nothing but the buzz of rattles and then a faint and muffled, sing-song chant, and rhythmic beatings of a hide drum. Had he stumbled into an Apache encampment? He doubted that. From the viewpoint he had had on the mesa, he had often looked across to this side of the canyon and had seen nothing that resembled such a place. He did recall the lone vigilance of the Apache who had sent the smoke signals from a point above and not far from the cliff dwellings, and wondered if he were not in close proximity to that location now. Was the brave keeping watch at some Apache holy site? Perhaps the pit of snakes was some portal to the spirit world of their superstitions, and the Apache keeping vigil, a holy man. If so, Colt intended to use it to his advantage and give this "holy man" something to talk about around the campfire on cold winter nights—*"The time he heard from the spirit world."* Colt again emitted his ghostly cry, then suddenly cut it off abruptly, following it up with as hideous and evil a laugh as he could muster. Listening, he heard the chanting and drum beat stop and all was silent, save the rattlers' buzzing.

It was plain that any escape from this place was not possible, not with the formidable obstacle of the snake-pit and Lord only knows how many Indians lurking about outside that portal of light. With sinking heart, Colt heard the chanting and drum beat resume, this time louder and more fervent than ever. Reluctantly he began the descent back down the chute, to check the last and final passage way, hoping against hope that it might lead him to freedom. With devilish inspiration, he periodically made his haunting call and evil laughter while making his way down, knowing it would sound to the Indian, like the evil spirit was retreating back into the bowls of the earth. Maybe he could instill a dread of the place for the redskin. If he could scare him off and figure out a way past the snakes, he might still have a chance of getting out. Colt had to quit the evil cry though. As he descended deeper into the darkness, he found that he was the one being instilled with a dire sense of dread—he was scaring himself.

By the time Colt reached the main cavern, his second candle was nearly burned out. He had one left, and vacillated on whether or not to return to the prison cave for more, or try to explore the third and final tunnel first. He knew if it took too long, and he had to go back, he could be caught when the mine slaves returned, and he most assuredly would be found out by the guards. They may even now be aware of his absence. Time was of the essence.

His ribs ached. He was tired, hungry, hot, dirty and sweaty and would soon be in the dark once his final candle was gone. He estimated he would need at least a quarter of it to retrace back to the prison vault, which meant he could not explore more than one quarter—maybe a third at best, of the candle's light, down this last tunnel. With a heavy sigh of weariness he stood and made his way into the third and final tunnel.

This tunnel was much like the second, it followed a fairly level plain with definite signs of having been chiseled out of the living stone. There were only slight bends and irregularities and the floor was level and relatively easy to walk along. Stones and pebbles fallen from the ceiling were the only impediment to his progress, that and the dark, of course, and he was grateful to be able to walk upright here.

He rounded a slight bend and stopped. Somewhere far ahead, he could hear the slight tinkle of falling water and then his heart leaped into his throat. He thought he saw a ghostly light moving off in the distance. He strained his eyes for it seemed to appear then disappear. He rubbed his eyes and looked again, listening hard and scarcely breathing. Only the indistinct sound of falling water could be heard. Cautiously, he started forwards again, straining his eyes. *What was it? There it was again.* He stopped and focused—were his eyes playing tricks on him? Maybe the flickering candle flame was making his eyes tired. He kept on, moving cautiously forward, and the apparition appeared again, but this time it seemed lower. He moved his head and it disappeared. He moved it again and it reappeared. *Was the thing watching him, hiding and appearing at will?*

Suddenly Colt felt his ears burn with embarrassment. He took a quick step to the left and the apparition appeared and he realized that he had been watching a distant patch of light that faded in and out of view as he walked along, due to the irregularities of the tunnel wall. "*Boy, what a knot-head I've been,*" he thought, "*here I been thinking I was seeing a ghost and all along it's light up there. I've fallen victim to my own haunting.*"

Something was still wrong though, as he steadily approached the patch of light, it did not appear to be at the end of the passageway or in the ceiling, but in the floor, and it shimmered and wavered unnaturally. Why would it do that? He felt totally disoriented and nervous, and for a moment he had to put out his hands and steady himself against the cold stone walls to stop the vertigo.

Eventually, he came to a place where water dribbled from a crevice in the tunnel wall near the ceiling and drained ahead of him towards the light, and when he finally got close enough to realize what he had been looking at he found he was staring at a square cut hole in the floor of a hollowed out room in which the tunnel he was in, ended abruptly. It was filled with water through which the light shimmered from an outside source and was filtered, with a bluish tinge, giving mute testimony of the sky outside. Shadowy light danced on the walls of the tunnel with the water's movement from where the stream trickled in. It revealed two portals, one on either side of the tunnel, that opened into rooms or vaults cut out of the stone, not unlike those Colt had seen in the mountain stronghold of Victorio.

He stepped into one and nearly stumbled over an ancient suit of armor. Holding the candle high, he saw several suits of the armor with helmets, swords and shields of ancient Spanish design, such as he had seen in pictures. This must have been an armory of some sort, but what was the body of water through which the light from the outside was coming? He knew of no lakes or ponds in these mountains. If he dove in, how far would he have to swim under water and stone before he reached the surface and could he hold his breath that long?

Colt knew he had to try, but not knowing what awaited him on the other side, he decided to arm himself, and picked up one of the swords from the floor of the cache, and tucked it under his belt. He removed the leather pouch at his waist and blew out the candle. Setting these on a ledge by the doorway of the anteroom; he climbed down into the water and found he was standing on a stone step. Taking several deep breaths, he ducked under the surface and swam with his eyes open, towards the light. It took several strokes for him to pass under the dark ceiling of stone and come out to surface in a pool of water that had been cut into the living rock. Somehow it seemed strangely familiar. Then it dawned on him; he was in the water reservoir of the cliff dwelling that he and Penny had visited; the very same one she had gone swimming in.

Laughing joyously, he waded out of the pool onto the floor of the cavern and collapsed in a puddle of sunlight. "Free. . . I'm free at last, thank you Lord," he breathed fervently. He lay there in the sunlight catching his breath and drying off in the warm sunshine. Then he fell asleep.

Colt awoke in the twilight, the sun having dropped behind the west wall of the canyon, and sat up with a groan. His clothes were nearly dry, but the bandage about his rib cage had come loose. Carefully he rewound it, and then donned what was left of his shirt. Feeling somewhat better, he moved carefully to the edge of the cliff to peer down into the mining camp. All was in shadow but still light enough for him to see the usual evening activities.

He intended to sneak into the village after dark and try to gain entrance to the store, for he would need an outfit to trek across the wilderness—food, a pistol or rifle, and walking boots. He would have preferred taking a horse and heading down stream again, but dared not be discovered a second time and besides, a horse would be missed. He also needed to learn the whereabouts of Penny and figure out how to bring her with him. He decided to wait a few days, taking a few items from here and there where they would least likely be missed. These he would bring back to the cliff dwelling hideout. He would cache the stuff in one of the empty pueblos until he had his outfit together, just in case someone should come to investigate this site, and await his opportunity to make good his escape.

Absently, his eyes sought out the long, low, adobe structure that housed the women who were unmarried or unattached. He would look for Penny there first, and keep watch during the daytime to learn the movements of the camp. His eyes followed a rider who rode east, up the creek and disappeared from view on the trail, east of the camp. He saw the changing of the guard on the lower river trail and figured they had one posted on the upriver end of the camp as well. He would have to be careful to not alert this man when he climbed down from the cliff dwellings, for by this time, they would be on high alert, looking for him.

For the next few hours, Colt mulled over in his mind his plan of escape. He would take the same route they had brought him in on. It was supposedly a secret trail, but had been used frequently enough that he felt certain he would be able to follow it back to the Texas border and the Rio Grande. He would need to avoid the main trail, perhaps paralleling it at a distance, in order to not leave any obvious tracks for Hutch's Indian tracker. He and Penny would slip out over the rocks some dark night in a week or so, giving it enough time so that L.T. Jones' interest in his whereabouts would die down. Then he'd grab Penny and be gone—at least that is what he hoped for.

He would need some sort of distractions at the time of his leaving, to pull the guards in from their posts, and he wished there was some way to sabotage this whole corrupt operation. The idea of some wealthy, Eastern, New York City Syndicate getting rich off the backs and the misery of those enslaved here, rankled him.

Escape to the north was out of the question due to the Apache and Geronimo's stronghold in that direction and going south, deeper into Mexico while traveling in disguise was risky, with the Federales always on the lookout for the "Gringos." West, over the Devil's Backbone, would be even more difficult, traveling into unknown mountains and besides, it would be going the wrong way. It was too bad the snakes and the Apache blocked the exit from the mountain caverns, for that would be the ideal exit from this God-forsaken country.

Sometime after one o'clock in the morning, Colt stealthily made his way down the rock chimney from the cliff dwellings and paused to study the river trail before crossing the scree of loose rock and boulders at the cliff wall's base. He was just about to go on down, when a faint movement below and off to his right caught his eye. He saw a man stretch and yawn then slump back down to doze over a rifle he was holding. This must be the guard, he thought. With utmost care, Colt removed his boots and, in stocking feet, he moved carefully through the slide area, all the while keeping larger boulders and rocks between himself and the guard's position. At one point, he heard the man snoring and was satisfied he had passed him undetected. He hurriedly pulled on his boots and disappeared down the trail towards the camp. Stopping first at the little hut he had shared with Penny, he listened at the window, but could hear no sound, so carefully tried the door. It squeaked loudly on its hinges until he lifted up on the handle and swung it open.

The place was just as he had left it. From under the bed he recovered a couple of gunny sacks and from the cupboard shelves, he took salt, pepper, coffee and a one pound bag of beans. He added a frying pan and a tin cup, plate and butcher knife, along with a box of matches and a box of cartridges. These he stuffed into one of the sacks, then filled the other with a rain slicker and an extra pair of pants and shirt. He was about to leave, glancing around the room in the dim light, when his eyes fell on some rawhide leather rolled up in the corner, this he stuck in the sack and then stepped outside. Around back, he found a coil of rope and added it to the sack and left both bags behind the building.

He turned and headed down the path that paralleled the canal which brought water to the sluices and irrigation ditches. When he passed the arastas and smelting shed, he stopped. "There should be some dynamite around here somewhere," he thought.

Going over to the ore wagons that would be making a run up to the mine in the morning, he peered in. The first two were empty but the third one was only partially unloaded. Here he saw a box under the seat and on closer inspection in the starlight, he found it was marked T.N.T. Carefully he lifted out the box and carried it back to the hut and secured it under the bed. *This will come in handy when it comes time to leave,* he smiled grimly.

Retracing his steps, he then snuck through the backyards of the village and raided a couple of gardens, taking melons, carrots and corn, but being careful to leave no tracks. From three different spring-houses, he found butter, eggs and in one, a slab of bacon. Picking up an old wicker basket from under a clothesline, he placed his provisions in it, and headed back for the hut and his sacks.

The guard was stretching and stood to relieve himself, as Colt reached the rock slide to the pueblos. He kept to the shadows, creeping up the pathway behind the guard. When he reached the chimney, he set the basket down and placed the two sacks into it. Tying off the coil of rope to its two handles, he waited until the guard moved off towards the village, as the sun was lighting the eastern horizon. When he was out of hearing, Colt shinnied up the chimney with the rope in tow and hauled up his supplies.

Folks were just beginning to stir in the camp below, by the time Colt had hid his stores away and sat down to munch on a carrot and slice open the melon. He wished for bacon and eggs, but dared not light a fire, in fact, when the sun hit full light on the pueblo later, he must not be seen even moving around up here, for it might be visible in the village below.

A little later, he watched as a Mexican woman berated a little girl in the yard with the clothesline, where he had taken the basket. He felt bad for the child having to bear the blame for his theft, and made up his mind to try to return it that night. He watched a work detail finish unloading the third wagon and witnessed a Mexican boss abusing one of the workers when the missing box of dynamite was discovered. The worker was sent to the store for another.

By the end of the third night, Colt had accumulated a pair of hiking boots with walking heels, a sombrero, two blankets, and a rifle complete with double bandoliers, which had been carelessly left on the porch of one of the guard shacks.

He spotted Penny being led from the women's barracks to a hut, where the horse Reese Hutchinson rode was tied. He seethed inside at the abuse the girl must be suffering at the hands of that coldblooded killer.

After a week had passed and his whereabouts remained a mystery to the inhabitants of the camp, life seemed to return to some semblance of normalcy. The guard was removed from the up-river location, thus clearing the way for Colt's nightly excursions into the village, but the other guards remained at their regular posts downstream and on the eastern trail.

Colt had secured most of what he thought they could carry, hiding it in one of the vacant pueblo dwellings out of sight. Now he was intent on finding Penny and sneaking her away. He intended to bring her to the cliff dwellings before they made their final escape, and wait for the right time. He knew what building she was in, but without going inside, he had no idea which room and bunk was hers. He decided that tonight he would try to enter the women's quarters, having secured a woman's dress and scarf from another clothesline for this purpose.

After dark, he made his way to the women's barracks, and with his jeans rolled up to his knees, a shawl over his head, and the large dress sweeping the ground, he crept to the back door of the building and watched. Sometime around midnight, the door opened and a large Mexican woman hurried from the building and down the path to disappear into the privy. With catlike steps, Colt slipped through the back door and found himself standing in a long hallway with rooms off either side. Moonlight shone through a window at the end. He began to check the rooms, opening the first door on the right. A single window allowed enough light to see four bunks, two on each side. The sleeping occupants were either women too old, or children. He closed the door and moved to the next room. It wasn't until he tried the fourth door that he found a room with girls Penny's age, inside. He had just stepped over the threshold, when the outside door behind him opened and the old woman from the outhouse came through. Quickly, Colt pulled the door of the room he had entered closed and waited. Holding his breath, he listened to her shuffle down the hall. When he heard a door open and close, he breathed easier and turned to look at the girls.

Penny was in the second bed and came awake with a start and low cry of alarm, which he quickly stifled with a hand clasped over her mouth. Her eyes flashed about wildly then opened in surprise and recognition, after he removed the shawl from his head. Holding a finger to his lips, he removed his hand from her mouth and motioned her to follow him. Penny rose quickly to her feet, clad in a light cotton gown, and slipped into her shoes. Catching up her clothes from a nail on the wall, she reached under her bed and pulled out a sack, then quickly stuffed her clothing into it and followed the cowboy to the door. Colt opened it and stepped into the hall, leading the way to the back door, while Penny followed. He reached it and turned the knob, when a voice behind them demanded, "Where do ju theenk ju are goink?"

Colt froze; but Penny, reacting swiftly, stepped up close to him and merging with his outline in the dark, she turned while slipping him her bag.

"To the privy, if that's alright with you," she answered.

The stout Mexican woman took a few steps down the darkened hallway towards them, peering questioningly in the darkness, "Who is dat wi ju?' she demanded.

"Just my sweetheart and lover," Penny said sarcastically, "who'd you think?"

Colt stepped swiftly through the door and around to the side of the building where he was out of sight, as the Mexican matron walked the rest of the way up the hall. There was the sound of a slap and then the matron stuck her head out of the door looking this way and that.

"Doan ju geet smarts weeth me, ju leetle puta," she said and shoved Penny out the door. "Do jor beesnus and geet back to thee bed." She waited until Penny disappeared into the outhouse, then turned muttering, and went back into the building, shuffling down the hall. Colt heard a door click shut behind her, waited a few minutes, and then shut the door from the outside loud enough so that she could hear it and would think Penny had returned.

Penny must have been watching, for no sooner had the door closed than she was out of the privy and joining Colt. Together, they slipped away through the shadows and made their way back to the cliff dwellings.

The next day, they could see from their vantage point on the cliffs that the camp was in turmoil. Guards were racing about to block the exits, while others were conducting a building by building search for the missing girl. Colt knew that it would not be long before Jones and the others put two and two together and would figure out he was still in the vicinity. Undoubtedly, they would redouble their efforts to find him.

"Everyone had given you up for dead," Penny said. "Some of the Mexican workers said spirits had come and taken you."

"Hardly," Colt scoffed. "I found a way out through the caverns. There's a whole lot more to them than what they think there is."

"How do we get away?" she asked anxiously.

"I'm studying on that, I think we're safe up here for the present. We will just have to watch for an opportunity and be ready to leave at a moment's notice."

Penny looked badly used. She had lost weight and sported bruises. Her eyes, once so bright and mischievous, now were dark and hollow and listless, though they seemed to follow his every movement, as though conditioned by fear.

"I knew you would come for me," Penny said. "When I heard you were missing, I packed my bag and hid it under my bed—I knew you would come."

"I'm sorry it took so long—did they treat you so very bad?"

Penny turned her head away and did not answer him. He could see she was struggling to keep her emotions under control and he sensed her spirit, if not broken entirely, was badly damaged—maybe beyond repair. The one spark in her seemed to be an earnest desire to get away, to flee the confines of this camp, and Colt prayed it would sustain her throughout the ordeal ahead of them.

Penny sighed then and said, "I hope we can leave this place soon, if I have to stay here much longer, I don't want to go on living."

"Of course you do, Penny, life is worth the living. Someday you'll look back on all this and remember the pluck and sand you had that got you through it all, and you'll be able to tell your grandkids all about it."

Penny looked at him sadly and shook her head. "There will be no kids and there will be no grand-kids—they have ruined me—degraded me beyond redemption—I shall never marry."

Colt's heart went out to this girl. She sat with elbows on her knees, chin in hand and eyelashes wetting the rusty freckles on her pale cheeks. He reached out his hand and gripped her shoulder, "There's nothing that's beyond redemption, Penny," he said, "least of all you."

"You don't know how badly I have been debased," she said passionately. "If I ever get the chance, I will kill that Reese Hutchinson."

"Penny," Colt said with alarm, "don't say such things. Nothing is so dark that the light of God's love cannot shine through. You will live and laugh and love again, you will see."

"I don't see—not even God could look on me with favor, given what I've been made to do."

"But that's just where you are so wrong, it's those who are lost and without hope that He is looking for the most. Don't you know Jesus?"

"I thought I did, but then all this stuff's happened to me and He seems to have disappeared. I don't know what I said or did that was so terrible that it would cause Him to let all this happen to me and not even hear my prayers, let alone answer them. You want me to trust

Jesus? Give me one good reason why I should! Where was He when I needed him? Where was He when you needed Him? How come, Colton? You trusted Him, how come He has let these awful things happen to us?"

Colt was silent for a moment. She was asking some hard questions and he was not altogether sure he understood the answers himself.

"I don't know, Penny, I can't answer that question right now, but one thing I am sure of, Jesus is altogether trustworthy. If He wasn't, then He put His life on the line for nothing, and this whole thing's just one big, bad, cruel joke—Reese Hutchinson and his kind win and evil trumps good."

"So," she said, the bitterness heavy in her voice, "where does that leave us?"

"That's just it, girl, don't you see—it doesn't. We haven't been left. Good always winds up on top in the end. As for you and me, we better hang around and watch to see how it does, that's how we learn to trust Him. Won't you trust Jesus in this, with me?"

Penny looked at him with hollow eyes. He thought he saw a little glimmer of hope there. "How can He fix it? What's been done has been done and can't be undone. What has been stolen and violated and destroyed, can't be restored."

"No, maybe not undone, but Jesus knows a way for you to make new meaning out of it all—the day will come when you can attach new significance to all of this."

"I don't know if you fully understand me, Colton," Penny said. "I did not oppose all that happened to me, some of it at first seemed fun and exciting—even thrilling, but I had no idea it would lead to such awful debasement and degradation. How can I expect God to overlook that?"

Colt thought for a moment, "You ask Him to forgive you and He will."

"That's it?" she said.

Colt nodded, "Would you like to?"

"You mean ask His forgiveness?"

Colt nodded again.

"Don't you have to do something first to prove you're really sorry?"

"Like what?" Colt asked

"Oh, I don't know, penance or something—vow never to marry or have kids—you know—something connected to that kind of stuff, maybe go into a convent and swear off all sins of the flesh and live celibate."

"You think you could keep that kind of vow?"

She thought for a moment and then shook her head, "No, probably not. There's really not much left of me that is worth anything anyway—I have nothing to bring."

Colt chuckled, "That's right, but enough that Jesus figures you were worth dying for, that's all."

"He died a long time before I was born, how could He die for me when I wasn't even thought of yet?"

"Oh, but you were thought of. You were in the plan and foreknowledge of God before any of your parts ever existed and when Jesus was on the cross, He looked ahead in time and saw you, Penny Stauffer. He saw you and He knew you, and He knew what would happen here, and yet He still loves you just as you are right now—while He was up on the cross, you were on His mind. He took all your sin and shame and disgrace and defilement upon Himself and pinned it to the cross for you, so you could get off—that's why you can trust Him, will you?"

"Yes," she said, her voice low.

"Would you like me to help you?" he asked.

"No, I need to do this myself."

With that, Penny began to pour out her heart to God, releasing all the bitterness and anger and shame and even the hatred for those who had so despitefully used her.

When Colt heard that, he smiled a broad smile and looked at the girl's rapt face as tears of repentance and remorse flooded from beneath her closed eyelids and coursed down her cheeks, washing her soul clean. He knew that genuine repentance and a wondrous salvation had been worked out on the cavern floor of an ancient cliff ruin by the "Rock of Ages"—more sure than the very stone under their feet.

Chapter Eleven

Kathreen McClusky

Summer, 1870

Kathreen McClusky stepped down from the stage and dusted off her green satin traveling dress, tucked an auburn strand of hair under her hat, then looked around. "Same little, nowhere cow town," she mumbled to no one in particular.

"Where do you want your bags, Miss," the driver asked as he removed two leather valises from the boot of the coach and set them on the boardwalk.

"Just leave them here until I can secure lodgings," she replied. "The green trunk is also mine." She turned to walk into Munson's General Store and speak with the storekeeper's wife.

"Excuse me, do you know where Suzanne Kluseman might be at this time of day?"

Mrs. Munson looked up from the batch of mail she was sorting that had just arrived with the stage, and then smiled in recognition of Suzanne's friend.

"Aren't you Miss Kluesman's friend from Saint Louis—Miss McClusky, isn't it?"

"Yes," Kathreen replied. "Do you know where I might find her?"

"School is out for the summer, but she still spends a lot of time at the schoolhouse, just follow Main Street back towards the river and take the first turn to the right. You will see a little white building with a bell-tower."

"Thank you," Kathreen said. "Is it all right to leave my luggage on the porch step until we can pick it up?"

"That's perfectly fine, my dear," the postmistress said.

Kathreen walked back down the street and turned the corner and then saw Suzanne's buggy hitched in front of a small building with a bell tower. She tucked her chin and marched resolutely towards the schoolhouse and her friend.

"Kate!" Suzanne exclaimed and rushed from behind her desk to embrace her friend in the middle of the room.

For several minutes the two young ladies stood clinging to each other while the tears came unbidden and they cried on each other's shoulders. Finally, they broke apart, laughing and crying at the same time, and found a couple of desks to sit in, while wiping their eyes and blowing their noses in dainty handkerchiefs.

"Seeing you, Kate, is like a fresh breath of spring," Suzanne said. "I am so glad you are here."

"Suzanne, I just had to come, your letters were so sad, I knew you needed a shoulder to cry on."

Suzanne's eyes brimmed full of tears as she looked at her friend and felt the pang of her loss swell up in her throat. Before her was a girl who understood, to some degree, her pain for she, too, had loved Colt, and knew the devastation his loss created.

"Kate," she choked, "there are some days that I just don't think I can go on."

"I know, I know, it's tough isn't it? The only decent guy in the whole damn place and God or the Devil kills him."

Suzanne snorted a little chuckle through her tears at her friend's bold language, then blew her nose. "You're awful," she smiled, "Colt is not dead."

"He's not dead! Do you know that for sure?" Kathreen was staring with wide-eyed expectation. "I know you said that in your letters, but has there been any further information forthcoming?"

Suzanne shook her head sadly, "No—nothing you don't already know, except what my heart keeps telling me. . .I can't help feeling he is alive somewhere, but something is keeping him away."

"You poor thing," Kathreen said. "I bet everyone thinks you're crazy too, don't they?"

Suzanne nodded and gave a little, self-conscious laugh. "I am afraid they do."

"Well, phooey on them—does Sonny?"

Suzanne shifted uncomfortably under Kathreen's steady gaze, and then shook her head. "No, he has been very supportive—he makes me eat."

"Makes you eat?"

"Yes, when he got back from Colorado last year, he practically force-fed me for awhile. I had lost an awful lot of weight and he made me eat. He said if Colt was alive, he wouldn't want to find me looking like a scare-crow when he got back."

"Does Sonny think he is alive?"

"No, not really, I know he just humors me to get me to eat."

"Huh," Kathreen scoffed. "Well, he left off answering my letters—I have a certain bone to pick with that cowboy."

"Oh, Kate, I am so sorry—I know he has been paying way to much attention to me and I have tried to tell him but. . .I may as well try to stop a cyclone."

"I know how he is, and I think it is pretty low of him to be playing upon your sympathies to advance his own interests," Kathreen said.

Suzanne stared at her friend, red-faced. "I haven't encouraged him—in fact, I very pointedly told him he was wasting his time and disapproved of the shabby way he trifled with your affections."

"You did?" Kathreen seemed both surprised and relieved. "What did he say?"

"Oh, he just mumbled a bunch of nonsense about water."

"About water? I am confused."

"Sonny, my dear, can be like that, both confused and confusing."

"Well, never mind him, I'll deal with him later. What I want to know is would you like me to stay around for awhile and be here for you?"

"Oh yes, very much," Suzanne said, "could you?"

"Yes, but I will need to find lodging at the hotel."

"Oh no, you must stay with us."

Kathreen look inquiringly at Suzanne, "Are you sure your folks won't mind?"

"Of course not, where are your things?"

"Over in front of the General Store, if some scalawag hasn't run off with them."

"I am just finishing up here, then we'll get my buggy and go pick them up. Won't Momma and Poppa be surprised—oh my, won't Sonny be surprised, if he ever gets back that is."

"Back—where is he?" the redhead replied."

"He is off chasing wild horses."

"Wild horses, how come?"

"He says he wants to sell them to the Army, but I really think he is just trying to get back at me."

"Back at you, why would he want to do that?"

"I told him I needed a little space and he took it all the wrong way and left without a word."

"How long has he been gone?"

Suzanne gave a helpless smile and said, "A couple of weeks."

"When is he coming back?"

"I don't know," Suzanne sighed.

"Well, I don't care! I came to see you anyway. If I see him, I'm just as liable as not to shoot him."

The girls stopped the buggy in front of the General Store and were wrestling with Kathreen's steamer trunk in an attempt to load it into the back, when a deep voice spoke behind them.

"Can I help you ladies with that?"

Suzanne and Kathreen turned to see the acting sheriff swinging down from his horse and dallying the reins around the hitching post.

"Oh, Mr. Anderson," Suzanne said with a smile, "Yes, please. I am afraid this is a little too heavy for the two of us. Do you know Miss McClusky?"

Kathreen had been standing and staring at the big cowboy, watching with something akin to wonder at the attention he was paying to her friend. He had not even once looked her way until Suzanne called her to his attention.

Clay Anderson stood awkwardly, his hat in hand and looked up at the redhead and nodded, "How do you do?" he said.

"I am fine, Mr. Anderson, Clay isn't it?"

"Yes, ma'am."

"Didn't I see you at the barn dance the last time I was here?" Kathreen asked with a mischievous smile.

She was amused by the big cowboy's befuddlement. He reminded her of a big bear with a star pinned to it that was being attracted to a beehive and enduring the stings in order to get at the honey.

"Yes, ma'am," he said again.

"If I remember right, you never asked me to dance, Mr. Anderson, might I inquire as to why?"

Clay Anderson's face turned beet-red and he looked down at his feet.

"I don't know, ma'am. I'm not much of a dancer.'

"I noticed you had no problem with Miss Kluesman here, in fact, if I remember right, you asked her to dance more than once."

His ears glowing red with embarrassment, Clay Anderson mumbled, "I know Miss Kluesman a little better—where do you want this trunk?"

Suzanne gave her friend a cautionary look and said, "Right here in the back will be fine."

Clay grasped the steamer trunk in one big hand and swung it up into the space behind the buggy seat as if it were filled with thistledown. Both girls stood smiling in appreciation, Kathreen in particular, enjoying his confusion from her teasing.

"That was very thoughtful of you," Suzanne said sweetly. "Thank you, Mr. Anderson, or should I call you Sheriff?"

"Clay'll do fine, ma'am."

At that point, two of the Box 7 cowboys walked out of the General Store carrying several letters and packages in their hands. They saw Anderson fidgeting like an ant on a hot griddle, in front of the two pretty young ladies, and one of them, a fellow called Bud, elbowed the other in the ribs and nodded in the direction of the trio on the street.

"Get a load of Anderson," he said.

His partner, a fellow called "Two-Bits," for his propensity to bet Two-Bits on just about anything, said, "I'll betcha Two-Bits the Swede's as tongued-tied as a trussed up spring calf."

"Hey, Swede," Bud called. "Whatcha doin' with those two pretty gals, are you fixin' to roomance 'em both?"

Suzanne and Kathreen stared up in amazement at the two mischievous cowboys, who were untying their horses from the hitching rack and swinging into the saddle. Clay Anderson visibly gulped, his eyes opening wide and his face growing even redder. Without saying another word he clapped his big hat onto his head and turned on his heels. That was when his spurs hung up on each other and sent him sprawling into the dust of the street.

His friends rode past him snickering and Bud said, "Looks like another good man's down—fallen victim to the course of true love." He tipped his hat to the schoolmarm and her friend and the two of them trotted up the street laughing.

Clay Anderson untangled his legs and sprang into his saddle with amazing dexterity for a man of his size, and with his hat pulled low over his eyes, he trotted after his friends without another word.

"Well, I declare," Kathreen said. "Here we have another fine example of what I have already begun to suspect. All men are boobs."

"Poor Clay," Suzanne said. "Kate, that wasn't very nice."

"Aw," she said dismissively and waved her hand as if brushing away flies. "He'll get over it—it's good for him."

"Good for him? How do you figure that?"

"Did you see the size of him? If he ever took a notion to run rough-shod over a girl—pity the girl. It's best we keep him just a little bit scared of us."

"Kathreen, how can you say such a thing? Clay is not like that," Suzanne said.

"Good, let's keep him that way. We don't want another maverick like Sonny Saber running around loose." Kathreen stepped up into the buggy and sat down.

Suzanne stared after her friend in wide-eyed amazement, then climbed up to take the reins and pop them against Checker's rump.

"Kate, you are pretty upset with him, aren't you?"

Kathreen did not answer right away but sat staring at the jogging withers of the pinto in front of them. "Wouldn't you be?" she asked.

Suzanne said, "I don't know, maybe."

"You don't know, why not?"

"Well," Suzanne replied, "I guess it all depends on what understanding we had."

"Understanding? What's to understand? He romanced me, made love to me and gave me all that sweet-talk. He even wrote love-letters to me for awhile."

"Yes, but that is no more than you did to him. What was the understanding between the two of you?"

"What do you mean?' the redhead said. "Isn't it obvious? We were sweethearts."

"Yes, but long-distance sweethearts, you the big-city girl and Sonny the home-on-the-range, country boy. I thought you two had agreed it was an impossible mix."

"Well, we did talk about that," she said, her voice a little crestfallen, "but then I never figured on my heart getting in the way."

"Kate," Suzanne said, "do you love him?"

"Yes, but I'll be darned if I am going to let him know it and you better not let him know it either—promise?"

Suzanne shrugged her shoulders and gave a look at her friend that said, Are you sure you know what you are doing?

"Promise me, Suzanne," Kathreen insisted.

"I promise."

Kathreen frowned and without looking at her said, "He has been paying court to you, too, hasn't he?"

Suzanne gave a helpless scoff and shook her head once. "He has tried."

"I thought as much. If it was anyone else but you I'd. . ." she let the thought go unfinished.

"I thought you came here to help me," Suzanne said wistfully, "not claw my eyes out."

"Oh, Sue, I am sorry." She reached a gloved hand across and squeezed her friend's arm. "You are right, this is not about me or Sonny. I am here to see you happy again, please just ignore what I said."

Suzanne said, "I have no desire for, nor do I wish to, encourage anything other than Sonny's friendship. He is Colt's brother and has been a great support to me during Colt's absence. It is Colt who holds my heart. I will hold him in my dreams until I can hold him in my arms once again."

Suzanne's folks welcomed Kathreen into their home and soon had her comfortably lodged in with Suzanne. When Kathreen saw the unfinished wedding dress standing in the corner of the bedroom, she walked over and began to inspect it.

"You never finished this." She said.

"No," Suzanne sighed.

"Why not, I would think you'd want it ready when Colt gets back."

"Oh, Kate, I just haven't had the heart to work on it. Whenever I see it standing there so unfinished, it reminds me that he and I are unfinished too. If I finish the dress and he doesn't come back, I don't think I could bear it. The dress would be done and we would still be undone. What would I do then?"

"Finish the dress," Kathreen said dryly, "I will help you."

The girls spent long hours sewing and working on the dress and Suzanne seemed to take a new lease on life. With the vivacious redhead as her constant companion, except for those times she was at school, Suzanne lapsed less and less into melancholia and regained much of her previous good humor.

The girls took evening walks, enjoying the antics of Nuisance while engaging in long talks. Suzanne told of the attack by Bollinger and of Clay Anderson's rescue and the ensuing hearing with Judge Roy Bean and of her refusal to go into the saloon.

"I've heard of him," Kathreen said, "did you get into trouble?"

"No, I think he actually was proud of me for not going in. He said I was, 'Just like the Jersey Lily.'"

Kathreen was incredulous and stopped walking. Grabbing Suzanne's arm she turned her round to look in her face. "He said that?"

Suzanne nodded.

"Huh! Who would a thought that? That's not what I heard he was like."

"Oh, he was nice enough, at least to me, but he sure sent that little tin sheriff and his cronies packing, at least what was left of them."

"Gee, I would have liked to have been there. Suzanne, you even got the likes of the notorious Roy Bean eating out of your hand. Do you own all of West Texas?"

"Hardly," the girl replied with a modest blush and resumed walking.

Walking on, Suzanne brought Kathreen up to date on all the latest gossip around Wade's Landing and Kathreen filled her in on Saint Louis. The talk finally got around to the Sabers, Sonny in particular. Suzanne related to Kathreen her last conversation with Sonny at the graveside, and how he had left shortly after that to hunt wild horses. It had been several weeks since anyone had seen him.

"I don't care if I don't see him," Kathreen said. "I am not sure I can trust myself to behave in a lady-like manner."

Suzanne grinned at the petulance of her friend. "Maybe it would be good for you if you did talk things over with him. At least you would know where you stand."

"Do you know where I stand— with him?"

Suzanne paused in their walk, looking guilty. "Not really," she said unconvincingly.

Kathreen saw through her ruse to avoid the question. "Really, Suzanne, if he was paying court to you, he must at least have offered some sort of explanation as to our relationship. Even if he didn't, you surely questioned him?"

"I did."

"Well—what did he say?"

"I asked him if he was going to just brush you aside like he had done Margarita, and wondered what might be in store for anyone else down the line."

"You mean like you?"

Suzanne stared straight ahead but said nothing.

"Well, never mind, what did he say, what did he say?"

"He mumbled some mumbo-jumbo about it taking some cowboys longer than others to make up their minds about who they liked—or something like that."

"Why that wishy-washy, trifling, boob-hatch, is that all he said?"

"Pretty much, except for the part about water."

"Water?" Kathreen looked puzzled.

"Let's see—some water's good for wading in, and some is good for swimming in, and some is so deep you can fall right in and never be seen again—guess which one you are?"

"Which one you are?"

"Yes, he said that to me."

"What do you think that's supposed to mean?"

Suzanne fidgeted uncomfortably under her friends inquiring gaze and started walking again. Kathreen stared after her friend and then followed.

"I think he was implying that I was the deep water," Suzanne said.

"And which one am I, the wading kind?"

"No—that was Margarita."

Kathreen walked beside her friend then without speaking. Finally, she sighed and said, "I guess that leaves me somewhere in the middle, doesn't it?"

"I told him he was wasting his time, my heart belongs to Colt."

"I should hate you Suzanne—first you take Colton and now Sonny away from me. I don't know what ever possessed me to come to this God-forsaken hell-hole anyway, except I love you too much to let you dry up and blow away."

"I am so sorry, Kate, I really am. I can't help what others do and believe me I never encouraged Sonny's affection."

"I know you didn't, the darned, fickle-hearted cow-poker. In fact, you don't seem to encourage anybody, but you still attract men like bees to clover. What's with that big galoot of a sheriff, Clay Anderson anyway?"

Suzanne smiled, "Not much, I've danced with him a few times is all. He has been very nice."

"I've got a feeling, he'd like to be a lot nicer, given half a chance."

"Listen, girl," Suzanne said, "You turn heads way more than I do with that red hair. I saw those Box 7 riders staring at you."

Kathreen grinned, showing white, even teeth. "Yes, perhaps you are right. What Mr. Sonny Saber needs is a good dose of his own medicine. I think I'll go talk with Mrs. Munson, she said she could use a clerk to help out part-time at the General Store, while she's busy in the post office. I could meet a lot of folks in there."

Suzanne shook her head and chuckled, it looked like Sonny was in for it.

Kathreen snapped the till drawer shut and gave a tongue-in-cheek grin in response to the Box 7 cowboy's wink. "Got something in your eye there, Two-Bits?" she asked.

"Yep, you. When you going to take me on a buggy ride and picnic?"

"'Bout the same time hell turns to blue ice," Kathreen said. "What makes you think I'd do that?"

Two-Bits picked up the package of Levis he'd just purchased and headed for the door, his ears burning. Turning, his hand on the knob, he said, "I figured you'd jump at the chance to be with the Don Juan of the Pecos is all. I coulda showed you what you don't know how."

"Ha," Kathreen shot back, "I wrote that book, Mr. Two-Bits, and by the way this is the third pair of jeans you've bought in the past month. What's the matter, you getting' too big for your britches?"

"Nope," he said, "just keepin' a clean pair handy 'n case I get to go on a picnic or somethin'." He tipped the brim of his hat, a big grin on his face and stepped out the door and was gone.

Mrs. Munson looked up from the mail she was sorting and peered over the glasses perched on the end of her nose, "My, Kathreen, how you do carry on with those poor cowboys. Have you no mercy?"

"What do you mean?" Kathreen asked innocently.

"Oh, I think you know quite well what I mean, you get those poor hands ridin' into town near every day to buy one thing and another, especially Bud and Two-Bits from the Box 7. They are running up a tab here that will take all of next month's wages just to settle their accounts."

"Well, good," Kathreen said. "At least they won't be spending it on wine, women and song. Don't you appreciate the business?"

The storekeeper's wife smiled and shook her head. "Well, of course I do, but I never figured on you keeping every ignorant cow nurse on the range broke just so they can come in here and endure your barbed witticisms."

Kathreen laughed, "It's good for them," she smirked, "gives 'em something to do."

"Well, I suppose you do provide a spot of color in their rather drab and dreary lives alright, just be careful one of them doesn't fool you and capture your fancy."

Kathreen looked up and studied the face of her employer but did not respond with the usual quip. She turned to wind up a ball of string, feeling Mrs. Munson's eyes on her.

"Oh, I see," the postmistress said, "That's already happened."

Kathreen tossed a red curl from her eye and said, "Not so's one would notice—not anymore at least."

The storekeeper's wife pursed her lips. "He's had his hands full with your friend, you know."

"That's what bothers me," Kathreen said.

"When Colt died, we came very near to losing her. If it hadn't of been for Sonny, we would have."

"Well, he didn't have to fall in love with her, did he?"

Mrs. Munson gave a short laugh and shook her head. "No, I guess not, not that it's done him any harm, or much good either, for that matter. Suzanne is still convinced Colt is alive somewhere, even though she no longer says it. We all know she thinks it and I doubt very much Sonny stands a chance of dislodging that notion from her head or her heart. It is probably why he's interested in her in the first place."

"What?" Kathreen asked, "What is why?"

"It's the old saying, you know, we always seem to want what we can't have."

Kathreen looked at her employer and suddenly felt like a specimen under a magnifying glass. "You mean me, don't you?"

"Well, no, not entirely, but if the shoe fits. . ."

"Sonny Saber can go to blazes as far as I am concerned and as soon as he gets back I'm going to tell him so, and you can accept my resignation then because I will be on the next stage out of here."

On a Saturday afternoon a week later, Suzanne and Kathreen packed a picnic lunch and drove to a spot along the river that was used by the town folk as a park of sorts. They enjoyed watching a pair of robins feeding their babies and the sights, sounds and smells of summer. When lunch was finished, they rested on an Indian blanket spread upon the grass and stared up at the incredibly blue sky through the green growth on the trees.

"I don't understand something," Suzanne said.

"What's that?" her friend replied.

"How come God would take Colt after sparing him so many times?"

Kathreen raised herself up on one elbow and stared at her friend. "What do you mean?" she asked.

"The Indians," Suzanne said. "Time and time again, Colt was kept from harm—from the Comanche, from the Kiowa and from the Apache. Did you know he was barely scratched that time that the Kiowa captured us, even though he had over fifty braves shooting arrows at him? All they succeeded in doing was to outline a cross-like shape on the ground where he lay. That was nothing but a divine miracle."

Kathreen nodded her head in understanding. "Don't forget his and Sonny's escape from the burning cabin."

"I know, so why would God deliver him all those times just to let him die in the end?"

Kathreen sensed her friend's heartache and reached out a comforting hand. "Doesn't it say somewhere in the Bible that God knows what He is doing?"

Suzanne's eyes brimmed with tears. She forced a smile and gave a slight nod.

"And aren't we supposed to rest in that?" Kathreen went on.

"Yes," Suzanne blinked away a tear, "but it just doesn't make sense to me that he is gone. . . I won't believe it."

"Well, don't then. Just keep on trusting in Jesus."

They lay silent then, watching the robins bringing the groceries to their offspring in the nest above them. Presently Kathreen spoke. "Suzanne?"

"Yes?" her friend answered.

"Can I pray for you?"

"Yes," Suzanne said quietly.

"Okay. God—I don't know how to do this very well and Suzanne talks to you a whole lot more than I do, but I just wanted to ask, don't you hear her? She has poured out her soul to you regarding Colt and him missing and it seems to me, if you are such a good Father; the least you cold do is let her know what happened and where he is. I am not trying to boss you, I just want you to know that I agree with all she is asking of you. Someone said that when two agree on something that you pay better attention. Well, I cast my vote with Suzanne. Find Colton Saber and bring him back to her. That's it. . . that's what I have to say!" She paused for a moment and then said, "Amen."

Suzanne smiled through her tears at her friend's straightforward prayer and patted her hand. "Thanks," she said.

"Well, look what we have here," a familiar voice drawled. Both girls started up and turned to see Two-Bits Thompson sitting his cowpony on the trail above them, with Buddy McLeod alongside on his own horse. Both riders were wiping sweat from their faces on dusty shirt sleeves and grinning down at the two girls.

Kathreen spoke up, "I suppose you two knights of the range just happened along this particular trail today in search of dragons to slay and fair damsels to rescue."

"Naw," Buddy said. "Ol' Two-Bits here thought you might of come down here and he said we might be able to get a drink of lemonade, if we was to find ya."

"No-siree, Bud," Two-Bits said, "it was you what wanted to come down here, once Swede said these gals went on a pic-a-nic."

"Oh, I did not," Bud said. "He's yarnin' ya, but Swede Anderson did say you came this-a-way. You got any lemonade, I'm powerful thirsty?"

"Well, come and get it then," Kathreen said, "Do you expect us to pack it up there?"

The two cowboys unhorsed and, dropping the reins, strolled down the embankment to accept glasses of lemonade from the girls.

"Where is Mr. Anderson now?" Suzanne asked. She felt comfortable around these fun-loving cowboys, but kept a wary eye on Kathreen McClusky, for she knew how Kate enjoyed badgering them.

"Aw, he's back in town sittin' under the chestnut tree playin' sheriff. He don't know much about relationshippin' with purty gals," Two-Bits answered.

"And you do, Don Juan?" Kathreen said witheringly.

Two-Bits gave the redhead a big smile and said, "Sure, we're at your pic-a-nic, ain't we?"

Suzanne hid a smile behind her hand and held her breath.

Kathreen spoke, "That's right and with a gold lettered invitation, too, I dare say."

The cowboy shrugged, "You can't pick apples unless you come to the tree. What were you two talkin' about?"

Kathreen glanced at Suzanne and gave her a wink. "Actually, Mr. Two-Bits, we were praying. Would you two boys like to join our little prayer meeting?"

Standing red-faced at a loss for words, both cowboys' mouths gaped open and they swallowed hard, then began to fidget with their hats. Finally Bud said, "We ain't much on praying, ma'am, we was just thinking to get to know you a little better—and the schoolmarm, too," He added this last as an afterthought, with a nervous glance at Suzanne.

"Do you cowboys pray?" Suzanne asked curiously.

They both shook their heads. "Not regular like," Two-Bits said. "We don't bother God much, lessin' it's somethin' important like Comanches or a grizzly bear, or somethin' like that."

"Why not?" Kathreen cut in, her voice challenging.

The two hands looked at each other, then Buddy spoke, "I've seen some folks treat God like He's some sort of errand boy, doin' this and doin' that for 'em and—well, I figure that ain't right. Since God's busy feedin' birds and makin' rain, then I don't need to be pesterin' him with stuff I can just as well handle m'self."

He finished this lengthy declaration, let out a big breath and then turned to his partner and grinned as though he had just delivered the Gettysburg Address. Two-Bits stared at him with something akin to wonder on his face and solemnly nodded his agreement. Both men turned back to the girls with satisfied smiles and stopped twirling their hats.

"So, you just ask God for help when you need it, is that it?" Kathreen asked.

"Yep, that's about it," Buddy said. They both nodded in agreement again.

"Did you ever think you might need His help getting invited to a picnic?"

The two cowboys looked as though somebody had put sugar in their beans.

"What?" Bud said, "No, why would we?"

Kathreen smiled like a cat toying with a mouse. "Because otherwise, you haven't got a prayer of ever getting such an invitation."

"Huh?" Two-Bits said.

"C'mon, pard," Bud said, "I think we've worn out our welcome 'round this apple tree."

"What did she say?" Two-Bits asked as they turned and headed back to their mounts. "What just happened?" They reached their horses and swung up without looking back. Bud was explaining to Two-Bits as they rode out.

"We just got un-invited to their pic-a-nic."

The two girls watched them ride away, smiles on their faces as they listened to the pair of them arguing.

"You owe me two-bits," Thompson was saying.

"No way," Bud replied, "We never got no invite."

"We sure did, we got invited to have a glass of lemonade."

"That t'wernt no invite, that sassy redhead just asked if we expected 'em to bring it up to us."

"They still gave us lemonade," Two-Bits insisted.

"Yeah," Bud replied ruefully, as they rode out of sight, "and that's about as sweet as it got, too."

Chapter Twelve

In search of Hank and Oscar

Somewhere on the Sweetgrass, 1870

"We've had company," Sonny said as they rode up to the wagon. There was stuff strewn all over from out of the wagon and at least one bed roll had been knocked into the mud of the seep. The mules were gone and several fresh tracks of unshod horses were about, indicating a small band of Indians had passed by during the day. They had messed up the rocks lining the spring and it looked as though they had deliberately destroyed the water holding tanks, for they were now mud holes more nearly resembling the wallow they had found here in the first place than the clear, cool pools of water they had created.

"Why would an Indian want to trample a nice spring in this hot country?" Rusty asked. "Just look at my blankets."

"Who can figure the wild Redman," Lance mused.

"Better see if there's anything left of our grub," Sonny said. He threw a leg over the horn and slid lightly down to stride over to the wagon and peer inside. "Sugar's all gone," he hollered, "bacon and hams, too." He turned and set the camp table upright while the other two began to collect pots and pans and the rest of their equipment. "Coffee and flour is dumped all over the floor in the wagon, we might be able to salvage some of it." Sonny muttered. "Who wants to go knock over a couple of prairie chickens for supper?"

"I'll go," Lance said, "Rusty's got to wash out his blankets."

"With what, mud?" Rusty groused.

"We can clean the seep out again," Sonny said. "Lance, you keep an eye out for them blasted, red devils, they may still be lurking about looking for some scalps to hang from their lodge pole."

Sonny and Rusty worked with bucket and shovel for over an hour and found that most of the stones were still in place. They relocated the few that had been dislodged, cleared the seep and the runoff channel of mud, and soon had clear water flowing again. While Rusty washed his blankets, Sonny got a fire burning and turned to recover the flour and coffee.

Rusty was hanging his dripping blankets over a couple of tree branches, when, off in the distance, they heard a pistol shot, soon followed by two more.

"Supper," Sonny predicted, then added, "Rusty, if you pull up a couple of tumbleweeds and drape your soogan over them, it'll dry quicker."

By the time the wagon was cleaned up, Lance was back with three prairie chickens and had sat down to pluck them

"What about our mules?" he asked, "We gonna go after 'em?"

"We'll trail 'em," Sonny said, 'There'll be a moon out later—trouble is, by the time we catch 'em they'll probably already have killed and roasted one, if not both of them. Comanches love mule meat, we'll probably just be wasting our time."

"So, how we gonna move the wagon?" Lance asked.

"We could use our saddle horses," Rusty said. "Lance, you and me could make 'em pull it if we rode 'em bareback."

Sonny was skeptical, "You think that'd work?"

"Yeah, they won't like it much but we can do it."

"We better go get the mules," Sonny said. "We'll track 'em after we eat."

Fortunately, the Comanche had not discovered the salt and pepper cans under the wagon seat, or if they did, chose to ignore them. The cowboys were also able to retrieve the spuds and onions from where the Indians had thrown them. They made a supper out of fried prairie chicken and spuds and onions.

"Why didn't they take the spuds and onions?" Lance asked, "Don't they eat 'em?"

Sonny said, "If you was traveling fast and light, would you want to be totin' a sack full of taters?"

"What about beans or flour?"Lance said.

"Indians eat these, too, but are not nearly so dependent on foodstuffs as we white folk. They can go days without food, kill a deer or buffalo and gorge on it all night, and go for days more, perfectly content. They do not require three, or even two, square meals a day like we do."

"Yeah, Lance," Rusty put in, "if you miss eatin' even one meal you act like you're starving to death."

"So do you," his friend shot back.

"Just pass me some more of that singed canary you call fried chicken and quit cher belly aching," Rusty answered.

Sonny concluded from the tracks that there were six Comanches and that they were riding fast. The hoof prints showed deep toe marks and long strides. The three cowboys had left camp upon completion of their meal and were maintaining a steady lope while following a plain track left in the sand that headed north towards distant, rolling hills.

Sonny rode in the lead, his experienced eye reading the sign as the two younger boys kept pace behind. When the twilight deepened, and before the moon's light was of much benefit, he called back to the two cowboys.

"You fellers keep right behind me. If we loose the trail, I don't want you tramplin' it all up in case we have to backtrack."

"How many do you reckon there are?" Lance asked nervously.

"Looks like six of 'em," Sonny hollered back, "That makes it two to one, their favor. They're still quite a ways ahead of us, and making good time."

"Where you think they're headed?" Rusty called from where he rode last, behind his friend.

"Those hills yonder, maybe to the rest of their band," Sonny said. "Keep a sharp eye out, one or more of them could double back and lay an ambush for us."

Lance looked back at his friend and both boys cast anxious glances at both sides of the trail. Rusty's hand reached to check on the Winchester jouncing in its scabbard under his leg. It was secure.

The trail led into a brushy area, necessitating a slowing of their pace, and Sonny said, "Either of you boys fight Injuns before?"

Both boys said, "No, not really." Rusty added, "Other than that time at the ranch this spring," then asked, "You think they might ambush us?"

"Not too likely now," Sonny replied. "They may have sent someone back earlier on, but we got such a late start he probably gave up and rejoined the band. I look for them to hole up somewhere in those hills for a mule barbeque."

"What we gonna do when we catch up to 'em?" Lance asked worriedly.

"We'll have to see what we're up against first," Sonny said. "One thing for sure, we can't go bustin' in on 'em ridin' like this. We're going to have to slow down."

The moon was tracking to the western horizon by the time the cowboys reached the hills. It cast long and worrisome shadows for at least the two younger riders, for every bush, rock or tree seemed to harbor an unseen Comanche intent on lifting their scalps. Their nervousness was passed on to their mounts and the horses began to head-shy and snort at the shadows, while pulling at the bit.

Sonny raised a hand and reined up. "I smell smoke. You boys climb down, we'll tie off the horses here and go in on foot."

The three riders tied their mounts and slid their rifles from the scabbards. Sonny chambered a round and set the hammer on safety. Rusty and Lance, wide-eyed, followed his example and looked at the older cowboy expectantly.

"We'll Injun up on 'em and see what we can find," Sonny whispered. "Hopefully they will all have stuffed their gizzards with roast jackass and be sound asleep."

"If they've killed the mules," Lance said, "what's the point?"

"Not much, I guess, but we gotta go see," Sonny said grimly. "Maybe they haven't killed 'em yet."

The track led up a slight incline to top out on a brush-covered hogback. As they neared the top, the smell of smoke was stronger and the threesome paused.

"If they have posted a guard, he most likely will be watchin' this back trail," Sonny cautioned his two companions. "Rusty, I want you to sneak off to the right about two hundred feet and Lance, you do the same on the left. I'll watch for you to both get set and then we'll all creep up to the top and have us a look."

"What we supposed to do once we get up there?" Lance asked.

"That depends on what we find," Sonny said. "If all six Injuns are down by the fire and you can see all their horses, and if our mules are dead, then just meet me back here. If one of the redskins is missing, then sit tight until we can locate the varmint. Once we know that, we can figure out the next step."

"What if there's only one mule dead?" Rusty said."

"One mule is still our mule," Sonny whispered tersely, "Hank or Oscar, we need 'em back."

"Man, I hope I don't get scalped over one lousy, lop-eared jackass," Rusty said.

Lance looked at his friend, his face blanched white in the moon light. "Me too," he nodded solemnly. Both boys looked to Sonny for corroboration.

"Okay, you guys, I know you're a little bit edgy about this. Just keep your wits about you and follow my lead. If you don't know what to do next then don't do anything. Sit tight until you do—then do the next best thing. Now go on and keep quiet."

Sonny waited as he watched his two friends move silently off on either side of him. He nodded his head in approval at Rusty's stealth and heaved a sigh of relief when Lance finally waved his hat. "If that kid don't get us all scalped, it'll be a miracle," he thought.

He began to creep to the crest of the hogback and upon reaching it, Sonny peered down into a shallow hollow in which a small campfire was burning. Seated around it and cutting chunks of meat from a roasting spit were five Comanche braves. Six ponies were tethered to the willows nearby and the dead carcass of one mule lay on the ground, barely visible at the edge of the circle of firelight. The other mule was nowhere in sight. Sonny caught a slight movement beyond the seated warriors and his breath caught in his throat.

Lying on the ground were two small children, bound hand and foot with gags tied across their mouths. "They've taken a couple of white kids captive," Sonny groaned quietly, "Well, looks like our work's cut out for us now. I wonder where that other Indian is?" He turned to the sound of a slight tread in the grass. For a brief instant he saw the hideously painted face of a warrior loom up in front of him. There was an explosion of light and then all went black for the tall cowboy.

Sonny awoke with a dull throbbing in the back of his head. He tried to figure out where he was and what had happened. He was lying on his side and when he tried to move, he found that both his hands and feet were bound tight with rawhide. A low groan escaped his lips and then a moccasined foot rolled him over onto his back and the cowboy saw a Comanche warrior wearing his hat and staring down at him with an evil grin. The brave said something and then laughed in scorn and pointed Sonny's Winchester at the rider's forehead. Sonny could see his six-gun belted about the Indian's waist. From this new position in the Indian camp, Sonny counted five other Indians and realized that he was now their captive. He mentally berated himself for his carelessness. He had done the very thing that he had warned the others not to do and walked right up on the unseen sentry.

"Well," he sighed, "I guess I found out where the other Indian was." He was kicked soundly in the ribs by his leering captor for the comment.

Deciding to keep his thoughts to himself, Sonny shut up. He searched about to see if his partners had been discovered, but there proved to be no indication that they had. Good, he thought. Now if I can keep from getting scalped while those boys figure out a way to get me out of here, it'll be even better.

The cowboy looked over to where the two children were tied and saw that both were small girls with golden curls. One was about six or seven, he guessed, the other perhaps a year or two younger. They were staring at him in desperation with wide, tear-filled eyes.

Bound for slavery and adoption into some Comanche band or else for trade to the Comancheros, Sonny reasoned. He recalled his father telling of such practices by the Comanche and of the fondness they seemed to have for yellow-haired little girls. Well, if he had anything to say about it, here were two kids who were not going to end up like that. It was up to him and the boys to rescue these poor little waifs.

The problem was, it didn't look like he was going to have too much to say about it, and if Rusty and Lance didn't act before daylight, chances were that they'd be discovered, too, and then all their gooses would be cooked. He began to cautiously work at the rawhide thongs about his wrists and study on a way to get out of this situation.

Lance Gilles sat huddled in the shadow of a large sagebrush and watched anxiously down into the Indian encampment. He had heard the quick blow and the low groan when the sentry had discovered Sonny's position and brained him. He watched helplessly as the Comanche drug Sonny's inert form down the embankment and raised his rifle twice to fire at the brave, only to lower it again.

What had Sonny said? "If you don't know what to do—do nothing until you do."

Well, he didn't know what to do, but he was pretty sure that if he shot the one Indian, the others would do for Sonny Saber before he and Rusty could finish them all off. Where was Rusty? Maybe he would know what to do.

Rusty was quietly making his way along the backside of the hogback to where his friend knelt watching the Indians. He, too, had witnessed Sonny's capture and his heart thudded against his ribs as he subconsciously thought of the times he and the other kids had played pioneers and Indians in the woods back home. He had practiced his skill of the stalk and sneak and now realized that all that training was paying off. He moved like a shadow from bush to bush until he reached Lance's position.

"Lance," Rusty whispered.

"Yikes," Lance gasped under his breath. "You scared the pea-waddin' out of me. I didn't even hear you come up."

"Never mind that," Rusty said. "We gotta figure out a way to rescue Sonny and those two kids."

"What two kids?" Lance said, peering down at the camp in confusion.

"There—beyond the fire, beneath that bush. Two little kids all trussed up just to the right of Sonny."

"You mean those piled up blankets or whatever they are?"

"Try two little kids—little girls, I think, see the yellow hair?"

"Oh good Lord," Lance said in dismay as he leaned forwards with hands on the ground staring intently. Rusty saw his friend tremble as he stared at the scene. "What'll we do?" Lance turned back to his friend. "We gotta rescue them."

Rusty stared wide-eyed at Lance and nodded. "Maybe they'll go to sleep and we can sneak down there and cut Sonny loose, grab the girls and make a run for it."

Lance shook his head, "We'd never make it. They'd be on us before we were halfway up this hill. . . besides they'll post a guard."

"Yeah, you're right. I wonder why they've kept Sonny alive?" Rusty whispered. "I figured they'd just kill him right off."

Lance shrugged, "Who knows, they probably want to take 'im back to the rest of their band and torture him."

Rusty nodded grimly. "If we rush them, they'll kill him for sure, and the kids, too. It looks like one of them has Sonny's six-gun and rifle. You see any other firearms?"

"No, but that don't mean they ain't got 'em."

His friend nodded slowly and then lapsed into silent thought.

"If we could create some sort of a diversion, maybe raise a ruckus with their ponies, we might get the drop on 'em long enough to cut Sonny free," Lance said.

Rusty said, "I could sneak down and cut those ponies loose while you pumped a couple of rounds into that campfire. I'll bet we could set them afoot, but what do you suppose would become of Sonny and those little girls?"

Lance thought a moment, shaking his head slowly in the dark. "Unless I miss my guess, Sonny's waiting for just some such stunt from us. I'll bet he is working at his bounds right now."

"I don't know," Rusty frowned in the dark, "This ain't no game like what we used to play as kids in the woods. Somebody's likely to die and we better fix it in our minds that it's going to be them and not us."

Lance looked scared, "I ain't never shot nobody before," he said.

"Me neither, but I sure can't stand by and let 'em kill Sonny and those poor little kids."

"Okay," Lance said, "I'll back your play—what'll I do.

"Give me about a half-hour to get down to their ponies and then you work your way over to that big boulder 'bout halfway down there." Rusty pointed to a big rock. Lance nodded. "Work your way down to there and fire a couple of rounds into the camp. Once all hell breaks loose, you try and keep the redskins pinned down while I try and get away with the horses. Make sure you cover Sonny if an Injun goes for him, and keep firing until I am away.

"Then what'll I do?"

"The Comanche will probably chase after me and that'll give you a chance to get down there and cut Sonny and those kids loose."

"Where will I meet up with you?"

"You guys just head back on the trail we came in on and I'll find you. I need to get back to our horses and get yours and mine out of there. Those Indians will be going to look for Sonny's horse any time now.'

"Rusty, you sure?" Lance looked at his friend uncertainly.

"No," Rusty shrugged, "but we got to open the ball and see how she dances. So long, pard, I'll see you up the trail."

"Yeah. . . so long," Lance mumbled. He was looking intently down into the Indians' camp and fingering the Winchester nervously with clammy hands.

———

Snake-Who-Talks sat quietly in the bushes watching back the way they had come. He was quite certain the white-eyes, whose mulos they had taken, did not follow, for there had been no one about the camp that they raided and it looked as though they had been gone for sometime. This is good, the young war chief thought, it gave them time to be far away before the theft and wreckage was discovered. He chuckled silently to himself, thinking of the stupid intruders' anger at the destroyed camp.

But Snake-Who-Talks had not become the youngest war chief in the band by being careless. He knew that even a blind Mejicano could follow the trail they had left and even though it had been several hours since the raid, if the camp they had despoiled was one of the accursed Tejano's, then he would be wise to stay alert. He almost hoped one would follow, he would like nothing better than to return to the people with a Texican's scalp hanging from his coup stick.

Snake-Who-Talks waited in the shadows and glanced briefly at the youthful braves around the fire below him. Five young men, not yet twenty summers, who had joined themselves to the young war chief because of his fierce hatred for the white man and his defiance of the old ones and their traditions. He gave a self-satisfied smile at the way they had backed him in challenging the elders, especially Two-Dogs and his silly superstitions and dreams. The Spirits of the dead do not go into trees or stone—at least none that he ever saw, and though he had seen the "*Weeping Lodge,*" he did not believe it was as the older chief had claimed. If it was medicine, it was not good medicine. Perhaps the foolish Two Dogs should have smoked his *"dream-pipe"* a little longer, maybe then he would have seen the fire-balls and the exploding hornets and Snake-Who-Talks would not have been stung in the back of the head and had his best war bonnet destroyed, along with most of his scalp lock.

At the memory, he felt the blood flush to his face and was thankful the young braves by the fire could not see him now. It had been humiliating enough to have been so cowardly attacked by the exploding hornets in front of the watching band and he was still bewildered at how the "Weeping Lodge" had dispelled them. But to have been attacked thereafter by the invisible demon that nearly tore his throat out and pulled him from his pony to dump him flopping like a beheaded chicken in front of the others was almost more than the young war chief could bear. Many of them had sided with Two Dogs after his disgrace and revealed how he had plotted to go against the older Chieftain's orders and how he had mocked the medicine sign. When he was summoned before the war council for countermanding those orders, he had been obliged to prostrate himself before Two Dogs and take a blood oath to never go against him again. Even then, it was all that he could do to not have to meet Two Dogs in the *"Knife-Circle."* Not that he was afraid of the stodgy chieftain, he could have easily disemboweled him, but it would have only put him further out of favor with the people.

Though he agreed with the others to never again approach the "Weeping Lodge," Snake-Who-Talks still believed the white-man was not invincible. He had vowed to prove to those elders that the whites bled just like everyone else, even if they did posses strange enchantments. He had not fully recovered the use of his voice after his experience and spoke with a horse, raspy tongue that made him sound more like a specter or night creature, than a powerful war chief of the Comanche.

Two Dogs had been quick to capitalize on his dishonor, putting the entire blame for the humiliating defeat handed to them by the white-eyes upon Snake-Who-Talks. Once he learned of his plan to rush the Tejano's lodge on his own, he pointed the lance in the young chief's direction when they returned to the village and told the elders that Snake-Who-Talks had angered the ancient ones with his defiance and spoiled the medicine for the battle. He was the one responsible for the dead and wounded of both warriors and ponies.

Snake-Who-Talks came near to being banished from the tribe and his lodge was ordered to be pitched at the end of the encampment, while Two Dogs' status as a chief rose in the eyes of the people after the others told of seeing the "*Weeping Lodge,*" weep.

It had taken two full moons to convince these youth to accompany him on this raid, ones who had not seen his disgrace on the first one, and now he was returning to the band with two of the sunlit-haired girls and a fat mulo. He would wait until the moon passed beyond the ridge and if no one came he would go down and join his braves in the feast.

Snake-Who-Talks' eyes were on the top half of the moon still showing above the trees on the ridge. He would wait the predetermined time he had set for himself in spite of the cramps in his legs. A warrior was best tested by his ability to do what he had set for himself to do and not take any shortcuts. He would wait until the moon was no longer visible for he had learned to trust his own medicine.

He paused, what was that? He had heard something. His keen ears trained towards the sound. Was someone or thing moving up the back trail? He peered cautiously down the backside of the hill and made out a tall figure moving stealthily through the brush. The man wore one of the wide-brimmed headpieces of the Tejanos and the moonlight glinted from the barrel of a rifle.

Silently, the war chief waited, his hand gripping his war-club. The Tejano glided, ghost-like, past the spot where Snake-Who-Talks waited and then crouched down a few steps away to stare at the camp below.

Snake-Who-Talks scoffed silently, hardly believing his great, good fortune. Two Dogs would say the spirits had favored him, but he knew better. It was his own vigilance that had placed his enemy before him like this. Still, he waited, his eyes studying the back trail. There may be others. It wasn't until he heard the white-eyes make an indistinguishable sound in his throat, that the Indian warrior silently rose to his feet, raised his war-club and took two quick steps to bash the Tejano in the head.

For a brief moment Snake-Who-Talks saw the white man turn, his eyes open wide in surprise before he slumped to the ground unconscious.

The blow should have killed him. Snake-Who-Talks intended for it to kill him, but the Tejano's wide-brimmed headdress cushioned the force of the blow to where the man was only in the unknowing sleep. The war chief grunted in satisfaction, stuck his war-club into his waistband and then stepped over the man's inert form to pick up the wide headdress. If it protected the paleface it should protect the head of an important war chief like himself. He removed the two eagle feathers from his scalp lock and stuck them into the hatband and placed the Tejano's headdress upon his own head.

Picking up the white-man's rifle, Snake-Who-Talks smiled. It was one of the sought-after repeating rifles that Two Dogs had coveted. The older chieftain would be envious. He ran his hands over the smooth surface of the weapon with genuine satisfaction. His braves had stopped, one by one, from eating the mulo to stare up at him, silhouetted in the waning moonlight. He bent, unbuckled the gun-belt and pulled it from the white-man's waist, and then buckled it about his own. Straightening, he stood, the holster and gun hanging in front of his breechcloth and raising his arms above his head in a salute to his watching warriors, he pumped his arms once in the air in triumph. Then he bent to grasp the unconscious Tejano by the shirt collar and drag him down the hill and into the circle of firelight.

The younger braves came crowding around to stare. A couple sneered in contempt and one bent to roll the unconscious man onto his back.

"How come you no kill?" the youth asked. "His scalp will look good hanging in front of your lodge."

"Kill later," Snake-Who-Talks said. "First, we take back to village and test to see how brave he is. Him heap malo enemy, one of the Tejano—hard to kill. See, my war-club did not crack his skull."

The younger braves peered close in the half-light of the fire, but could not discern any blood on the unconscious Tejano's head. Snake-Who-Talks saw them stare in awe at him. He proudly stuck out his chest, hefted the rifle over his head and danced three steps by the fire. Suddenly he whirled around to his companions and croaked, "Snake-Who-Talks will count much coup on this strong Tejano. He will be long in dying for his affront to the people. We shall see how strong his medicine is and show the old ones that our medicine is better. Bind him hand and foot while he is still in the unknowing sleep."

The younger Comanche bound the hands and feet of the white-eyes, while the chieftain drew his knife and sliced a crisp piece of meat from the spit and then squatted on his haunches to eat.

One of his braves asked, "Were there any others with the Tejano?"

"No, I do not think so. You drag the white-eyes over by the little ones with the sunlit-hair and keep watch. I will go and find his horse in a moment.

The Indians examined the rifle and their chief even let them handle the six-gun, while he finished his meal. Finally he strode over to the white-man and rolled him onto his back. The Tejano was awake, his eyes looking around in bewilderment. Snake-Who-Talks sneered in contempt at his captive and thrust the barrel of the rifle against his forehead. The Tejano only stared back, looking baffled and then said something without fear, which the war chief did not understand, but he kicked him in the ribs anyway. His braves were watching intently to see if the white-eyes would cower in fear. The captive shut up and Snake-Who-Talks turned to snap at one of his braves, "You go—follow our back trail like the spirit wind and find his horse. See if there are any others and bring the horse to me."

Rusty crept silently back to where their horses were tied and paused long enough to untie his and Lance's mounts. If the Comanche came looking, they would only find one horse tethered in the dark. Sonny's mare, Penny, chuckled low in her throat and turned sideways to stare after the other two horses as they followed the young cowboy and disappeared into the shadows of the night.

Rusty led the animals in a wide, circuitous, route west of the camp. When he came to the draw in which the Comanche had their fire he stopped. They were several hundred yards up the draw and out of sight, but he could easily smell the smoke as it wafted on the night breeze into his face. At this point, the ridge of the hogback had lessened considerably, enabling him to lead the horses over a slight hill and tie them off to some willows where they immediately began to browse on the leaves.

Checking his load in the rifle, he began a stealthy approach up the draw until he was just about to the Indians' camp. Here he came upon the second mule. It was Hank and he had been tied farther back than the Indian ponies on the other side of the wash. A little ways beyond their ponies, the Indians were seated about the fire, stuffing themselves with the meat of poor Oscar.

As he studied the scene before him, he was wondering how to take the Indians' horses without being discovered, when Hank suddenly startled him by lifting his tail and emitting a loud, continuous, burst of gas.

For a moment Rusty feared discovery, for the loud sound caused the Indians to peer into the darkness in the mule's and his direction. He crouched in the shadows only to witness the Indians break into laughter and begin to accuse one another of making the indiscretion.

Huh! Rusty thought grimly, some things don't change. He snuck to the mule who turned suspiciously and side-stepped to strain at its tether and stare wall-eyed at the dark figure coming towards it. Then Hank broke into a loud braying and short-stepped nervously, until the cowboy caught him by the halter and pinched his muzzle shut.

"Shh," he whispered. "You wanna end up stayin' for lunch?" The mule quieted down with a few more chuckles low in its throat. Rusty listened intently, but the Indians only renewed their laughter. He head the word "Mulo" spoken and then more laughter. Apparently, the Comanche thought Hank had given them the "horse laugh."

The red-haired youth untied the mule and, standing on the shadow side, he led him to the Indians' ponies, using Hank as a shield. The mustangs shifted nervously as he crept amongst them and began to cut their tether ropes and bunch them next to the mule.

It was at this point that he heard a clatter up the hogback and saw one of the braves leading Sonny's mare down the embankment and into the camp. One of the Indians gestured for the brave to tie the mare with the other ponies and the Indian led the horse over and tied her to some willows while looking back to the fire and speaking to the others seated there. He did not see Rusty hiding two horses away in the shadows.

The cowboy again heard the word "Mulo" in the otherwise, indistinguishable chatter of the Comanche, along with more laughter, and figured they were acquainting the newcomer with the mule's breaking of wind and their hilarious take on it. The young brave turned back to his companions with a dry comment and shook his head as though failing to see what was so funny.

While the talk continued around the fire, Rusty worked quickly until all the mustangs were loose and bunched together, with him holding the lead ropes. He was sure most of the time he'd told Lance to wait had passed, and his friend was about to open the ball.

Once again Rusty's thoughts were interrupted by Hank passing another staccato burst of gas. The Indians looked towards where the animals were tethered and the sound triggered another outburst of laughter, along with more banter back and forth, amongst them.

Rusty was reminded of an incident that had happened when he was a kid back on his father's farm on the Brazos. When he was about thirteen, his father had sent him to the field to plow a couple of acres for a corn patch, a chore of which he was not particularly fond. He moped about most of the day without getting much done and had stopped to rest in the shade of a large oak and roll a homemade cigarette. Since tobacco was in short supply and also forbidden to him, he had rolled some corn silk up in a piece of old newspaper and was attempting to get it lit when the old jenny he had been plowing with lifted its tail and let a long, continuous expulsion of gas, much like what Hank was doing. Wondering why it was called gas he had spontaneously stood, walked over and held the lit match under the mule's tail to see if it would burn. He had been totally unprepared for what happened next. A blue flame shot out from the back of the mule while the startled animal let out a loud bellow and bolted off across the field in a kicking, braying, bucking frenzy. The plow was yanked from the ground and bounded along behind, touching down every six or eight feet or so, and then proceeded to mow down a split-rail fence along the edge of the field that the jenny was racing past. Both the fence and his dad's new plow were totally demolished.

The incident, Rusty thought ruefully, produced some serious consequences for the young boy's backside, of course, but now he wondered, since this old jackass here was such a windbag, just maybe he could use that experience to his advantage. Digging into his pants pocket for a match, while still gripping the mustangs' leads, he patted Hank and slid his hand along his side back to his rump and waited.

The seconds ticked by. Rusty could barely see Sonny's form lying on the grass, the girls just beyond. Hank lifted his tail and Rusty placed a thumbnail against the head of the match. The mule's tail relaxed, then the animal peered around at the cowboy, its ears askance.

Just like an ornery jackass, Rusty thought, never does what you want when you want it to. The mule swung its head back to the front, then stretched its back slightly and lifted its tail. For a moment it seemed as if Hank was making a statement of what he thought of all cowboys and him in particular. Then there was another loud expulsion of pent up gas and Rusty popped the head of the match.

Lance sat motionless by the big boulder, watching the Indian camp below. He did not have a pocket watch so had to guess at how long it would take Rusty to get to the Indians' horses. The moon was beyond the horizon and he tried to count off the seconds; "one-potato, two-potato, three-potato, four. . ." It was no good, this would take forever and he abandoned the task as a bad idea. He would just have to watch and make his best guess.

His eyes on the camp, he saw one Comanche, who appeared to be the leader. He seemed a bit older than the others. The Indian got up and walked to where

Sonny lay and rolled him over with his foot. When he put the muzzle of the rifle against his forehead, Lance raised his own rifle and drew a bead on the back of the warrior's headdress, but relaxed when the chief turned and barked a command at another Indian then went and resumed his seat by the fire.

Alarmed, Lance saw the younger warrior start up the hill towards his position and centered his sights on the beaded wampum of the brave's chest, while shrinking back deeper into the shadows of the boulder. When the young Comanche reached the rock, he passed heedlessly by, unaware of the watching cowboy crouched in the shadows just a few feet away.

Lance breathed a sigh of relief as he watched the Indian pass on up the trail and out of sight over the crest. Shifting his position to where he could watch both directions, he kept his eye on the encampment and the back-trail. He did not wish to be taken by surprise from behind.

The minutes passed slowly. Off in the brush came the sound of a horse breaking wind. He shook his head, amused as the Indians broke into loud laughter. The cowboy waited in the dark, watching the good natured banter around the fire. There came another sound of horse-gas followed by the raucous braying of a mule. "Well, I guess we know where the other mule is," Lance mused silently. "I wonder which one they ate, Hank or Oscar."

A sound behind him caused him to look towards the ridge in time to see the Indian brave skyline, leading a horse. Remaining motionless in the shadows, he watched as the brave led Sonny's mare past his position. The mare shied sideways and cocked her ears at Lance as she clattered past, but the Comanche did not pay any attention to her antics or snorting.

The mare was led into the camp and then over to where she was tied off to a clump of willows. Lance saw the saddle horse turn to stare alertly into the darkness and give a low whicker of recognition.

He figured Rusty probably had the Indians' horses nearby. He decided to give his partner a little more time to be sure he had all the animals released, but eared back the hammer on the Winchester in preparation. The youth swallowed hard, his mouth dry.

The little dell where the Indians were camped suddenly lit up with a blue light. A terrified bellow, more like a scream, split the air. Startled, the Indians leaped to their feet as one man, to see a frenzied mule streaking towards them out of the darkness, its tail aloft and a foot-long blaze of blue flame jetting out from its rear end, propelling it onward. Close on the heels of the panicked mule came the six horses of the Comanche, all squealing in fright and racing after the crazed mule, who disappeared up the gully, into the night.

For an instant the Indians stared after the bedeviled mule and their fleeing horses as the animals raced up the draw and off into the dark, then they burst into action, charging off after their stampeding ponies.

Lance watched in amazement as the Comanche disappeared up the draw, then he jumped from behind the rock. His rifle at the ready, he rushed down the embankment towards the captives. Reaching the older cowboy's inert form, he saw Sonny's eyes light up in recognition and drew his belt knife. Stooping, he bent and snicked his knife through the rawhide bounds about Sonny's wrists. A sound behind him caused him to whirl, his knife at the ready.

Rusty was lumbering up, dragging at the reins of Sonny's horse, Penny, and he flashed a grin at the wide-eyed stare of his friend.

"You cut 'im loose?" he questioned.

"Rusty! Jeepers you gave me a fright. I thought you was a Comanche."

Sonny said, "You boys might want to palaver after we quit this part of Texas. . . cut me loose."

Lance quickly cut Sonny's feet loose while Rusty stood guard, looking after the Indians. Sonny sat up, rubbing his wrists and flexing his fingers while Lance crossed to where the little girls were huddled. The two of them stared up at the cowboy in big-eyed fright, as the lad carefully cut loose their bounds, but left the strips of cloth about their mouths in place.

"Don't worry," he whispered, "we are going to get you out of here and back home safe."

Lance led the girls over to where Sonny was painfully mounting his horse. He lifted the smaller girl up to a place in front of Sonny while Rusty lifted the other girl up behind the saddle.

"What did you do with our horses?" Lance said.

"Follow me, I left them down this draw a ways.

Quickly the cowboys made their way down the draw, the Comanche nowhere in sight.

Chapter Thirteen

Savage Justice

Guaynopa mining camp, summer, 1870

Reese Hutchinson stood stock still, his hands clutching in frustration. The little freckle puss that he'd had big plans for that evening had turned up missing this morning and nobody seemed to know where she was. Jones was fit to be tied and everyone was on high alert, certain that the kid L.T. had taken a fancy to was behind it all. Hutch had his own ideas about that and wanted in the worst way to get his hands on the smart-aleck pup, himself, for he had not fully vented his spleen on the young cowboy, nor tested his fighting ability. As for the girl, an evil leer came to his face. He was not finished with her yet, either.

His eyes fell on the cliff dwellings as the late morning sun crept slowly down the west wall of the canyon and flooded the ancient pueblos in light. "Nobody ever goes up there," he muttered. "I wonder. . ." He withdrew his pistol, checked the loads, and then returned the gun to its holster and started out at a brisk walk through the camp and towards the upper river trail.

Penny had curled up on a blanket and was taking a nap while Colt had decided to wash out the rags he had been using for bandages around his ribs. He was bent over the shallow outlet of the pool where it drained off to seep away onto the rocky floor, and was rinsing the cloth strips when a sudden clatter of heavy boot steps behind him caused him to turn a split second before Reese Hutchinson was upon him.

Colt dodged the vicious kick aimed at his head and sprang out of the way, rolling over in the shallows to come up on his feet and turn to meet his attacker, his guard up and every fiber of his being on the alert.

"So, holed up here in the cliff dwelling with my little sweetheart are you?" Hutch sneered, "I figured you for some stunt like this. You know, you're not too bright kid, you shoulda skedaddled out of this country a long time ago instead of trying to save this little whore. Did she tell you what I done to her?"

Penny had sat up and was watching in wide-eyed horror as the big man circled about the cowboy. Colt felt a white-hot stab of anger flash through him, but held his peace, and then turned cold inside. His mind seemed to sharpen and focus on his adversary. His nerves went cool, calm and collected. He waited. This was a big and dangerous man who enjoyed the fight—lived for it—anticipated the beating of his opponent, and relished the letting of blood and even the kill. Circling him, Colt knew he was toying with him like a cougar he once saw tormenting a cornered bobcat.

"Well, did she," Hutch taunted, "Did she tell you how much she liked it—what it was like to be with a real man?"

Colt knew he was trying to bait him and he let the remarks fall on deaf ears. The last thing he needed to do was let these filthy lies goad him into breaking his concentration. A grim smile crinkled at the corners of his steel-blue eyes and his jaw set as he stepped away from the water and planted his feet on dry ground.

Hutch continued circling him, eying the bruises on his body. "Looks like I mighta busted a few ribs on ya, sonny-boy, why don't you come over here and let me finish bustin' the rest of 'em for ya?"

"Okay," Colt said unexpectedly, and took two quick steps to close the gap between them, and then slugged a hard fist into the leering mouth of the big man. Taken momentarily by surprise, Reese's head snapped back as his lips were smashed against his teeth and his mouth bloodied. He grappled wildly for Colton, but the fleet of foot cowboy eluded his grasp and danced away towards the edge of the cliff.

Hutch's eyes lit up with an evil gleam and he grinned as he spit blood and stared after Colt.

"First blood," he said and spit again. "That's gonna make this all that much sweeter, why don't you try that again?" The big guard was walking slowly towards Colt, his huge fists doubling and clenching as he spoke.

"I got a better idea," Colt said and taking a quick step towards his opponent, he aimed a kick, as hard as he could, into the groin of Reese Hutchinson and doubled the big man over gasping in pain. He followed up by grasping Hutch by the hair and driving a knee upwards into the face of the stricken man, propelling his head downward. There was an audible pop as Colt's knee smashed into Reese's nose.

Hutch snapped over backwards to land flat on his back, his head cracking against the granite floor. He lay there twitching and shuddering like a blade of grass in a high wind.

Colt waited, watching. Reese's face was covered in blood, his nose mashed and swelling and oozing blood back down his throat to where he was choking on it. Colt stepped to a place just above the downed man's head and could see indescribable hate in his bulging eyes. Reese raised halfway up on his elbows, spitting more blood and coughing to clear his windpipe, then began to laugh. It was a cold-hearted, evil laugh without humor but, strange as it might seem, Reese Hutchinson seemed to be actually enjoying himself.

"That was pretty good, kid," he rasped between clenched teeth, "Maybe I finally found somebody worth whipping. Now let me show you what a real drubbing's like." Suddenly the big man lunged to his feet and made a grab for Colt, almost catching him about the knees.

Colt danced backwards and pushed aside an extended arm then delivered a punishing blow to Hutch's ear, setting it to ringing. Hutch shook it off and, with a roar, charged the cowboy again. Colt sprinted away across the cavern floor with Hutch in hot pursuit. He saw Penny watching, her eyes filled with horror at the vicious contest unfolding before her.

He redoubled his efforts and gained a lead on Reese, who finally slowed and then stopped to bend over, his hands on his knees, panting like a dog. Colt stopped and turned to face him, breathing hard.

"What are you, some damned rabbit?" Hutch panted out. "Just once, let me get my hands on you and I'll fix your bacon."

Something about the way Hutch was lumbering towards him, reminded Colt of the time he had leaped over that Texas longhorn cow, and with hardly a second thought of what he was doing, he charged back towards the big man in an erratic pattern, noting the confusion this created in his eyes, and then moments before they made contact, he sprang into the air and drove both his boots into Hutch's face, then twisted and fell heavily backwards to tuck and roll, breaking his fall.

Hutchinson was whipped off his feet like he'd been clotheslined, the kick sending him over backwards and skittering him across the cavern floor towards the edge of the precipice, where he lay stunned

Landing hard, Colt lay on the ground, watching his enemy and catching his breath. He was poised to spring to his feet the moment Reese showed signs of renewing his assault. He wondered at the big man's stamina. He had already withstood more than any ten men should have. If this game wasn't so deadly, he could almost admire the man's sand, but he had little time or care for such thoughts, for Reese Hutchinson was sitting up, laughing his wicked laugh, while passing a big hand over his face to clear his vision.

"Dammit, kid, who taught you to fight? I ain't never seed nobody do stuff like that, you're plumb squirrelly, but it just so happens, I like squirrel stew, so come to papa," He stood to his feet and beckoned Colt towards him. This time he stood waiting, watching him like a hawk, as Colt approached on the balls of his feet. The youth was fresh out of ideas and breathed a silent prayer, "Lord, help!" He knew he could not stand and slug it out with the big guard and he dared not let him get his hands on him. He would just have to wear him down with quick in-and-out punches. Maybe he would eventually pass out from loss of blood or something.

He began to dance about Hutch, feinting like a prize fighter the way his father had taught him to do. He landed some solid punches both to the head and body of the big man and he might as well have been slugging a longhorn bull for all the good it seemed to do. All it did was infuriate the one-eyed man.

Colt played to the blind side of Reese, keeping him turning in that direction, while raining blows about the ears, eyes and head of his opponent. Then it happened. His foot slipped on a loose pebble on the cavern floor and he momentarily lost his footing. The delay in his rhythm was just enough to allow Hutch to close a huge mitt around his right arm and with a powerful blow the big man drove his fist up from the waist in a wicked uppercut that struck Colt on the point of his chin. The blow lifted him off his feet and sent him flying backwards, skidding on his bare back, to the very edge of the rocky shelf. He lay there stunned, half unconscious, his head swirling with dizzying speed.

Hutchinson laughed gleefully and approached the downed cowboy, his hands clutching, claw-like, opening and closing in eager anticipation. "Now, you jacksnipe," he said, "I'm going to stomp the rest of your ribs before I stomp you below the belt like you did me. After that I'll just see if I can kick you all over hell till there's nothing left."

Colt's head and neck were over the edge of the cavern floor and he was vaguely aware of the sounds of the river far below. He struggled to rise up, his head still swimming, when a sudden, crushing pain seared through his side as Reese's heavy boot stomped down into his stomach. A wave of nausea swept over him and he nearly passed out. Futilely, he tried to protect his abdomen with his arms and roll to his side.

Hutch laughed maniacally and made to leap up into the air to land with both feet in the middle of the stricken youth. He did not see the figure that streaked towards him from his blind side, until a scream of terror and rage broke through his chortling laughter while he was in mid-air, intent on stomping the very life from the prostrate and helpless youth.

Penny Struthers, in a desperate effort to save Colt from being brutally killed, rushed against the man who had treated her so vilely and leaped upon his back to clutch his hair and sink her teeth into the back of his neck. The force of her attack struck the big man in mid air and the impact of her body carried them both over the precipice in a long, desperate scream that was cut short on the rocks below.

Colt was stunned. He lay there, retching and gasping for breath, scarcely able to breath from the intensity of the pain in his side. Slowly, he managed to raise himself up and peer over the edge of the cliff into the shadows below. He saw the crushed and broken bodies of his assailant and the poor, desperate girl, who had saved his life. Tears welled up in his eyes as a great awareness of the senseless tragedy overwhelmed his spirit. With it came a profound sadness for Penny's young life cut short. She'd had the spirit to overcome unspeakable atrocities and only this morning had agreed to make the decision to trust the Lord for her life, and now this. He found he could hardly believe it. She was just here a few moments ago and they were talking about getting out of here and now she was gone. He would know her no more—not in this life.

The shock and ever enlarging realization of what had just happened seemed to move in upon him like a huge, black, gathering storm cloud, and he felt as if he was being swallowed up—engulfed in it and loosing his ability to see. Then the anger and frustration set in.

"God!" he cried, "How come you did that?" His voice cracked and he began to sob. "She never deserved this—never deserved any of it. Why! What's wrong with you, where is the justice and rightness of this?

You should never have let her be stolen from her home and raped by those animals you call men, in the first place." Colt spoke out of the bitterness of his soul while the cavern chamber echoed back his voice in eerie, haunting, mockery. "I'll kill 'em," he sobbed, "I'll kill every last, rotten, son-of-a-bitch," he swore. "It's just not fair!" His sobs began to subside and he gritted his teeth at the hopeless sense of futility. "I was just about to get her out of here—we were ready to leave, I was going to take her home to her mom and dad, and you had to let that miserable bastard, Reese, find us. Dammit, dammit all to hell, God—Why?"

Colt's rage stormed through him as he lay wounded on the cavern floor, until the emotional torrent blew itself out and left him as spent and empty as an old mesquite bean pod, and that's just the way he saw himself lying there. Wearily he sat up and peered over the edge once more. He could see people moving near the bodies below and then staring up at the cliff dwellings.

"Won't be long and they'll be up here," he muttered through the pain. "Well, they won't find me, but they'll wish they had before I'm through with them." He got unsteadily to his feet, wincing against the pain, and made his way to the pueblo where his pack was stashed. He spent the next half hour ferrying everything through the underwater portal to the inside cavern, after which he collapsed in exhaustion. Cold and wet, he fell asleep.

He awoke sometime later, shivering. The passageway to the pool was dark and he knew night had fallen. Taking the rifle and some shells, and wrapping matches in a piece of oilskin, which he stuffed in his pocket, he slipped into the cold water to swim to the outer pool. Carefully, his head broke the surface while he paused in the shadows of the overhanging cliff, listening, but he heard nothing. Evidently they had come, probably made a thorough search of the place, and finding nothing, had gone back down. His suspicions were confirmed when he waded from the pool and noticed that Penny's bag was missing. He hoped Jones would figure that just Penny had fled to the pueblos in hopes of meeting Colt there, and that Hutch had ended up finding her. That in the ensuing struggle, the two of them had gone over the edge. He had little doubt that a guard would be posted on the trail below again, and that they would be watching for him.

"Well, they better be because here I come," he said grimly. Colt shouldered the rifle by a strip of rawhide he'd attached earlier and headed for the chimney chute and the trail below. Stealthily he crept up to the chimney and peered downwards. He could see nothing, but could smell tobacco smoke floating up. His eyes fell upon a slab of rock, perhaps a foot or so across, and he picked it up, hefting it. It weighed around thirty pounds, and he held it suspended over the chute and proceeded to kick several small stones down into the chimney of rock. These rattled as they fell, and he waited until a dark shadow moved at the opening below, then dropped the rock while whispering, "Hey, amigo." It could not have worked more perfectly, the stone struck the guard full in the face at the same moment he looked up, and the man silently slumped to the ground.

Colt waited for about ten minutes and when no one else came to investigate, he shinnied down the chimney and rolled the guard over. It was Lute Berry, one of the men who had been party to his and Penny's recapture. Colt noted with grim satisfaction that he was dead, his neck broken. He dragged the body to the side of the trail and propped it up into a sitting position and shoved the man's rifle into the hollow of his arm. Colt removed the gun belt and buckled it around his own waist, then checked the loads and returned the .44 to the holster, tying it down. Searching through the man's shirt pockets, he found a couple of cigars and a box of dry matches. These he put in his own damp pocket, then turned down the trail towards the mining camp.

First, he went to his old hut and found it still empty. He slipped inside and dragged the box of dynamite out from under the bunk that he and Penny had shared. A momentary pang of sadness swept over him, and he swallowed hard at the lump in his throat. "Penny, they're gonna pay for what they did," he gritted under his breath. With a determination to wreak havoc on this evil nest of vipers, he added, "and this dynamite is just the thing to do it, too."

He spent over a half hour tying the sticks together into bundles of six, and cutting and attaching varying lengths of fuses to each. The last three sticks he kept as singles with a six inch length of fuse attached to each. These he left on the bunk and slipped out into the still dark of the night.

The first bundle of explosives he set under the foundation of the locked smelting shack where the melt furnaces were. The second went under the arastas where the ore was ground. Two bundles were placed under the long sluice boxes by the canal, and then he went to the head of the reservoir that fed the irrigation canal and sluices and set two more charges in the earthen dam that held back the water, one on either end.

It was two hours before daylight when Colt stepped back into the empty hut, took out one of the cigars and struck a match. He and Sonny had puffed on cigars a couple of times before, but had never really smoked them. Soon he had the end glowing red in the dark. He picked up the three single sticks and stuck them into his hip pockets, took one last look around and went out the door.

The sluices were the farthest away and these had the longest fuses. He bent swiftly and blew on the end of the cigar, then touched the tip to the first wick. It spit and began to sputter and he hurried to the other and lit it. Running to the arastas, he lit that fuse and then touched off the one under the smelt shack. Dogs started barking at him as he ran full speed to the dam and lit the first fuse there, then raced across its top, for the last and final charge.

A shot rang out and he heard the angry whine as a bullet whizzed past his head. He turned and saw a guard running towards him and shouting. It looked like Toby Rolland, Reese's other henchman who had been in on the recapture. Colt jumped down and held the stogie to the end of the last fuse and dove to the side as Rolland pumped two more shots into the dirt next to him.

Clenching the cigar tight in his teeth, Colt drew the .44 and shot the man, sending him spinning backwards to land in the dark water just as the first blast went off. The charge lit up the night sky, sending splintered remnants of the sluices high into the air. In rapid succession the arastas and then the smelter shack blew, and Colt paused in his flight on the other side of the reservoir, as the dam charges went off, sending mud, rocks and water raining down all around him. A section of the dam held at its center, and Colt pulled a stick of dynamite from his hip pocket, lit it, and flung it towards the middle. The charge broke the top loose and the next two sticks finished the job, sending a wall of water five feet high rushing down towards the mining encampment, sweeping everything in its path before it. He saw the little adobe hut he'd stayed in hold out against the flood, only to finally give way and collapse in the torrent. Smiling grimly, Colt turned and headed back for his hideout.

He stopped and collected an armful of pine knots and then paused at Lute's dead body to remove his hat and try it on, it fit fairly well. Next, he shinnied up the chimney, removed all of his clothes and dove into the water to the internal tunnel and retrieved a rope from his cache of supplies. He swam back out, slipped on his pants and boots, and returned to the chimney. Climbing down, he tied the rope around his bundle of pine knots and then struggled back up to haul the sticks up behind him. By the time he reached the pool's edge he was exhausted and collapsed, his side paining something awful.

"Hope no busted ribs are gonna puncture my lungs," he groaned. From off in the distance he could hear shouting and hollering in the camp below, but felt no remorse. "There," he said, "that oughta do for starters. It'll be a long while before those vultures in New York will be getting any more gold out of this place." He closed his eyes for a minute to rest.

Dawn was lighting the eastern rim of the canyon by the time Colt finished transferring the pine knots to the inside tunnel, and made one final inspection trip to remove all traces of his passing. The escape tunnel carved out of the living stone by the ancient cliff dwellers would enable him to flee his enemies as well. Now all he had to do was figure out how to get past the snake pit and the Apache medicine man, or whoever he was.

He sat down in the dimly lit tunnel and rested, his side paining him greatly with every breath he took. He knew he should eat something, but had no appetite. He rested for a few minutes more and then began to struggle into his wet clothes, while taking a mental inventory of his possessions. There was the rifle and bandoleers of shells, along with the gun belt strapped around his waist. The old Spanish sword, he would have to leave, for in his injured condition and given the miles he had to travel, there was just too much to carry. He pulled on the hiking boots, gratified to find they had dried, and discarded the sombrero for the guard's hat. He chose one of the two Mexican blankets and rolled up the eggs and butter in that, before stuffing it into a gunny sack along with beans, salt and pepper, a few left over carrots, spuds and some ears of corn. A slab of bacon was added along with some tin ware, pants, shirt and a slicker. By the time this was all stuffed into the sack, he had a pretty bulky pack. His eyes fell on the pouch containing the gold he'd left on a ledge. He found a place in the bag for it as well, knowing he would eventually have need of money to buy a horse and saddle and a decent outfit, once he reached Texas.

Colt tied the end of his rope around the bundle of pine knots and took one last look around. The remnant of his candle and packet of matches lay on the ledge where he had left them, and he put these into his shirt pocket. Sitting on the floor of the compartment, he tied off the neck of the sack with rawhide thongs and attached it to the bandoleers where they crossed in the back, then shrugged into them, thus effectively creating a backpack. Struggling to his feet, he picked up the rifle, slung a full water bag over one shoulder, the coil of rope over the other and began to trudge up the tunnel into the darkness, dragging the pine knots on the floor behind him.

When he reached the spot that he could no longer see the pool's reflected light, his progress slowed while he felt his way along the tunnel wall. He knew this passage to be fairly uniform and decided to save the candle for the more difficult assent, once he gained the big room. He estimated it was more than an hour before he reached that chamber, and then he stopped to light the candle while the sounds of his passing echoed off the high ceiling.

Regaining his breath, he struggled across the broken floor to the chute on the far end that led upward, and gave a big sigh. This was not going to be easy and his side was paining him furiously. He sat down and rested, leaning back against the wall without removing the pack, easing the weight of his burden. His eyes heavy, he decided to nap, blew out the candle, and returned it to his shirt pocket. It was blacker than the inside of a coal miner's boot, and he leaned back taking shallow breaths. "I guess no rib's going to puncture my lung or it would a done it by now," he murmured, and shut his eyes.

But sleep eluded him. He could not get his mind off what had happened to Penny and again felt the too familiar feelings of despair and frustration with God. The unfairness of it was almost more than he could comprehend, it just didn't fit in with his understanding of who God was and something within his soul cried desperately for understanding. "Jesus said, '*Love your enemies,*' but how could anyone—even God—love somebody like Reese Hutchinson?" he asked the darkness. "I suppose He does because, theoretically, He loves everybody, but He is supposed to be just, too, where was the justice in Penny's lost life?" Colt quietly voiced thoughts were troubling. "Why did it take sacrificing her, to stop the likes of that miserable Hutch? In fact, why does it seem that something good always has to be surrendered to compensate for the bad stuff?"

He was angry with himself, too, not only was he on shaky ground with God for his outburst against Him, but he had failed Penny. He had not come through in the crunch and just when he thought he had the best of his adversary, the table was turned and he was at the non-existent mercy of Hutch. Had Penny not intervened, he most certainly would be dead now. Why couldn't he have kept his wits about him like his dad had said? He'd done it before with others—had intervened to help Willow and Kathreen and Suzanne and Carlotta and even had a vague recollection of the girl, Sarah, fleeing across the river. Why had he failed Penny? It made no sense, and as he sat there in the dark, mulling it all over in his mind, he began to have serious doubts about himself.

Was he ever going to get out of this fix and get back to Suzanne—and would he even be the guy she thought he was when he did? He felt the darkness closing in around him—it was like he was buried alive—stuck in the bowls of this mountain—closer to hell than heaven and an unreasoning fear seemed to clutch at his heart. The only way out was up and it was going to be a painful struggle. Could he even make it? He didn't know, but right now he was just going to sit here and rest. Finally, he fell asleep.

Colt awoke stiff and sore and for a moment was at a complete loss as to where he was. His eyes were open but he could see absolutely nothing. Had he gone blind? He reached out a hand and felt cold stone and his memory came flooding back. He was in the cavern and he carefully felt for the candle and matches. The light flared up with the match and dispelled the darkness. He rose to his feet and started up the passage, wincing at the pain in his side. He was mindful of the need for God's help in getting out of this place, for his own strength was indeed small, and then he was surprised to find himself wondering if he even wanted God's help. If the Lord had failed him on the cliff dwelling floor, what made him think He'd help him now? Just because he was in need, it didn't necessarily mean God was going to show up with a band of angels and haul him out of this miserable place. "Well, the Lord helps them who help themselves," he quoted the old adage as though it were Scripture.

Colt gritted his teeth against the pain and yanked the bundle of pine branches past an obstructing rock, then inched forward and upward slowly. His pack caught and wedged him into a narrow part of the chute and he felt an overwhelming desire to cuss. He paused, breathing hard, and waited until the feeling passed. Had his cursing earlier made it easier to cuss now? In the darkness of this place it seemed to make no difference and he thought, "Who cares!" but then he knew his mother cared. Jessica Saber cared, his mind seemed to say, and she'd have something to say to you about it, too. He smiled sheepishly and backed out of the tight spot, resisting an urge to look around to see if anyone was watching.

Wearily, he removed the pack and crawled through the narrow spot and then reached back to drag his baggage past the obstruction. Maybe he did need the Lord's help. He could certainly imagine his mother assuring him he did. Feeling guilty about the things he had said and the hard thoughts he'd had towards God, he said, "Lord, I'm sorry for cussin' and for gettin' mad at you, and if you wouldn't hold it against me—would forgive me, I'll try and do better—and I could use your help on gettin' out of here."

Like a mole burrowing through the garden or a rabbit down a hole, Colt walked, crawled, squirmed on his belly, and sweated his way up the ancient lava tube until at last he stood in the serpents' chamber. A late afternoon sun was streaming radiant shafts of light down into the slithering, sliding mass of rattlers in the snake pit. He had made it this far and he stood staring at the light. "Funny how the sun is shining light right down into that snake den—showing me where the danger lies," he thought. "Now if I can just get across it."

Colt untied the rope from his pine knots and held one to the stub of candle, it began to smoke and then burst into an oily, orange flame. He took from his pocket the sling he'd fashioned while waiting at the pueblos, and finding an egg-sized chunk of granite, he set the stone, then lit two more pine knots from the first. As the chamber began to fill with smoke, the rattlers began to set up a din and Colt stepped to where his view could command the opening of the hole to the outside.

When he saw a shadow pass across the opening and the painted face of an Apache warrior appear, he swung the sling in one quick circle and released the rock, which flew true, and cracked the Indian on the bridge of the nose. He gave a low groan as his eyes rolled up into his head, then he pitched forward to fall through the opening into the den of snakes below. His body convulsed as several snakes struck it, but he didn't know for he never regained consciousness.

Colt placed another rock in the sling and waited for about ten minutes, but when no one else appeared, he was satisfied that the Indian had been alone in his vigil. He carefully donned his pack, slung his rifle and the rope and canteen over his shoulder and stooped to light several more pine knots. These he dropped into the pit forcing the snakes to clear a path. Holding a blazing torch in his hand, he slid into the pit and crossed to the other side, brushing the retreating snakes back on either side as he went. Some struck at the torch, but most slithered away. Holding onto the torch, he had to crawl up the other side, seeking toe and hand holds until he reached the opening. He was just about to drop the torch back into the pit and reach out of the hole to pull himself up, when he heard the ominous buzzing of a rattler. Coiled in the sunlight on a ledge was a huge diamondback rattlesnake, just a few feet from his head. Colt made a lightning quick sweep of the torch and caught the serpent in mid-strike to fling it hissing, past him down into the slithering mass of its companions.

The next instant, Colt pulled himself up through the opening and rolled out onto a rocky table of stone. A small fire was burning next to a pile of green brush and a smoke blackened Indian blanket lay close by. He lay there breathing in great, lungfuls of the fresh, pine-scented mountain air. He was mindful of shots being fired and screaming and yelling in the distance. Rolling to his hands and knees, he unslung the rifle, then got cautiously to his feet and hobbled over to the edge of the cap rock to look into the valley below.

He was struck dumb at the sight that met his eyes. The entire mining camp appeared to be on fire and was under the long-awaited attack of the Apache. He saw Indians racing about on horseback, shooting the fleeing inhabitants of the camp, Mexican and whites alike. His eyes went to the Jones' hacienda on the hill. The rambling structure was ablaze and he saw what looked like L.T. Jones and Evita drug from the porch. He watched helplessly as Jones was shot point blank in the head and Evita was stripped and violated by an Indian brave before his very eyes. The distance was too great for him to fire with any affect, but her pathetic screams reached to Colt's ears and he turned away, sickened at the sight. There was a single shot and her cries were cut short. Colt turned back in time to see one of the savages dragging her naked body by the hair, behind his running horse and then hurl it over an embankment out of sight. He shook his head, but felt little sympathy for their wretched end.

It was time for him to make good his escape, while the Apache were thus engaged, and with scarcely a thought for those doomed in the camp, he struck out west to intersect the trail he had been brought in on, in oblivion, nearly two years before.

The country was some of the most rugged he had ever seen. The brush covered ridges and hillsides often presented formidable barriers even for travel on foot. Some of the thickets were so thick, Colt found them impossible to get through and he would have to go around, often back-tracking, to climb steep embankments or slide down others in his attempt to cut across country toward the trail he sought. The place was a maze of rolling hills of granite at the higher elevations, and looked as though the stone had flowed in waves of liquid rock to crash into craggy mountainsides, and then instantly solidify.

Nothing in Texas had prepared the cowboy for the wild, primitive, savagery of this land. His travel was further hindered by his injured side, which he suspected included a broken or cracked rib or two from the brutal attack of Hutch.

From the vantage point of the Apache lookout, he had been able to see the trail leading into and out of Guaynopa Canyon and the mining camp. Having struck out in a southeasterly direction to intercept it, he had descended off the ridge only to drop into a veritable jungle of manzanita and creosote brush that choked the hillsides and draws. After attempting to leave the Indian track, which wound away in a confusing pattern, to beeline to the trail he wanted, he found himself lost in the brush, his sense of direction totally confused and disorientated. Reluctantly he retraced his steps until he regained the Indian path.

Something Pops Cranston had told him came to mind: "When trying to cross rough country, keep to the ridges. If you drop off the top to side-hill, you will invariably work your way down hill and end up in a draw or canyon and play hob trying to get out."

Colt sat resting in the shade of a scrub manzanita bush and caught his breath. He took a long pull at the water bag, adjusted his pack and with a sigh, pushed to his feet. Picking up the rifle he slung it over his shoulder and followed the path back to where it had crossed the ridge. From here he could once again see the route to the mine. Trudging up an eroded embankment, he gained the top of the ridge and started following it back down. "Pops was right," he said, "this is easier going."

It was nearing dark when Colt slid off another embankment, the tin ware clanking in his pack as it hit a rock. Nervous at the sound he'd made, he landed in a cloud of dust on the trail that led out of the canyon. Looking off towards the palisaded battlements of the cliffs towering up from the Rio Aros, he could see smoke billowing up from the doomed mining camp.

"Looks like they've torched everything," he said. "I better make tracks out of here. That bunch of Apache could be heading back this way." He turned to study the fresh dirt where he had slid down onto the trail and then thought, "making tracks is just what I do not want to do." Locating a dead cluster of manzanita, he carefully swept the embankment and trail free of his footprints and then, keeping to stony ground, he headed east on the horse path until he gained the crest of the hill that led out of the canyon.

Chapter Fourteen

The Box 7 Riders

The Pecos River, summer, 1870

Kathreen giggled happily and watched the dust settling on the brush alongside the trail. "Guess we tied a can to their tails," she smirked.

"Kate, I'm not going to have a friend left in all of Upton County if you keep on tormenting these cowboys," Suzanne said.

"Huh, like that's going to happen. I'm telling you, you need to assert yourself more or these fellows will just keep on creeping out of the woodwork to get at you."

"Kathreen," Suzanne said. "No one is trying to get at me."

"They're not, huh? What about Clay Anderson—worse yet, what about Sonny Saber? You have your heart so set on Colt and him missing, that you just have no idea how vulnerable you are."

"Vulnerable? What possible vulnerability do I have to these others?"

"Listen, my sweet, innocent friend," Kathreen asserted with a knowing nod of her head, "there is a great big, vacant hole left in your soul, and even though you long for Colt to come back and fill it, if he doesn't, someone else eventually will."

"Oh, Kate," Suzanne sighed, "I do miss him so. We were so close. I desperately miss the intimacy we had. I just can't imagine anyone else ever taking his place."

"Well, I can, I see these Box 7 riders coming around, and it doesn't take much to encourage them either," Kathreen said.

Suzanne smiled then, "They're after you."

"And that's why I go out of my way to discourage them—besides the fun of teasing them, that is. Can you imagine me taking the likes of the 'Don Juan of the Pecos' home to meet my mother?"

Both girls had a good laugh at this and then the redhead said, "Whew it's hot, I'm going swimming."

Suzanne looked skeptical. "How? I do not have any swimming costume."

"Me neither," her friend replied, "We'll just not use any."

"Kathreen, what if somebody comes—what if the Box 7 cowboys come back?"

"Then we will just have to give them a good dressing-down again," her friend declared.

Suzanne hesitated, "I don't know, it is awfully hot but. . ."

"Haven't you ever gone swimming pickle before?"

"Pickle, what's that?"

"Swimming without anything on," Kathreen said, amused at her friend's wide-eyed stare.

"No!" Suzanne cried, "Certainly not! Why do they call it pickle?"

"I don't know," Kathreen shrugged, "they just do. Come on, I'll race you to the river."

The two girls ran down a cattle trail to the edge of the Pecos River. The water ran sluggishly between low banks, a weak coffee and milk color. Kathreen sat down on the grass and pulled her shoes off then began to disrobe. Slowly, Suzanne began unbuttoning the front of her dress.

You are going to leave your under things on?" Suzanne asked, looking worriedly at her friend.

"Suzanne," Kathreen said in exasperation, "look around you. There's nobody here, we're surrounded by brush and I have no wish to soil my nice, white under things with this brown river water. Don't be such a prude, get your clothes off."

Kathreen tossed her pantaloons over a buffalo berry bush and waded into the water at the river's edge. "Eeek, it's cold," she cried and then ducked under the water with a little screech only to burst back up gasping for breath and giggling. She looked like some kind of elfin wood nymph, with water streaming from her naked body.

Suzanne removed her dress and stood nervously on the bank in her chemise with her arms clasped over her bosom. She enviously watched her friend cavort in the water, launch into a back-float and drift slowly around in a little eddy of the pool she was in. The redhead was enjoying herself and Suzanne wished she could be as uninhibited as her choleric friend. But to undress, here in the wild—what if somebody should see her uncovered like that—unveiled? That thought called to mind the things Colton had said to her about her unveiling and she smiled sadly. She had been ready—more than ready—to unveil herself for him that night on the Sweetgrass after their escape from the Kiowa but he would not allow it. She supposed he was right, but still she wished they had, for now he was gone, lost to her and she feared that the long desired coming together that they had yearned for, would never be.

With a heavy sigh, Suzanne sat down on a log and clasped her arms about her knees. She was not going to unveil. Her beauty, what there was of it, would remain hidden, lost to the world as Colt was lost to her, she didn't care if it was ever uncovered if it could not be uncovered for him.

"What are you doing?" Kathreen's question startled her back to the present. "Aren't you coming in?"

Suzanne shook her head, "I've never gone swimming without anything on before, not outside like this," she said.

Kathreen treaded water against the current and looked skeptical at her friend. "Not even with Colt? I thought you and he got pretty cozy on that camping trip."

"Kathreen, I was never like that with him—or anyone else either, for that matter."

"Like what?" Kathreen said with a smirk. Suzanne could not even say the word.

"Like you—pickle, or whatever it was you called it."

"Ha ha," her friend laughed, "you can't even say the word. It's naked, the word is na-ked."

Suzanne blushed scarlet. She wondered at her intuitive friend. Did Kathreen know that she had been ready to get like that with Colt that night in the teepee? She had never said anything to her. What about the time at her bath in the creek, when Colt came upon her unexpectedly? She blushed red, at the memory.

"You can't fool me," Kathreen said, "I know what its like, and I know that even someone wrapped as tight as you are will unwind once the right strings are pulled."

"Oh, you do, do you," Suzanne perked up and stared back at the girl in the water in defiance. "Well, for your information, Miss Smarty Pants, Colt pulled a lot of strings and I did go swimming with him in their pond, so put that in your pipe and smoke it."

Kathreen burst out laughing at her indignant friend. "So you did go skinny-dipping with him then, I thought so." She nodded her head knowingly.

"I did not," Suzanne declared hotly, "I kept my underclothes on, so there."

"Fat lot a good that would have done."

"What do you mean?"

"Come on in. . . right now, just like that with your chemise and knickers on."

Suzanne hesitated, what was this impish redhead up to now? She stood and took a few steps down the riverbank to stand at the edge of the water and watched Kathreen moving towards her.

"Are you coming in?" her friend said.

Suzanne stuck her toe into the murky water, "Oh, it is cold."

Kathreen stood in water to her knees. Suddenly scooping handsful of water, she began to splash her reluctant friend. Suzanne let out a piercing scream when the water hit her, and stumbled backwards to trip and fall on the muddy bank.

"You big stinker," she moaned and turned to examine her backside. "I'm all muddy now."

Kathreen stood giggling, "Look at you," she said, pointedly.

"What?" Suzanne looked down at the front of her drenched chemise. The wet fabric had become nearly transparent with an abundance of pink flesh showing plainly through.

"Oh, you," she declared hotly, "you are such a brat." Suzanne scooped up a handful of mud, her jaw set with determination.

"What did I tell you?" Kathreen asserted positively. "If you went into the water with Colt, like that, you might as well have been naked."

"No, I might as well not have! You make me so mad!" With that declaration the blond girl flung the handful of mud at her sassy friend and splattered it all over the front of her.

Kathreen let out a loud squeal and ducked under the water to come back up clutching a handful of slimy river bottom. Suzanne shrieked and jumped up, as her friend threw the mud at her, then, grabbing up a chunk of mud and sod from the edge of the river, Suzanne rushed into the shallows to plop the gooey mess, on top of the Saint Louis redhead.

The two young ladies, one naked and one nearly so, losing all sense of propriety, launched into a full-fledged mud fight, while laughing and screaming and splashing each other with the otherwise languid waters of the south-flowing Pecos River on its way to the Gulf of Mexico.

Suddenly the frolicking girls were interrupted by a loud clatter of hooves and turning, were startled to see two cowboys galloping down the trail towards them. For a moment they stood, wide-eyed in fright, in all of their unadorned glory, watching Two-Bits Thompson and Buddy McLeod leap from the saddles of their plunging mounts with pistols drawn and look back and forth from the girls, to up and down the river.

Both girls screeched like a couple of deranged owls, and dove for the cover of the river. When their heads popped back up above the surface of the water, they turned to stare angrily at the cowboys.

"What the hell is going on?" McLeod roared.

"Yeah," Kathreen said, swallowing her fright, "what the hell is going on, and what are you two nincompoops doing busting in on our swimming hole?"

"We heard you screamin' and figured the Comanche got ya," Two-Bits said.

Buddy slowly lowered his pistol into the holster and pushed his hat to the back of his head. "You girls are alright then?" he asked.

Suzanne slowly nodded and shivered under the water. Embarrassed, and mindful of her state of undress and, as Kathreen had so patently pointed out, its revealing nature, she dared not raise up with the two riders staring, bug-eyed at them.

Kathreen, however, immediately took the two cowboys to task. "Of course we're alright, you clodhoppers, there are no Comanche around here, just you two voyeurs trying to get your beady little eyes full. You can just climb back on those nags and get the blazes out of here."

Two-Bits looked confused and turned to his partner, "Wha'd she call us—voyagers?"

Nonplussed, Buddy scoffed, "She says we're Peeping Toms."

"What? Peeping Toms? What's that?"

McLeod shook his head and turned to catch the trailing reins of his cowpony. "It just goes to show ya, no good deed will go unpunished."

"That's right," Kathreen snapped, "now you two ninnies haul your sorry tails out of here before we turn into a couple of prunes."

Buddy stepped up into his saddle, but Two-Bits got a huge grin on his face and walked over to where the girl's clothing was draped over the bushes and poked his gun barrel under the edge of Kathreen's chemise. "Looks like you ladies may be missing a few things," he said.

"Come on, Two-Bits," McLeod said, "let's vamoose."

"In a minute, in a minute. First I think we oughta 'splain a few things to the schoolmarm's, sassy little friend here, and, you'll excuse me, ma'am," he said, nodding to Suzanne as he walked over to sit on the log, "if I take over educatin' this city slicker from Saint Louey for a moment."

Buddy shrugged, hauled a leg over his saddle-horn to relax and scratched the back of his head, wondering what his partner was up to now.

Kathreen scowled and shivered. "Mr. Two-Bits, I have neither the time nor the inclination to sit here in this cold water and listen to you concoct some cock and bull story. We're about to turn blue and if you don't want to witness two *blue* females, naked, you better put an egg in your shoe and beat it right now, 'cause I'm coming out of here."

Both cowboys chuckled and Two-Bits said, "Naked blue females, eh. I hain't never seed no naked blue ones, Bud, have you?"

"Nope," Bud said, shaking his head.

"You miserable C*retian*," Kathreen said, "I'll get you for this."

"Wha'd she call me. . . a Cretian, what's that?" he turned a bewildered look on Bud.

Buddy shrugged, "Don't know, pard, but it can't be good, probably some bad actor in Saint Louey."

"It's from the Bible, you lunkhead, 'All Cretian's are liars and lazy, slow-bellies,' better known to you as rascals," Kathreen flared, "now get!"

Two-Bits let out a long, pent up breath, pushed his hat to the back of his head while his eyes flashed fire. "I ain't no liar, missy, and if you was a man I'd call ya on that. We're goin', but first you're gonna sit right there and listen, your high and mighty highness, to what I have to say. This ain't no park in Saint Louey and that ain't no highfalutin swimmin' pool you're in either. You happen to be in the wilds of West Texas. It's crawlin' with Comanche, Kiowa and Apache Indians, to say nothin' of renegades, thieves, outlaws, Mexican Banditos and Comancheros, all who would like nothin' better than to get their hands on a couple of purty white girls, or even blue ones, for that matter. Throw in a river full of quicksand, water moccasins and an occasional snappin' turtle that could take a finger off—or somethin' else—and you got the makin's for some serious trouble. The onliest thing standin' between you and all that grief, is us 'lunkheaded knights of the range,' as you put it, and when we hear girls screamin', you can bet we come-a-runnin'."

Two-Bits went on, "Now, the fact that you are down here hain't no major concern of ours since we already know you're meaner than a striped snake with a toothache and pity the poor Injun or desperado that ended up with you for a captive. But since we're all kinda partial to our schoolmarm here, when we heard you-all screamin' we figured we should had oughta come and see if *she* was in some sort of trouble, or not."

Two Bits stood to his feet, dusted of the seat of his britches and took the reins that Buddy handed him. "Now that we know that *she's* okay, and you're just as sociable as ever, we'll bid you good day and go find us a swimmin' hole of our own to cool off in—one without any blue females." The cowboy swung into the saddle, tipped his hat to Suzanne and followed his pard along the river trail upstream.

"Well, I never," Kathreen gasped and stood up from the water to stare in bewilderment after the departing riders.

Suzanne waded to shore and found a spot in the sun to lay down on the grass and dry off. She watched Kathreen come to shore and retrieve her clothes.

"Who dressed who down?" she asked.

The redhead's eyes flashed fire and her cheeks burned as she stared back at her friend. "I'm going to fix their little red wagons," she vowed and began to put her clothes on.

Suzanne rose up on one elbow, mild concern on her face and said, "What are you going to do?"

"They said they were going swimming, didn't they?"

"Yes," Suzanne said guardedly and sat up.

Kathreen was buttoning up the front of her chemise. "You don't suppose they brought along any swimming costumes, do you?"

"Never gave it a thought, but no, probably not— why?"

"That's what I figure, come on, get your clothes on, we're going to go teach those boobhatches a lesson they won't forget."

Suzanne looked dubious at her friend, "You can't really blame them, Kathreen, they were right to come to our aid if they thought we were in distress. This is dangerous country, you know, why I was even attacked by the local sheriff's deputy, no less, and that was just outside of town."

"Well. . ." Kathreen seemed to have some doubts. "Maybe so, but they didn't have to stay and try to get their eyes full and torment us by keeping us in this cold water all that time. That Two-Bits makes me so mad."

Suzanne lay her head back down on her arms in the grass and giggled. The sun's rays felt hot on her back and her underclothes were drying out rapidly. "I can't get dressed until I dry off."

"I can't get dressed 'til I dry off," Kathreen mimicked her, "I told you not to wear your underclothes into the water. My clothes are all dry and still clean and I am ready to go cowboy hunting."

"Now, just hold your horses," Suzanne said, "you may be biting off more than you can chew."

"Them?" Kathreen scoffed. "When I'm done with them, they'll think they collided with a run-away circle-saw."

Suzanne rolled over onto her back and shielded her eyes from the sun. "Just what do you intend to do?"

The redhead thought for a moment, "What's this business of having a burr under your saddle, you Texans are always talking about?"

"Kathreen, you wouldn't!"

"Oh, wouldn't I?" Kathreen picked up Suzanne's dress and tossed it to her. "Put this on and come and find out."

The two girls followed the trail along the river. They could see the fresh hoof prints of the horses the cow-boys had been riding and moved carefully, to not make any noise that Two-Bits or Bud might hear. Presently they came to a spot where a huge old oak spread its branches out over the water, and here they found Buddy's and Two-Bits' horses tied to some willows.

Carefully, Kathreen plucked a handful of cockleburs and walked over to the cowponies. Lifting the back of each cantle, she slipped a couple of burrs in under the saddle blankets and grinned at the disapproval on her friend's face.

"That ought to prove interesting."

"Kate, I don't think you should do that," Suzanne said.

"Huh!" her friend scoffed. "Now for their clothes."

Shaking her head, Suzanne watched in amazement as Kathreen marched over to the pants, shirts, underwear and boots piled on the bank. She watched her friend tie knots in the pants legs and shirt sleeves and then toss them along with the underwear and boots up into the branches of the oak. It took her several tries to get the boots to stick up in the tree and when she was finished, she dusted her hands together and said, "There, that ought a fix em."

It was while she was finishing up playing the tricks on the cowboys, that they appeared, on a couple of pieces of driftwood, floating out in the river. The two swimmers saw Kathreen make her final toss of a boot and yelled.

"Hey, get away from our stuff, you crazy woman." They let go of the logs and started swimming furiously towards shore, shouting at the girls while wearing nothing but their hats.

Suzanne and Kathreen ran quickly out of sight back up the trail to where they had left the buggy. When the two of them reached their picnic spot, Kathreen hurriedly stuffed their things into the back of the rig while Suzanne untied Checkers and climbed to the driver's seat. She clucked to the mare after Kathreen jumped in and drove the buggy up to the road, heading back towards town.

A ruckus broke out back towards the river with horses squealing and the cowboys hollering. It sounded like a regular rodeo. Kathreen settled back in her seat with a satisfied grin and began to whistle Dixie.

Suzanne pulled Checkers up behind the house and the two girls jumped down from the buggy. Suzanne began to unhitch the pinto while Kathreen began to collect the picnic things from the back of the rig.

"Two-Bits and Buddy are going to have it in for us," Suzanne declared, "and I don't think it's fair, what you did to them."

"Who cares?" Kathreen responded glibly.

"I do, I have to live in this town, and those boys have been nothing but nice to me."

"Yeah, and I am sure they will keep right on being nice to you, too," the redhead answered. "You've got nothing to worry about, your majesty, all your loyal subjects will continue to bow and scrape, whenever you pass by."

Suzanne was surprised, "Kathreen, what is the matter with you? That was downright mean!"

Kathreen gave her friend a dark look and flounced off to the house, slamming the door loudly behind her. Shaking her head, Suzanne led her pony into the barn and put her up in the stall.

At the supper table that evening, Suzanne was unusually quiet, while Kathreen chatted happily along with her friend's parents, as if nothing was wrong. The whole time, she directed mean looks towards Suzanne whenever her folks weren't looking.

They had just about finished dessert when the sound of galloping horses was heard out in front of the house, accompanied by yelling and shouting. Whoever it was had pulled up and stopped out in the street by their gate. Glancing through the parlor window from where she sat at the table, Suzanne caught glimpses of Two-Bits and Buddy riding back and forth, and then she heard Two-Bits calling for Kathreen to come out. It was obvious from the sound of his voice that he had been drinking.

Gunner Kluesman scooted his chair back and went to the door. Opening it, he called, "What do you boys want?"

The Box 7 riders reined up and Two-Bits sheepishly pulled his hat off and held it to his chest. “Beggin' your pardon, sir, we have a little business matter to discuss with that redhead you got in there. Could you send her out here for a minute?”

“Miss McClusky is at supper and is just finishing her dessert. It looks to me like you fellas have looked at the bottom of a shot glass one too many times and I suggest you ride for the ranch and sleep it off, and come back some other time, a little less rowdy.”

“Okay,” Two-Bits said, “but you tell that Saint Louey a-ris-toe-crat that Bud broke an arm and I busted my butt, after she stuck those cocklebIurs under our saddles.” This last announcement he made by raising his voice and looking past Gunner through the open door, to shout loud enough for the girls and Mable to hear.

“That'll do,” Gunner thundered, “You boys hit the trail.”

A couple neighbors had come out on their porches and were watching the proceedings, as the Box 7 cowboys wheeled their horses and vigorously applied the ends of the reins to the animals' haunches. Whipping them into a gallop, they disappeared in a cloud of dust up the road out of town.

Gunner walked back in and sat heavily down in his chair. He picked up his fork, cut a piece of peach pie and put it in his mouth and then chewed it slowly, as if such things were an everyday occurrence. Suzanne was about to say something to him, but quickly closed her mouth when Kathreen pinched her under the table.

Gunner studied the two girls and then took a swallow of coffee. “Whatever happened today, I don't wanna know, you gals just be careful, you can provoke these cowboys only so far. . .then the next thing you know, you got something like the *Alamo* on your hands.”

At bedtime that evening, the two girls were getting ready for bed with neither speaking. Suzanne was in a quandary as to why Kathreen was acting as she did. For the life of her, she couldn't think of any reason why her friend should be mad at her. She was about to ask but changed her mind and, slipping her cotton nightgown over her head, she turned to pour water into a basin and rinse out the under things that had been stained with river water.

Kathreen got into bed and was holding a book upside-down, pretending to read. After a few moments she said, without looking up, "I don't know why those stupid cowboys think you are the only one worth riding to the rescue for."

Suzanne could not help noting the petulance in her voice. She turned to look at her friend, "Kate, they don't think that."

"Huh," the redhead scoffed, "you heard 'em, '*We're all kind of partial to our schoolmarm here,*'" she mimicked in a snotty voice, *"'We wouldn't want anything bad to happen to her.'* Boy, Suzanne, you sure got everybody bamboozled around here with your poor little, lost-love pose."

"Kathreen," Suzanne cried, "I am no poser."

"Aren't you? Then why do you keep Sonny and that Clay Anderson both stringing along? You know you like them, it's about time you made up your mind and chose one of them so everyone else can get back to normal around here. You got every dadgum cowboy on the range feelin' sorry for you and acting like Sir Galahad on your behalf."

Suzanne sat heavily down on her side of the bed, her shoulders slumped. "You're wrong," she said quietly, "it's not like that. My heart is gone—it was taken away to I don't know where. I suppose I do pose some,

I go through my days acting as if things were alright and sometimes I even forget about my heart for a little while and actually do see the light of day, but mostly the sun has ceased to shine for me. You have come and with you has come a breath of fresh air—for the most part, but now you've turned on me and I just don't understand why."

Both girls sat silently for awhile, Suzanne's last remark hanging awkwardly in the air while the lamplight flickered their shadows on the wall. Finally, with a sigh, and feeling blue, she lifted the covers and got into bed, her back to Kathreen.

Kathreen turned the page, pretending to read. At length she swallowed hard and said, "I just don't know why every darned cowpoker has to be in love with you. The other girls in this town must hate your guts."

Chaffing under her friend's comment, Suzanne said nothing, but just pulled the covers up around her chin and thought, *"Meaner than a two-striped snake with a toothache."* Two-Bits had it right, she mused and made a slight scoff.

"What are you scoffing at?" Kathreen demanded, "It's not funny."

"Your book's upside-down, you big whiner," Suzanne replied.

Kathreen looked down at the book and then threw it across the room to where it thudded against the wall. She blew out the lamp plunging them into darkness, and flounced down into the bed, causing the springs to squeak in protest, then she yanked at the covers. Suzanne giggled at her friend's irritation, and yanked the covers back.

Kathreen lay all tense for a few moments and then finally relaxed and rolled onto her back.

"It's not funny," she said again, then reached to prod a finger into Suzanne's ribs.

Suzanne jumped and made a little screech, then broke out laughing.

"It is, too," she said. "That Two-Bits Thompson is head over heels in love with you, even if he does think you're meaner than a two-striped snake with a toothache."

"No-he's-not," Kathreen said, and taking up her pillow, she tried to bury Suzanne's head under it. The two girls struggled and began to fight over the pillow until Suzanne grabbed up her own pillow and smacked the redhead in the dark.

"Oof," Kathreen grunted and then said, "That was a striped snake, you ninny, not a two-striped snake," and she hit her with the pillow. . ."get-it-right."

The battle with the pillows waged on, with the girls making grunts and squeals until Suzanne's father called out, "You two young ladies think you might finish your socializing any time soon and seek your repose?"

"How far does this road go?" Kathreen asked. She and Suzanne were walking on the road north of town with Nuisance one evening after supper a week later. Kathreen had wanted to see the place where Deputy Bollinger had attacked her. Suzanne had reluctantly agreed since it was a nice evening for a walk, after the heat of the day.

"I am not sure," Suzanne said. "I know it goes past the Nelson place and the Box 7 is some miles this way too." She gave a quizzical look at her friends to note her reaction to that bit of information.

"Can we go out there?"

Suzanne scoffed, "Where, the Box 7? Why would we want to go out there?"

Kathreen shrugged, "No particular reason—I thought we could take a horseback ride to someplace on this road and that seems like as good a place as any. Have you ever been out there?"

Suzanne said, "I'll tell you what, I've been meaning to visit the Nelson place for some time now. I have a few things for Carla and Emeline. Why don't we pack a lunch and pay them a visit tomorrow, and if we still have time I can take you out to see the Don Juan of the Pecos, if you must."

Kathreen gave her a withering look and said, "Yeah, like I'm just dying to see that bow-legged toad—of course you could see where your Sheriff Anderson calls home, too, couldn't you?"

"Alright, enough teasing. I would like to see the Box 7 spread. I have never been that far out. Do you want to ride the horses or take the buggy?"

"Do you have a lot of stuff to take to the Nelsons?" Kathreen asked.

"No, just some articles of clothing and our lunch."

"Let's ride then," the redhead said, "that way we won't have to stick to the road."

Suzanne frowned, "What do you mean—we have to take the road to get there."

"I don't know, maybe we'll want to go down by the river—maybe we'll want to chase jack rabbits out in the sage or something. I might even beat you in a race."

Suzanne smiled and shrugged, "Okay, but we better not stray too far from the road, there is still the danger of Indians and desperadoes lurking about, as I well know."

Kathreen looked skeptically at her friend. "Indians, desperadoes—we could bring a couple of guns along, can you shoot?"

"Of course I can," Suzanne replied, "I shot that big buffalo bull whose robe you saw in my room. I can shoot, can you?"

"I've never tried, but I bet I could. Do you have one of those little hand ones?"

"I have both a rifle and a pistol that Colt bought for me. We will bring them along and you can wear the handgun on your hip like a rootin'-tootin' buckaroo."

Chapter Fifteen

Aurora and Ida

Rusty led the way back down the draw in the dark. A low nicker off to their right led them to where the horses were tied. Rusty and Lance each took one of the girls from Sonny and placed them behind their own saddles, leaving the injured cowboy free to ride unhampered. They quickly mounted and rode on down the draw, following it until it eventually led out onto the prairie. In the starlight they could just make out the tracks the Comanche band had made in their earlier passing, and urged their horses into an easy lope to put distance between themselves and any pursuit.

They had been riding for about fifteen minutes when the little girl behind Rusty began to tap on his shoulder. He turned to look back at her and saw a look of urgency in her eyes. Thinking she was still frightened of the Indians, he gave her a reassuring smile, patted her leg, and spurred his pony faster.

The little girl tapped him again, this time more insistently, and Rusty realized she wanted him to stop. He held up a hand to the others and pulled his pony in.

"What are we stopping for?" Lance called.

"This kid needs something," Rusty said, "just a minute." Turning to the girl he asked, "What's wrong?"

The girl mumbled something from behind the gag in her mouth and the cowboy realized they had not undone them on either girl. He quickly reached back to loosen the knots of the gag and told Lance to do the same on the girl behind him.

"I gotta go potty," the older girl told Rusty as soon as he removed the gag.

"Oh, brother," Rusty said and glanced back in the direction they had come. He slid a leg over his pommel and jumped to the ground to reach for his young charge.

The girl behind Lance began to whimper when he removed her gag, and she tried to climb down from the horse when she saw her sister on the ground.

"She has to go, too," the older girl said.

Reaching back, Lance placed an arm around the little towhead, and handed her down to Rusty. He took the girl and set her beside her sister.

Sonny lifted his head and said in a dazed voice, "What's going on?"

"Gotta make a quick stop," Lance told him, "These kids need to find a bush."

Rusty directed the two children to a spot just off the trail and pointed at some milkweed. "That weed's pretty good for wipin'. . . use the soft side. Now hurry."

Sonny reached for the canteen tied to his saddle and took a sip. "My head feels like my brains are scrambled," he said when he had finished taking a few swallows.

"You going to be alright to ride?" Lance asked.

"I reckon there ain't no point in hangin' 'round here to see if them Comanche have any headache powders," he shrugged. "Where's those young'uns?"

The two little girls came back from behind the bush, the older one leading the younger by the hand. They stopped in front of Rusty and waited for him to lift them to the horses, but then the younger one let go of her sister's hand and ran to where Lance sat his horse. Reaching up to him, she waited for him to help her. Lance reached down, took her by the arm and smiling at her, lifted her up to set her in place behind his saddle. The child wrapped her arms about his waist and snuggled against his back.

"Huh," Rusty scoffed, "looks like you finally found a gal that likes you."

"Let's ride," Sonny said.

Rusty mounted and kicked his boot free of the stirrup and held out a hand to the older girl. She tried to reach the stirrup but couldn't until Rusty pulled her up by the arm high enough for her to put a foot in it, after that she was able to swing her leg over the horse and settle to a seat behind him.

They started out again at a brisk gallop, with the children clutching the backs of their rescuers, and rode on south through the night towards their camp. As the animals began to tire, they slowed the pace to a lope and then finally to a trot which was maintained until they rode up to the wagon. They had been in the saddle for more than three hours and the girls, in spite of the rough gait, had to be awakened, then lifted down.

There was no indication of pursuit by the Indians, but Sonny told Rusty to stand watch and indicated Lance should tend to the girls. "I gotta lay down," he said and wandered off to find his blankets.

Rusty took his rifle and walked to a large clump of mesquite along their back-trail. Here he took up a position to watch.

Lance tied the horses and then came back to poke about the fire pit and feed some grass and sticks to a few embers glowing there. The two little girls came sleepily over and stood there watching as he coxed a small blaze to life.

"What are your names?" he said.

The older girl answered, "I am Aurora and she is Ida."

"How old are you?"

"Seven, almost eight—she's only five," Aurora said. Ida held up five little fingers and smiled shyly at the cowboy.

"Are you girls alright? Did those Indians hurt you or do anything bad to you?"

Both girls looked at each other and slowly shook their heads. "No, they just taked us," Ida said. She stepped to where Lance was kneeling, feeding sticks into the fire, and placed a hand on his shoulder.

"She means took us," Aurora explained, with a knowing nod.

"Well, how did they get you? What were you two doing?" He reached an encircling arm about Ida.

Aurora said, "We was down by the creek picking blackberries and they just came out of nowhere and grabbed us and carried us away before we could even make a sound." The girl made this declaration while walking around in a tight little circle with her arms lifted in an extended shrug of bewilderment, as though she still couldn't believe that such a thing could happen. She finished up by saying, "Mama is going to be so mad at us."

"Does your mama get mad at you often?" Lance asked.

Aurora looked at him puzzled, "No," she said. "Not very often."

"Not unless we do something really, really, really bad," Ida put in, "Then she does."

"We were not supposed to go out of sight of the house unless we were with a grownup," Aurora said, "I'm afraid we did this time—now we're in for it."

Lance swallowed a chuckle, "I'll bet she will be so glad to see you she'll forget all about being mad at you," he said. "Where is your mama?"

"She's at home," Ida said matter of factly.

"Yeah, with papa," Aurora added.

"What's your papa's name and where do you live?"

"We're not supposed to talk to strangers," Aurora asserted as though suddenly remembering these instructions.

"Oh, pardon me, my name is Lance Gilles, how do you do?" Smiling, he stuck out a hand to the two children, who promptly took it and shook it vigorously, saying they did fine. Lance took a few minutes to explain that he was cowboying for the Cross Sabers, who Sonny and Rusty were, and that they had been catching wild horses when the Indians wrecked their camp and stole Hank and Oscar.

"Now that we are no longer strangers," Lance chuckled, "do you think you can tell me who your papa is and where you live?"

"Our papa is Mr. Carlson, Hans Carlson, and we have a farm on the Nueces River."

"Mama's name is Hildegard," Ida said. She pushed past her sister and tried to climb into Lance's lap. Both girls crowded the cowboy and seemed fearful of the dark.

"Where'd that other man go?" Aurora asked and looked off in the direction Rusty had taken.

"Rusty is standing guard to protect us from danger. He will sound a warning if there is any trouble. Are you girls hungry."

Both of the girls nodded their heads. "But we don't want no mule meat, those brutal savages killed a perfectly good mule and ate it," Aurora asserted.

Lance smiled to himself and rose to his feet. He patted the girls on the back and said, "I think there is some leftover prairie chicken and a biscuit or two, would you girls like that?"

Both girls nodded again with solemn expressions on their little faces. It was plain to Lance they were remembering their manners and waiting to be offered something to eat. "Well, take a seat there by the fire and I'll see if I can rustle you up some grub," he said.

Lance dug about the wagon and found the food and brought two plates over to hand to the girls.

Both girls took the food and bowed their heads. It was clear to the cowboy they expected him to give thanks for the meal.

The young cowboy shifted uncomfortably and glanced to see if Rusty or Sonny were listening, then quickly muttered, "Lord, bless this food, in your name, amen."

"Amen," both girls echoed, then Ida asked, "Do you have any jelly?"

"Say, please," Aurora corrected.

"Please."

Lance laughed and tousled the littler one's hair. "Afraid not, how about some molasses, would that be alright?"

"Yes, please, that will just hit the spot," Ida said around a mouthful of prairie chicken.

The cowboy chuckled and went in search of the sweetener.

While the girls ate, he fixed a couple of blankets for them on the grass near the fire and then prepared his own bed nearby. When the girls had finished he sent them off to go potty and then helped them to their blankets. Once he had them settled, he rolled into his own and was nearly asleep when little Ida crept over and lifted the covers to snuggle in beside him. Soon Aurora joined them with her blanket and snuggled against his back.

Later, Rusty found them like that and hesitated to wake Lance for his turn at guard. "I wonder if he planned that," he muttered and nudged his friend with the toe of his boot.

The next morning, the camp was awakened by a loud clatter when a bucket was knocked over and went rolling off to bang into the wagon wheel.

Rusty sprang from his blanket, his pistol drawn to stare in the direction of the sound. The early morning sun rays were filtering through the trees and dappled the side of Hank, their missing mule. The animal was nosing about the wagon, looking for something to eat.

"Would you look at that crazy mule," he said.

Sonny sat up, a hand to his head, and said, "Hank, is that you?" He stared bleary-eyed at the mule, who turned to stare back at the cowboy. The mule's tail was held aloft from a very singed and sore bottom. When Hank spotted Rusty, he broke out into a loud, staccato braying. It was obvious to all, he held no high regard for his assailant of the night before.

Lance came running into camp, wondering what was going on, and then, spotting the mule, stopped short. "Looks like ol' Hank's back," he laughed. "Look at that tail, maybe we should rename him Skyrocket, after last night. Rusty, what in tarnation did you do to him anyway?"

"He setted his tail on fire," Ida declared with a positive nod of her head.

Rusty grinned sheepishly and then began to chuckle at the spectacle the mule made. He got up and walked over towards the braying mule. Hank stopped his racket and hurried away from the approaching redhead.

"He ain't havin' nothin' to do with you," Sonny growled. "I need some coffee, after breakfast we'll catch him and doctor up his behind. Is there anything left to eat?"

"Awhum, you said 'behind,'" the little five-year-old said. Her older sister prodded her to be quiet.

Sonny squinted against the morning sun at their two little visitors. Chuckling, he scoffed and then moaned as the movement hurt his head. "Who're the little wild roses?"

Lance squatted down and began helping Ida put her shoes on. "Boys, meet Aurora and Ida Carlson, two little yellow roses of Texas.

"I can tie my own shoes now," Ida said and pushed Lance's hand away. "I am five years old."

Rusty and Sonny came over and squatted down next to where the two girls sat on a blanket.

"Howdy, yellow rose," Rusty said, looking at the bigger girl. "My name is Rusty Chambers, now which one are you?"

"Her name is Aurora and he's a girl and he's not a boy and he's not a rose either," Ida stated emphatically.

"He's not eh? You sure about that?" Rusty chuckled, amused with the child's confusion of he and she.

Ida puckered up her brow in exasperation and with hands on her hips stated loudly, "Yes I am."

"She's not a yellow rose of Texas?" Rusty asked in surprise. "Just look at all this yellow hair—are you sure?"

Aurora sat there grinning while her little sister got to her knees and said, "He's a girl." Giggling, she pushed Rusty over backwards, making him lose his balance and fall to a sitting position.

Laughing, Rusty warded of the rambunctious child and said, "You look like a yellow rose, too, maybe I should call you Rose, what do you think about that?"

"My name's Id-aah!" she cried, "I ain't no rose."

Sonny was laughing and joined in, "But you are pretty as a rose with all that yeller hair, ain't cha?"

Ida turned to look at Sonny with a big smile and then rushed to clasp Lance's legs about the knees. Shyly, she looked back at the tall cowboy over her shoulder and said, "Yes I am."

"Well, Lance," Rusty spoke up, "Looks like you have a new conquest."

Sonny turned his attention to the older girl who stood watching the antics of her younger sister with an indulgent smile.

"How about you, young lady, you're purty as a yellow rose, too, aren't you? How come you're so purty?"

"I get my fine looks from my mother, it's true, but I am not as expressive with my affections as my younger sister," the older girl said soberly.

Sonny swallowed a chuckle and held out his hand. "Let me introduce myself. My name is Sonny Saber, is your name Aurora?"

"Yes, Aurora Carlson, pleased to meet you." She made a little curtsey and shook his hand.

Ida stepped over next to her sister with her eyes shining in anticipation and watched as Aurora met Sonny. When he let go of her hand and held it out to the littler girl, she took it, pumped it up and down vigorously and giggled. "I am Ida Carlson, pleased to meet 'cha, too. Are you the man that was sleeping with the Indians?"

Sonny stood to his feet with a grin and tousled her hair. "Reckon I am, little darlin'," he said.

"I didn't like sleeping there, I'm glad you got away."

"Me neither and I'm glad you got away, too. I don't think those Indians know how to appreciate little roses like you two," Sonny said.

With the introductions out of the way, everyone got busy fixing breakfast and straightening up camp. The two girls had adopted Lance and were constantly under foot until he set them to gathering wood for the fire with a stern warning to not go out of sight.

When breakfast was over, Sonny and Rusty set out to catch Hank, while Lance supervised the girls in cleaning up the breakfast things and getting the wagon packed.

Hank would not let Rusty get anywhere near him and Sonny finally had to rope the mule in order to doctor his burned hind end. Whenever Rusty came over, the mule would break into a frenzied bucking and lunging against the rope. It was all he and Sonny could do to get him tied off to a tree. They finally had to call Lance over to help, but it wasn't until Rusty moved back away, that Hank let the other two riders near him. Sonny quickly tied a rope about his neck and then caught a loop around a hind foot. He passed the end of that rope up through the one about the mule's neck and pulled the foot up tight and tied it off. Hank was left standing on three legs.

With the mule disabled, Sonny directed Rusty to bring the carbolic salve from the wagon, but when Rusty came over, Hank once again broke into a fit of lunging and kicking, until he lost his balance and fell in a heap at the end of the rope.

"What the heck did you do to this jackass anyway?" Sonny said, "He just plum don't like you."

Rusty started laughing. "Can't say's I blame him much. Did you know that farts are explosive?"

"What?" Sonny looked at his young friend in unbelief. "Where'd that spring from?"

Rusty shifted a little uncomfortably while handing the salve to Sonny, then told how he had wrecked his father's plow when he was a kid. Lance had been listening and both cowboys had a good laugh.

"I figured, if it worked with Dad's jenny, it would work on this ol' windbag here, so I touched him off there in the glen last night."

"Well, it sure spooked those redskins and I'll have to admit, it boogered me some, too," Sonny scoffed. "Trouble is, I am afraid old Hank here isn't about to forgive you. Why don't you try and make up to him while we got him all trussed up like this, and maybe see if you can doctor his sore butt, maybe then he won't be tryin' to kick your head off every time you walk by."

Rusty approached the downed mule, who lunged at him with its teeth bared. He stood in front of the animal and talked low, soothing nonsense, and tried to scratch between his ears, but had to keep jerking his hand back each time when Hank tried to bite him. Eventually the mule grew tired and grumbled his disgust with a long chuckle in his throat. Rusty was finally able to touch him, and eventually Hank quit head-shying and let the repentant cowboy cajole him, and scratch behind his ears. But it was a good hour before Rusty was able to apply the soothing salve to the mule's smarting posterior.

Leading her little sister by the hand, Aurora came over to where Lance squatted near the fire, scrubbing out the frying pan. She began to tug on his sleeve.

"Mr. Lance," she said, "Ida stinks."

The cowboy looked up in surprise. He had noticed that neither girl was none to clean, and after all they had been through, he was not to surprised.

"Well, how would you girls like to have a nice, warm, bath?" he said.

"You can't see us without our clothes," Ida said with a solemn shake of her head, her lips pursed in a concerned frown.

Lance chuckled and tousled her hair again, "I won't, sweetheart, but did you know I have little sisters back home and I have given them baths before?"

This was a new concept for the five-year-old and she stared up at him in disbelief. "You bathed girls?" she asked.

Chuckling, Lance nodded, "Yep, not only did I bathe them, I changed their diapers too."

Ida looked at Aurora. "I didn't know cowboys could do that." she said.

Aurora shrugged, "We have no clean clothes to put on."

"How would it be if I fix a tub of warm water in the back of the wagon and you girls can be out of sight and have a nice bath at the same time? I even have some nice smelling soap and Aurora can help Ida get washed. Would you like that?"

The two girls nodded and looked expectantly at the young cowboy.

"If you give me your clothes I will wash them out, too, but you will have to wear them wet until they dry, or else sit tight in the wagon until they do."

With the patience of the very young, Aurora said, "We will sit tight in the wagon until they dry."

"We will not sit in the sun because it makes freckles," Ida asserted with a knowing look and her eyebrows raised.

Lance built up the fire and heated water and after making some room in the back of the wagon, he proceeded to fix a bath in the tub. The girls were helped up and he had them toss out their dirty clothes, which he washed out in a bucket of warm water and then draped over the wagon tongue in the sunlight to dry.

"How we going to pull this wagon with just one mule?" Rusty asked.

"I been thinking on that," Sonny said. "I guess we're not. I thought you boys said you could hitch your saddle horses."

"Yeah, we did, but that was before we got the mule back. We sure can't hitch no mule and a horse together."

Sonny nodded in agreement. "Let's see if we can fit these harnesses over your two cowponies."

Lance continued to putter about doing camp chores while keeping one ear tuned to the splashing and chatter in the back of the wagon. Sonny and Rusty harnessed the two younger cowboys' reluctant saddle horses, while Sonny's little mare, Penny, and Hank looked upon the proceedings with the indifference of their kind, since it didn't involve them. They just contentedly chewed on some mesquite bean pods that were lying about.

There came the unexpected thud of horses' hooves and four riders rode into camp. Sonny and Rusty left off tussling with the horses and walked over, while Lance stepped casually to the back of the wagon and hissed at the girls to not make any noise.

"Howdy," the lead rider said. He was a big man on a long-legged bay gelding, and sat tall in the saddle with an easy manner. He sported a bushy walrus mustache, wore a tied-down Colt on his right hip and had the silver star of a Texas Ranger pinned to the front of his leather vest.

Sonny stepped up, wiping his palms on the seat of his pants and nodded. "Howdy, step down and rest a spell, we finished breakfast but I reckon we still got coffee if you all would care to have a cup."

The big man said, "We'd be obliged," and swung down from the saddle. Two of the other three riders also wore Ranger badges but the last man had more the look of a dirt farmer than anything.

"I'm Captain Ellison and we're up from the Nueces River country, trailin' a band of Comanche for nigh onto a week now. The trail's led us to your camp," the captain said and accepted a cup of coffee from Rusty. "Have you seen anything of them?"

"I should shout," Sonny said, "the varmints wrecked our camp and run off two good mules, then ate one of 'em."

"How'd they manage that?" the ranger asked.

"Me and the boys here got a passel of broomtail mustangs corralled up in a box canyon a few miles east of here. We was up there when they hit."

"I see you got one of your mules back," the captain said looking to where Hank stood holding his tail aloft. "Wha'd they do, try to barbecue his behind while he was still alive? He looks a little singed."

"Yeah, he was, but it's a long story."

"How'd you get him back?"

"We went and got 'im," Sonny said.

The farmer-looking fellow stepped in front of the captain, an anxious look on his face. "You didn't see anything of a couple little towheaded girls did you?"

Lance strode over to where the men stood around the fire. "We sure did," he interrupted, "are you Mr. Carlson—Hans Carlson?"

"Yes," the man blurted out and turned to look at the youth. "What's happened to my little girls?"

"Got 'em right here, all safe and sound," Lance beamed. "They're in the back of the wagon gettin' cleaned up."

"Oh, thank God," Carlson cried and ran to the back of the wagon. "Rory, Idee, where are you?"

"Oh, Papa," both girls cried out at once, "here we are." Two curly blonde heads covered with soapsuds appeared at the back opening of the wagon. Carlson grabbed up both girls in a bear hug and began to laugh and cry and plant kisses all over both their happy faces.

"Papa," little Ida said, "Don't let those mens see us like this."

Both cowboys and rangers stood watching the happy reunion with big smiles, hiding moist eyes behind the rims of their coffee cups.

"You boys done a good job rescuing these young'uns from those savages," the captain said. "I wish all our expeditions ended this happily." His two men nodded in agreement.

It took nearly till noon to reach the entrance of the boxed canyon. Both boys had managed to harness their saddle ponies to the wagon and ride them bare-back while Sonny led the way. They bucked, balked, started, stopped, and nearly had a runaway twice before they traveled the few short miles up the valley to the canyon's mouth. Reluctantly, Hank followed along, tied on behind.

Sonny was down studying the tracks when they finally rode up. "Looks like the rest of the wild bunch came in here to water," he said. "I don't see any fresh tracks leading back out."

"You think they're in here?" Lance asked excitedly.

Sonny nodded, "You guys drop that wagon about twenty feet or so inside the fence and get your horses out of that harness and under saddle." He swung down and began to close the gate.

"Why we leavin' the wagon here?" Lance asked, "We had a heck of a time gettin' these cow ponies under harness."

"We need that wagon in the way so that the mustangs can't get a run at this fence and jump it," Sonny grunted as he dropped the heavy end of the gate and tied it shut.

Rounding the corner where the canyon opened up, the three riders soon spied the stallion and the rest of the wild bunch, trotting about nervously up near where the captured horses were watching and pulling at their anchoring logs.

"They'll probably make a run for it," Sonny said, "pick a horse and rope it. Hopefully they won't get by the wagon and jump out. I'm going for the stud."

Slowly, they rode forward, the alert animals watching their approach with ears pricked forward. The stallion began to pace back and forth, snorting through flared nostrils, and then with a squeal, he broke for an opening, sweeping to the far side of the cowboys, and the chase was on. The others fled after him, while Sonny shook out a loop and spurred for the big grulla. Lance and Rusty fell in behind, their horses not as fresh from having hauled the wagon earlier.

Riding around the bend at the opening, the riders saw the horses slow up and break in confusion around both sides of the wagon to come up against the fence, their momentum lost. Three ropes sang out almost simultaneously and settled over two colts and one stallion. Sonny had caught the stud and now a fight ensued that nearly made him wish he hadn't, for the horse began to buck, paw and snap at the rope viciously. Suddenly the stud bolted and ran at his captor with teeth bared. Penny, Sonny's quick little cowpony, ducked around the end of the wagon, fleeing from before the enraged stallion, but not before receiving a painful bite on the rump. The little mare squealed and swapped ends, causing the slack rope to pass between the legs of the charging wild horse, who was once again making another break for freedom. When the rope came taught, there was a loud pop and the little mare was nearly yanked off her feet, as the grulla stallion made a perfect somersault when the rope around its neck jerked his head down and back between his legs.

Sonny received a severe chafing from his gun belt when the rope cut back across his right hip, and would have been knocked out of the saddle had the rope not pinned his leg. The well-trained little mare quickly turned and backed, keeping tension on the rope. Sonny leaped to the ground and rushed to the downed stud. The horse was screaming in defiance and trying to get his legs under him, when the tall cowboy landed on its neck and deftly looped a pigging string around an up thrust hind hoof, and then hauled it up to take a quick wrap around a front foot. He leaped safely away, as the horse's head came up with bared teeth snapping at him.

"Dang," Rusty called, "I thought he was going to eat ya." The redhead had his own hands full with a line-back dun, and Lance was busy tussling with the palomino. The other horses had fled back up the canyon

Sonny mounted Penny and kneed her forward, taking up the slack in his rope. The stallion, still squealing and bellowing, kept trying to rise on two feet, only to fall heavily backwards each time. Sonny flipped a couple more loops around the downed horse's hooves and then stepped from the saddle to untie his rope from the horn. He coiled up the slack and tied the shortened rope off to the wagon axle, then reached in and retrieved another lariat before mounting back up.

"You fellers try hazing those colts you caught back up the canyon and get 'em tied off to a couple of logs, then meet me back here and give me a hand with this big boy. I'm going to go drag down the biggest log I can find."

By the time Sonny had drug a stout log back to the groaning stallion, Lance and Rusty were riding up. The captive horse lifted his head at their approach, the whites of his eyes showing, and gave one of those half squeal, half nicker, grunts of anger.

"Boy is he up-setted-off," Lance said.

"I reckon," Sonny replied and dismounted. Untying his lasso from the wagon, he retied it to the heavy log. "I'm going to try and free his legs now and I want you two to sit on his head so's he don't kick my brains out."

The boys approached the horse from behind and pounced on his neck. Lance and Rusty tried to hold his head down but were nearly thrown off.

"Don't let him get his teeth in ya," Sonny panted while grabbing at the rope, "Ear 'em down." He waited until Rusty knelt forward, caught one of the stud's ears in his teeth, and bit down on it. The horse squealed in pain and stopped thrashing, forgetting everything but his smarting ear.

Quickly Sonny loosened the coils of rope around the horse's feet. "Look out boys, he's 'bout to unwind."

They all three jumped back, Rusty scrambling away on his hands and knees before regaining his feet. The grulla kicked his feet free of the remaining entanglement and lunged up to run back up the canyon towards his mares.

There was an audible whoosh of air from the horse's lungs when the rope came tight, choking him down and jerking him to a stop. The drag log went sailing through the air to land with a thud behind the horse, which again bolted as he felt the rope relax about his neck, only to be brought up short a second time, the log launching anew. Breaking stride only momentarily, the big horse charged on up the valley, bouncing and pulling the log through the grass in a fast skid behind, while the cowboys stood watching in awe.

Rusty stared after the horse in grudging admiration, "Man, he's mean enough to fight with a snake an' give 'im the first bite." The others nodded in agreement.

A week later, out in the middle of the pond, Sonny eased up onto the back of the quivering stallion, while Lance and Rusty, one on either side, held fast to ropes running to the hackamore about the grulla's head. Sonny gingerly sat bareback on the stud and reached forward to draw the blindfold from under the headstall. When the mouse-colored horse could see again, he snorted at the withers-deep water he was standing in and vigorously shook his head. Lance and Rusty loosened their grips on the ropes and the stallion turned to look at the man on his back, the whites of his eyes showing, then with a curious sniff at the water he just stood there, his ears alternately twitching forwards and back again. The unaccustomed weight on his back was momentarily forgotten until he felt pressure on his nose from the hackamore. Sonny took a firm hold on the rope and gently kicked the big horse in the ribs.

The horse erupted into a wild, pitching, frenzy, boiling the water of the pond into a dirty, brown froth, as he kicked and bucked under the long-legged cowboy. Sonny wrapped his legs around the slippery, churning body and grabbed a handful of mane in order to hang on. He had a decided advantage over the bronco as the depth of the water hindered the stallion's ability to get airborne and dislodge him from its back.

For a full ten minutes, Lance and Rusty watched in awe, their mouths agape at the strength and stamina of the wild horse. How furiously the animal fought to regain his freedom. Lance was almost sorry to see him lose, but little by little, his bucking slowed to crow-hops and then finally to a prancing standstill.

Sonny patted the neck of the soaking, horse and said, "Atta-boy, easy now—that didn't hurt none, did it? You'll be just fine—just fine." With low, soothing words he talked to the heaving horse until the walleyes disappeared and the flattened ears came up. Sonny clicked a couple of times with his tongue and touched heels to the animal's sides while pulling on the hackamore rope to the left. The horse's head came around and the stud made a couple of quick, hopping, lunges towards the shore and then stopped. Sonny did it again and the smoky-looking horse crow-hopped some more and then began to walk into shallower water. Sonny kicked him into a trot around the edge of the pond once the water dropped below the horse's knees, and then reined him back and forth, starting and stopping him, until the stallion caught on and became responsive to his commands and the pressure on his nose and ribs.

"I'm going to bring 'im out on dry ground," Sonny called to the two friends. "If he unloads again, just let go the lines and let'er buck."

He rode the snorting horse up out of the water and began to maneuver him around the pond again. The grulla took about ten rough steps and then bogged his head and stuck his tail at the clouds, sending Sonny flying over his neck, to land in the bulrushes and tulles. The horse just stood there looking after him, his ears pricked forwards and then curling his lips, he opened his mouth in a silent horse laugh, showing Sonny his teeth.

Lance and Rusty burst into raucous laughter as Sonny came wading to shore, picking moss and duck-weed from his hair. He gave the two a sheepish grin and said, "One of you cackling crows haul my saddle over and see if ya can screw it down tight on 'im while I find my boots." He sat on the bank in just his jeans and hat and pulled on his boots while Rusty and Lance held and saddled the stallion. The horse humped his back at the unaccustomed weight of the rigging and pawed with a front hoof when the cinch strap was pulled tight. Rusty gained two more hitches by thudding a well aimed knee into the stud's belly after the animal puffed up his stomach at the feel of the cinch, and nearly got kicked for his efforts.

"He's salty enough," the redheaded cowboy said, "You sure you want to dryland 'im?"

Sonny nodded, "Yep, he already knows I can ride 'im in there and unless there's another flood, most of Texas is dry land. Let's show 'im what it's like haulin' my freight on terra-firma."

"On what?" Rusty seemed confused. "Oh, you mean on dry ground."

Sonny slipped his bandana under the headstall and over the stud's eyes and had Rusty loosen the lunge lines that the boys had been holding. He then grabbed the horn and swung into the saddle, catching the off stirrup with his right boot. Rusty jerked the blindfold free and scrambled for safety.

With a defiant bellow that brought every horses' head up in the valley, the stallion threw his head at the ground and showed his rump to the swallows. Sonny hauled on the hackamore rope and raked the bronc's shoulders with his spurs. With what could only be described as grunts and squeals, the horse bounced around the pond on stiff legs like a jack rabbit with a new pogo stick, but try as he might, he could not dislodge this creature and the clutching apparatus from off his back. Finally his head came up and he took off like the proverbial bat, in a dead run for the fence of the enclosure. In a single bound, he sailed over the top rail to land without breaking stride, and race off up the valley. Sonny, sitting easy, with the wind whistling past his ears and sawing at the hackamore rope, guided him and let him run. They rounded the bend at the lower end of the box canyon, swept through the open gate on out into the larger valley floor and raced away.

It was a full half hour before the two boys looked up from the horse they were saddling, to the sound of thunder rumbling from under the hooves of the wild stallion, and saw Sonny riding the lathered horse at full tilt back to camp. It looked like the horse would jump the fence back into the enclosure, but at the last moment Sonny hauled back on the rope and set him on his haunches, bringing him to a snorting, trembling, stop.

"Whooee," he cried, "talk about ridin' the wind—I might just as well be forkin' a tornado."

"Tornado," Lance called, "That'd be a good name for 'im, Tornado."

"He shore can run," Sonny drawled, "He took me clean back to the spring before I could get him turned around and headed back this way. Look at 'im, he's barely turned a hair and ain't even breathing hard, got a little suds on 'im's all—he's just gotten warmed up." It was true, the big stallion stood nosing the top rails of the fence with flaring nostrils and then at Sonny's urging, turned and trotted through the gate Rusty swung open, and on into the enclosure.

Chapter Sixteen

Through the Wilderness

Darkness overtook him while crossing a high grassy plateau. Fearing loss of the trail, Colt decided to make a dry camp at the base of a gnarled old pine tree. It had been struck by lightning so many times that the youth hesitated a moment, his eyes on the heavens. The stars were already freckling the night sky, even as the sun faded to a pinkish glow on the western horizon, back-lighting a panorama of rugged peaks, cliffs and mountains. Somewhere beyond all that, a beautiful girl waited.

"Don't look like much chance of rain," he muttered. "Reckon I can curl up here as well as anywhere. This old tree looks like a resident lightning rod, but it doesn't look like there's any danger of a storm up here tonight."

A warm breeze was blowing from the north. Risking a small fire, Colt shielded a match with his hat and touched it to a dried root wad of a small manzanita plant. The dead clump flared up like someone had poured kerosene on it, burning hot. Quickly he added some more short pieces of red Manzanita. Its curling, paper-thin bark blazed brightly, and he added some sticks of greasewood. He spent a few moments beating out the small flames that ignited the short grass around his fire site. Once the ground around it was singed black, he allowed the little blaze to burn down to glowing embers and then placed the frying pan from his pack over them. Digging out the bacon and eggs, he soon had strips of bacon sizzling and sputtering in the pan. He watched the grease as it popped over the sides, causing mini-flames to flare up and send bursts of light into the darkness.

"I'm not so sure this was such a bright idea," he said. "Some Apaches could easily smell this fire, if not the bacon, should they be downwind." Nervously he finished cooking the bacon and cracked a few eggs into the hot grease. Salting and peppering them, he removed the frying pan from the heat. Setting the pan on a rock, he moved a few yards away from the fire to allow his eyes to adjust to the darkness. Looking in the direction of his back trail, he listened but heard no other sound than the night wind sighing through the old pine and the yodeling cry of a coyote off in the canyon.

Returning to the fire, Colt took a stick and spread the embers then picked up the frying pan and checked his eggs. They were almost fried too hard. Carefully, he slid them onto a tin plate alongside his bacon and set the pan down. Hunkering down on his heels, he gingerly began to eat a hot strip of bacon with his fingers. He had forgotten to give thanks for the food, but instead of stopping to do so, he just kept right on eating while the thought that he should be more grateful played in the back of his mind.

This was a new thing for Colt. The food was good, the weather and his campsite comfortable, and the danger past, at least for now, and yet, instead of a thankful heart, he felt almost a resentment, as if God owed him and he put off asking the blessing or giving thanks. Finishing the meal, he began to clean up, all the while wondering at the hardheartedness he felt.

"Lord, I suppose I should be grateful—you got me out of that tomb of a mountain—but frankly, I'm still a little bit mad at you. The stuff that happened to Penny—that wasn't right and while I'm on the subject, the stuff that has happened to me ain't exactly right, either. What did we do to deserve any of this? And Suzanne, what did she do to deserve all this terrible upset to our life? Right now I feel more like an ant you are poking around with a stick, than a much-loved child of God. You're going to have to excuse me until I get over my mad and if you're going to kill me in the meantime. . ." he paused and thought about what he was thinking, hell had to be full of people who were all mad at God. He finished by saying, "well. . . I guess I'll just end up being stuck on mad, too." He knew it was a rather lame line of reasoning and thought about repenting on the spot, but then from out of nowhere, a stubborn streak kicked in and instead he rolled in his blanket, stuck the slicker under his head for a pillow, pulled his hat over his eyes and went to sleep.

A clap of thunder and a lightning strike that split the old pine tree into kindling and erupted it into flames, literally bounced Colton Saber awake. In terror, he grabbed up the blanket and slicker and ran as fast as he could away from his little camp. Another bolt of lightning struck the ground nearby, the thunder clap so loud he felt it nearly broke his eardrums. Stunned, he ran this way and that in the dark, dodging rolling blue balls of electricity that set the grass on fire and seemed to chase after him in the highly charged atmosphere.

Colt tripped over a rock and stumbled headlong into a patch of brush to land panting, face down and suspended a couple of feet above the ground. He struggled to regain his feet, his side paining him as he twisted about. To his horror, he saw one of the rolling, blue balls of Saint Elmo's fire sweep across the ground towards him. Starting at his feet, it engulfed his entire body and the surrounding bush with a snapping, crackling, blue charge of electrical current. The cowboy quivered and tingled until the charge went to ground, leaving him steaming in a strong scent of ozone.

With heart thudding in his chest, Colt saw ball after ball of electrical fire play about the camp and surrounding mountain top in a ghostly dance. The grass was burning, as well as the ravaged old pine and the rising wind was sweeping the flames higher and higher. Another ear-splitting thunder clap brought a cloudburst of rain with such fury that when the rain drops struck the burning debris of wood and grass they caused sparks to fly up into the air.

Colt scrambled from the bush to crouch beside it with the Mexican blanket wadded up in his lap and the slicker tented up over his head. Here he squatted and watched the downpour quickly douse the fires as the storm moved off to the west. He pondered the fury of the storm. Was that God? Was He trying to kill him? He doubted that—if He had wanted to, He would have. What then? Was he just trying to get his attention? Colt didn't know if God was trying to get his attention or not, but one thing he did know, spending the night in the mountains on top of lightning hill had sure got his.

Cold and wet and huddled under the slicker, Colt gritted his teeth against the pain in his side and shivered in the darkness. Occasional flashes of lightning illuminated the black crags and peaks of the *Devil's Backbone* off in the distance. He shifted his weight to sit down in the slicker and try to find a comfortable position of repose and wondered again at the blackness of the night. It was like the blackness that seemed to have collected about his life. Lost in a hostile and alien land fraught with danger, he sat and pondered the incredible shift his life had taken. Where it had once been all light and brightness and color and happy days filled with beauty, joy, and the wondrous love of his delightful Suzanne, it now found him adrift on this lonely, wind-swept plateau. The sound of the wind sighing through the grass seemed to echo the sentiments of his beleaguered soul.

What had really happened? How had he come to this place? How much time had really passed since Suzanne had so sweetly surrendered to his love and promised to be his wife? Where was she now? What was she doing and did she still wait for him?

Colt's thoughts turned to another dark and rainy night spent on a mountainside when he had vowed with certainty to Penny that he and Suzanne were of one mind and one heart—that she knew he was alive and waited for him. That was only a few weeks ago, but now he was not so sure. Did she really wait—still—after all this time?

Here in this dark place, the cowboy trembled in the night and steeled himself against insidious doubt. He would get out of this place and find his way back to her. The sun would shine again and he would know the wonder of her embrace and life would go on. He'd probably even find a way to talk to God again. But not now—he set his jaw, right now he had to try to get some sleep.

Colt came awake to the sound of something clanking. He had tumbled over onto his side during the night while still wrapped in the slicker and struggled to sit up. With the rising sun in his eyes, he turned towards the sound with a groan at the catch in his side. He looked to where the shattered and charred remains of the pine stood and saw his stuff where it had been left in his haste the night before.

Suddenly the gunnysack pack moved and then he saw a badger poke its head up. It was trying to pull his pack off to its den in a hole under a nearby boulder.

"Hey!" he yelled, "that's my stuff." He jumped to his feet and threw a couple of rocks at the animal and then ran to retrieve his pack. He was nearly on the creature when the badger left off worrying the pack and turned with an ominous hiss to face the man.

Colt made a sudden stop, realizing his mistake. There's not an ornerier critter than a badger when it's riled, and every one he'd ever had anything to do with had always seemed to be riled. This one was no exception.

The badger made a short run at him and he yelled, "Hey, you get!" and waved his arms about wildly. The badger growled and back-stepped in short, jerky, movements and then made another charge at the cowboy, its mouth open and sharp teeth snapping furiously. Colt drew his gun instinctively and was earing back the hammer when caution got the better of him. A shot might be heard by the Apache. He momentarily wished he had put more distance between himself and the gold camp, but soon forgot that as the badger rushed at him and backed him up once more. Colt turned and sprinted for the big boulder that was over the badger's hole and jumped up on top of it with the animal snapping at his heels.

The rock was a little more than four feet off the ground and maybe seven feet around. The smooth surface of the granite offered no toe holds for the badger, which kept jumping up the sides and sliding back down, all the while trying to get at the intruder and growling like a deranged dog with a sore throat.

Colt began to understand what badgering someone meant. The animal was positively relentless in its pursuit to sink its teeth into him. When it became apparent that it was not able to get up to where he was, Colt began to relax and started to laugh at the frenzied antics of the enraged critter. He sat down and decided to have a little talk with the screwy beast.

"You know," he said, "you remind me of some folks I know. Just look at you—stuck your nose in where it didn't belong and when you got caught you set about making such a fuss that you think folks will just overlook your faults if you make enough noise and get angry enough. What's the matter with you anyhow? Did your mother teach you to act like that? Come to think of it, she probably did, but that's no excuse, it still doesn't make it right. You're just lucky those sneaky Apache are hereabouts, else I'd ventilate your flea-bit hide and make me a nice Davy Crockett cap out of it."

Colt's chiding of the badger had little effect on its jumping, growling and snapping and he marveled again at its stamina and determination. "You'd think you would get tired after awhile," he grinned. "I don't think I've ever seen any critter act as stupid as you do." Suddenly he assumed an authoritative voice, one he imagined sounded like his father and shouted in a loud voice, "Now you straighten up!"

The badger stopped its jumping and stared up at him, its mouth frozen in a snarl. He could almost hear the animal say, "*Who you calling 'stupid'? Look who's perched up on that rock like some jaybird.*"

He grinned at the thought. "I didn't start this, you did," Colt said.

The badger hissed and then looked back towards the gunnysack pack.

"You leave my bacon be, that's my grub and you can't have it." The sound of annoyance in his voice caused the badger to whirl back towards him and resume its growling and jumping.

"Now, there you go again. Why don't you get a clue? You can't get up here and I ain't coming down until you beat it."

"Get off my rock and off the roof of my house!"

Colt's eyes widened in surprised glee. His imagination was working overtime. The expressions and actions of the badger were easily lending themselves to a fanciful dialog between him and the silly beast, and he began to chuckle.

"Your roof of your house, huh? Well pardon me. I'll be happy to get down if you'd just mosey your scruffy carcass down that burrow and stay put 'til I get my stuff."

"Leave the bacon." The badger had paused in a crouch and was looking sideways at his pack.

Colt smiled, "No, I ain't leavin' the bacon."

The Badger growled again and Colt, tiring of the amusement, thought of another time when he had been stranded on top of a rock in a stand-off. He had resorted to some unusual tactics and counted coup on ol' "Flour Print Shirt," the Mescalero Apache of Victorio's band.

Colt stood to his feet, causing the badger to renew its attack and then, glancing left and right as though someone might be watching, the cowboy undid his pants and made water in a steady stream down onto the enraged creature.

Surprised, the badger lost its footing in mid-leap, and fell, tumbling into a snarling, drenched, heap at the base of the rock. Jumping up, it snapped and snarled at the stream until it ended up biting at and chasing its own tail in circles for a frenzied second or two. Growling in rage, it finally managed to sink its teeth into its own rear end. The badger gave a startled yelp of pain and turned to dive down its hole.

Colt broke into spontaneous laughter and jumped from the rock. He walked over to gather up his things and stuff them in his pack. Shrugging into it, he glanced back at the badger hole and saw two angry yellow eyes staring out of the darkness.

He tipped his hat with another happy chuckle and said, "Good day to you, Mr. Badger. Now you know what it really means to get pissed off."

Colt adjusted the pack and made his way east, following the dim line of the horse trail across the grassy plateau. He was still chuckling inwardly over the incident with the badger when an unbidden thought came to his mind.

"That wasn't very nice."

He shrugged it off and said out loud, "Hey, I'm not to blame, I didn't make him act like that."

"Yes, but you know badgers are cantankerous," the voice in his head went on. *"Don't you think that was a bit crude, peeing on him like that?"*

"Naw! He deserved that—in fact he's mighty lucky I didn't plug 'im." Colt grinned at the thought.

"So you, the man here, can degrade creatures lower than yourself with impunity?"

"What?" Colt exclaimed. "I didn't degrade that badger. I merely showed him who's boss—you know, took the dominion God gave me. What do you think I should a done, pat 'im on the head and tell him what a nice little badger he was?" He rolled his eyes and solemnly shook his head, wondering at the bizarre conversation going on in his head.

As the lad made his way down the trail he began to encounter increasing clumps of manzanita brush and tried to thread his way through. He thought about the voice in his head, giving it serious thought, maybe for the first time, he wondered about it. It was a familiar voice, one he had known for along time and had always assumed it was just the normal workings of his own thought processes and still figured it was, too. But he knew that on his own, he didn't really think about, or even care much about a badger's plight, especially that particular thievin' fella, so why the sobering thoughts about what had happened? Was that his conscience? He knew that, at times, his conscience was part of the voice, but this seemed like more. It was so unexpected. Probably no one else on God's green earth cared about badgers either, and then he remembered that God sees the sparrow fall. He probably cares for badgers, too.

"Boy, Lord, is that you?" He heard no response and then reasoned that it might be. "Wow! Has this been you talking to me all this time and I haven't even known it."

But Colt knew not all the thoughts—the voices in his head—were from the Lord. There had been plenty that were not—some were of his own devising and many originated from the evil one, maybe more than he realized. How many of those had he assumed the blame for?

"So Lord," he said as he pressed past a clump of brush in the trail, "How am I supposed to know who's who?"

"You'll know," the answer seemed to come. *"If it's good and right and virtuous, it's of God, if not, it probably isn't."*

Colt studied on that for a moment. "So what's good about this?" he asked as he slipped and skidded down some loose shale in the path. "What was good about

Penny getting killed and what's good about Suzanne and me being separated for all this time?" There seemed to be no answer. Answering his own question, he suddenly blurted out, "Nothing."

It was as if a light went on somewhere inside him. If it wasn't good and right and virtuous then it wasn't of God—it was from that other character. Had he been blaming God all this time for things that had sprung from the very depths of Hell itself?

A wave of shame and humiliation brought him up short in the trail. Bowing his head, he said, "Sorry, Lord. I'm sorry for my anger and for spouting off and using bad language and blaming you for Penny's death. And for Suzanne's and my separation, and all that's happened to me, and for not asking the blessing or being thankful for my supper last night. I suppose I should be sorry for pis—peeing on the badger, too, but I'm not really, so you're going to have to help me with that if it's even an issue."

He grinned at that last and scoffed at himself, then went on his way down the mountainside whistling.

The trail Colt followed appeared to be more of a game trail than the oft traveled track of the Guaynopa caravan and he wondered if he had lost it somewhere along the way. The hillside he was winding down was a maze of manzanita bushes, all with a profusion of green berries in clusters. He thought he had heard that the Spanish word for apple was manzanita and he wondered if the berries were edible. Picking a few, he popped one in his mouth and bit into it. A tart juice seemed to pucker his tongue with a drying affect on the inside of his mouth. He spit out what remained of the berry and threw the rest away. "If the Spanish thought these were like apples then it would have to be little green ones," he mused. The berry, however, did leave a pleasant taste in his mouth that was reminiscent of apples. . . little green ones.

This observation made him think of the times he had noted the alluring scent of apples on Suzanne's breath, those times of their passionate lovemaking. That, in turn, provoked a profound yearning and longing for the blacksmith's sweet daughter. "I wonder what she is doing now," he said aloud.

Several routes through the brush converged and diverged, dissecting the hillside, but it wasn't until Colt saw the print of an iron-shod hoof that he determined he was in the right place. The track was old and he did not recall coming this way when he had been brought to the mining camp, but his memory was quite vague of that trip anyway and he could only hope he might see recognizable things. Apparently, the pack train traversed different routes up this hillside in an effort to leave as little evidence of its passing as possible.

Eventually, Colt came to the bottom and the track he was following led into a large pine forest. Here the ground leveled and travel was much easier. He marveled at the beauty of the morning sunlight as it streamed down in golden shafts of light, feathering through the overhead canopy of trees. There was a pungent odor of pine in the air, a warm, dry and pleasant scent that brought with it a sense of well-being and delight.

Here there was little underbrush to hinder his way and the forest floor was riddled with trails. Tracks of deer, elk and either buffalo or cattle, Colt could not be sure which, were everywhere. He even saw the smaller, cloven hoof prints of antelope, goats, or sheep, which caused him to wonder about their presence. Perhaps a Mexican herder pastured his flock in this area from time to time.

As he gazed through the woods, trying to determine the best way to go, he could not help but think that he was in a kind of park—a big, beautiful park, but one that had been left sadly neglected. Branches and blown down trees cluttered the pathways and trails, requiring him to step over, around, or under them as he went along. Without thinking about it, he would occasionally reach to toss a branch or limb from out of the pathway, as if it would impede a horse's progress, should one come that way.

"Huh," he scoffed, "what am I doing?" He was straining to yank a heavy pine bough out of the trail. "I'll never pass this way again and I sure don't have to worry about riding a horse through here." He let go of the branch and moved on. What was it about this place that made him want to straighten it all up? He saw the dead and downed trees as a marvelous source of firewood, something in scant supply on the prairies of Texas. He could almost imagine tying into each windfall with a good, sharp, bucksaw to cut and rick the wood.

In his mind's eye, he could see the forest put in order, the trees all tall and straight with the dead, dying and diseased wood turned into firewood and hauled off to a useful purpose. It was almost as though that was the way it was supposed to be—that something had gone wrong to bring all this clutter and waste and uselessness. He imagined a time, maybe back when God created it all, or perhaps at sometime in the future, a time yet to come, when things would be restored to their right order.

Again, he scoffed at himself. What made him think that this forest was out of order? "Every tree must fall," someone had once said, and that made sense. If it wasn't cut down to be useful to man, it would crash to the forest floor where it would become useful to the bugs and worms and grubs and eventually rot away its strength and might, recycled to enrich the soil for the next tree to take its place. The bugs and grubs and worms would nourish the smaller animals and birds and become part of the food chain, and it all was a part of a marvelous plan and order.

A smile crept over Colt's face as he walked through the woods. So, why did he want to fix this place? This was not the first time he had felt this way when looking out over some turbulent and wild landscape. In fact this was some of the wildest country he had ever seen—the mountainous regions he was passing through seemed to have been in the very throes of agony and disruption, caught in chaos and then solidified,—and it was a wonder to behold. Here was evidence of nature's excesses. In some bygone era, these mountains had been a flowing, writhing, river of liquid stone, like an alive thing that had suddenly been stopped, the force of it shut off, and Colt could not help but wonder what it had all looked like before the violence and upheaval took place. He was mindful of the destruction that could come, for he had seen a whole forest that had been destroyed by fire that time on Woulfeter Mountain, just a few years ago, and he had read of the devastation that high winds could do in a woods. There were raging hurricanes that sometimes slammed into the east coast of Texas, knocking down everything in their paths. Would there come a time when just the right trees would fall to nourish the soil and produce just the right number of bugs to feed the right number of birds and animals so that all was in perfect balance? Had it been like that in the beginning? Surely God had created an orderly universe. Even when God made the Garden of Eden and everything was in order before the fall, he still told Adam to go and tend it—to take care of it. What was that all about? Was this innate sense he felt to park-out this wood, a trickle-down of the original task God had set for Adam?

A happy grin spread over the cowboy's face. He felt as though another blind had been rolled up and God was showing him a picture. He could almost see Adam picking up sticks and piling brush in the woods. "I wonder if he was naked while doing that." he said with a chuckle, "could get slivers in something important. Was Eve there, too, helping out? If she was naked, too, I doubt they got much brush piled." Colt laughed at his own cynicism and then felt a pang of longing and desire for Suzanne. He wished she were with him—here, in this place. He quickened his pace—he must get back to her.

Colt came upon a small stream meandering through the woods and spied the remnants of an old campfire. Had he been here before? There was a sense of familiarity about the place and he wondered if they had stopped here when he was brought, an unwitting captive, to the mines. His stomach was reminding him that he had missed breakfast and, pushing thoughts of his abduction and previous journey from his mind, he decided to stop and fix a meal before pushing on. Those eggs in the pack should be eaten.

An hour later found Colt once again on the trail, his pack a little lighter and his stomach happier. He was following the stream, into rougher country, as it passed through gullies and rills, with noisy cataracts and swift rapids. Making his way along the rushing water, he crossed from one side to the other, choosing his line of travel along the path of least resistance. The trail followed the stream through breaks in what appeared to be timber-covered foothills that rose to higher mountains ahead. He occasionally passed through open meadows, rich with grass and wildflowers and lined with trees. He could imagine some pioneer hacking out a home in this wild and remote place.

Colt had just passed down a shallow ravine in order to skirt past a difficult set of rapids in the creek, when he thought he heard something scrabble through the rocks and gravel behind him. Whirling quickly, his hand on his gun, he turned to look, but saw nothing. An uneasy sense of danger caused the hair on the back of his neck to prickle.

The draw he was passing through was about ten or twelve feet in depth and as he continued on his way, he had the feeling of being watched. Something or someone had him in its sights. He moved his rifle from off his shoulder and checked the load. Satisfied that a round was chambered, he eased off on the hammer and kept on walking. He hadn't gone more than ten yards when he again heard something, this time above him on the embankment to his right.

He was being followed. Someone was stalking him along the embankment above, just out of sight and stealthily paralleling his position. Was it Indians? Ahead, Colt saw a place where the embankment had eroded and washed down into the gully. Quickening his pace, he reached the spot and cocking his rifle, he rushed suddenly up the bank to peer over the edge. Just in time, he caught the flash of a tawny rear end as it disappeared off into the brush. A mountain lion had been stalking him. Colt snapped a shot in its direction, but upon closer inspection, could find no evidence that he had hit the cougar. He continued on his way, but with his rifle at the ready.

"That ornery catamount was stalking me," he said. "I best keep my eyes and ears open."

For the rest of the day Colt traveled a vigilant trail but saw no further sign of the big cat. The stream he had followed eventually widened and flowed into a small river that wound its way through a broad, timbered valley, interspersed with numerous open meadows and grasslands. Here the trail was marked plainly and in spite of the pain in his side, Colt made good progress until darkness overtook him.

Finding a small brook that intersected the trail, on its way to join the river, he chose to follow it up for a couple hundred feet, far enough away from the river so that the sounds of the current would not interfere with his hearing. Finding a level spot on a gravelly bench away from the clatter of the river, he began to build a fire and prepare for the night. His ears were attuned to the night sounds and, still nervous about the mountain lion, he was alert to every little noise.

Colt pulled a couple ears of corn from the pack and set them to roast on the edge of his fire. He melted some leftover bacon grease in his frying pan and sliced a couple of spuds in, and adding salt and pepper, set them to cooking. "Too bad I don't have an onion for these spuds," he said.

While his food cooked, he busied himself with tying some new rawhide thongs for his sling as the old ones were frayed. At least with this he could secure a rabbit or sage hen, or maybe even a squirrel, without announcing his presence to the Apache, by firing a gun. He regretted the sound made when firing it at the cougar, especially since he hadn't hit it. Meat for the pot would be good, and he was running low on bacon. The spuds cooked to a golden brown and he removed them from the fire, along with the roasting ears, and then leaned back against a tree to enjoy his meal.

"Thank you, Lord, for this good food and for keeping that cougar from me, in your name, amen." For a moment he felt a little sheepish over his omission of the blessing the night before, but soon forgot it in the business of getting the hard butter to stay on the hot ear of corn long enough to melt and get salt and pepper on it.

His meal finished, Colt cleaned up and heated some water to bathe his side. The injury had turned a dark black and blue and was painful, particularly if he jarred it. It had caused him to gingerly navigate difficult places with special favor that day. The hot water felt good and he noted with some satisfaction that he could breathe a little easier and without as much pain.

His chores done, he built up the fire and leaned back against the tree again and gazed into the flames to think of Suzanne. Memories of her sweet embrace and kisses filled his soul with an ache and longing that carried his thoughts away, while visions of her pretty face danced in the flames.

He recalled the thrill of their first kiss when he had been so sure she had come to tell him of her love for another. Never had she seemed more beautiful than in that moment in the moonlight, yet somehow vulnerable, even open to and welcoming him as well. He smiled when he remembered how, with his heart in his throat, he took the chance and drew her to him, how her lips met his in surrender to their very first kiss.

The smile on his face sobered and turned to sadness as he recalled that fateful trip to Saint Louis only to discover her affections turned towards another, and the heartbreaking disappointment of the rejection he felt there. That had been a long hard winter followed by the devastating journey to Yuma and the lonely struggle to get back to her and see if she had meant the things she had said in her letters. He had fought the Apache, the desert, the distance and time, all which seemed to contrive to keep him from his heart's desire, and mixed with the uncertainty of what he would find when he did get back. He recalled the joy of finding, when he had returned, Suzanne contrite and hopelessly devoted to him, and the sheer joy of her love. The heartache and disappointment he had gone through disappeared in the warmth of her embrace. He mused upon the days that had followed, long and glorious days of sweetness and desire and discovery—of their camping trip to the Sweetgrass—guilt-edged golden days of allure and intimacy that were the most glorious days of his life. The days of sweetness and desire and discovery that grew and grew upon them until the two of them had moved into a merging of spirit and soul and had come dangerously close to the merging of their bodies as well.

"Huh," Colt scoffed, recalling their time together on the little hill. "It's a good thing God sent that Mojave rattler along. Lord, did I even thank you for that? Probably not, but I should have, so thanks—thanks for giving me such a precious and special love for such a precious and lovely girl. . . and Lord, wherever she's at tonight—right now—send her my love and let her know I am on my way back to her. In Jesus' name, amen."

His mind savored the memories as though discovering them again, after being hid away in some dark, dusty place for a long time, but now remembered and brought to the surface of his emotions and with the recall came the familiar longing and loneliness for Suzanne. There was a hole in his soul where Suzanne belonged and Colt knew he would never feel whole until she was back in his arms to fill it.

Restless, but still savoring the thoughts of Suzanne, he got up and moved to the edge of the firelight. With his mind soaring with the memories they had made together, it was without conscious thought that he stood in the shadows to attend to his toilet. Unmindful of the quiet of the night, his focus was on Suzanne and the journey ahead, along with a dim consciousness of the pain in his side and the fatigue of the day. Sleep and taking time to rest felt almost like a necessary evil, along with the darkness, both an irritating nuisance to his progress.

Gradually he became aware that something was amiss. He heard nothing, and that was what first alerted him. An uneasy sense of dread came over him, worse still, his gun belt and rifle lay where he had left them next to the tree. There were no sounds, just the silence. No chirping of crickets, no buzz of insects, or croak of frogs. No rustle of leaves, no sighing of the wind—just dead silence like that of a tomb. . . like that of Victorio's Peak, and the horror of that place seemed to creep over his soul like an icy hand, as every nerve in his being came alive.

He knew someone or something was watching him from out of the darkness, but he did not know what. Was it the Apache or banditos? If so, an arrow or bullet could hit his body at any moment, yet he stood immobile, unable to move. Had the cougar returned or maybe a bear or was it more sinister than that? He knew that jaguars were know to be in this part of Mexico and had heard of the big spotted cats stalking unwary peasants. Whatever it was, he knew he must not turn his back to it.

His hands were sweaty and he doubled them into fists and slowly stepped backwards towards the fire and his weapons. Whatever this danger was, Colt prepared to fight. *It might take me down,* he thought, *but not without me getting a piece of it first.*

A sudden flicker of movement to his left caught his eye and Colt instinctively turned to throw a mighty, right-handed punch. It caught a pouncing cougar square in the nose as it leaped at him out of the darkness. The blow knocked the big cat to the ground where it spat, hissed, and instantly rebounded back upon the startled man. Colt immediately grabbed the lion in a head-lock with a death-like grip. The animal's face and gleaming teeth were pressed sideways and away from the youth's chest while he held on for dear life.

The force of the attack bowled Colt and the cat over backwards while the cougar's right forepaw ripped at the coat on Colt's back. The animal's other paws were tearing at his legs and stomach. As the two of them fell heavily over backwards, he held on with a vise-like grip about the cougar's neck.

"You may be taking me," he gritted out, "but I'm keeping this head." Born out of terror, the ferocity of the onslaught and the challenge to stay alive, a sudden surge of fury and determination swept over the cowboy. As they fell backward, Colt landed on his elbow on the hard ground. There was a loud crack and instantly Colt's arm went totally numb—the arm which was encircling the predator's neck. The whole arm was now devoid of feeling but he dared not relinquish his hold. *I've broken my arm,* he thought, but still holding on, he bore down even harder with the strength of his other one.

More determined than ever to not allow the animal's teeth to come into play, he grappled with the cougar's neck, wrestling it in a desperate grip, while the big cat twisted and turned, snarling wickedly and clawing at the man. For moments that seem an eternity, they rolled about on the ground and Colt had the horrible thought that he was being killed—that this mountain lion would soon disembowel him and he would end up dead—lost to Suzanne and the world. He thought of her sorrow and screamed, “No!” He gave a might wrench to the creature’s neck and there was another loud pop, and then the cougar suddenly went limp. All movement ceased and the big cat lay still, but Colt held his desperate grip until total exhaustion and the rapid beating of his heart, caused him to black out. Anyone happening upon the two of them would have wondered why the cowboy was sleeping with a wild mountain lion in such a close embrace.

Slowly Colt regained consciousness and, finding the mountain lion in his arms, he quickly pushed the beast away and then lay panting for breath. He was hoping the big cat would not get up for he was utterly spent, so much so that he could not possibly get to his guns and shoot the animal should it renew the attack. But the cougar did not move. Slowly feeling crept back into his right arm and he flexed his fingers. Apparently he had just hit his crazy bone and his elbow was not broken. He looked again at the cat, aware of blood trickling down his back, his left arm, his belly and down both legs. The cougar’s head was twisted at an impossible angle and Colt realized that the loud crack he had heard was the breaking of the mountain lion’s neck when they fell. Its continued struggles had been its death throes and he had ridden them out. The catamount was indeed dead. He crawled into the circle of firelight to where he could reach his guns and grasping the .44, he drew it from the holster, then all went dark as he collapsed in a swoon.

Chapter Seventeen

Ridin' North of Town

"How much farther to the Nelson place?" Kathreen asked Suzanne. The girls had ridden north on the road out of town with Suzanne mounted on Checkers and Kathreen on a spirited filly named Petunia that she had rented from the livery stable.

"I don't know for sure," Suzanne replied, "I have never been all the way out there but it can't be too far, their children have to walk to and from school."

"And you say the Box 7 is on past their place?"

"Yes, we can ask the Nelsons how far it is."

"How long are you going to stay at the Nelsons?"

"Don't worry, you will have plenty of time to see 'the Don Juan of the Pecos', Kate."

"Well, for your information, Miss Blue-Belle of Wade's Landing, I happen to have important business out there." Kathreen held up a mysterious looking letter for her friend to see as they rode along.

"What business?" Suzanne said.

"Mrs. Munson just asked if I could deliver this registered mail to one of the hands on the Box 7, that's what."

Suzanne reined Checkers over next to her friend's horse and reached for the letter. "Who's it for?"

"Uh-uh," Kathreen warned and pulled the letter back. "This is private mail from the U.S. Post Office, and not for prying eyes."

Suzanne shook her head in annoyance and kneed Checkers over more, trying to see the address. "Well you could at least tell me who the letter is for," she said.

"Nope, it's private, registered mail and has to be signed for."

"You brat, you are not a postman, what makes you think you have any more right to look at that letter than I do?"

Feigning mock indignation, Kathreen pulled herself up in the saddle and said with a haughty voice, "I am a duly appointed employee of Postmistress Munson, who has charged me with the delivery of this envelope and its contents, to the person addressed on the front."

"Aw, balderdash, give me that letter." Suzanne spurred Checkers forward and made a grab for the envelope.

Kathreen's filly, prompted by the pinto's sudden rush, broke into a run, and Kathreen called over her shoulder, "Race you to the end of that fence line and if you can beat me, you can look at the letter."

Suzanne bent low over Checker's neck and yelled, "Get'er," and the race was on. Kathreen's long-legged horse had a good lead and it took Checkers over two-thirds of the distance to catch and pass the livery stable horse. Suzanne was laughing happily and holding the snorting Checkers in when Kathreen finally galloped up.

"This old nag can't run worth a hoot," Kathreen said as she pulled the horse in. "I should have known a horse named Petunia, wouldn't amount to much."

"Who's the letter for?" Suzanne taunted.

Scowling, Kathreen held up the letter to study the address. "One Godfrey Thompson—who the heck do you suppose that is?"

Suzanne shook her head, "Never heard of him. You said 'heck.'"

"Ye-gads, Godfrey Thompson," Kathreen eyed her friend sideways, ignoring the comment. "Who would name a poor kid Godfrey? Can you imagine a kid with a name like that trying to survive on the school playground? It would be worse than a bleeding hen in a chicken house."

Suzanne looked at her friend in surprise, "How'd you learn about stuff like that, big-city girl?"

"Huh," Kathreen scoffed, "my working at the general store hasn't been a total waste of time, I've picked up quite a lot of your country ways, my little Texas cow town gal."

"Well, I guess you have, big city girl."

Kathreen waved her hand, "Anyway, if I were a kid with a name like Godfrey, I'd be changing my name faster'n you could say Jack Robinson." Suddenly a slow smile grew across the redhead's face. "Say," she said, "what was Two-Bits' last name?"

Suzanne thought a moment, "It's Thompson, isn't it? You don't suppose that letter is for him, do you?"

Kathreen sat her horse with eyebrows raised and a mischievous smile toying about her lips. "I'd bet dollars to doughnuts it is," she said, then tapped the envelope thoughtfully against her chin. "Suzanne, we are just going to have to ride out and see that Mr. Godfrey Thompson gets his letter and it *is* going to be special delivery—definitely special delivery."

The road stretched out before them, mirages of water pools shimmering in the heat waves rising above the ground. Dustdevils twisted off across the range with an occasional jackrabbit hopping urgently away to hide, its feet and ears looking impossibly long.

"Are those jackass rabbits any good to eat?" Kathreen asked.

"Jackrabbits," Suzanne corrected, "and no, not usually, too tough and too stringy."

"I thought Colton said he ate them that time he got away from those Apache Indians."

"Well, yeah, a lot of people eat them when there's nothing else, but they're not very good, cotton tails are better."

"You ever eat one?" Kathreen asked.

"No," Suzanne said.

"Let's shoot the next one we see and cook it for supper."

Suzanne gave her friend an amused look, "You ever shoot a gun from horseback?" she asked.

Kathreen looked confounded, "No, why?"

"Unless that horse has been conditioned to gunfire, she'd probably toss you into the ditch and hightail it back to town."

Kathreen looked uncertainly at her mount and changed the subject. "How much farther to the Nelson place?"

"Another mile or so," Suzanne said, "let's kick these ponies into a trot, it's still a ways to go if we're going on out to the Box 7 after the Nelsons, and still get back to town before dark."

"I don't like trotting, it jiggles me about to much and bruises my fanny," Kathreen complained.

"It can be rough, but I think you will find it is not so bad if you ride the trot differently."

"What's wrong with the way I ride, I know how to ride horseback."

"Now don't get your dander up, I know you do. Just try pointing your heels down and your toes up and out a little, let your legs absorb some of the shock and let your hips swing with the movement of the horse. She is a little rough-gaited, but try that, it should help."

Urging the horses into a trot, both girls adopted the riding posture Suzanne had suggested and settled into the gait of their ponies. Kathreen allowed as how it was indeed easier to ride like that, and wondered why no one had ever told her that before.

It wasn't long before they came to a large field of cotton and could see a man and the Nelson girls dragging long sacks and plucking the cotton bolls. They rode past a fence alongside the road until they came to a high overhead, pole gate with a faded board sign that had "*The Nelsons*" painted in rude letters. They turned in here and rode up a driveway towards a rough, unpainted, clapboard house fronted by a full length porch. Scruffy cur dogs came bounding out to meet them, barking furiously at the strangers. The porch was littered with various odds and ends that ranged from trash and tin cans, to tools and harness gear. An old, half-open cotton bale looked like the dogs had claimed it as their own private bed, and had a good amount of cotton strewn about at one end.

At the commotion the dogs were making, a woman in a dirty gingham dress came through the door, wiping her hands on her apron. She yelled at the dogs to shut up but they ignored her until she picked up a billet and hurled the chunk of firewood at the nearest one. It yelped and fled under the porch, the rest of the dogs close behind. Nervously, Suzanne and Kathreen swung down from their horses, keeping a wary eye out for the dogs, then turned to greet the watching woman.

"Mrs. Nelson?" Suzanne said, "I am Suzanne Kluesman, your girls' teacher and this is my friend, Miss Kathreen McClusky. We have come for a visit."

The woman gave a big sigh and then said, "Now what have they done?"

"Oh no, Mrs. Nelson, Carla and Emeline are just fine. It was just such a lovely day for a ride, Kathreen and I though you might appreciate a little visit, we've brought a couple of things for the girls. Do you like tea?"

"When I can get it, which ain't often around this place," Mrs. Nelson replied. She brushed ineffectively at her dress and looked back over her shoulder into the house.

"May we come in for a few minutes?" Suzanne asked. "Kathreen works at the mercantile for the Munsons and has a special delivery letter to take on out to the Box 7, so we won't be staying long."

The woman nodded reluctantly and motioned with her head toward the open door. The girls tied their horses to a dilapidated fence that only half enclosed the yard, then stepped up onto the porch with packages in hand. Mrs. Nelson stood back, holding open a sagging, screen door and waved them inside. She eyed the packages suspiciously, but said nothing.

Suzanne and Kathreen found themselves in a cluttered front room with ragged, run-down furniture and a cold fireplace. Flies buzzed at the dirty windows and an open archway led to an adjoining kitchen. A stairway strewn with articles of clothing, led to the attic where the ends of a couple of beds could be seen. Two lean-to bedrooms held up either end of the house.

"Come into the kitchen," Mrs. Nelson said, brushing past them to lead the way. "I'll put a kettle on if you are wanting tea." There was a look of awkwardness about the woman and it was plain that the niceties of life were few and far between for her. Collecting some books and papers and a pile of crumpled clothes from off a couple of chairs, she indicated the girls should be seated.

"I figured it was Bonnie you come about," the farmer's wife said. She poked up the fire and added a few sticks of wood. "Just push that stuff on the table out of the way—did you say you brought some tea?"

Suzanne dug into the bag and produced a package of black tea, while Kathreen busied herself clearing a place on the table.

"Bonnie?" Suzanne said, "Wasn't she off to Saint Gaul for high school last year?"

Mrs. Nelson set the tea kettle on the stove and looked worriedly over at the teacher. "She was there, boarding out for last term, now she's supposed to be home for the summer, helpin' out gettin' the cotton in but I am afraid going to the big town's put notions in her head, she's nothing but boy crazy now and we can hardly get a lick a work outta her."

"Bonnie's a good girl," Suzanne said, "she'll settle down soon, you'll see. I believe we saw Carla and Emeline in the field with Mr. Nelson on our way in here."

While setting some cracked tea cups on the table, Mrs. Nelson had looked skeptical at the schoolmarm's assurances about Bonnie, but she nodded about the two younger girls. "They're pickin' cotton along with their father, what there is of it, hain't been much rain this year, you know."

The two girls nodded in agreement and chatted with the woman about the weather and how things were in town while the water boiled. When it was ready, Suzanne handed the lady the package of tea. She took it with barely a glance and began to spoon some into an old, china teapot that she had taken down from a top shelf, after blowing the dust off and wiping it out with her soiled apron.

While the tea steeped, Suzanne said, "The ladies at the church sent out a few things they thought you might like." Kathreen rummaged around in the sack and produced some tea biscuits and set them on the table along with a jar of strawberry preserves.

"Hain't much on going to church," the woman said, "don't have the proper duds."

"You may find some things in this package they sent along, "Kathreen said. "Do you like this?" The redhead held up a print dress for her inspection.

Mrs. Nelson's eyes lit up and she nearly spilled her cup of tea in her haste to set it down and reach for the garment. She stood and held it up in front of her, then sadly shook her head and handed it back. "We don't take no charity," she said.

"Oh, this isn't charity," Suzanne said. "The church ladies heard that you spin some fine cotton cloth and are offering you these items in exchange for a bolt of your spun goods. They wish to make some sheets up for the infirmary. Mrs. Munson has also said she would like to have a few bolts for her dry goods section in the store, and will take any you have on consignment if you so choose."

"All's I got is just plain home-spun muslin—it ain't much good for dressmaking but should make sheets alright." The girls could see a look of pride come over the housewife's face. She got to her feet and went into one of the back bedrooms and returned with two bolts of clean, white muslin cloth. "There's several yards here, I usually ask ten dollars a bolt but I will trade one for credit at the store if you think old Munson will go for it. Give the other to the church. Now what else you got in them bags?"

"Good," Suzanne said. "Kathreen will get this set up at the store and I'll see to it that the other gets to the Ladies Aid Society. By the way, besides the dresses and blouses, there are some under things in here for both you and the girls."

Mrs. Nelson sat back smiling and smeared some preserves on a biscuit. "Now tell me all about this Ladies Aid Society," she said.

The two young women visited with the woman for another half hour and brought her up to date on all the news, explaining the benevolent activities of the church ladies and the rummage sales where they collected the articles of clothing for redistribution. Mrs. Nelson sorted through the things they had brought with moist eyes and a happy smile, and allowed as how they might be able to start attending services after all, now that they had some proper "duds."

At one point, she asked Suzanne if there had been any new developments regarding her young man, but then immediately went silent when she saw the look of consternation register on the young schoolteacher's face.

Suzanne sadly shook her head and Kathreen quickly changed the subject.

"Where is Bonnie now?"

Mrs. Nelson sighed and said, "She is supposed to be fixing dinner for Lars and the younger girls, but I'm afraid she's off dawdling along the river somewhere. Can't seem to get much work out of her these days, she's too busy pickin' wild flowers and writin' letters to that boy in Saint Gaul."

"Is that safe—her being off down by the river like that?" Suzanne asked.

Mrs. Nelson frowned and then shook her head, "Safe as anyplace in this God-forsaken wilderness—she's within hollerin' distance of the house I reckon, why?"

"It's a fearful thing to fall into the hands of Indians, I know. My folks and I were captured by the Kiowa and would have come to a dreadful end if it had not been for Colton."

"I heard about that," the woman answered with a dismissive wave of her hand, "We ain't had no Injun trouble 'round here for quite a spell."

"How far is it to the Box 7?" Kathreen interrupted.

Mrs. Nelson looked at the redhead then said, "About five miles north of here." She scooted back from the table and stood up, indicating their visit was at an end. Suzanne and Kathreen stood, too, and followed her to the front door. The farmer's wife held the dilapidated screen door open for them to pass again.

"I reckon I best be fixin' some vitals afore my outfit shows up hungry as a bear. If you see that gal of mine, tell her to hightail it home, pronto, and good day to you both—thanks for the goods."

She pulled the screen door to and disappeared back into the house. The two girls could hear her poking up the fire and banging pots and pans around while they stuffed the bolts of cotton into the saddle bags of their mounts and swung astride.

Riding out of the Nelsons' yard Kathreen said, "That's what you are going to end up like."

"What are you talking about," Suzanne said as they trotted to the road.

"You go and marry some broke-down cowboy or farmer and that'll be you in a few years."

"Kathreen, have you no aspirations for a home and family? Families such as this are the backbone of America."

"I have no aspirations of picking flies out of my tea," Kathreen said flatly.

"It will get better," her friend said. "This country is growing and it will get better—Oh, is that Bonnie down there—good heavens, where are her clothes?"

The road ran parallel to the river and through an opening in the trees and brush, some fifty yards away, they could see a slender girl lying on the grass next to the river, sunning herself with no clothes on.

Bonnie jerked to a sitting position and snatched a thin dress in front of her when she heard the schoolteacher and her friend ride up.

"Miss Kluesman," she cried, "you gave me such a start, I didn't hear you ride up until just now."

Suzanne gave the teenager a skeptical look. The girl had recovered quickly from her alarm, once she saw the two women on horseback, and casually slipped the dress back over her slim figure.

"It's a good thing we weren't some of the Box 7 cowboys riding along here," Kathreen said dryly. "Running around like that, you might be found guilty of corrupting their morals."

"Or the Comanche," Suzanne put in. "Bonnie, it's not such a good idea, being off by yourself like this. I would hate for anything to happen to you."

"I was just trying to get a little sun," Bonnie said sheepishly.

"Well, your mother is looking for you, aren't you supposed to be fixing dinner for your father and the others?"

Bonnie jumped to her feet. "I completely forgot," she said. "Thanks, Miss Kluesman, I better get back." She called, "Goodbye," and hurried, barefoot, back towards the house.

Both girls rode silently back to the road and turned their mounts towards the Box 7. "I can't blame her for wanting to get a little sun," Kathreen said. "I like to get a little myself now and then."

Suzanne looked sideways at her friend. "There's no such thing as a little sun in Texas, why if I laid out like she was, I'd burn red as a lobster."

Kathreen seemed surprised, "Haven't you ever sunbathed in the nude?" she asked.

"No, and I'm not about to either."

"Too bad, nothing makes you feel quite as free as stretching out in the all-together and letting the sun's rays warm your skin."

"I should think, with your complexion, you'd burn to a crisp if you did that, to say nothing of the immodesty of it all."

"Now, Suzie, you need to unravel a little bit, you're only young once, try letting the mud squish between your toes once in a while, it makes getting cleaned up all that much nicer."

Suzanne gave a wistful smile, "Oh, I've felt the mud between my toes a few times," she said. She was recalling the time Colt had caught her bathing in the creek. Kathreen was right—there had been an element of freedom and recklessness, coupled with both excitement and danger, energizing her then. It had made her feel so alive, the unwitting feel of the sun and the cold of the water on her body. She knew exactly what her friend was alluding to and with the realization came a desperate longing to feel alive like that again. Why was she living only half-alive now, just marking time and using up oxygen? Was Colt ever going to come back—really? Inwardly, she trembled and felt the old stab of doubt, that all those golden days were over and she was left just a shell of a woman. Her true self, her heart, had flown and was lost in the darkness of the unknown. Her only hope was in the Lord; that He knew the answer for her soul's deep questions, and would ultimately reveal them to her. In the meantime, she would press on, do her duty, and be who she was supposed to be—a good, dutiful woman.

Kathreen was rambling on about the fun of skinny-dipping and sunbathing, reminding her of their recent escapade on the Pecos when Two-Bits and Buddy had shown up.

"Now be honest, Suzanne, wasn't that fun? If I remember right, once you got out of your dress, you had a pretty good time, didn't you?"

Suzanne hesitated, then nodded. "It was fun but the trouble was, I was with the wrong person."

Frowning and a little confused, Kathreen said, "The wrong person? What's wrong with a couple of friends skinny-dipping?"

"Oh, nothing," Suzanne sighed, "That's okay, it's just not anything like it is with the right person."

A look of understanding came knowingly over Kathreen's features. "You are talking about you and Colt in the pond again, aren't you?"

"Yes, that and—oh, never mind, there are just some things that are private and nobody else's business, but I do know what the sun feels like on my skin—all of it, okay?"

Kathreen grinned at her blonde friend riding next to her, "So, best friend, there is more to the story than just you two in your underwear, what happened?"

"Did you get that part about it's nobody else's business?" Suzanne said, her eyebrows arched.

"I'm nobody else," Kathreen was exasperated. "I am your truest and dearest friend and I am here to watch out for you, so fess up, how can I pull the arrows out of your wounds if I don't know what ones are stuck in you?"

The earnest look on Kathreen's face brought a giggle from Suzanne and had her marveling at her friend's cleverness in trying to worm from her the intimate details to which she had so foolishly alluded.

"I'm not telling you. I should have never said anything about it in the first place."

"You were naked with him, weren't you? Where—where were you? Were you in the woods, out on the prairie, in the barn or the pond—where were you?"

"None of your business."

"Come on, Suzanne," Kathreen whined, "I know you two were like that, you said as much when you said the sun was on all your skin. Where was that?"

"I didn't say Colt was like that," Suzanne corrected.

"You mean just you were? My, this is getting more interesting by the moment. Come on girl, tell me—what happened?"

"It wasn't all that much, my inquisitive little friend. Colt just happened upon me one time, on our trip to the Sweetgrass, when I was taking a bath in the creek."

"He did? What did he do—what did you do?"

Suzanne laughed uncomfortably, "He swallowed his tongue and near fell into the creek and I shrieked and ducked under the water—that's all."

"That's all! What did he say, what did you say?"

"I asked what he was staring at and he said he wasn't staring at anything and when I offered to stand up and give him a better look, he just squawked like a strangled hen and ran off."

"Did you really do that—offer to show yourself?" Kathreen looked skeptical."

"Yep," Suzanne said cryptically.

"What were you thinking—why did you say that?"

Resigned, Suzanne gave in to her friend's questions. "We had just come back from the Kiowa camp when Colton was rescued by that Indian girl. Then they let us go."

"What's that got to do with it?" Kathreen was confused.

"She was beautiful, that's what. He spent a lot of time alone with Seeaugway when he took her back to her people that time, and when I saw her, she wasn't wearing anything but some pretty, buckskin dress."

"How'd you know that?"

"I saw her dismount from riding astride. Now I know why civilized women ride sidesaddle when wearing a dress.

"I still don't see how that has anything to do with you presenting yourself in the altogether to Colt."

Suzanne grew defensive, "If I saw her that way, Colt must have seen her that way, too, maybe several times. I was just trying to find out if he found me prettier than her and if you tell anybody I did that, I'll snatch you baldheaded."

Kathreen laughed at the other girl with something akin to wonder. "Surely you were not worried about some Indian girl, Suzanne, Colt adored the very ground you walked on."

"Then why did he run away?" she asked plaintively.

"You tell me. Do you think he wasn't interested in seeing you that way?"

Suzanne sighed and relaxed in the saddle, "No—he was—he told me I could not unveil my beauty like that until after I was his in Christ."

"In Christ, what does that mean?"

"Marriage, he said that once our union was sanctified by God in marriage, then the veils could be stripped away."

"Huh, I never heard anything like that before. Do you suppose that's why folks are supposed to get married before they take their clothes off?"

Suzanne nodded, "I do."

Kathreen was thoughtful and said nothing for awhile. The clopping of the horse hooves on the road was the only sound as they rode along together.

Finally, she said, "Rape is such a terrible intrusion, it violates every secret part of you."

Suzanne reached across to touch her friend's arm, "I am so sorry," she said.

Kathreen patted Suzanne's hand, "That's okay, Colt told me that Jesus fixes those things and He does. I just wonder sometimes though, what would things have been like if that hadn't happened? Sometimes it's hard to feel pure and innocent again. I envy you that."

Suzanne grimaced and nodded. "Yes, pure and innocent and lost. Will he ever come back to me, Kate?"

"He will," her friend assured her, "and it will be worth it all in the end, don't lose heart."

Suzanne and Kathreen topped a small rise and saw an impressive two-story house with a wide porch supported by columns running across the front, behind a white picket fence that enclosed a spacious yard that held large elm and chinaberry trees, which seemed to issue an invitation to escape the hot sun in their cool shade.

"That must be the home place of the Box 7 Ranch," Suzanne said.

Someone had artfully piped water to flow through a gurgling fountain to a small pool that fed a ditch on its way to water a large garden just off the kitchen door. As the girls approached, a pig-tailed Chinaman appeared at the back door with a bucket of scraps, which he carried to a nearby chicken pen and dumped over the fence to a flock of clucking hens.

Several outbuildings, some with shade trees, spread out down a gentle incline from the house and ended at a large storage barn, granary, and a long, one-story bunkhouse that sported several windows and a front porch.

All of this, the girls took in at a glance as they pulled up by the front gate. An English birddog came rushing from the porch of the house up to the gate, waggling his tail happily and barking loudly to welcome the newcomers. The front door opened and a tall, distinguished looking man, dressed in a tweed jacket with leather elbow patches, and a white shirt open at the throat, and jodhpur breeches with knee-high riding boots, stepped out. He called to the dog, "Heel." The dog immediately stopped his barking and trotted back to the porch to stand behind his master.

The man seemed surprised to see the two lovely young ladies sitting their horses at his gate, and hurriedly knocked the coal from a pipe he had been smoking against the porch rail, stuffed the pipe into his pocket, and came quickly down the steps to meet them.

"Good afternoon, ladies," he said. "To what do we owe the honor of your visit to our humble enterprise?"

Suzanne and Kathreen were both staring at the striking man. Tall and muscular, he was immaculately dressed in expensive clothes of obvious European cut, and was just about the last thing either of them expected to find on a working ranch. He was well groomed, with neatly barbered black hair and a stylish, close-cropped mustache and his frank gaze and smiling eyes swept over the two girls with genuine admiration and welcome.

"Allow me to introduce myself," he said, "I am Gareth Hazelhurst, absentee owner of the Box 7—now no longer absent, as you can see."

A broad smile accompanied this last remark as the ranch owner stepped to Suzanne, the nearer of the two girls, and offered a hand to her. "Please, won't you ladies step down and let me offer you some refreshment?"

Suzanne noticed the fine lines at the corners of his eyes and sensed that here was a jovial and expansive man who enjoyed life. Swinging a leg over the cantle, she felt a steadying hand at her elbow while she stepped down, then murmured a polite, thank you, as Hazelhurst stepped around her horse to help Kathreen dismount. She could see the sparkle of deviltry in the redhead's eyes as Gareth approached.

"May I help you down, Miss?" he said with an even, white-toothed, smile.

Kathreen smiled happily back as she brought her off-leg agilely across the pommel of her saddle, and kicked her nigh foot loose of the stirrup. This left her sitting sideways, facing the waiting cattleman.

"You certainly may," she quipped, and then slid from her seat to fall, unexpectedly into Gareth Hazelhurst's arms.

The rancher quickly caught her and set her on her feet. Laughing heartily, he said, "My, aren't you a spontaneous lassie?"

"Thet I am," she said, affecting a Scottish highland brogue. "An whut hah brrung a highlanderr such as yerrself, to th brroad plains o Texas?"

Gareth laughed heartily again and bowing from the waist, he said, "I guess I am guilty of raising cows. Now whut highland lassie do I have the pleasure of addressing?"

Kathreen gave Suzanne a knowing look and a smile of triumph. Holding out her hand to the rancher, she said, "My name is Kat'a'rreen McClusky," and she deliberately rolled her r's as she pronounced her name. Reverting back to her normal way of speaking, she said, "I would *love* to share a little refreshment with you."

Suzanne was aghast at Kathreen's bold and obvious flirtation with the man, and wondered if a Mrs. Hazelhurst might not be watching from the ranch house. Gareth Hazelhurst had bent to kiss the back of Miss McClusky's hand, but did a double-take at her remark, his face registering a mild, yet amused, befuddlement. His poise and good humor returned with a slight shake of his head and a low chuckle, then he turned to face Suzanne.

"And you are?' he said, reaching to take her hand.

"I am Miss Kluesman," she replied extending her hand to shake his. "Miss Suzanne Kluesman."

The rancher took Suzanne's hand, and with a gracious bow, likewise gently kissed the back of it. "Welcome to the Box 7," he said.

His were impeccable manners and Suzanne felt herself enjoying the genteelness of the whole thing. The introductions lasted but a few minutes, but volumes were written into those few moments. Who would have expected to find such refined manners on the frontiers of Texas? They were all the more meaningful for their usual absence, and the little schoolteacher from East of the Pecos felt her desolate soul sucking up the graciousness of the man, like a dry waterhole in a sudden rain squall. It was no wonder that Kathreen had so readily succumbed to his charming manner, his was a huge contrast to the rough, tongue-tied cowboys, one usually met. Here was a man who definitely knew how to treat a woman like a lady and make her feel like one, too.

"Ladies, will you join me?" Gareth swung the gate wide and motioned them up the walk towards the porch.

"Thank you," Suzanne said and led the way. Kathreen curtsied as she passed Hazelhurst and placing a slim finger to the collar of her blouse, she murmured, "Whew, isn't it hot."

"Yes," Gareth said, "It is cooler on the porch, there is a bit of a breeze there. I will get Wrong to bring out some sweet tea, do you ladies like iced tea?"

When they had affirmed that they did, the rancher went off to notify the Chinese cook and once he was gone, Suzanne turned to her friend.

"Kathreen," she scolded, "you are horrible, have you no shame? What if he is married, what if his wife saw you throw yourself into his arms like that?"

Kathreen scrunched up her upper lip and shook her head. "I don't think so, he's not married. Isn't he delicious, I'll bet he has been all over the world—New York, Paris, London. I'll bet he's from London."

"Kathreen, haven't you learned anything yet? He is old enough to be your father! How do you know he is not another Pierre LaRoush?"

"He's not, and he is not that old either, I'd bet he is rich, too, just look at this ranch."

"Money can't buy you love," Suzanne reminded her.

"No, but it can sure make the down payment on it," her friend replied as she fingered the petals of some roses sitting in a vase on a small table.

Just then Hazelhurst returned, "Down payment on what?" he said.

Smiling, he indicated that the girls should be seated in some large, round-backed, wicker chairs spaced around the small table that held the roses. The two girls were seated and then looked at their expectant host. It was obvious he was waiting for an answer to his question.

"Oh, nothing," Kathreen said. "How long have you owned this place?"

"I bought the Box 7 as an investment several years ago with an eye to introducing some of our Scottish and English strains of cattle to the rich grasslands of the Texas plains, but other than a brief visit at the time of purchase, I have not lived here until recently."

"Who runs the place when you are away?" Kathreen asked.

"Clay Anderson is my foreman, or at least he was until Roy Bean made him the sheriff. I wish they'd hurry up and elect a new one. Anderson's a good man and I need him back here."

Nodding her head, Suzanne said, "He is a good man."

"Oh, do you know him?" the rancher said.

"Suzanne is the reason Clay Anderson is the sheriff now," Kathreen put in.

Hazelhurst looked surprised, "Are you the schoolteacher that Anderson rescued from that brigand?"

Suzanne nodded, "I owe a huge debt of gratitude to Mr. Anderson."

"I dare say you do. Allow me to express my regrets for your late unpleasantness."

At that moment the Chinese cook appeared carrying a tray with three tall glasses of iced tea, a mint leaf garnish and real chunks of ice floating in them.

"Thank you, Wrong Way," Hazelhurst said.

"No! No! belly bad," the Chinaman corrected, "it Wong Wey, Wong Wey. I keepee tellee you, Wong Wey." He walked off muttering under his breath while the rancher and his guests chuckled to themselves at the ruffled dignity of the little cook.

"It seems wrong way is the wrong way to say Wong Wey," the unflappable Englishman said to the added amusement of the girls, for his response elicited outright laughter from them.

"So ladies, what brings the two of you to the Box 7?" Hazelhurst asked, "Is this business or pleasure?"

Kathreen said, "Actually, my friend and I had other business out this way and the postmistress at the Mercantile where I work asked if I would bring a special delivery letter to the Box 7, on our ride out today."

"To whom is the letter addressed?" the rancher asked.

"A Godfrey Thompson," Kathreen replied with obvious relish. "Do you know who that is?"

"Godfrey? There is nobody here by that name that I know of unless—you said Thompson? Could that be Two-Bits' real name?"

"Well, he has to sign for it," Kathreen said, "Where will we find him?"

"A bunch of the boys are breaking out horses down at the corral, would you like for me to send someone for him?"

A mischievous smile came across Kathreen's features, "No, I think I would like to see if Mr. Two-Bits is Godfrey Thompson for myself. Did you say he was riding wild buncos or whatever it is you call them?"

Gareth gave an amused smile, "I think he is, He's one of the best bronc busters on the place."

"Broncos, yeah, broncos is what you call it. Come on, Suzie, let's go watch Two-Bits busting broncos."

Hazelhurst stood, "May I escort you two ladies to the corrals then?"

Kathreen's demeanor changed and she sat back in her chair.

"Oh, there's no hurry, tell us more about the ranch—are you from London?"

Gareth Hazelhurst sat back down. "Yes, London and Devonshire. My family has a large estate there and I have been experimenting with the cross-breeding of cattle, but you ladies do not care about such things. Tell me a little of yourselves, I suspect that neither of you are native to these sand hills and dusty plains."

"Saint Louis," Kathreen said, "we're both from Saint Louis and received our formal education there."

"Well, it is delightful to have you visit the Box 7. How did you end up at a place like Wade's Landing?"

"Well, I came to visit Suzanne and decided to stay for awhile but I must be returning soon," Kathreen said, "Suzanne?"

A smile tugged at the corner of Suzanne's mouth at her friends assumed formal manner. "My father is a blacksmith and moved the family here a few years ago to run the smithy at the Landing," she said.

"Do you have family?" Kathreen asked, once again assuming control of the conversation.

Hazelhurst was not fooled by the veiled question and smiled tolerantly. "I have a younger brother and sister back in England, living with my mother. My father is deceased and I have inherited the responsibility of maintaining the family fortune. I have yet to start a family of my own."

"Good," Kathreen said, satisfied with his answer. "That's good," then to Suzanne's surprise she boldly asked, "What's the holdup?"

Gareth Hazelhurst broke into hearty laughter. "You Westerners certainly believe in laying your cards on the table, don't you?" he said. "Why—are you interested?"

Kathreen feigned shock, "Mr. Hazelhurst, I barely know you, what would my father say?" She preened a little, turning her profile to the older man, while smoothing her riding dress with her hands.

Suzanne could see a smile beginning to form at the corners of her mouth as she lifted her chin slightly. The young schoolteacher was incredulous at her friend's antics and just a little bit uncomfortable, too, with Kathreen's coyness.

Hazelhurst took it all in stride. It was obvious he was comfortable with the wiles of women and had navigated such waters before.

"I imagine he would say I am old enough to be your father," the rancher said with a chuckle.

Kathreen's demeanor collapsed like an eggshell on a railroad track, her face growing redder than her auburn curls. She stood hastily and said, "I need to deliver this letter," and moved towards the porch steps.

Slowly, Suzanne rose to follow her friend while Gareth Hazelhurst stood with a broad smile and gave the schoolteacher a slight wink.

"If you ladies would excuse me, I believe I have pressing business elsewhere. You will find the corrals down beyond the bunkhouse—that long low building with all the windows. Just follow the lane on down towards the barn and you will see it, if you don't hear the ruckus those lads are making first. Good day to you, Miss Kluesman, Miss McClusky, it has been a pleasure having you here and, Miss McClusky, anytime you would like to discuss my future family plans further, I would be most happy to engage in that conversation with you."

"That man was making fun of me," Kathreen said angrily, once they had reached the gate.

"You mean because he called attention to the obvious?" Suzanne scoffed.

"Obvious nothing," Kathreen said bitterly, "there's lots of older men who marry younger women."

"Oh, so now we're down to marriage, are we? What did you expect, Kate? You go barreling in and try to take the bull by the horns, it's no wonder that now and then one's going to toss you on your ear, and if you ask me, it serves you right."

"Nobody asked you, so you can just shut up." Kathreen set her jaw, her mouth a determined line, and marched across the ranch yard with Godfrey Thompson's letter firmly in her hand. Amused, Suzanne followed behind her towards the noise and dust that rose from a high pole corral, where several cowboys sat.

Chapter Eighteen

Breaking Horses for the 4th Cavalry

By the end of July, they had cut and green-broke all of the males of the bachelor herd except one promising young black that they turned out with the mares in the larger valley. They gentle broke, Indian style, the half dozen they planned on keeping. Rusty had selected a brown colt with the black legs that spoke of Morgan blood somewhere in his lineage and a buckskin, two-year-old with a white star on its forehead. Lance had spent hours in the pond and on dry ground, gentle breaking his palomino and the blaze-faced red, both flashy colts that showed a lot of promise. Sonny had contented himself with the stallion, its grulla markings running to a smoky gray-blue color, which was even more striking as it darkened to charcoal black on his legs. He had the dark mane and tail and a dorsal line up his back of a lineback dun, not unlike a blue roan-buckskin, as Lance had described him. The stud was quickly catching on to working stock and herded the other horses, only this time with a man on his back.

"We're gettin' low on grub," Sonny said, "We'll finish those last two colts tomorrow and head for Fort Concho and San Angelo. We can collect on these broomtails there, how'd that be?"

"Suits me just fine," Lance said.

Rusty gave his friend a wry grin and nodded his agreement. "You never did tell us why you call working a horse in the water like that, Injun breaking them," he said.

Sonny took a swallow of coffee and tongue spit some grounds into the fire. "Two things," he said, "One, they keep a horse from water for a few days until that's all the cayuse can think of and while the parched critter is finally taken for a drink and is busy slakin' his thirst, they crawl on its back so that it hardly notices 'cause it needs to drink so bad. "Case you hadn't noticed, horses ain't the brightest match in the box, they got a one-track mind you might say—sorta like some cowboys I know. Secondly, redskins ain't all that found of gettin' bucked off onto the hard ground—it's a lot better taking a dunkin' than a bruisin', wouldn't you agree?"

"Yeah," Lance said, "I notice that the horse can't buck as well in the mud and water too."

"Seems kinda chicken to me," Rusty scoffed, "taint hardly like real cowboyin', takin' up with Injun ways."

"I suppose not," Sonny said sarcastically. "Real cowboys ain't afraid of havin' their head kicked off on the way up and havin' it handed back on their way down. That way they can tuck it under their arm before they go bouncin' off across the gravely-bosom of Mother Earth."

Lance laughed and gave his friend a shove as Rusty grinned sheepishly and then mumbled, "Reckon I kinda like the water when it's hot out."

It was a two-day ride from the wild horse canyon to the middle fork of the Concho and Rusty led the remuda of horses by taking point. Sonny brought up the rear on the stallion that seemed to delight in nipping his former adversaries, keeping them on the move. Lance rode either flank and by the time they had reached the fort, the herd was trailing well.

Sonny left the boys with the herd on the opposite shore and splashed the big grulla across the river to ride up to the open gate of the stockade. He told the sentry on duty he was there to speak to whomever was in charge of buying horses. The sentry waved him on through the gate and directed him to a low sandstone building with a flag pole out front, where Captain G. Hunt was in charge.

Captain Hunt received the tall cowboy and dismissed the orderly who had shown Sonny in, then waved the cowboy to a chair at the side of his desk. Hunt took a seat in a large leather-bound, swivel chair behind it, reached for an ornate humidor and offered the young civilian a cigar. "Sonny Saber, huh?" he said.

Sonny declined the smoke with a shake of his head and watched the officer select one of the cigars, hold it to his nose a moment and then bite off the end and spit it into a wastebasket. He lit a match on the sole of his boot which was propped up on his desk, leaned back, and slowly turned the stogie to the flame until it was burning to his satisfaction. Then the captain blew a long, blue cloud of smoke towards the ceiling, and looked across the desk at his visitor.

"You part of that Crossed Sabers outfit west of here?" he said.

"Yes sir," Sonny replied, "Grant Saber is my father."

"Don't you have a brother—ah—what was his name. . . he passed through here a couple of years ago?"

"Colt was through here summer before last," Sonny paused, uncertain as to why the captain asked.

The captain saw the look of concern on Sonny's face and chuckled, "Where is that scalawag, I'd purely like to meet him."

"You would?" Sonny was surprised, "What in the world for?"

Captain Hunt dropped his feet to the floor and leaned forwards with his elbows on the desk looking like a kid headed for a watermelon patch. "Your brother corralled three of my junior officers after they had ganged up on him, and relieved them of their britches, blouses and sidearms, then forced them to run in their long johns with the flaps hanging down, through a crowd of dignitaries at our dedication ceremonies. The next morning the pants and blouses were flying from the post flag pole at reveille for the whole troop to see."

"Huh," Sonny chuckled, "that sounds like Colt—funny he never said anything to me about it."

"Well, is he here? I'd like to see him, I never did get all the facts on what happened that night."

Sonny swallowed hard, his Adam's apple feeling like it had grown two sizes too large in his throat. "He's dead, sir, killed in a fall with his horse a year ago last spring."

"Aw, that's a damn shame," the captain sat back in his chair and studied the end of his cigar for a moment then turned back. "Well, Mr. Saber, what brings you to the Middle Fork?"

"Heard the Army was buying horses," Sonny said, "got about thirty head of green-broke mustangs across the river and I was wonderin', might you be interested in them?"

Captain Hunt turned all business-like and took a pull at his cigar. "Might be, trouble is, with you Texas cowboys green-broke means you forked them one time and probably rode them to a standstill. It plays hell on a parade ground at morning muster to have bucking broncos tossing my men all over heck's half acre."

"Well, sir, these were Injun broke," Sonny said, "Your three-year-old granddaughter could ride any one of them to Sunday school."

The captain looked skeptical, "They'd just about have to be that gentle for some of these children they been sending out here." He turned to look out the window, puffed a cloud of blue smoke and then said, "How many mares in the bunch?

"Nary a one," Sonny replied.

"Forty bucks a head and I'll take 'em off your hands."

"I was thinking more like sixty," Sonny said.

"Fifty then," Captain Hunt said, "after all, it's you taxpayers' money I'm spending."

"Beggin' your pardon, Captain, but that's just it, what with the provisional government doubling our taxes here in Texas, we're just having to get top dollar in order to pay 'em. I reckon I'll go see Joe Hansen over at the Mercantile—hear tell he might be buyin' up horses for the trail drives comin' through here."

"Dang it, Saber," Captain Hunt clamped his cigar between his teeth, "You might just as well hold a gun to the President's head. Don't you know it's the U. S. Government you're holding up?"

"Sorry, sir, I thought the U.S. Government was tryin' to help us poor folks in Texas get back on our feet after whuppin' up on us the way they did in the late unpleasantries."

Hunt withdrew his cigar and studied the end of it while blowing a long stream of smoke from his nostrils. Sonny watched the smoke curl in the sunlight streaming through the window pane, and imagined the captain as a medieval, fire breathing dragon, like what he'd read about in school.

The captain gave a sardonic little laugh, "I reckon you are brother to that other Saber that blew through here and took our britches. Sixty dollars a head then, if they are gentle enough to walk around without getting your head stove in. Let's go take a look at the bunch of 'em, the quartermaster'll pay you in army script if the horses pass muster. You can convert it to gold at the new bank in town."

Captain Hunt rode around the milling mustangs looking them over with a practiced eye. He dismounted and checked a couple of the horses' teeth, finding them approachable and nodding with approval, he said, "I reckon they will do. I'll send Sergeant O'Keefe down with the script. It's been a pleasure doing business with you, Sonny, and I'm genuinely sorry to hear about your brother."

Sonny bade the captain goodbye and rejoined his comrades by the river. The boys had a small fire going and were boiling the last of their coffee.

"How much didja get?" Lance asked when he saw the satisfied look on his boss's face.

"Enough to keep us in coffee and beans," Sonny smiled, "How's fifty bucks a head sound?"

"Fifty bucks, whoopee," Rusty said, "sounds mighty good to me."

"Then sixty bucks a head would sound even better, wouldn't it?" Sonny grinned at his open-mouthed riders.

"You're kiddin', Lance said, "You got sixty dollars a head for these nags?"

Sonny gave a self-satisfied grin. "Yep," he drawled, "you just got to know how to parlay with the Yoo-nited States Gov'ment."

They were interrupted then as Corporal Ronson and First Sergeant Beauregard O'Keefe, quartermaster of the post, splashed across the river and rode up to the three cowboys.

They introduced themselves and when Ronson learned Sonny was Colton's brother he launched into telling how Colt had rescued his girl from a wild cow after a Lieutenant Stevenson had abandoned her and climbed up a tree to escape. For the next half hour the cowboys listened in astonishment to the story Ronson told of the lieutenant's cowardice and of how a few days later, he and two of his friends, had ganged up on Colt and given him a beating. Colt got even with them during the dedication ceremonies, by chasing them through the crowd of dignitaries in their underwear and running their pants up the flag pole.

While Ronson sat his horse chatting, First Sergeant O'Keefe stepped down and walked through the band of horses, lifting a foot here and checking teeth there. O'Keefe said, "How come you be bringing us all these mustangs, here now, they be as worthless as milch-cows, in the column."

"What do you mean? Sonny said.

"Now don't ye be givin' me none o' your blarney, you know as well as I do that wild horses in the column are a recipe for trouble."

Sonny feigned innocence, "Why, sergeant, what on earth are you talking about?"

"Huh," O'Keefe snorted, "Ye wouldn't be a keepin' broomies such as these in your own remuda, come trail-drivin' time. They get a whiff of the free range and like as not they be kickin' your teeth in, particularly if there be any of the wild bunch about."

"I expect these won't give you any grief," Sonny assured him, "and Captain Hunt said he'd take 'em, though he tried to beat me up on the price."

"Huh," O'Keefe scoffed, "twas it himself what had to nursemaid these broomtails, he'd probably sent ye a packin'."

The sergeant was counting out paymaster script into Sonny's hand for the thirty head of horses and muttering "sweet Mother Mary and Joseph, sixty dollars a head," when three uniformed riders came splashing across the river. The lead rider, a young lieutenant called out, "Hold up there, O'Keefe. The three of us are looking for mounts befitting our status as officers—we'll make the first pick."

"Blast it now, Lieutenant Stevenson, and be ye havin' the captain's okay on it then?" The quartermaster said with obvious annoyance.

"Never mind that, did you include that pretty sorrel and the palomino in the purchase?"

"No, and mind ye, they be not for sale," O'Keefe said.

"Why not," Stevenson said. The other two riders, both second lieutenants, had ridden over to inspect the horses that Lance and Rusty had picked out to keep. One of them dismounted and was looking in the mouth of Rusty's Morgan.

"Ask himself, he be standing right here," O'Keefe growled.

Lieutenant Stevenson turned to stare mildly down at the three riders and with a superior sniff said, "Why are these horses not included?"

Feeling like a bulldog barked at by a chihuahua, Sonny chafed under the condescending tone and said, "Who wants to know?" He had already pegged this arrogant officer for the same lieutenant that Colton had run into.

A frown crossed Stevenson's brow and he tried to rein his horse about to face Sonny, but the balky animal only half turned, fighting the bit and leaving the lieutenant talking backward over his shoulder. "Apparently you do not know who you are addressing," he said. "I am Lieutenant Stewart Stevenson, attached to the 4th Cavalry of the U.S. Army and assigned to Fort Concho. These other two gentlemen are my brother officers, Lieutenant Faust and Lieutenant Renchler." He indicated his companions who left off examining the horses and strode over to observe the proceedings in time to hear Sonny answer.

"I know who you are. You're the chicken-livered, yellow dog who obviously likes to hear himself talk, yet runs off and leaves damsels in distress while you save your own skin. The gutless wonder who doesn't have enough sand in his craw to stand up to a man in a fair fight without your two idiots here, holding him down."

Stevenson looked nervously at the other two officers and then glared at the grinning O'Keefe and Corporal Ronson. "Who the hell are you?" he demanded.

Sonny made a mock bow and swept his hat off his head, "Sonny Saber, brother to Colt Saber, who I understand you've already met. I believe we have a few things to discuss about three against one."

Stewart's face went white then flushed red with anger as recognition dawned upon him. With a snarl he said, "You obviously are related to that low-bred scum that came drifting through here a year or so ago. It beats all understanding how the likes of you people think you can claim half the State of Texas with your so-called cattle empire. Somebody needs to teach you about your betters."

"Well, I'll tell you what, Mr. High 'n Mighty, I'll bet the payment of this entire herd against your and your two monkeys' pantaloons, that me and these two boys' here can show you how us lowlifes stake a claim."

"You what," the lieutenant's mouth fell agape. "Are you challenging us officers of the 4th?"

"I don't see no officers," Sonny said, "just a mealy-mouthed blowhard, dressed up in blue with a yellow stripe up his leg that goes right on up his back. I got eighteen-hundred dollars here against you guys' trousers that says you'll see 'em flyin' from the flagpole in front of the captain's office before the day's out." Rusty and Lance sidled up to stand just back of Sonny with big grins on their faces at the lieutenants' obvious embarrassment.

"Men," Stevenson called to his friends, "What we have here is a failure on the part of these shit-kickers to recognize their betters. This tall, loud-mouthed one is kin to that sneaking bastard that got the drop on us and humiliated us in front of the whole outfit a while back, and now this one thinks he's going to do it again. What do you say we take his money and teach him a little respect for the officers of the 4th?" Stevenson dismounted and turned to face his friends, unbuckling his side arm. Slowly they followed suit.

O'Keefe spoke up then, stepping between the contestants, "If it tis to be a fight then, lads, and sure if I didn't see it a comin', then it's to be the Marquis of Queensberry Rules, with bare knuckles now, lord love ya, and nothin' else. Mind you, there'll be no eye gouging or hittin' below the belt and should one of ye go down, ta other is to step back for the count. There'll be no gangin' up, two against one or three against two, if'n you know what I mean. I'll be holdin' the stakes then and the last man standin' shall be declared the winner for his side. Lieutenant, I'll be takin' it ever so kindly if you lads be handin' over your britches."

"What, you expect us to fight without our pants on?" Stevenson's face flushed red.

"That be the stakes," O'Keefe said, "that and this script here." He waved aloft the wad of bills Sonny had just handed back to him, a big grin on his face.

"I have no intention of lowering myself to back alley brawling with this bovine riffraff, without proper attire," Stewart Stevenson said stiffly.

Sonny scoffed, "I told you he was yeller, let the crybaby keep his britches, I can take 'em off him after he's whupped."

"Let not one brag when he buckles on his armor as one who takes it off," Stevenson quoted with an air of contempt.

"Alright now, enough of yer patty-fingers," Beauregard O'Keefe said, "on the count of three, come out fightin'. . . one. . . two. . . three."

Lieutenant Stevenson and the other two officers had removed their jerseys and stood with suspenders dangling. Stevenson stepped in front of Sonny and took a prize fighter's stance, fists doubled and arms cocked at the elbow. His legs were bent at the knee with one foot planted firmly behind the other. His two companions paired up with Rusty and Lance, Rusty facing Lieutenant Faust, who was a couple of inches taller and several pounds heavier than he, and Lance in front of Lieutenant Renchler, who looked to be four or five years his senor, but who had a look of dismay at this sudden turn of events. It was plain that neither man was too eager to take on these "devil-take-the-hindmost" Texas cowboys. Stevenson's friends gave sidelong glances at his stance and, like monkeys on parade, assumed like postures in front of the boys.

Steward Stevenson began dancing around Sonny Saber, who turned in a slow circle watching him like a wolf at a rabbit weir. The lieutenant was feinting and making quick little jabs in the air and dancing in and out towards Sonny on the balls of his feet. His friends watched him for a moment and then began circling their opponents in like fashion.

Sonny waited and the next time Stevenson danced toward him, he said, "Aw, nuts," and swatting the lieutenant's guard aside, he stepped in with a powerful, up-sweeping blow and landed a heavy fist into the midsection of the astonished second lieutenant, 4th Calvary, U.S. Army, at Fort Concho, Texas. Stevenson's breath whooshed from his lungs and he bent double to stumble forwards and go to his knees, gasping for air.

The other two officers stopped to stare at their fallen comrade and Rusty and Lance stepped in to fetch each of them a ringing blow, Rusty hitting Lieutenant Faust on the chin, sending him flying over on his back, out cold, and Lance slugging Renchler on the nose, causing that individual to howl in pain and grasp at his injured proboscis. Lance continued to pummel Renchler while Rusty busied himself stripping off the unconscious Faust's trousers. Finally, Renchler could stand no more and fell to the ground and began to hurriedly shuck his pants. Lance stood over him with fists clenched, and watched as the vanquished second lieutenant, bereft of his trousers, lunged to his feet and ran to his horse. He mounted and, drumming his heels into the startled animal, he fled across the river in a spray of water and disappeared towards the fort, never looking back.

Lieutenant Stevenson gazed at the carnage from his knees and finally managed to pant out, "Quarter, I ask for quarter." He held up a hand to O'Keefe who pressed a hand against Sonny's chest.

"Tis it quarter then ye be wantin', Lieutenant, and does this mean you be quittin' the field of battle and ceasin' all hostilities?"

The lieutenant got slowly to his feet and turned a malicious eye on Sonny, "It means that discretion is the better part of valor and due to superior numbers," he eyed the watching Lance and Rusty, "I withdraw to fight another day."

"Then I'll be takin' your overalls if'n ye don't mind," the first sergeant said, and held out a hand waiting, with mock seriousness on his face.

Stevenson removed his pants and threw them at O'Keefe. "Take them and be damned," he snarled, then turning a hateful look towards Sonny he walked over to Faust who was slowly getting up. He gave him a quick kick to the hip and then went to mount his own horse. Lieutenant Faust joined him and they swung their mounts around and trotted towards the river in their red flannel underwear, looking for all the world like a couple of turpentined, French-cut poodles with too much dignity to yelp.

"Well, b'gosh and begorra," O'Keefe said, "It looks as if the likes of the high and mighty himself got that what's been a comin' to him ever since the last time. You ever see the beat of it, corporal, and can't ye just wait to be a tellin' the outfit over a pint or two now? 'Ere's your money, lads, and three pairs of trousers, and if ye don't be mindin' a little suggestion, the best time to be flyin' them pantaloons from the flagpole will be when the boys are at their tucker in the mess hall. That'll be twenty minutes or so, now, you hear? This'll be better'n when who put the overalls in Mrs. Murphy's chowder."

"Much obliged, gentlemen," Sonny said and swung up into his saddle with the pants over his arm. Lance and Rusty mounted and catching up the leads of the spare horses they were keeping, followed their boss back towards the fort with big grins on their faces and friendly nods to Corporal Ronson and Sergeant O'Keefe.

———

The cowboys followed the meandering trail along the creek that led to Suzanne's Hill. They had pulled out of San Angelo shortly after sunrise, having spent the night in the hotel after treating themselves to baths, some new duds, and a store-bought dinner in the hotel's dining room. It was while there that they overheard the conversation about the three lieutenants disgraced for losing their trousers, and that the captain had put them on report, again. It seems as though the three pairs of pants found flying from the flagpole had provided a great source of hilarity for the troops as well as the locals, and it was rumored about that the soldier boys who lost their pants were swearing out revenge.

Their business completed, Sonny thought it prudent to leave town and head for home. It was with some misgivings that he turned off the trail to go to the line cabin, for it was a solemn reminder of his brother and Suzanne. "*What transpired between those two at this beautiful and isolated spot?*" he wondered, but found he didn't really want to think about it. Rusty and Lance were arguing about the encounter with the lieutenants.

"Too bad you aren't part of the one-punch club," Rusty said. "How come it took you so long to get the best of that greenhorn shave-tail?"

"Huh," Lance said, "mine was twice the size of yours and if'n yours hadn't a had a glass jaw, he'd a prob'ly cleaned your plow."

"Glass jaw nothin', he went down like he'd been kicked by a Missouri mule. You need to toughen up some, boy," Rusty patronized, "work on your punch."

They rode out into the meadow then, and Sonny pulled up. "Something's wrong," he said. He was riding Penny and leading Tornado and kicked his horse into a run, galloping towards the hill, with the other two close behind. Sonny halted his mount at the top near the spring and stared down at the charred remains of Colt and Suzanne's cabin. A sickening sense of finality settled over his spirit.

"What happened?" Lance said, looking around. The barn and corrals were blackened rubble and the only other sound breaking the silence, was water tinkling from the exposed end of a bent pipe and a raven cawing in the distant forest below.

"Indians," Sonny said. "They wrecked the place, then burned it to the ground."

The riders looked at each other uneasily, none of them daring to voice the unspoken thought of what might have happened to the young couple, had they been living here at the time.

"What a shame," Lance said, voicing all of their sentiments.

Snake-Who-Talks pulled up his pony and signaled to his braves for silence. His black eyes narrowed, a hand shading them against the late morning sun while he peered through the trees at the three riders leading extra horses and racing across the meadow towards *The Perfect Hill*. It was a place where the Kiowa claimed the spirits sat for council whenever they came down from the sky-lands and they had been greatly disturbed when the Tejanos had built the cabin and barn on the very top of it.

Snake-Who-Talks could not be certain, but it looked like the three riders were the very ones who had set fire to the mulo's tail and stampeded their ponies a few weeks earlier. His ears burned with shame as he recalled the fear that had gripped him when the devil mulo had rushed at them out of the darkness. A great war chief would not have rushed mindlessly after the horses and allowed the captives to have escaped, especially the tall Tejano whose weapons he now carried. It was with some satisfaction that he had been able to flaunt these back in camp in front of Two Dogs and had celebrated by reining his pony about, holding the coveted rifle aloft for all to see. Two Dogs had turned in disgust and disappeared into his lodge while Snake-Who-Talks gave a hoarse victory cry after his retreating figure. However, when the word got out that he and his braves had lost their captives and the mulo, after being frightened by the animal with its tail on fire, most of the band had had a good laugh at his expense. The final conclusion was that Snake-Who-Talks' medicine had definitely not gotten any better. This idea became further entrenched in the collective mind of the band after watching the young war chief shoot his new weapons with little effect. He had shot up nearly all of the bullets in the belt, but was still a long way from mastering the rifle and pistol.

It was the need to acquire more of the cartridges, along with the dismissive attitude shown to him and his braves, that led Snake-Who-Talks, with his few followers, to quietly slip away early one morning before the rest of the camp was up and stirring around.

For the past week they had been riding in the hunting grounds shared with the Kiowa, in hopes of finding a poorly-defended supply wagon or settlers' caravan traveling to or from the stockade. With luck, they would find both goods and captives to bring back to the camp and have the last laugh on Two Dogs and the old chiefs with their silly superstitions.

Now his luck was with him, if it even was luck. He believed he made his own luck—his own medicine as the people said, and just as he had captured the tall Tejano before, so his foresight to go looking for just such an opportunity had once again put his enemy within sight.

The small band of Comanche watched the three riders reach the top of *The Perfect Hill* and stare down at the blackened ruins. The Kiowa had done well to destroy by fire the white man's buildings from the sacred spot. The white-eyes had no business building on *The Perfect Hill* in the first place, although rumor had it that the white man who was to live there was a powerful spirit-shaman and many of the Kiowa had been against burning him out. It had been something about an enchanted, crossed-stick sign, and that the Tejano was invincible, protected by the Great Spirit and was a close personal friend of his son. The whole tribe had been unable to kill him after they had attempted to shoot him with arrows.

The war chief scoffed at the idea. Would the people ever abandon the ridiculous ideas of the old women who called themselves chiefs? Apparently some Kiowa were as easily duped as some of the Comanche he knew. If the white-shaman had such strong medicine, then how come his cabin and out-buildings were so easily burned? Fortunately, the wiser heads of Crows Foot, the medicine man, and White Bear, the head chief, prevailed and *The Perfect Hill* had been purged of the desecration.

Snake-Who-Talks smiled to himself at the obvious dismay of the riders surveying the damage. He watched from the concealment of the forest as they dismounted and sifted through the rubble, to find nothing but ashes and charred logs on top of *The Perfect Hill.* Turning to his braves he said, "Yonder are the white-eyes who chased away our ponies and stole the little maids with the yellow hair. Their horses and weapons await you on top of *The Perfect Hill.* If you fight bravely and well today, we shall have much cause to celebrate when we return to the Badger Clan with the rifles, pistolas and the captive Tejanos.

His braves looked questioningly at the young war chief.

Laughing Otter said, "They are on top of *The Perfect Hill* of the Kiowa, its medicine is strong and may not be good for the Comanche."

A look of scorn crossed the features of Snake-Who-Talks, "The Kiowa do not have exclusive right to *The Perfect Hill* or the Spirit Councils who sit there. Even if there was such a thing, the Comanche are greater in number and would have a greater claim on the Spirit Council. They will fight for you this day. Would you not like a rifle of your own?" He held up the Winchester and saw the light of anticipation in the eyes of his braves. "We will count coup and capture the Tejanos, their weapons and much goods."

Dismounting, the young war chief took a small tin from a buckskin pouch at his waist and began to apply war paint to his face. His braves eagerly dug out their own war paint and followed his example. Carefully, Snake-Who-Talks drew a black circle around his pony's eyes. This would insure the animal would have keen vision, then he slapped black hand-prints on the horse's chest, legs and withers to help his strength not fail.

Once the braves were prepared for battle, he led the way quietly to the place where the white-eyes had left the wood and entered the meadow. Here they would wait in ambush for the Tejanos.

———

A sadness enveloped the cowboys as they descended the little hill and retraced their trail. "Why do bad things happen to good people?" Sonny wondered. Colt and Suzanne had such high hopes invested in this place. Sometimes he wondered about the goodness of the Lord. Did a person's prayers even really make any difference? He felt certain that both Colton and Suzanne had prayed for the Lord's protection on this little place, and he had, too, at least when he was here and they were building it. Now it was all for nothing, all that hard work gone up in smoke. What if they had been living here when the raid took place, could the two of them have held off a large force of hostiles bent on burning them out? There was no escape cellar built under this place, why had Colton overlooked that after their ordeal at the line shack?

Sonny was at a loss to figure it all out. Now Colt was dead and Suzanne was lodged deep in his own heart. "Thank God, she wasn't here," he thought and then scoffed at his own cynicism. "Maybe you do know what you are doing, huh, Lord?"

They were fifty yards from the edge of the meadow when a covey of quail suddenly flushed from the buffalo brush along the edge of the trees. Sonny reined in Penny and held up a hand, Rusty and Lance pulling up as well. From behind him, Tornado nickered, the big stallion's ear's were cocked, pointing towards the trees ahead.

"Indians," Sonny yelled and jerked his Winchester from the scabbard. "Make for the hill!" He whirled his mount about and tugging at the lead rope of the stallion, he sunk his spurs into the mare's side and bent over the horse's neck. A bullet whined past him followed by the report of a rifle and the blood-chilling war-cry of the Comanche.

Rusty and Lance turned their ponies about in an attempt to follow the lanky cowboy to the top of the hill, but became entangled by the horses they were leading. There was a struggle to get the extra mounts turned and finally the two boys had to let go of the leads and run for their lives as several Indians came galloping from the trees in their direction. The delay with the horses had given enough time for the attacking Indians to come within arrow range and an arrow struck Rusty's horse in the neck, causing it to go down in front of Lance's mount.

A wild-eyed look of panic emblazoned across the pale face of the redheaded cowboy as he kicked his feet free of the stirrups and turned to look at his close-following friend. Clutching his rifle, he reached out his left arm to Lance as his horse carried him down.

Lance's horse swerved to avoid colliding with the downed animal, but the young cowboy shifted his rifle to his other hand, leaned far out of the saddle and reached to grab Rusty's arm. Dragging him free of the tumbling animal, Lance launched Rusty up through the air to land behind his own saddle. Like a cat crawling out of a rain barrel, Rusty scrambled for a seat on the plunging back of the horse until he managed to get astride, then the two of them raced away for the top of the hill, the Comanche close on their heels.

Sonny spied a huge pine log lying off to the right of the burnt cabin and kneed Penny towards it. He quit the saddle in a running dismount and jumped over the log just as another bullet smacked into a large tree standing there. Turning to take cover behind the log and return fire, his attention was suddenly arrested by a huge Mohave rattler that he had nearly jumped on top of. Only an arm's length away, the snake had stopped its slithering for the cover of the log and was coiling its long body to strike.

A Comanche warrior, following close behind the two cowboys riding double, pointed his rifle at Rusty's back, and pulled the trigger but the gun did not go off, dropping the rifle, the warrior drew a pistol and brought it to bear on the fleeing riders. Lance and Rusty leaped their foam flecked horse over the pine log just a few feet away from Sonny and jumped from the winded animal to take cover. The huge rattlesnake was momentarily distracted by the other riders and quick as a flash, Sonny snatched it behind its head and flung it up and away.

Like something from a bad dream, with a long whirling arc, the green serpent sailed through the air and caught the Indian brave about the neck just as he jumped his pony over the log. The six-foot snake whipped about the surprised Indian, wrapping several times about his neck in a tight coil until its head stopped face to face with the warrior.

Startled, Snake-Who-Talks dropped the pistol in his haste to pull his pony to a stop. He stared transfixed into the malevolent, beady eyes of the rattlesnake, and could see the black, forked tongue flick rapidly from its mouth. Then, in fascinated horror, he watched the serpent draw back its head, saw the mouth snap open, and felt a deadly hiss propel into his face. The young war chief of the Comanche saw two white fangs protrude from the pink roof of the snake's mouth to stand forth in hideous display, drops of clear poison dripping from their deadly tips.

For one long moment, the idea crossed his mind that the medicine on top of the Kiowa's *Perfect Hill* was not in his favor. Somehow he must have angered the ancestral spirits, for them to send him this snake to wear. He who had boasted that he was as wise as a snake-who-talks, now found himself face to face with this horrifying serpent, with nothing to say.

Snake-Who-Talks began a low wailing death chant, his eyes following the snake's head as it slowly moved from side to side, as if charmed by the sound. Nervously, the chief's pony turned back towards the others, walking to where the astonished Indians had pulled their heaving ponies to a stop. When the rest of the Comanche saw the flying serpent wrap about their chief's throat, they halted in frightened amazement to watch the fascinating death song of their leader. Motionless and awestruck they sat their horses listening, as the war chief sat talking to the snake.

The hoarse chanting of Snake-Who-Talks began to rise in volume and intensity and with the increase in sound, the snake's movement grew faster. The Comanche chief's wail rose to a crescendo, when suddenly the serpent struck. Snake-Who-Talks saw a blur of movement and felt the fangs strike his face again and again. Soon he would join the old ones in the spirit world. He must remember to ask them what the snake had said.

Totally unnerved, the other Indians watched the snake strike the face of the young chief. Forgotten were the white-eyes and the battle, their attention riveted on the chief as he rode past them back down the hill, his death song fading into silence. He fumbled his fingers helplessly at the encircling snake about his throat, his movements growing feebler, until at last he lost his balance and fell, headlong, from his skittish pony, to lie convulsing on the grass.

Fascinated, the braves saw the six-foot-long snake uncoil and slither off out of sight. The medicine of this place was strong. For them to have sent the flying snake to speak with him in such a way, it was obvious the ancestors were angry with the way Snake-Who-Talks had disregarded the power of *The Perfect Hill*. His boasting against them was a powerful sign to the young Comanche that the old ones would not tolerate such irreverence.

Abruptly, the warriors turned their ponies and followed to where their chieftain had fallen. Laughing Otter and another brave swung a leg over their ponies and slid to the ground while one of the others caught and held the slain chief's horse. Quickly, they picked up his dead body and slung him across the back of the waiting pony, then leaping astride their own ponies, they galloped from the meadow towards the woods, ignoring the grazing horses of the Tejanos. Clearly, they were not welcome here. The Kiowa could keep *The Perfect* Hill with its spirit council. Let the white-eyes trespass here all they wished, this was no place for the Badger Clan of the Comanche and once the band heard what had happened here, it was certain this place would be given a wide berth.

———

"Jumpin' Jehoshaphat, did you see that?" Lance exclaimed. Both boys had piled in next to Sonny behind the log and had been feverishly working the actions on their rifles, preparing to shoot, when the attacking Comanche had stopped. Now they watched in amazement as the retreating Indians gathered the body of their stricken comrade and rode towards the woods.

"Where the heck did that snake come from?"

"I threw it," Sonny said, breathing hard.

"You threw it?" Rusty said. Both boys looked at Sonny questioningly.

"Yeah," Sonny replied absently, his eyes intent on the Comanche riding across the meadow. "I durn near jumped on top of it."

"Jumped on top of it?" Lance questioned, "Why would you do that?"

Sonny shook his head and gave the blond cowboy a depreciating look. He rose to sit on the log, still watching the retreating Indians and said, "Oh, I figured I needed to add a little excitement to my life, riding with you two can be so dull."

Lance's ears turned red in embarrassment while Rusty grinned at him and then turned to Sonny.

"That was quick work, good thing it didn't bite you—it didn't, did it?"

When the Comanche drew abreast of the loose horses the cowboys had left in their flight, Sonny raised his rifle to his shoulder and drew a bead on the lead warrior.

"Naw—and those redskins better leave our horses alone."

The younger cowboys looked in the direction he was aiming and immediately raised their own weapons with the hammers eared back. For several tense moments the riders watched as the hostiles rode on past the grazing horses to disappear into the woods, then with a collective sigh of relief, they relaxed.

"Good thing," Sonny said, "we worked too hard catching these broomtails to be makin' 'em a gift to those redskins."

"They kilt my horse," Rusty said.

"It's a good thing you got that Morgan," Lance said to his friend, "reckon we better go and catch them."

"Yeah, thanks for saving my bacon down there, my fat was sure in the fire."

"Sure," Lance said nonchalantly, "nothin' you wouldn't a done for me."

Rusty nodded and the two boys turned to follow Sonny on his way to their waiting horses. He bent and retrieved both the rifle and six-gun the Comanche had dropped in his haste. Then walked over and picked up the hat with the two eagle feathers from where it had fallen from the Indian.

"I'll just take this back," he said. His two friends said nothing but watched with amazement as Sonny replaced the new hat he'd bought in San Angelo with his old one.

"This is my hat and shootin' irons. Those must have been the same Injuns that rustled our mules and kidnapped our little Texas Roses." He stood shaking his head and staring down from the perfect little hill and across the meadow. "If that don't beat all."

Riding off the hill and heading back to where they had left the wagon and mule, Sonny dreaded having to tell Suzanne of this final collapse to the fragile house of cards she had held onto. As far as he knew, she had never even seen the cabin.

Chapter Nineteen

Joaquin Davilia

Colt lay for sometime in a half-real, half-dream state. It was daylight, yet he could not see. It was as if his eyes would not open. Somewhere far away he could hear a dog barking and he seemed to be floating weightless above the ground, spinning lazily around, yet he had the uncomfortable feeling of laying on something hard against his bruised ribs, a stick or stone. His hands reached to grip the ground and try to stop the spinning and then he felt something warm and wet licking his face.

With a start, he instinctively tried to sit up, pushing away at whatever it was. Darts of pain shot through his body and clouded his consciousness. He rolled over with a groan and struggled to hold onto the light behind his eyes, but it seemed to be receding, swallowed up in an ever-encroaching darkness. Dimly he heard a far off voice speaking sharply as though to a dog, "Sit," and then the darkness settled in around him again.

Joaquin Davilia pulled the border collie off the prostrate man and ordered him to sit. He had followed the barking dog up a small stream, after leaving his small flock of goats nibbling at the grass along the main trail.

"Wha has dees fool animal found now?" he wondered aloud. The dog was an excellent herd dog and for him to leave the flock with such purpose, caused the wizened old herder to consider it best to take a few minutes to investigate. He was not at all prepared to find a gringo all torn up and lying beside a dead puma. His seasoned eye quickly took in the scene which told of the attack and ensuing struggle. Hurrying to the man, he knelt and rolled him over. There was a low moan but no signs of life otherwise. The Mexican lowered his ear to the man's chest and listened. He could hear a faint heartbeat, and rose to stir up the fire.

"He ees alive, Taco," he said to the dog. Taco watched quietly and thumped his tail as if to say he already knew that.

Adding fuel to the fire, the Mexican goat herder took water from the stream and set a pan to heat, then turned to the stricken man. Blood was on much of his clothing, some of it fresh, but most of it crusted and dried.

"How long ju lay like dees, senor?" he muttered and began removing the lacerated boots from the man's feet.

For the next two hours, Joaquin tended to the white man's injuries. From the look of his clothing, he supposed him to be an Americano, probably one of the Tejanos from across the border. The man's clothes were largely in tatters thanks to the big cat's claws raking him. He removed the jacket and shirt from the gringo's back to discover bloody claw marks, most of them superficial, but one or two that were deeper and still welling blood slightly. The man's attempt to push off the dog had obviously reopened the scabbed-over wounds. There was another serious scratch on the

Tejano's left arm and one across his belly. The lower legs of his trousers were lacerated and hanging in shreds. Here were the most serious injuries—had the man not been wearing the heavy hiking boots, his feet would have been torn to ribbons. As it was, there were serious and deep scratches, all caked with dried blood.

"Dees man weel na be walking anytime soons," he muttered. The dog gave a low whine from where he lay on the other side of the fire, his head resting on his paws and his ice-blue eyes watching the two men.

"Go, Taco, watch thee miserable goatas," Joaquin said and waved the dog away. Taco leaped to his feet and bounded off down alongside the little brook towards the flock, his tail flagging.

Colt felt as though he were being tumbled about and prodded with a burning stick. He moaned and tried to force his eyes to open. Someone was working over him and he could feel cool water bathing the burning places. His mouth was dry and his breath came in short pants. "Water," he managed to croak. He felt his head lifted and then cool water was trickled into his mouth. He drank feverishly and then lost consciousness once more.

When he awoke again, he was being jounced along as though suspended and there was a clatter of poles over rough ground. In the distance, he heard a tinkling of bells and the bleating of goats, accompanied by the barking of a dog. Opening his eyes, Colt could see trees rising above him and gliding past under the blue of the sky.

His was mass confusion. Where was he and what was going on? He had just been dreaming of Suzanne and they had been walking, hand in hand, on a golden prairie through a sea of knee-high buffalo grass towards a brilliantly hued sunset. The wind was blowing her golden hair and she subconsciously had swept a strand of it from her face as she turned to look at him with the penetrating gaze of her incredibly blue eyes. She had asked him, *"Am I a part of this?"* When he awoke, he lay there pondering his answer, an answer he was formulating to assure her that not only was she a part, but that she was the whole. Now he was being bounced along on some sort of conveyance and the dream with its unspoken answer faded off as he came fully awake.

He tried to raise his head but ended up groaning, and let it fall back as a shooting pain coursed across his belly. With the sound he made, the bouncing stopped and the conveyance was lowered to the ground. A kindly face appeared; that of an old man with a thousand wrinkles and a bristly, white beard. A battered sombrero was pushed to the back of his head by a weathered brown hand and kindly dark eyes looked questioningly down at him.

"Ah," the man said, "alas' ju awake. How do ju feel?"

"What happened?" Colt groaned. "Where am I?"

"Ju hab been clawed by thee puma, ba ju hab broken hees neck. Ween ju are more better, ju maus tell me, how ju deed dees."

"Who are you?" Colt asked, looking around in bewilderment. A black and white dog was herding a flock of fifteen to twenty goats beyond them.

"My name ees Joaquin Davilia and thees are my poor, miserable goatas. I hab a cabana na far from heers and I jam tooking ju back to make ju moor better. Try to rest now, eet ees na mucho farther."

Colt lay back and closed his eyes. Joaquin had fashioned a crude litter from a couple of poles and one of his blankets and he bent over to pick up the ends of it. Once more, Colt felt himself born along. His mind grappled with how he had come to this. He remembered the cougar's attack from out of the darkness and the ensuing struggle, but what he did not seem to comprehend was how he had managed to kill the beast. . .and with his bare hands, too. He thought of Samson in the Bible and how he had, "rent the lion in twain" by tearing its jaws apart, but he knew he wasn't that strong. Probably, Samson wasn't either except for the enabling power of God's Spirit. Had God empowered him to destroy that cougar? How had he known of the danger? Something had warned him and prepared him to fight for his life when everything went silent in the woods. Had that been God's Spirit? And the fall that broke the mountain lion's neck, what were the chances of that happening? Surely it was miraculous that he was even alive and it was a miracle that he had been found by this smelly old goat herder before he had bled to death, as well. A deep humility and gratitude settled over him—he couldn't wait to tell Suzanne. Of all the unusual things that had happened to him since he had been separated from her, certainly this was the most amazing. Colt drifted mercifully back into slumber as the old man plodded along with his burden.

Colt spent the next two weeks convalescing, tossing restlessly on Joaquin's rude bunk while the old herder doctored his wounds and battled infection. His feet were the most difficult and slowest to heal, paining him in the extreme whenever he had to hobble to the privy. Joaquin had sewn stitches across the deep wound in his belly with the comment that, "Thee puma would hab deeseemboweled ju had thees wound been eeny deepers." Stitches had also been used to close the gaps in his left arm and across his back. The old Mexican was convinced that the jacket Colt had been wearing was the only thing that had prevented worse injury there.

After his feet, the wound across his belly was the most troublesome, for Colt found that practically every bodily function he had sent painful jolts across his stomach muscles. A simple thing like a cough or even laughter soon ended with a gasp and a moan. A sneeze was devastating.

Slowly, with the gentle care of Joaquin and the simple but nourishing food, he began to mend. He was immensely grateful when the day came for the old man to remove the stitches and he sat patiently, enduring the twinges of pain, as Joaquin snipped through the threads with a small pair of scissors and withdrew them from his flesh.

Colt found the Mexican herder to be a man well read, and of some education. He learned that at one point in his life he had spent time in a monastery and had studied for the priesthood. Books lined the shelves of his simple, one room, log cabin and often the two of them would sit on the porch and discuss some of the saints of old. Saint Francis of Assisi was of particular interest to the young protestant and Colt began to realize that not all Catholics were the idolaters he had been led to believe. Joaquin had a genuine faith in both the Bible and the Lordship of Christ.

The herder's place was in one of the small clearings in the forest and was situated along a small stream that eventually flowed into the river, although it was some distance away. Here he tended his flock of goats, raised a large vegetable garden and, with the help of his dog, Taco, kept the goats from a fenced off section of the meadow where he was raising hay to cut for the winter. His one-room log cabin had a full covered porch and a woodshed attached. There was a rudimentary pole shed and corrals and a one-hole privy completed his little homestead.

Chores of tending the garden, chopping wood, packing water and fixing meals were fitted around herding the goats to various grazing spots in the surrounding meadows and forest. Often the Mexican left the injured man to recover while he went about his daily routine.

Slowly, Colt mended to the point that he was able to manage, somewhat awkwardly, getting about with a pair of rude crutches Joaquin had fashioned for him. Finally he was able to attempt to accompany him on his outings, at least as much as his sore feet would allow.

"Ju maus na rush theengs, Senor Colton," Joaquin said, when Colt insisted on accompanying him with the goats one day. "Jor feet need thee times to heal."

"I can't stand being cooped up in here any longer," Colt said. "Even if I have to herd goats—it's still better'n doing nothing."

"Aw, thee cowboys doan like thee goatas, I forgeets dees. Doan worry, I won' tell anybodies wha ju do."

"How come you got goats anyway?" Colt asked. "This place has the makings of a pretty good cattle ranch."

"Cows too mucho troubles," he said. "The goata ees cheap, has the leteel bebe twice in thee year, makes bueno milk and cheeses and is muy good carne. He eats practically everytheengs and can prosperar where thee vaca, he starve."

"Well, I have to admit the meat's a whole lot better than I thought it would be, the way you fix it," Colt said. "Only one other time have I eaten it when it was any good and that was fixed by a Mexican, too. What are you doing to it?"

"Ju hab to slow thee cookeeng with mucho herbs and spices," he said.

"Well, it is good the way you fix it."

"Thee golden haired senorita, she weel na save ju, ju know."

They were sitting in the sunshine on a boulder that overlooked a meadow a few days later, watching Taco try to chase a couple of kid goats off another big rock nearby. The two young goats stood end for end and would attempt to butt the collie whenever he would rush at them from the ground. Now Taco lay on his belly watching them and waiting for his opportunity.

Colt turned to stare at Joaquin in surprise.

"What did you say?"

"Thees Senorita Susanna, she has thee golden hair, no?"

"Why yes, how did you know that? She is lovelier than the sun in the morning and her hair is like spun gold," Colt asserted with a fond nod of his head.

"She weel na save ju," the old man said again.

"Why do you even say that and what makes you think I need saving anyhow?"

"I heer ju talking to dees wan wheen ju are out of jor head weeth thee fevers. Do ju love her?"

"More than anything else in the world, I can't get back to her soon enough. We were about to be married, you know."

"Peety thee mans who theenk the answers lie weeth thee womans—peety the womans, too," Joaquin said.

Old Davilia was studiously tamping tobacco from a soft leather pouch into a home-made corncob pipe as though the conversation were ended.

Impatient for him to go on, Colt blurted out with some uncertainty, "What answers?"

The old man did not deign to answer until after he finished loading his pipe, struck a match against the rock, and had it puffing good. Shaking out the match, he took a long pull at the pipe and blew a cloud of smoke upward. Finally he took the stem from his mouth and with a knowing look said, "Thee answers to life."

Colt watched him for a moment and then turned back to look at the stand-off between the dog and the goats, but with far-seeing eyes.

"She holds some of them," he said with a sigh. "At least as far as I am concerned."

The smell of Davilia's tobacco smoke wafted past Colt's nostrils and he inhaled the smoke and absently thought, "*If I ever use tobacco, I am going to smoke a pipe.*"

Finally Joaquin said, "Si, thee woman can be thee source of mucho happiness, ba she ees na thee streams of joy, aleese na by herself."

"Then what is?" Colt asked, a little nettled. He could not imagine anything more lovely than Suzanne, no greater prize to win, and nothing greater than their love or more worthy of his devotion and his pursuit to make her his own. When he at last had her in his arms and in his bed, he would give her his strength, and his manhood would be complete, the woman in her, fulfilling the man in him. Then together they could face anything.

When he voiced as much to the old herder, the Mexican gave a wan smile and sadly shook his head. "All my streams of joy are in ju," he quoted.

"What?" Colt said, "in you. . . who, in me?"

Again the old man shook his head and removing the pipe from his mouth, he pointed with the stem upwards and looked knowingly towards the heavens. "No—in ju," and again he gestured upwards.

"What does that mean?" Colt asked.

"San Francisco, he says there ees a God shaped vacuum in thee heart of every mans and eet remains eempty unteel he fill eet weeth Dios—weeth God.

"I know the Lord," Colt said somewhat defensively. "I have invited him into my heart and I know Suzanne can't save my soul—I don't expect her too."

"Then why du ju steel look to the senorita to save ju?"

"I don't—she is the love of my life, that's all. Why are you confusing that with my salvation, haven't you ever been in love?"

A twinkle appeared in the corner of the old man's eyes and they seemed to moisten a little. He puffed for a moment and nodded his head.

"There was thee golden haired senorita een my life when I was jung, eekcep her hair was black as thee raven and so long—to her waist. Meeny happy hour we speend together—and some not so happy, too."

"What happened to her?" Colt asked, "Where is she now?"

"Een thee grave—no weeth thee Senor, thee Lord een heaven. We were married for a time, ba she perish een thee birth of our son and wheen she die, eet tore such a hole een my soul, I abandoned God and my new-born son and weent to live for the Diablo—the Devil."

"Well, you can't live for the Devil and expect to find happiness," Colt said.

Dat ees jus my point, I had made Juanita the ceenter of my juniverse and eet took meeny long and painful jears to learn that God was at thee ceenter of my juniverse. He is thee jealous Dios, he weel hab no others before heem. Juanita had to be removed from thee ceenter een order for me to see Heem there. Na unteel he was at thee ceenter deed I descober all my streams of joy were een heem."

"Are you trying to tell me that God killed your wife because you loved her more than you did Him?" Colt was incredulous.

"I jam telling ju dat thee answers to life—who ju are, wha ju are dueeng heer and where ju are goeeng, are nah found een jor golden haired Suzanna. She may be geebin to ju as a geeft from God, ba reemeembers, she ees geebin as thee helpmate, taken from thee man's side to help ju een thee battles and adveentures of life. Do na confuse her weeth thee adventure, or even thee battle ju maus fight, but rather thee wan to fight thee battle weeth."

"Then how come it seems that the battle to woo and win her seems to be life's greatest adventure and battle?" Colt asked.

The old man chuckled, "Eet ees God's way of depe-ecteeng thee greater truth. Thee adventure, thee battle, and thee beauty are geebin to us as a peecture of the greater adveenture, battle and beauty—the wans only found in Heem. Sadly, too meeny mens settle for thee lesser and ween thee golden haired beauty becomes thee hag, thee bag, and thee nag, then they turn to wha' eber habits they hab, to lose themselves. They finish their days as eemposters, weeth wine, womens, and songs, never knoweeng their true selves, jus filling thee God-shape weeth other theengs. Worse yet, they neber find that all thee streams of joy are een Heem."

"So, are you saying that I love Suzanne too much?"

Joaquin looked at the youth and removed his pipe. At last he spoke, "I jam sayeeng that she daus na hold thee answer to who ju are, wha ju are dueeng heer and where ju are goeeng. Only Dios knows thees theengs and ju maus get thee answers from Heem, na Suzanna. Only wheen ju have answered thees questions can ju eenvite her to come along weeth ju. Only then du ju hab thee strength to offer her—thee real mans for thee womans."

"So, have you found the answers to these questions?" Colt asked.

Again, the old Mexican laughed. "Partly, ba moslee I jam steel descobereeng that all my streams of joy are een Heem, too."

Joaquin knocked the dead coals from his pipe, stood and picked up a stone to throw at the two goats on the rock. Distracted by the clatter of the stone, the two kids turned to see what caused the noise and Taco rushed in to nip their heels and send them scooting back to their mothers' sides.

The days of summer were passing into autumn while the painful wounds Colt had sustained from the cougar healed. Joaquin was interesting company, but Colt could not help but feel the old goat herder had never known love in the same way that he loved Suzanne. In fact, he wondered if anyone else had ever known love like that. Had his parents? Had Suzanne's? Had Joaquin loved his Juanita that strongly? He tended to doubt it, otherwise he wouldn't be saying the things he said.

He had said that Suzanne could not be at the center of his world—that he wasn't to orbit around her like the moon around the earth, or the earth around the sun. Was he doing that? Joaquin had insisted that Colt needed a much bigger reason than her to know who he was, and that only after he had discovered his mission, his purpose and his name, could he come to the woman and offer her his strength. Until then, he wasn't fit for her, that it was only when he had answered these three questions that he could have anything to invite her into to share.

It all seemed a bit confusing to the cowboy as he pondered these things—confusing and annoying as well. The old man made it sound as if he had been feeding off of Suzanne's beauty, that his glorying in her beauty and loveliness was somehow depleting her, that her affections and admiration of him, her approval, was somehow validating him, but at her expense.

"Huh," he scoffed, "that old man has no idea of the things I have gone through for this girl. I've fought off Comanche, Kiowa and Apache; have faced bullies, outlaws, and banditos, and even cold-blooded killers. He thought of the would-be suitors, friends, and even family, that cast an envious eye in her direction; the kidnappers, scoundrels, and even some serious contenders for her hand, that he had had to overcome. I've forsaken all others, turned my back on other women—some who had more than a passing fancy—and remained devoted to her. I've endured danger and privation; the heat and the cold, hunger and thirst, captivity and pain; all as a direct result of my love for Suzanne Kluesman, refraining from the delights of her ultimate embrace, keeping myself only for her. So don't tell me I haven't fought for her—shoot, I am still fighting for her and trying to get out of this wilderness. If it hadn't been for that blasted cougar, I would probably be with her right now, maybe even married. I'll give her my name, too, I know what it is. What is he talking about? I am Colton Saber and Suzanne is going to be Mrs. Colton Saber, and I got a pretty good idea of what I am doing here and where I am going, too. I am here because I got dumped here by some cruel quirk of fate and I am going back to her, just as fast as I can get there."

He knew the earth was beautiful, at least much of it. Someone had said that the world is not primarily functional but beautiful, and Colt tended to agree. The sky was another thing that was beautiful—clouds, sunsets and sunrise, the stars and moon at night, all beautiful and all made by God. They told of God's beauty in their own way and he understood that. And women were beautiful, at least most were. Suzanne certainly was, and he loved to behold her in spite of what old Joaquin said. But to behold the beauty of the Lord—how did one do that? He got the part of seeing the good things God made, the beautiful things. . . "I bet that's part of it," he said, "but to look on the face of God, who could do that?"

He began to wonder if that was what the old man was talking about, the quest—to learn how to behold the beauty of the Lord. Was this the journey he was supposed to be on? King David in the Bible had said *"To behold the beauty of the Lord"* was the one thing he desired, and that he would seek after. Maybe he was to be seeking after that, too. Wasn't David the man after God's own heart?

"Huh," Colt mused, "if that is the quest, then it can just as well happen on the journey I am on now and that is getting back home just as quick as I can, to behold the beauty of my Suzanne."

Colt watched Joaquin slice a long butcher knife through a fresh loaf of bread and set a slice of it on a plate along with a generous piece of cheese. The old man handed it to him and began to cut another for himself. The cowboy was delighted with the taste of the simple fare, who would have guessed that just bread and cheese could be so satisfying. Picking up his own plate, Joaquin led to a spot on the porch where they could enjoy their lunch in the shade.

"How am I supposed to find out who I am, as you put it?" Colt asked around a mouthful of food.

"Wha can ju be trusted weeth?" Davilia asked.

"Huh? Trusted with? I don't know, I never thought about it before."

"Thee true test of a man's characters is wha he can be trusted weeth."

"I think I am trustworthy—at least I try to be."

"Some mans ees good only wheen others are aroun' to see heem behave, otherwise they doan always be so good."

"I try to be good—most of the time," Colt said reflectively.

"God ees good all thee time, theese ees how we can know who He ees."

"You mean that being good defines a man's character and our character reveals who we are?"

"Si, ween ju can be good all the time, then ju weel be like Jesus."

Colt scoffed, "Who can do that?"

"Na so meeny mans, ba wha ju can be trusted weeth; thees tells me who ju are. Thees is easier to be seen in others than in jorself."

"What can you be trusted with?" Colt asked.

Joaquin chuckled, a twinkle in his eye. "Ah, now ju come down to thee hearts of thee matters. Why doan ju tell me wha I can be trusted weeth?"

Colt thought on that for a moment and smiled. This wise little goat herder had very cleverly maneuvered him into understanding concepts of goodness he'd never considered. He intuitively knew that Joaquin Davilia was a man who was good, one who could be trusted. Colt had, in fact, trusted him with his very life—trusted him when he was helpless to do otherwise—and Joaquin had graciously and selflessly gone out of his way to tend to his wounds and nurse him back to health, asking nothing in return. In fact, he had seemed to thoroughly enjoy the chance to do so. He knew this had sprung from a basic goodness deep from inside the man, a genuine goodness of the heart that was good in and of itself. Colt observed that this little hermit, sequestered away here in the woods of Mexico, like some monk in a primitive monastery, had found true goodness and, with it, a contented happiness.

"You're good," Colt said, nodding his head several times. "I trust you."

Davilia smiled again, bit off a crust of bread and chewed slowly. "I know my leemitations, ba deed ju know tha beeing good ees fun? Virtue ees eets own rewards."

Colt pondered that for a moment. He thought of those times he had done things for others with no other motive than to be helpful, and remembered the satisfaction he'd felt latter. Old Davilia was right. Funny how he had never noticed it before. He sure noticed it when he didn't do "good things," and the dissatisfaction that came with that. He supposed that by its very nature, this kind of goodness didn't call attention to the fact that it was good—at least not initially. It might afterward, but by then the deed was done, and if the motive was pure and not contrived, a sense of personal integrity might result.

"What about bad?" Colt finished his bread and cheese and reached for a cup of water.

Joaquin shrugged, "Eet ees na thee same theeng. Bad can na exheest een and ob eetself like good can."

"What do you mean?"

"Good stands alone because God made eet tha way, ba evil is only good gone bad. No theengs, na even thee Devil started out bad."

Colt's mind went to the bad things that had happened to him and the bad people involved. As much as he hated to admit it, he had to begrudgingly acknowledge that such people had not been bad at their beginning. Even Reese Hutchinson had been an innocent baby at some point. Boy, that was a hard concept to put into the corral of his experience. A silly grin crept over his face as he pictured Hutch as a mean two-year-old, beating up his mother.

"Why do ju smile?"

Colt took a swallow of water. "Nothing really, I just got this ridiculous picture of an evil person I knew. I was trying to picture him as an evil toddler." He chuckled, "It didn't quite work."

"No, eet doan work, no wan starts out bad—flawed, si, ba na bad."

Davilia stood up and set his tin plate on the box he had been sitting on, then stretched. "Eet ees time for my afternoon siesta," he said. "All dees talk has made me sleepy."

A few days later, Colt bade Joaquin Davilia goodbye, patted Taco on the head, shrugged into his makeshift pack, and then took the trail east by northeast, headed for Texas. He had a lot to chew on, running through his mind. "What about ticks and mosquitoes?" Colt said, "I can't quite conceive them as ever having been good, even in the beginning."

Colt plodded steadily along, crossing mesquite-covered volcanic hills and ravines; occasionally finding a spring or creek in what was otherwise a hot, dry, and desolate land. The cool forestlands of Joaquin's river bottom dropped behind him, and were sorely missed by the cowboy. He had been greatly refreshed by his convalescing there, but the time had been a source of much impatience for him as well, and now he was anxious to complete his journey. He rationed his food supply and limited his travels to the early morning or late evening hours while holing up during the heat of the day in some shady spot to rest and nap. He was constantly on the alert for the Apaches, but after seeing no sign of them for the first few days, and now having passed an extended time with Davilia, he had hopes of having eluded the Indians and of having made good his escaped from Guaynopa Canyon, undetected. They were certainly preoccupied with the raid on the mining camp when he left.

Five more days on the trail found him tired but determined to get out of this maze of canyons and mountains and unfamiliar terrain. He estimated he had not traveled more than one hundred miles east since leaving Joaquin's valley. "I wonder if this is the area we traveled through blindfolded," he said aloud and found his own voice sounding unnatural to him.

In the multitude of his thoughts, he had heard no audible voice other than his own groans and grunts, since he had left Davilia's place. Colt chuckled to himself and smiled. "It's alright to talk to yourself, just as long as you don't answer yourself back," he recited, recalling the old homespun adage he'd often heard his mother use as a gauge against going crazy. "I wonder if that's true?" he said, then shrugged the makeshift pack on his back and moved on.

The trail he followed was often well defined and at other times hard to see or make out, especially at the higher elevations on the volcanic rock. Often he would have to choose from such vantage points, which of the ravines to follow and occasionally he chose the wrong one. He would double back until he located the one with signs of the caravan's passing. It took all of his tracking skills and a steeling of his will against the frustrating loss of time, for his heart was set on reaching the blonde-haired, blue-eyed girl waiting for him on the Pecos.

The memory of Suzanne and her sweet love sustained and drove him onwards in a steadfast determination to reach her loving arms again. At night he recalled those sweet moments of their first kiss. He rehearsed through his mind's eye the look of her—the lines and soft form of her figure, the blue of her eyes, the blush of her lips, her sweet scent and soft touch—all of these seemed to cause the grueling miles and hot sun; the thorns, and sand burs, and hardships, to fade into insignificance as he trudged on.

He often called out to her that he was on his way, whenever some cliff or hill or rockslide, hindered his progress. He'd struggle on through, around, or over the obstacles. In ways, it was not unlike his trek across New Mexico Territory, except that then, he'd had little hope of Suzanne's love and affection, now he knew he was headed for the arms of the sweetest girl in the world. How surprised she would be to see him—how they would fly into each other's embrace never to be separated again.

The miles passed underfoot as he dreamed of making her his bride, of their honeymoon in the little cabin on the hill he'd built for her. "Suzanne's Hill," he whispered, savoring the sound and magic of it—a perfect little hill for a perfect sweet girl—the place where he had begun his discovery of her, and the place where he intended to finish that discovery and make the blacksmith's beautiful daughter his wife—one with him forever.

Some days later, Colt stumbled down out of a rocky draw onto a well-defined wagon road that paralleled a broad, slow-running river flowing out of the northwest. He hurried to the water's edge and bent over to quench his thirst and wash off the grime, only to recoil in shock at the whiskered, hollow-eyed, bedraggled image reflecting back at him from the water. "Could that be me?" Colt removed his tattered clothing and the worn down boots the Mexican had repaired, then waded naked into the coolness of the water and bathed his tired and bruised body. Sitting on a flat rock, he rinsed out his worn jeans and the Mexican shirt he'd brought from the camp and draped them over some bushes to dry while he found a shady spot under a cottonwood and fell asleep.

The creaking of wooden wagon wheels brought him awake with a start, and instinctively, he reached for his pistol. Coming up the road was a peasant's two-wheeled cart towed by a long-eared burro. It was led by a middle-aged Mexican man whose large sombrero hid the upper part of his face from sight. The cart was loaded with melons and was followed by a Mexican woman and two small children, a boy and a girl.

The cart came to a stop and the man called out, "Hey. hombre, where are jor close, I have thee senora and thee leetle wans heer. Can ju make jorself decent?"

Colt started, then made a beeline for his pants as the Mexican woman turned away and the two little kids stared wide-eyed.

"Look, papa," the little girl said, "Dat man has no sombrero on, he weel geet hees head burned."

Chuckling, her papa said, "Si, my leetle dove, thees gringo could learn a lesson from ju."

"Hold up there, Senor," Colt called as he struggled into his clothes and then sat to pull his boots on. "Where does this road go?"

"Thees road?" the Mexican said, "Why eet goes to Del Norte—El Paso Del Norte, eet ees jus aroun' thee next beend ob de reeber. We are taking thees melons to sell in thee market there."

Colt shrugged into the bandoleer-backpack and picked up the rifle and hurried over to join the little family. "Then this is the Rio Grande and that's Texas over there?" he said, indicating the far side of the river.

"Si," the Mexican answered, his eyes looking uncertainly at Colt and his firearms.

"I've just traveled from the Sierra Madres over in Sonora and need to get to El Paso. Do you mind if I walk along with you and your family?"

"Si, jes, eet ees bueno—good ju travel weeth us. Maria, cut a slice of thee watermelons for thee senor. Would ju like a slice of thee melons?"

"Yes—si," he nodded with a smile towards the lady, "That would really hit the spot right now."

The Mexican nodded, "Heet hees spot for heem," he said with humor. He and his wife and the children began to laugh.

Colt watched the peasant woman carve a generous portion from a large watermelon and hand it, dripping, to him. He laughed, too.

Colt walked across the bridge into El Paso, Texas and was amazed at the changes that had taken place since his last visit, two years before. There were several people coming and gong at will, most of them Mexicans, when a sudden clatter of hooves behind him caused him to quickly jump to the side to avoid being trampled by two cowboys who were racing their horses past him.

"Out of the way you stupid bum," one of them sneered and then laughed to his companion as the two of them galloped by. Colt watched the two young toughs, run their ponies carelessly across the bridge, scattering the pedestrian traffic this way and that, with no concern for life or limb.

Shaking his head and a little bit embarrassed for his countrymen, Colt stopped to help an elderly Mexican woman recover a bag of oranges she had dropped in her haste to get out of the way of the rowdy cowboys.

"Gracias," the woman said when Colt handed her the bag. She reached in and took out one of the oranges and handed it back, a grateful look in her eye.

"Thank you, Senora," he replied. He took the orange and walked on across the bridge, peeling it as he went. It had been sometime since he had tasted the fruit and he smiled as the pleasant sweet juice, ran down his throat.

There were businesses and storefronts all along the main street, some even extending to side streets. Upon inquiry, he learned which building was the assayer's office. Here he went in to exchange the gold nuggets he had for cash. Colt had left several of these in an empty coffee can for Joaquin when he had left the herder's cabin, but still had a pretty good poke left. He came out of the assayer's office with over two-hundred dollars in his pocket and the clerk staring after him, his unanswered questions cut off with the closing of the door.

Next, he stopped at the mercantile to purchase a new outfit and although Gimble, the proprietor, kept staring at him, he didn't seem to recognize him as the cowboy who'd had the jewels for sale two years earlier. Colt was browsing amongst the dry goods in search of some new clothes when he heard a familiar voice, one aisle over. He turned a corner to see the minister's wife, Mrs. Blankenship, chatting with another woman, apparently a young soldier's wife from Fort Bliss. She was inviting her to attend Sunday services in the newly constructed Baptist Church, the next day. He was delighted to see a familiar face, although it had been over two years since he had made the ill-fated ride to Yuma on the stage with the Blankenships.

He took a step towards the two ladies, intending to introduce himself, and had just removed the battered hat from his head as a sign of respect, when the two of them turned to look his direction. Both ladies' eyes opened wide and, with startled shrieks, they clutched their packages and fled as one, out of the store.

There were several patrons in the store who looked up at the outburst, along with a young clerk wearing a bib apron and sleeve garters. He hurried over to address Colt.

"Sir, you are going to have to leave," he said nervously.

"I just got here," Colt replied.

"We can't have you disrupting our regular customers—that was the minister's wife you frightened out of here."

Colt stared back at him in amazement.

"I know that was her, I was just about to speak to her when she took off like that— what's going on?"

The clerk seemed reluctant to talk to Colt, but anxious for him to leave.

"Perhaps you should give some attention to your appearance before you come to town," he said.

"That's what I'm trying to do," Colt answered. "I need to buy some new clothes."

"I should say you do. Do you have the means?"

"The means? If you mean money, then of course I do, what did you think?"

"Never mind then," the clerk said stiffly. "If you will step back over to the men's section, perhaps you will allow me to assist you in selecting a more suitable attire." He looked nervously over his shoulder to where two elderly women stood near the front of the store, speaking to one another surreptitiously behind their hands, and glancing his way.

The clerk grabbed Colt by the arm and hurried him around the corner into the next aisle and away from prying eyes. As they passed a full-length mirror, Colt caught sight of the clerk escorting a scraggly, long-haired, bearded bum and realized with a start it was he. Suddenly he burst out laughing, he had forgotten how shabby he looked.

The vivid picture the minister's wife and the other lady must have had was obviously enough of a fright to send them fleeing like a couple of old biddies with their tail feathers on fire, from the wild-eyed, crazy man from Borneo. It tickled his funny bone, and he chuckled until he caught the disapproving look in the clerk's eye. It was obvious to him, it was no laughing matter.

"I do not see what is so amusing," he scowled, "if you will just. . ."

"Don't get yourself all tangled in the traces," Colt interrupted and shook the man's hand from off his arm. "Here's ten dollars against my purchase, you go and tend to those ladies up front. I'll pick out my own outfit and see you at the counter."

The man fingered the bill gingerly as though it may harbor some rare exotic disease, gave him a skeptical look, and then turned and walked back to the front. Colt could see Gimble casting a baleful eye in their direction and remembered his attempts to swindle the jewelry of Empress Carlotta, the last time Colt was there.

Colt grinned, "Probably don't remember me, with this brush on my face and my eyes looking like two holes burned in a blanket," he thought. He purchased jeans, a couple of shirts and the rest of the clothing he needed and then added a black Stetson with a silver concho hatband and a matching belt. Then on a whim, he added a new gun belt and holster, also in black with silver studs and a nickle platted .44 with pearl handled grips. He wanted to look his best when he saw Suzanne. A new pair of black boots and silver spurs completed his purchases along with a black satchel and some items for the trail. Taking his packages, he headed for a two story building with a sign that read, "West Texas Hotel."

"I'd like a room," he said to the clerk behind the desk.

The man turned the guest register for him to sign and asked, "How long will you be staying?"

"Until the next stage rolls through for San Antonio," he said.

"Well, that'll be a couple of days, I'll need five bucks in advance." He passed a disapproving eye over Colt's bedraggled appearance.

Colt paid the man and asked, "Is there a barber around, I could use a shave and a haircut?" The clerk nodded his agreement and pointed out the window to an establishment across the street that sported a barber's pole.

"I could use a bath, too," Colt added."

"End of the hall," the clerk said, "towels are five cents extra."

Colt flipped a nickel onto the counter while the clerk pulled out a folded towel and handed it across to him. Colt thanked him and took his packages, towel, and key, then went up the stairs to his room. A glance in the mirror on the bureau and Colt said, "No wonder the storekeeper didn't know me, I hardly know myself." He studied his reflection, "I've lost weight," he muttered to the scarecrow starring back at him in the glass. He wondered if he should keep the beard. "Naw," he said, "I wouldn't want to scratch up Suzanne's pretty face."

Colt felt like a new man. It was surprising what a bath, shave, haircut and new duds could do for a feller. He trashed the old ragged clothing he had been wearing, then hesitated for a moment before tossing the battered hat, taken from the mine guard he'd killed, wondering that he felt no remorse. It had been a hard time and, with the discarding of these rags and the old hat, Colt put that part of his life behind him and turned with purpose to the stage depot to get his ticket back to the life and the girl he once knew.

Chapter Twenty

Godfrey and Ol' Strawberry

The cowboys were hollering and yelling encouragement to a rider who was trying his best to stay in the saddle on top of a bucking horse, and they did not hear the girls as they walked up. A quick glance between the corral rails revealed Two-Bits Thompson astride a strawberry roan that was just about the ugliest animal Suzanne had ever seen.

With a big Roman nose and little pig-eyes, the horse was animated in a squalling frenzy, trying to dislodge the man on his back. The cowboy flapped about like some disjointed puppet with its strings tangled, but still managed to keep his seat.

The horse's little eyes were rolled to the whites and blazed a baleful anger as the animal hit on all fours and then rose up on its hind legs, nearly toppling over backwards with the rider. Suzanne gave a short scream, while the cowboys cheered Two-Bits, calling, "Stay with 'im."

"Look at 'im sunfish," a cowboy in a blue shirt cried.

"He's one, sunfishin' son-of-a-gun, his belly's turned clean up to the sun," another man agreed.

The horse was bouncing around the corral, hitting on all fours with punishing force on each jump and Suzanne wondered why anyone would ever put up with such a ride. What was the matter with these men anyway? This was absolutely insane.

"He's sure a frog-walker," a thin cowboy with a black vest said. "Hook 'im, Two-Bits." He turned to elbow his companion on the right, "I got a dollar that says 'ol Two-Bits pulls leather afore he's done."

Suzanne saw he was talking to Buddy McLeod who sat scowling on the top rail, his arm done up in a sling.

"I'll take your dollar," McLeod said, "My pard'll never pull leather."

"You're on," the thin cowboy said. "Look how high that crowbait can jump, he only lacks wings to be on the fly."

The ugly roan came down with a bone jarring thud, again hitting on all four feet at once and then with dizzying speed, he swapped ends and bounded higher than the top rail of the corral.

"Look at him," Buddy cried, "He just turned on a nickle and gave ya the change."

Down the horse came again in that same brutal stance and then with a mighty leap, he rose in the air and twisted with a wicked kick at the clouds. To everyone's amazement, Two-Bits Thompson seemed to go sliding off, upwards and backwards, away from the horse, and higher into the sky. Still holding the hackamore ropes, there was a surprised look on his face as he watched the bronc drop away from between his legs and when he reached the end of those reins, they jerked him into a forward somersault and propelled him back to earth. He literally bounced when he hit the ground, the wind driven from his lungs.

For a moment, the cowboys were stunned into silence as they listened to the low moan coming from the crumpled heap of their pard, as he struggled to pull air back into his pancaked lungs. Suzanne was sure the cowboy was dying.

"Uuuunh," Two-Bits gasped. Finally he managing to suck in enough air to light into cussing the roan's birth.

"Dad-gum-it," he panted. "You dad-burned, dog-gone, gimp-eared, knock-kneed, stinkin', mangy, flea-bit, hoppin' toad." He rolled over and got to his knees, warming to his task. "You weed burnin', pea-brained, hunk a dog meat wrapped up in horse hair. You squinteyed, pin-headed, son of a seabiscuit-eaten jackassed cross between a hyena and a pole cat. You bobtailed, butt-bustin', bag a bones. You ain't nothing but a sway-backed, jugheaded crow bait bound for the glue factory, and I'll ride your sorry carcass all the way there and pay 'em to take you. Oh, that the sun had refused to shine on the day you was born—that the coyotes had kilt your mama and et ya afore ya ever opened your eyes or drew breath. You should a drownded in a flash flood, been pounded to death by a hail storm, burned in a prairie fire, carried off by a tornader and got buried by a sandstorm." He took a deep breath and finished by saying, "And if that ain't enough, let me catch my breath and I'll tell ya how I really feel."

Two-Bits got slowly to his feet and arched his back, then stretched his neck, trying to realign his battered vertebrae, while the rest of the hands looked on in awe.

"Well, pard," Buddy McLeod said, "you get an F in ridin' but we'll give you an A-plus in airin' the wind."

With a low whistle, the fellow with the blue shirt said, "That was the most colorful bending of the King's

English we've ever heard, do you think you could give us lessons?"

Thompson gave both of them a sour look and said, "You can both go to and stay put," then he turned to where a couple riders had caught up the roan. "Put the blinders back on and yank that bronc saddle off, and slap my leather on 'im and open up the gate. Screw it down tight, too, cause I'm gonna fork this miserable cayuse and run his sorry tail into the ground or know the reason why." Seeing the fire in his eyes, the two riders were quick to comply.

Suzanne followed Kathreen, who had climbed to stand on the third rail to where they could just peer over the top pole of the corral.

"Hey, **Godfrey,**" Kathreen called, "got a letter here for you to sign for."

Two-Bits froze in mid-mount, one foot still in the stirrup and one on the ground, then turned to look over his shoulder at those on the fence. Slowly he lowered his foot from the fidgeting roan, while everyone stared open-mouthed at the two girls.

For a moment, Two-Bits stood there staring at the toes of his boots, his head bowed. Then he scrunched his eyes shut, threw his head back and reached to push past the brim of his hat and rub his forehead. This could not be happening to him—not now. That smart-alecky redhead from town had somehow found out his real name, and now here she was, blabbing it out in front of all his pards. Some days it just didn't pay to get out of bed.

"Wha'd she call him?" Blue-Shirt said.

Black Vest shrugged his shoulders, "Don't know, sounded like gadfly or somethin'."

"She said, 'Godfrey,'" a third cowboy spoke up.

"Oh, my Lord, Two-Bits," McLeod called. "Is your front handle Godfrey?"

"I have a special delivery letter for one, *Godfrey* Thompson," Kathreen announced, placing undue emphasis on the front of his name with a belittling laugh. She stepped up one pole higher and waved the envelope aloft for everyone to see. "You have to sign for it," she went on, "Godfrey Thompson, right here, see?" She pointed to an attached, tear-off portion of the envelope. "Who is Godfrey Thompson?" she said, while she fixed her eyes on poor Two-Bits.

All hands watched as Two-Bits shoved his hands into his hip pockets, turned slowly around with a shake of his head, and strode resolutely towards the aggravating female on the corral poles.

"Are you *Godfrey* Thompson?" she said in a voice loud enough to flush pigeons from the barn.

"Yes," Two-Bits mumbled.

"Speak up," Kathreen goaded him, "I can't hear you."

"Yes, give me my letter, you little imp."

"Now, just a minute, I thought your name was Two-Bits, isn't that what they call you?

"Yep, that's m'name."

"Then how do I know that you're Godfrey? I've got to be sure to deliver this letter to *Godfrey* Thompson, special delivery."

"That's the handle my mother hung on me," he said with a helpless gesture to the grinning cowboys on the fence. They reminded him of a flock of buzzards watching a gut-shot wolf.

"Can anyone here vouch for you—that you are, in fact, Godfrey Thompson?" She turned the question to the men on the corral, but they all just exaggeratedly shook their heads. while enjoying the hoorahing this gal was giving their pard.

"For cryin' out loud, I'm Godfrey Thompson! Give me the dad-blamed letter and quit your gallin' me." Two-Bits made a grab for the letter but Kathreen jerked it away.

"You must sign for it first. Has anyone got a pen and ink so *Godfrey* here can sign for his letter?"

The cowboys were snickering and whispering back and forth.

"Is his name really Godfrey?" one said.

"Who'd name a kid Godfrey?" another said witheringly.

"My lord, I'd sooner be called a girl's name," Blue-Shirt spoke up.

The others turned to look skeptically at him.

"You sure about that?" the first one said.

"I surely would," Blue-Shirt vowed in an attempt to save face.

"All right, fellas, meet Shirley Wood, now we got two new hands at the Box 7, Godfrey Thompson and Shirley Wood." He gave the befuddled rider a shove from the top rail with a contemptuous hoot, while the other cowboys roared their delight.

In confusion, poor Blue-Shirt landed with a thud in the dust. Just moments before he had been privy to the razzing of ol' Two-Bits and now all of a sudden, he himself, was sitting in the dust of the corral, a victim of the other riders' merciless hazing.

It was too much for the cowboy, he sprang to his feet, grabbed the man who had shoved him, hauled him off the top rail and gave him a solid punch in the nose. The two began to slug it out to the delight of the on-looking cowboys and while they were momentarily distracted, Two-Bits hurriedly took the pencil Suzanne had dug from her pocket, and signed his name for the offending letter Kathreen had bandied about.

"Now give me the dang letter," he said.

Kathreen made him jump twice for it, before she let him snatch it from her hand and stomp back to the hands waiting with the strawberry roan. They stood with mouths agape at the unusual goings on.

While the fight behind him wound down, Two-Bits paused to open the envelope and scan the contents of the one page letter. Slowly he folded it back up, put it back in the envelope and stuck it in his hip pocket. A look of sadness came over his face, then with an angry shake of his head, he stepped up on Strawberry and jerked the blindfold free. He jammed his spurs into the roan's flanks with a cry nearly as loud as the horse's squeal. "Open the gate!"

With an angry bellow, the bronc exploded into a frenzy of bucking again, intent on dislodging the rider as before, but Two-Bits stuck to the saddle like a burr to a fleece-lined coat, and when the horse found he could not dislodge him, it suddenly bolted through the open gate in running jumps and disappeared across the yard and out onto the prairie in a cloud of dust; taking Godfrey Thompson, his humiliation, and whatever distressing news was in the letter, with it.

Kathreen gave a self-satisfied smirk and hopped down from the corral poles. "One letter delivered special D," she said, and walked back towards the house.

Suzanne left the equally amazed cowboys roosting on the fence, and followed her friend back to where their horses were tied. She wondered if Kathreen might not have overdone it this time.

Both girls had just regained their seats in the saddle when Gareth Hazelhurst stepped out on the porch. "Leaving so soon, ladies?" he called.

Kathreen cast him a dark glance and then, without a word, she smugly turned her nose in the air and spurred her mount towards the road back to town. Suzanne held Checkers in long enough to reply to the rancher.

"Yes, Mr. Hazelhurst, we should be starting back before it gets too late. Thank you for the refreshment."

"I am afraid I may have upset your friend," Gareth said apologetically as he came down the walk.

Suzanne smiled indulgently with a slight shake of her head. "That girl is a bundle of surprises just waiting to happen," she said. "I wouldn't be overly concerned about her feelings, if I were you."

Hazelhurst gazed up the driveway at the disappearing cloud of dust and chuckled, "She certainly seems to be in a large hurry." He turned to Suzanne and held out his hand, "It has indeed been delightful to make your acquaintance, Miss Kluesman, and that of your friend as well. Please feel free to visit the Box 7 at anytime—nothing brightens up the place like a couple of pretty ladies."

Suzanne shook his hand with a blush and bid the cattleman goodbye, "Thank you again for your hospitality," she said, and then waving goodbye, she cantered her horse out of the yard after Kathreen.

Kathreen McClusky let Petunia run for awhile, something the head-strong animal was eager to do, seeing they were headed back towards town and the barn. Kathreen was feeling a mixture of glee at having put one over on Godfrey Thompson, and resentment at having been put in her place by the suave rancher. She did not pay a lot of attention to her riding and immediate surroundings, but was mindful that the reckless pace seemed to match her mood. At length she began to try to slow the horse down, pulling the filly in, to allow Suzanne to catch up, but the stubborn animal fought the bit, its blood high, while the young woman battled for control. She finally managed to slow

Petunia to a skittish walk and, keeping a tight rein, she turned in the saddle to look back at the distant cloud of dust that marked her friend's progress as she galloped to catch up.

Suddenly the rental horse shied violently sideways and came to a stop, standing trembling by the side of the road. The horse had been alarmed by a Gila monster that was making its way across in front of them. Kathreen, being nearly unseated, gave a shriek and grabbed the saddle horn. Her eyes followed the horse's gaze to stare horrified at the big ugly lizard. The reptile stopped its progress and blinked beady eyes at the intruders, its black tongue flicking in and out of its lipless mouth.

This is one of those poison lizards they told me about, she thought. *It looks like it is about to attack.* Anxiously, she began to fumble in the saddlebag for the .38, her eyes riveted on the motionless Gila. Petunia was side-stepping backwards across the road when the girl drew the gun and cocked it, and when the Gila monster made a short run at them, she screamed again and pulled the trigger. Amazingly, the random shot struck the dirt in front of the venomous creature and sent up a shower of dirt before the bullet went whining off across the sage. The effect was that the Gila monster stopped in its tracks, but the stable horse had other ideas.

In no hurry to catch up, Suzanne had Checkers in a slow lope, figuring to allow Kate time to collect her thoughts and come to her senses. She heard the distant scream and saw her friend nearly fall from the saddle. Alarmed, Suzanne kicked her horse into a run to see what the trouble was up ahead. Then she heard another scream accompanied by a pistol shot. She saw Kathreen nearly tumble from the saddle again, when the rental horse bolted at the unfamiliar gunfire. To her amazement, the redhead's horse leaped from the road over a ditch, and went racing pell-mell, off across the prairie towards the river.

Kathreen fell backwards over the horse's rump, her feet still locked in the stirrups, when Petunia jumped the ditch. She was desperately fighting to sit back up on the racing horse, and try retrieving the reins, which she had dropped in her fright, along with the pistol. Fortunately, the reins were tied together and were now caught in the filly's mane, looped up around its neck, behind the ears. Kate screamed a couple of more times as she bobbled about trying to regain her balance. She had a stranglehold on the saddle horn, but this only seemed to urge her mount to run faster in its head-long dash toward the fast approaching Pecos River.

It was in this manner that she passed Two-Bits some distance off. The cowboy was riding a subdued strawberry roan from out of the sage, back towards the road, and chaffing under the news of the letter. His father was doing poorly and his mother wanted him to come back to Iowa and run the hog ranch. For a moment, Two-Bits pulled the bronc to a stop and just stared at the crazy spectacle a hundred yards distant. Was that that smart-mouthed, redhead from Saint Louey, bouncing about on the back of that runaway? He could not be sure but even as his judgment warned him he'd regret it, he jerked the roan's ugly nose about by the hackamore rope and sunk his spurs into the bronco's flanks to give chase. Strawberry exploded in a series of running bucks that carried him and his rider about half the distance to the running horse's line of flight before the game little mustang lined out in a dead run after the fleeing stable horse and its screeching female burden.

Suzanne reached the spot where Kathreen's horse had left the road about the same time that Two-Bits gave chase to the runaway filly. Checkers was fidgeting, and pulling at the bit and she had to turn the spirited horse in a tight circle to keep her from jumping the berm and racing after the others. Finally bringing the pinto under control, and relieved that the cowboy would help Kathreen, Suzanne stopped her mount and stepped down to retrieve the .38 from where it had fallen in the recent ruckus. Blowing the dust from the barrel, she pocketed the gun, remounted and set out at a fast trot to follow Kathreen's flight towards the river.

Badly bruised from the buffeting she'd taken, Kathreen managed to regain an upright position and was still holding onto the saddle horn for life itself, when the ground before her dropped away in a long, gentle slope to the Pecos. She screamed again as Petunia made a long leap over the crest of the hill and ran madly down the incline towards the slow-moving river.

Like a giant, brown snake, the river coiled back and forth, eating into the bank here and leaving muddy shallows and sandbars there. When the panic-stricken rental horse Kathreen was riding reached the river's edge, it made one last heroic leap from the three-foot-high bank to land with a resounding splash up to its knees in the sluggish current, and there the filly stuck fast.

With an ear-piercing scream, Kathreen was launched from the saddle and sent flying over the horse's head to land some distance from shore, with a splat in the shallows of a muddy sandbar. Soaked and dirty, she scrambled to her feet, but to her horror, felt herself sinking into the soft, sucking, clinging mud. Petunia was thrashing about and whistling in fright and Kathreen knew that both she and her horse were caught in the deadly quicksand of the Pecos River.

In the despair of this realization, Kathreen saw Two-Bits Thompson come thundering up on the fiery strawberry roan. He pulled the horse to a ground-squatting stop, sending rocks and chunks of turf splashing into the water.

"Help, Two-Bits!" she screamed, "Quicksand —I'm sinking!"

To her relief, she saw the cowboy untie his lasso from the saddle while the roan pranced about on the bank. Expertly, the cowboy held his mount in while at the same time building a loop with the rope. The broncy mustang, head-shied and lunged backwards, as the unfamiliar rope twirled about his head and went singing out over the water, causing Two-Bits to miss his toss.

"Hold still, you dashed jug head," Two-Bits said and pulled to retrieve his wet rope.

Kathreen stared in wide-eyed fear when she saw the cowboy was casting his loop towards her horse and not her.

"What are you doing, you fool?" she cried. By this time the mud was to her knees and in spite of her struggles, she was unable to pull either of her legs free.

Two-Bits stuck the hackamore rope between his teeth, guiding the mustang with his knees, and hauled in the lasso, yanking it back until he was able to catch the flying end and shake out another loop. This time, while goading his horse forwards, he was successful in dropping the noose neatly about the struggling filly's neck. Tying the rope quickly about the horn, the cowboy spurred the roan around and up the slope while the girl screamed at him.

"Forget the stupid horse—save me!"

With bucking crow-hops, the sturdy mustang stretched the rope to near the breaking point, but finally enabled the desperate filly to regain her footing to where she could scramble free of the clinging mud. Half-running, half-dragging, they pulled the rental horse to shore and up the embankment where it stood streaming water and heaving for breath.

"Two-Bits," Kathreen screamed, "I'm sinking, save me."

Two-Bits merely glanced in the redhead's direction and kneed his horse over to the trembling filly. Calmly, he removed his rope and then caught up the dragging reins of the riderless horse and rode over to where he could tie it off to a cottonwood. Methodically, he recoiled his rope and then, building another loop, he edged the roan to a spot opposite the stranded girl and just sat there studying her.

The mud had oozed over Kathreen's knees by this time and for one awful instant, she realized that she may have taunted this man once too often. Before her was the fellow that she had belittled, mocked, and depreciated in front of others so many times, that even though she had done it mostly in fun, there now came a realization that, at best, she had never once taken him seriously. She had diminished him as a person and probably alienated him to the point that he hated her. Could it be that her only hope of rescue now sat there on the shore, disinclined to take her plight seriously? What had she done?

"Two-Bits, please," she pleaded. "I am sinking deep in this miry clay, won't you please toss me your rope? I am going down. I am sorry for all the bad things I have said and done to you. Please—help me!"

The cowboy stepped down from his horse and turned to tie it to the brush. He then squatted on his heels on the bank, his rope clutched in his hand and hat pushed back on his head.

"Is the mud above your knees?" he said.

"Yes," the girl cried, "hurry, I'm still sinking!"

"I don't thinks so," Two-Bits replied. "You haven't moved any in the past five minutes or so."

"How do you know? I can't move! Throw me your rope and pull me out of here—pleeese!"

"Nope, not with this horse and not with that filly either. The angle is too sharp, you'd most likely break both your legs. I won't try it with an inexperienced roping horse—too dangerous."

Kathreen grew a little bit irritated with the lackadaisical cowboy. "Well, what do you expect me to do? I can't stay here even if I am no longer sinking!"

"I'm going to get you out of there, but you have to do exactly as I say. As soon as I throw you this rope, I want you to put it around you under your arms and tie it off with a granny-knot. Can you do that?"

"Yes," Kathreen answered with a quaver in her voice.

Two-Bits whirled his rope and threw it out to let it land in the slow-moving current just above the stranded girl. It floated down to where she could catch it, then he watched her tie it about herself as he had instructed.

"Now, I want you to sit down in the water."

"Sit down?" Kathreen said with consternation, "I'll just sink even more."

"I don't think so, you're broad enough across the beam for the mud to hold you."

"I'm what?" she said nettled at the indelicate inference in spite of her predicament.

"Just do as I say, I'm trying to yard you outta there."

It was at that moment that Suzanne crested the top of the slope and took in the scene and her friend's plight below. She quickly spurred the pinto down to the water's edge, pulling up beside the waiting cowboy and hurriedly dismounted.

"Kathreen," she called anxiously, "are you alright?"

Shakily she replied, "I think so, if Two-Bits doesn't drown me first."

His lips in a tight line, Thompson grimaced, "She's fine, she needs to do what I tell her." Then he yelled, "Sit down!"

Kathreen leaned back until she could feel the soft mud at her derriere. This action brought the muddy water nearly to her chin.

"Alright, now I want you to slowly work one leg at a time, back and forth. Allow water to come in alongside until you can pull it free."

Kathreen complied with the rider's instructions and was relieved to find that, once her weight was off of her legs, she was able to work first one and then the other free of the clinging mud. Seated as she was, she barely made an indent in the mud, the water holding her up and, in fact, she actually began to bobble and then float as she pulled her other leg free.

"Don't try standing up, just let the current carry you," Two-Bits called, "I will guide you to shore."

Soon the redhead was scrambling up the slippery bank to where she fell panting on the grass, while muddy water streamed from her soiled clothing. Finally she rolled over and sat up next to her amazed friend and the grinning cowboy. She pulled her boots off and dumped the water from them.

"Before you waste your breath asking," Two-Bits said dryly, "I had to pull the hoss out first, its weight was taken 'er down a whole lot faster than what yours was, and since I ain't no hoss-whisperer, I couldn't tell that other filly to sit on her rump and pull 'er legs free.

Besides that, you didn't want to have to walk home and pay for a dead hoss, did you?"

Kathreen looked skeptically at the cowboy and then at her grinning friend. With a mysterious look in her eye, she pushed to her knees, reached out a muddy hand and clasped Two-Bits Thompson by the front of his shirt and pulled his face down equal with hers. She then proceeded to plant a big, wet kiss of gratitude on the shocked cowboy's lips.

"Dang woman!" The cowboy said and stumbled backwards, nearly falling. "You're more notional than this muley bronc here." With that declaration the cowboy righted himself and then clambered into the saddle, all the while coiling his rope.

"At least when ol' Strawberry humps his back I know what to expect." Jerking the hackamore rope free, Two-Bits put the roan up the slope in a series of running crow-hops before the game mustang lined out in a dead run and disappeared from sight.

Laughing delightedly, Kathreen called after him. "Godfrey Thompson, I'll have you know, my rump is not all that big."

Two weeks latter, Kathreen McClusky sat on board the stage bound for Saint Gaul, while they waited for Silas Wade to bring the flat-bottom boat to shore. She had bid farewell to Suzanne moments before in a tearful goodbye, but was satisfied that her friend's outlook on life had much improved during her three-month-long visit and now it was time to return to Saint Louis and home.

Mrs. Munson was sorry to see her leave for she had been a decided asset to the General Store, having attracted many customers from both near and far, just to be served by the vivacious, if somewhat prickly, clerk. Customer goodwill was at an all-time high.

Twice more, since the episode at the river and her fright in the quicksand, Kathreen had seen Two-Bits. The first time was at Munson's Store, when he came in to pick up mail for the Box 7. He barely nodded to her and without speaking, he quickly finished his business and fled the store.

The second occasion had been last Sunday afternoon. Suzanne was otherwise engaged, playing music at the Trinidads' town house in preparation for the evening's song service at church. Kathreen was walking Nuisance along the tree-lined lane that led from the Trinidads' place towards Main Street, when Two-Bits rode up.

"Good afternoon, Mr. Thompson," Kathreen said brightly.

"Afternoon, Miss."

Two-Bits had slowed his pony to match the red-head's pace, but had no further comment.

Kathreen could see his sober expression, and asked, "Are you feeling alright, Godfrey?" She couldn't help giving the usually, happy-go-lucky cowboy a little dig.

"No," he said, "and don't call me that name."

"Why, Mr. Thompson, what do you want me to call you, surely after all we have been through together, we might be on a first name basis?"

"Two-Bits is fine," he said dryly.

"I'm going home soon," she said, watching his reaction.

Two-Bits seemed to slump in his saddle, "Yeah, that's what I heard. I don't suppose there's any chance of your. . ." he broke off in mid-sentence, reined his horse up, then sat looking at her with a rather forlorn look in his eyes.

"Of my what?" she prompted. Suzanne had said this cowboy was in love with her, but she had disbelieved it. Now she was not so certain.

"Some of the fellas at the ranch—oh, dash it all. Miss McClusky—Kathy, will you write to me once you get back to Saint Louey?"

"Write to you? Why Mr. Godfrey Thompson, whatever for?"

The cowboy was flustered and not seeing she was trifling with him, began to bluster nonsense.

"Well. . . to let me know how you are, how things are going in Saint Louey and such. . . you know what I mean."

"You mean like sweethearts?" she asked.

Two-Bits turned about two shades of red and fidgeted with a knot in his horse's mane.

"Well, you did kiss me," he said.

"I did, indeed," Kathreen replied. "But that was for saving my life from drowning in that nasty Pecos River. You don't figure that made us sweethearts, do you?"

Two-Bits shrugged. "It made me one," he said matter-of-factly.

"Very well, Mr. Two-Bits, I shall add you to the list of my would-be suitors and shall be happy to correspond with you, once you have written to me first."

"Does that mean you will?" he asked in amazement.

"Yes."

A visible change came over the cowboy. With a broad smile flooding his face, he urged his pony close to Kathreen and reaching both hands down, he clasped her about her shoulders, lifted her a foot off the ground and leaned over to kiss her on her very surprised mouth. Setting her back on her feet, he whipped his hat off his head, popped his prancing horse on the rump and with a loud, cowboy "yippee," went galloping off up the lane.

Kathreen smiled and straightened her clothing while Nuisance sat looking at her. "What are you looking at, Shep?" she chided the pooch, "He's a bit o' alright."

The only cloud over her trip had been the fact that Sonny Saber had never put in an appearance. She had not had a chance to confront the sanguine cowboy regarding his jilting her, and she was leaving with a sense of frustration and of things unresolved in that regard.

She had seen and greeted Sonny's folks at the little church on Sundays, but had declined going out to the ranch. She did not wish to revisit the scene of so many, now painful, memories.

The flat-boat ferry thudded into the dock and Kathreen absently watched as a wagon with a mule tied behind got off the ferry, followed by two riders leading several horses. One, on a dark grayish colored horse paused to pay the ferry-man and then came on to pass by her window just as the coach started down to board the boat.

With a start, Kathreen recognized Sonny Saber. He seemed darker, more sober, not the devil-may-care cowboy she remembered, and somehow he seemed bigger, taller in the saddle and more in command.

For a moment he glanced her way then turned back, intent on leading the horses past the rumbling stage coach. Kathreen sat stricken, her hand to her bosom and struggled with a torrent of emotions, not the least of which was anger. Anger at how he had treated her, anger at herself for having given her heart to him only to be rejected, and there was sadness, too, sadness at her loss. Still, she felt some gratitude that he had stepped in to help Suzanne in her time of need.

With resignation, she sat back in her seat. Although she wanted to jump from the stage and go tell him what she thought of him, it was just as well. Plainly, she was now a part of Sonny's past, and she may as well let bygones be bygones.

The ferry boat lurched and slowly began to draw away from the dock when Kathreen heard shouting and someone yelled her name. There was a clatter of hooves and she stuck her head out of the window in time to see Sonny Saber galloping a big horse down the landing road and out onto the dock. To her amazement, she saw him leap the horse over six feet of water to land with a crash on the fan-tail of the ferry boat.

Kathreen sat with eyes big and mouth agape, as Sonny, with a droll grin on his face, kneed the grulla stallion up alongside the coach and said, "Well, hello, darlin', where'd you spring from and where you goin'?"

At the sight of his laconic insolence and audacity, something flashed inside the redhead and ignited her Highland ire. Forgotten were all her noble and self-sacrificing thoughts. This West Texas cowboy was going to pay the piper for the tune he'd danced with her.

She spied a large Bowie knife in a sheath on his left hip and in a flash she was out the door and plucking the blade from its sheath on her way down, She landed on her feet in the narrow space between the coach and the horse and rider.

Sonny's horse neighed and shied suddenly, rearing up. Sonny grabbed leather and yelled, "What in tarnation are you doing?"

As the half-broke bronc went up, the saddle girth was exposed on the horse's underbelly, while Sonny fought to keep his seat and get the animal under control.

Quick as a cat, Kathreen slid the flat edge of the Bowie knife under the cotton webbing of the cinch and with a flick of her wrist, cut it in two.

There was a loud pop as the girth gave way and the saddle came loose and started to slide off the back of the grulla. At the same moment, Kathreen caught hold of Sonny's leg and heaved upwards for all she was worth, causing Sonny and his whole rigging to dump from the horse's back and land with a huge splash in the river to drift to the downstream side of the ferry. The horse, suddenly relieved of his rider, head shied and nervously back-stepped on the swaying deck until it cleared the coach. Then, turning with a clatter of hooves, it sprang awkwardly into the river and swam back towards shore.

Kathreen stepped around the coach to the railing of the ferry and called to the bobbing figure struggling to hang onto his saddle and keep afloat. "Since all I am good for is water to swim in, you can just enjoy this swim on me, with my compliments." With that, she turned back to the coach, climbed in and slammed the door. She was still clutching the Bowie knife, to the amazement of the other passengers. Her last view of Sonny was his dark-faced visage drifting slowly downstream with the current of the muddy Pecos River.

Chapter Twenty-One

Something About Hands

Suzanne came slowly awake lying on her bed as a warm breeze ruffled the curtains at her open window. Her eyes focused on the sunlit pattern of leaves from the big oak in the front yard that was casting shadows on the opposite wall. She could tell without conscious thought, it was going to be another hot day. Her mind was still mulling over the lingering remnants of a dream that came to her in ragged pieces, like patches of clouds blown by the wind.

She stretched languorously on the bed and kicked the remaining sheet off onto the floor, then lay there in her light cotton gown, her body seeking the coolness of the breeze, yet somehow more alive and awake than she was.

She closed her eyes and tried to pull back into the dream, willing it to continue. There was something about hands—big hands—who's were they? Colton's—Clay Anderson's—Sonny's? She willed them to be Colt's but sensed that in the fickleness of dreaming it was more than him. She knew she was making that part up. If truth be told it was all of them, one wandering into the other, meandering in and out in some unseen pattern, the way dreams sometimes do. The hands had been all over her—touching, caressing, fondling—and she had enjoyed it—liked the way it made her feel.

Suzanne came fully awake now, realizing the sensuality of the dream with some embarrassment. She blushed deeply and looked uncertainly around, even though no one else was there. It was good to have her room to herself again. She stretched again, conscious of the light cotton garment brushing over her skin, and smiled at the delicious sensation of being alive and aware of just how sensitized the dream had made her feel. At the same time, she was thankful for the privacy of her bedroom.

She sat up and put her bare feet on the floor, then stepped in front of her bureau dresser and studied her reflection in the mirror. She thought herself just an ordinary girl, what was it that drove men like Claude Bollinger or Elwood Langton to such distraction that they would risk assaulting her? She turned sideways to profile her figure in the mirror and saw how the gown hung away from her ribcage and draped from the prominence of her bosom.

Slowly she pressed the gown at her waist, stretching the fabric taut against her, then again studied her reflection. The breeze blew over her, bringing with it a sense of life as though every pore of her body was lighting up. She turned this way and that, then profiled once more. She pressed her hands to the cloth beneath her bosoms, outlining them in bold relief, and wondered at the eloquent affirmation of her youthful femininity.

"They are kind of nice," she murmured, "I wonder why men are so enthralled by these?"

Memories of Colt's devotion and his gentle adoration and lovemaking swept over her, bringing with it a stirring, aching longing. She looked at her lower body, knowing she was in the full bloom of life and ready to have the promised fulfillment of becoming a wife and mother. She sighed in despair, for the bee that would carry that pollen to her was not to be. She scoffed at her cynicism, then shivering, she felt her skin pucker into goose flesh and began to dress.

Kathreen had left, and Sonny was back. She wondered, with both anticipation and dread, if he would come to see her today. Suzanne put the dish in the cupboard and hung the towel on the rack

"Mama, can I ask you something?"

Mabel Kluesman wrung out the dishcloth and draped it over the pump handle at the sink. Turning to her daughter she said, "What is it, dear?"

"Why do men pay so much attention to a woman's figure?"

Mabel Kluesman's face registered momentary shock, and then flustered, she smoothed her hands down the front of her apron.

"Decent ones don't."

"They don't? Are you sure?"

Her mother gave a self-conscious smile, "Well," she hesitated, "not so you'd notice, they don't."

"Well, I notice, and it's not just the fellas my own age either, older men look at me and even the boys in my schoolroom do—even the little ones."

Suzanne's mother raised her eyebrows, then said with a sigh, "I suppose it's just the nature of the beast."

"Sometimes it makes me feel a little bit funny, like there might be something wrong with me, but then I'll see them looking at other women like that, too, so I know it's not just me. Do they look at you like that?"

Her mother grew red in the face and shook her head. "It's not considered ladylike to talk about such things."

"Mother, who else can I talk to about it? Kathreen's gone and she wouldn't be able to give me a descent answer anyway. She says all men are boobs."

"My darling daughter, God has blessed you with an unusually amazing figure, one that attracts the stares of men, like honeybees to wild roses."

Suzanne smiled uncomfortably, she was not used to speaking with her mother on such frank matters.

Her mother went on, "You have come by it honestly enough, I suppose, seeing as how I've garnered my share of attention in such matters, so you might as well relax and learn to live with it. That's what I've had to do."

"Mother!" Suzanne was aghast, "You mean to tell me—aha! They do look at you like that, don't they? What does daddy think?"

"Your father?" Mabel got an affectionate smile on her face. "He just sticks out his chest and acts like he's won a blue ribbon for the best heifer at the fair."

"Daddy does?"

"Yes," she snickered, "it's alright though, whenever that happens, it makes him appreciate me more."

"So is it okay then, looking like this?" Suzanne cast her eyes down at her front while posing the question to her mother. "Aren't we supposed to try and hide them if they are this obvious?"

Mabel smiled and shook her head. "Some women do and I suspect it stems from a false modesty or perhaps, self-consciousness, but the opposite side of that is true, too, others will flaunt themselves and end up being a snare to men, perhaps for the same reasons."

"I'd never want to do that."

"I know you wouldn't, honey. What's prompted you to all these thoughts?"

"I don't know. I had this dream last night, something about hands, and it has made me more aware of my feelings along those lines. Colt was so enamored with me, not just in that way, but all of me, too. With him I felt so at ease with his delight of me—of my figure, it made me glad I was a woman and it all seemed so natural and good."

Suzanne's mom got a reflective twinkle in her eye. "When it's the right man, it does happen like that, and it is good."

"I suppose it's wrong of me, but that's one of the big things I miss from losing Colton, and I can't talk to anyone about it. I can't even imagine being with anybody else like that, like we were, and it frightens me sometimes. If he is dead, do you think I will ever find another '*right*' man again?"

Mable Kluesman grew quiet and pondered her daughter's question.

"Do you think he is dead?"

Suzanne's heart dropped. "Oh, I don't want to. As long as I could hold onto the hope he was alive, life seemed to make sense somehow, in spite of all that has happened, but now it has been so long. Sometimes I wonder if things—like maybe my own body even—are telling me to move on."

A troubled look came over her mother's face. "Just how intimate did you and he get," she asked.

Suzanne blushed, "We kept our clothes on, if that's what you mean, but there was never any question that we were meant for each other. He was the right man, Mama."

Mable Kluesman relaxed then, a look of relief in her eyes.

"Good, I figured as much. Colton was a fine young man."

"He was, Mama, and honorable, too. He said if we went beyond what was right, it would be like he was stealing me from God and you and papa, too."

Her mother smiled, "He said that?"

"He did. He said something else, too, that has bothered me since he disappeared. He said we had already done more than what someone else would find acceptable, if he should be killed and I were to end up marrying another."

"Had you?"

Suzanne felt uncomfortable under her mother's inquiring gaze, almost like one of her students might feel under her own.

"Well, maybe, I wouldn't ever want him to have paid court as passionately to someone else, as he did with me."

"And do you think someone else, Sonny for example, would want to come in behind him, and find that Colton had paid court to you that passionately?"

"Sonny's a poor example, Mama. I can think of at least two other women that he has paid passionate courtship to."

"Hmm," Mable gave a long sigh. "It's a broken world isn't it, my dear?"

"Mama, do you think people can change?"

Her mother looked thoughtful and then nodded slowly, "Yes dear, under the amazing grace of God, people can and do change every day. Why do you ask?"

Suzanne gave a gentle scoff. "Sonny—I think he's changing."

Mable got a tender look in her eye. "I think you're right, he is changing. That boy is turning into a man. He just might be worthy of your consideration."

"He said he loved me. Becky said he's never said that to anyone else before."

"Then maybe he hasn't, do you want him to love you?"

"Yes—no—I don't know. I want him to love me, but I don't want to love him, not like Colt and I loved. What about all his passionate courtship of others?"

"What about your passionate courtship?"

"That was different, Colt and I were in love—deeply in love—we were pledged to each other. We weren't wandering around in little wading pools just getting our feet wet, the way Sonny puts it."

"You thought you weren't, and I will give you that, but fate or God, call it whatever you will, intervened and now you have this history. What are you going to do about that?"

"What can I do?

"Forgive yourself and forgive others their history, too, then look to God's grace, and move on with your life. There is nothing like genuine repentance for starting over."

"You mean Sonny, don't you?"

Her mother gave her a smile that said no further words were needed and turned to fold another dishtowel.

"Mama, thanks for talking with me. Some of these things, you can't talk to just anybody about, and I love you for being here for me. Sorry if I disappointed you with what I said."

"You mean about Colt's and your passionate courtship?"

Suzanne slowly nodded.

Mable Kluesman put the dishtowel on the rack and turned to enfold her daughter in her arms and give her a hug.

"Don't worry, honey, I understand perfectly and so does your father—and so does God."

"Do I have to repent?"

"Do you want to repent?"

"No, never," Suzanne said hastily. "I loved him with every ounce of my being and if I could do it over, I would do it all again, and marry him immediately. At least we might have had a child to remember him by."

"But that didn't happen."

"I know, I suppose I should rethink it, but somehow loving him the way I did cannot be wrong, if anything, I didn't love him enough while I had the chance."

"As long as you feel that way, you will probably never see what needs repenting of."

"Well, I don't."

Her mother looked at Suzanne, recognizing the young woman before her as an adult in her own right, and that she had been for sometime. She was no longer under her chain of command, and not wishing to push her away from her chain of council she graciously said, "Then there is nothing you need to repent of, is there?"

"What about Daddy, will he think I need to repent?"

"I will speak to your father about this, you needn't worry about him."

"Oh, I hope so, I would hate to disappoint him, too."

"Honey, I'm not disappointed in you, and he won't be either. We both understand, we really do."

As realization dawned on her, Suzanne said in surprise, "Mama, have you and Daddy had stuff you needed to repent of, too?"

Mable Kluesman got a protective look in her eye and pushed her daughter towards the door. "Just you never mind, the past is under the blood—go walk your dog."

Suzanne and the dog made their way towards town, her eyes passing over the horses tied at the hitching rails in front of the mercantile. She was searching in vain for Sonny's little mare.

She paused to sit down on the bench in front of the barbershop, which was now closed, and slipped off her shoe to remove a pebble. Resting a moment, she absently watched the few riders and wagons as they passed by. This was the same seat that the two rowdy cowboys had been sitting on when Colt took them to task for their somewhat earthy, if not rude remarks. Their inept attempts of expressing their appreciation for her figure and form had been unusual, for most cowboys were so tongue-tied you could scarcely get a word out of them. Perhaps it had been the liquor talking.

There was sadness in recalling Colton's gallant and forthright manner in challenging the two for voicing their thoughts, and the thought that he would never do that again. Sadly, she shook her head with a little smile. He had already been defending his claim on her as his mate against all contenders, whether he knew it or not at the time was beside the matter. She smiled again at the ways of men. Apparently all men were like that to some degree and had such thoughts regarding a woman's figure. If her mother was right, it just wasn't proper to voice them. She decided convention and society had not really moved them all that far along on the pathways of civilization and away from these basics—probably it never would.

While lost in her thoughts, a shadow fell across her and she looked up, shading her eyes from the westering sun, to see Clay Anderson standing there.

"Evening, ma'am," the acting sheriff said. "I was wondering if you might be walking your dog this evening."

He squatted on his heels and scratched the reclining Nuisance behind the ears. The half-grown pup lay supine on the boardwalk with one front leg hanging over the edge and his two back legs spread out doing the splits at impossible angles.

"Evening, pooch," Anderson said.

Nuisance cocked one ear and looked up at the big man then thumped his tail a couple times on the boards.

"Good evening, Mr. Anderson," Suzanne said, "How's the sheriffin' business?"

Clay smiled nervously and pulled his hat off, "Good," he said.

"Why don't you sit down here by me and tell me all about it?" she invited, scooting over and patting the bench beside her.

Anderson's eyes darted to the seat, looking like a robin listening for a worm, and then self-consciously he stood up, bent easily at the waist, and lowered his large frame to sit halfway on the edge of the seat. He perched at an angle next to her, being careful not to touch her or get too close.

Suzanne stifled a smile. He appeared to be wound tighter than a dime-store clock and looked like he was about to spring to his feet at the slightest provocation.

"Do you like being sheriff?" she asked.

"Not really," he said.

Suzanne waited for him to enlarge upon his comment, but the conversation was dropping into a familiar pattern. If she wanted to know his thoughts she was going to have to coax them out of him. For a brief moment she wondered if he had had any of *those* thoughts regarding her figure, and blushed at the idea. Imagine trying to coax any of those kinds of ideas from him. Not in a million years, she thought. Again there came the stab of regret and loss in recalling how Colton had so freely, and eloquently, and passionately, praised and adored her.

"What is it about the job that you don't like?" she asked, her eyes wandering to stare at his huge hands. The fingers were tense and spread wide over his knees, and her dream of the night before pushed unbidden into her mind, sending a little shiver up and down her spine.

"I don't much like tellin' folks what they have to do," he said. "Most folks already know it anyway."

Suzanne looked up in surprise. This had to be one of the longest sentences he had ever spoken to her. She studied him and, feeling her eyes upon him, Clay turned his head slightly towards her, but still looked sideways and said no more.

"Clay—may I call you that?"

He nodded and awkwardly adjusted his seat on the bench.

"Clay, please sit back and relax—now tell me more. What about those who disregard the rules? Shouldn't there be some restraint for them?"

Swallowing hard, Clay Anderson finally scooted back on the bench and began to fumble with his hat. Suzanne had the distinct impression he was sweating, although she could not see that.

"Reckon they have to be stopped alright," he said.

What was it about him that reminded her of a Jerusalem Cricket that had just hopped into a pen full of turkeys? She smiled at the imagery. Slowly she reached forward and took the hat from his fidgeting fingers, then calmly set it on the boardwalk.

"Clay, are you afraid of me?" she asked.

"Yep," he nodded without looking at her.

She giggled, "Why—you think I might beat you up?"

He chuckled then, "No—not that."

"What then?" she said. "Look at this."

She reached over and took his off-hand, noticing him start at her touch. Placing it palm up, she spread her small hand, palm down, on it and for a moment they both sat there in silence staring at the picture it made. The incongruity of her dainty hand resting in his huge mitt was enormous. It looked like a small child's hand in his by comparison.

With a cute little laugh, she said, "Look at that, do you actually think that poses any threat to you?"

Anderson chuckled silently and then visibly relaxed, "Naw, I suppose it doesn't."

"What then? I'm not going to eat you up, you know."

He started to pull his hand away but she said, "No, I want to look at your hand for a moment, do you mind?" She turned her pretty blue eyes on him questioningly.

He shook his head no and relinquished the hand to her.

Suzanne began to trace the lines of his fingers and palm with her finger and asked him again, "What is it about me that frightens you?"

Clay seemed uncomfortable with the question. "It's kinda hard to put into words, ma'am," he said, his eyes following her finger as she felt about a callous.

"Try," she said, only half conscious of the conversation and fascinated with his big hand. *What would it be like to hold it up to her face?*

"It just pleasures me to be near you and—well—I'm afraid you might not want to be around me one of these days."

Suzanne looked up at him and smiled, "I like to be around you, Clay, may I ask you something?"

"Yes ma'am."

"Will you let me hold your hand up to my face?"

"Do what, ma'am?"

"Your hand—let me have it for a moment."

He shrugged, "Sure, if you want to."

Suzanne took his hand with both of hers and lifted it up to her face and held it spread out in front of her. She was right; his hand did cover the entire expanse of her face. A satisfied smile was on her lips; *"Curiosity killed the cat but satisfaction brought it back,"* she mused.

Suzanne had been unmindful of the occasional sounds of passersby in the street and so paid no particular attention to the sound of an approaching horse and rider. It wasn't until the animal stopped opposite them and she heard the horse snort, blowing loudly through its nostrils, that she looked up. Peering through the spread fingers of Clay Anderson's big hand, she was surprised to see Sonny Saber on a big dark horse, sitting his saddle with a cynical look on his face.

"Oh!" she cried and jerked Clay's hand down, dropping it as though it was red hot.

"Sonny, you're back!"

"I heard you was walkin' out with him, but I never figured you was a holdin' hands," he said. "Good evening, Miss Kluesman." Sonny touched the brim of his hat and spurring the flanks of the stallion; he trotted off up the street and into the gathering darkness.

For the next two weeks, Sonny busied himself about the ranch and avoided going to town. Even on Sundays, he managed to be somewhere out on the range and was thus unable to make it to services. He was in a blue-funk over the blacksmith's daughter, on the one hand yearning to see her and declare his love and desire and on the other, resenting her willful rejection of his suit, while at the same time she was not at all indisposed to accept Clayton Anderson's attention. Who could figure women? That was it—he decided to continue to distance himself from Suzanne. He had hoped that his absence, while hunting wild horses, might have caused the schoolteacher to view him in a new light, only to despair, for apparently that was not the case, especially since Becky had told him of the attack by Deputy Bollinger on Suzanne and of Clay Anderson's rescue, and that they had been keeping company ever since.

Sonny was riding back to the home place one evening mulling this all over in his mind. "Even that danged pup made no difference," he said bitterly to Tornado. "She takes the little mutt out walking each evening and Anderson's Johnny-on-the-spot to hold her hand. I ought a plug the big Swede." The stallion just snorted and picked up his pace for the ranch.

On a hot, late-summer afternoon, a few days later, Sonny stopped below the house while on the way in from the range, and in an attempt to cool off, shucked his clothes and dove into the pond down along the creek. He was treading water out in the middle when he heard voices and saw Becky and Suzanne coming down the trail from the house.

"I saw him ride down this way a little while ago," Becky was saying to the blond girl. "Oh, there he is in the pond. Sonny, look who's here."

For a moment Sonny felt totally exposed. Not only was he without his pants, but there was no place to hide. In the water up to his chest, he thought about ducking under, but knew that was useless. With nowhere to disappear to, he squatted lower and steeled himself. Adopting an "I-don't-care" attitude, he turned to face the watching girls.

"I'll leave you two alone," Becky said, and turned to walk back up the trail, displaying a wisdom beyond her years. With mixed feelings, Sonny watched her go, and then waited to see what Suzanne's attitude would be.

Suzanne was nervous. Gone was the dismissive regard she had so often shown for this tall, lanky, cowboy. She had failed to take him seriously so often in the past, mainly because he himself had not taken life seriously, approaching it with a cavalier, devil-may-care manner. Even in his affairs of the heart, he had shown himself to be callow and non-committal. Now as she stared at him up to his neck in the water with an inscrutable look on his face, she wondered just how badly she had misjudged this man. One thing she did know, she did not like being out of favor with him. No, it was more than that, she had genuinely missed him and his attention. She missed his company, his support and care, and the encouragement he had given all through the dark days of her grief and loss over Colton. In fact—she was forced to admit it—she missed his courtship of her, too. She didn't believe she actually loved him, but she did care for him and she wanted him to—well, to love her anyway, and even though she recognized the selfishness of such feelings, it was with all this in mind that she had made the drive to the ranch to see if she could somehow patch things up between herself and Sonny Saber.

It had been more than eight weeks since she had last seen him, other than for that time in front of the barber shop with Clay Anderson. One thing was certain, she had not expected to find him like this, soaking in the pond with his clothes in an obvious pile on the bank.

"Hot out today," she said lamely.

Sonny nodded and allowed his feet to drift to the bottom of the pond and stand in the cool mud.

"That looks nice and cool," she said. She had the distinct impression, had he not been something of a captive audience, he would have turned and walked away. Again, Sonny nodded and said nothing.

"I never got a chance to thank you for my puppy before you left. Nuisance is such a delight."

Sonny finally spoke, "Nuisance, is that what you call him?"

Suzanne nodded her head and looked to a spot on a log lying in the shade of the oak to sit down on. "That was the name you gave him, remember?"

"Uhm," Sonny nodded once again and then waited.

"Sonny, I've missed you," she said. She could tell by the skeptical look on his face, even across the water between them, that he didn't believe her. "You don't believe me, do you? It's true, I have—a lot. How come you took off like that? That's no way to treat a lady. . . a woman. . . your friend?"

"You asked me to give you some space," an accusation was implicit in his voice, "so I am."

Suzanne felt frustration rise up in her. *"What was the matter with these Saber boys? He was acting just like Colt!"* She recalled the time Colt had left her at her grandfather's in Saint Louis and she had wanted to shut the door because she was letting in the cold. He had gone off with an attitude and shot up his new hat in anger and frustration. Now Sonny was acting the same way.

"Sonny, I hardly meant for you to abandon me altogether and I think you know it," she said. "What has really put the sticker under your saddle blanket, as you cowboys say?" She tried to say it with humor, knowing it was supposed to be a burr, but also knew it fell short.

Studying the feigned witticism of the girl, he said, "I think that would be a burr, you mean there." A slight smile twitched at the corners of his mouth but she could not see it.

"Well, a burr then, how come you just up and abandoned me? I would really like to know."

"Suzanne," his voice rang across the pond, low and in earnest. "I am not Colton, never have been—never will be. I know you loved him, I know you miss him—that you have not gotten over him and I'm beginnin' to wonder if you ever will. But Colton's dead and I'm not, and if you can't tell the difference, then there's no use in me hangin' around holdin' your hand and hopin' you will. I think life's worth the livin' and if a person can't live life with the one they want, then perhaps it's time for them to move on and find someone they can live life with—that's it—that's how come and that's my 'sticker' as you so quaintly put it."

Suzanne's face paled. It was a blistering rebuke, although he had spoken it calmly enough, and she shrank under the onslaught of it. Was it her fault she had loved Colton so? She didn't think so, but perhaps she had misjudged his brother's depth of feelings for her. One thing she did know, the thought of Sonny disappearing from her life on top of the loss of Colt was more than she wanted to bear.

"Don't," she said. Her lower lip began to tremble and tears started to well up in her eyes. "Don't Sonny," she repeated, "don't you go away from me. I know you are not Colt and I don't even want you to be. I want you to be you—I have missed you." Feeling the turmoil inside, she hid her face in her hands and wiped at her tears, hoping he could not see them.

"You have?" he said with a tinge of awe in his voice. He took a short step towards her. "What about Anderson, you two looked pretty cozy the last time I saw you?" The accusation came back into his voice.

Suzanne dropped her hands and lifted her head. "Clay Anderson has been a perfect gentleman and a good friend and was there when I needed someone to protect me from a vicious assailant, something that I shall, and you should, be forever grateful for. And just where were you? Off chasing brush-tails or whatever it is you call them. Don't you try and throw him up in my face—he is reliable and doesn't go off in a snit if I don't happen to say everything in just the right way."

Sonny studied the flashing eyes of the girl on the bank and he bit his lower lip in an attempt to quell a smile but failed to stop a couple of silent chuckles.

"I suppose next you are gonna tell me he's just a friend, too, aren't you?"

"That's right, Mr. Saber, he *is* just a friend and a darned good one, too—at least he doesn't go off and leave me when the chips are down."

"Miss Kluesman," Sonny said in mock surprise, "What would folks say if they knew their schoolmarm was using language like that?"

"I don't give a tinker's—darn—what folks think and you can just go suck a pickle, Sonny Saber." She got up from the log and started up the trail towards the house.

"Suzanne, wait!" There was a sound of command in his voice that caused her to pause. "You stop right there and cover your eyes while I get my britches on, there is something I have to tell you."

Suzanne obediently hid her eyes, happy to comply with his command, and elated he was stopping her, but she was careful not to let it show. She heard him splash to shore and put on his clothes.

Presently he said, "All right, you can turn around now."

She turned to find him sitting on the log, a sock in one hand, ready to put on his boots.

"Come over here, there's something I need to tell you."

Suzanne walked back and he held out a hand to her. She took it, then seated herself on the log next to him before letting it go. "What is it?" she said feeling a rising sense of apprehension.

"It's not good news, but you might as well hear it from me as well as from someone else. The Comanche burned the cabin Colt built for you two on that little hill. Burned it clean to the ground—there's nothing left."

Suzanne's eyes went wide, "Our cabin—Colt's and my cabin is gone? Oh, what a shame, and I never even got a chance to see it, how sad—all Colt's work and everything. . ." she broke off in silence.

Sonny sat next to her, both of them staring at his bare foot and letting the news sink in. Finally Suzanne gave a big sigh and said, "That's just as well, I guess—we were never going to get to live there anyway."

Somewhat startled, he couldn't help noticing the tinge of bitterness in her voice and looked over at her. She saw the look on his face and nodded at his unasked question, "Yes, I know now—Colton is not coming back." She reached out a trembling hand and touched his cheek briefly and he saw a crystal tear making its way slowly down her own.

Chapter Twenty-Two

Leaving El Paso

Colt stopped in to see the lawman he'd turned the two wanted men over to on his last visit to El Paso. The sheriff looked at him with a critical eye and then recognition came over his face.

"Say, ain't you the young bounty hunter that came through here a couple of years ago? You got any more desperadoes for me?"

Colt shook his head, "Not exactly, but you probably should know about an operation going on across the border.

The sheriff's name was Samuel Loomis, and when Colt told of his ordeal in Guaynopa Canyon and of the enslavement being carried out there by some New York firm, the Sheriff turned grave and asked if he knew the names of the people involved.

"Never heard any names, and as far as I know they never shipped any of the gold out of that place either. Probably, they never will." He told how the Apache had massacred and set fire to the whole encampment and that Geronimo was holed up in the mountains just north of there.

"You better report this to the colonel over at Fort Bliss," Sheriff Loomis said, "there's talk of the Army cleaning out that nest of vipers along with Victorio and Cochise. He'll probably want you to guide them back in there once the powers that be in Washington work out an agreement with Mexico City for us to cross the border and get the rascals."

"That ain't going to happen Sheriff. I've been gone most of two years, and I am making a beeline for home."

"Where's home," Loomis asked?

"Upton County over on the Pecos, my dad has the Crossed Sabers spread just out of Wade's Landing.

"I hear tell that's a pretty big spread, you must be anxious to get back to your folks if you've been gone that long—you say they have no idea where you've been?"

"No, I don't guess they do, I reckon it'll be a pretty big surprise when I come ridin' in."

"You know son, the Army picked up a little gal, naked as a jay bird, wading across the Rio a year or so back. She had managed to escape a bunch of Comancheros that had kidnapped her from her home on the Trinity. She made her way to a troop of soldier boy's out of Bliss and she mentioned they had a white fellow about your age—might that of been you?"

"I think so, I don't remember that very well, I guess I had amnesia for a spell after being hit on the head one too many times. Do you know what the girl's name was?"

"Sarah, Sarah Lambert. We bundled her onto the stage and sent her to San Antone after wiring her parents."

"I vaguely remember a Sarah, but couldn't tell you much else."

He bade the sheriff goodbye and headed for the street. It bothered him that he could not recall the events of his capture. He knew some things, but could not bring his thoughts into focus on much that had happened during his memory loss. That was still garbled and unclear, and he figured there was much he did not recall at all.

Once he had visited the Sheriff, he turned his attention to getting something to eat and found a small corner restaurant where he was able to watch passersby while enjoying a finely cooked steak. After supper, he walked about town a bit, noticing the new stone-structured bank building, along with several other important business establishments that had a look of permanence about them.

Colt was not in the habit of frequenting saloons and had never done more than peer curiously over the swinging doors of the Branchwater Saloon in Wade's Landing, and maybe one or two others in Saint Louis and San Antoine. Perhaps it was the salt from his supper, as he had become unused to it in his recent diet, or maybe it was the strength of the onions he'd eaten, but he found himself an hour later with quite a thirst. He did not care for beer, having tried it once while in Saint Louis, but had developed a taste for sarsaparilla. While in that city, he had discovered the soft drink was served in soda parlors. There was no such thing as a soda parlor in El Paso that he knew of, but he wondered if he might not be able to find the soft drink in one of the many saloons along River Street here in El Paso.

His mother would disapprove of course, and he could just hear her say, *"Idle hands are the Devil's work shop,"* but he had a powerful yen for a sarsaparilla, so it was with some trepidation, that he pushed through the batwing doors of a low-brow saloon called T*he Jacks* *n'Aces*, and made his way through the smoky room up to the bar.

The man behind the bar took him in at a glance, his eyes lingering on the low-slung black holster with the pearl handled, nickel-plated, tied down Colt. The newness of his outfit along with the black hat, and the silver concho hatband, gave him the look of a young aspiring gun hand, and more the dude than anything else, but Colt was unconcerned. He really didn't care what folks thought, he wore what he liked and could put up with a little hazing when it came down to it.

The bartender gave him a quick once over and Colt could tell what he was thinking. He just looked mildly back, with a hint of a smile tugging at the corner of his mouth. The barkeep was a burly fellow in a collarless white shirt with the sleeves rolled up to the elbows revealing brawny, hairy arms. There was a tuft of dark hair showing at his throat where the top button was undone and his thick neck extended upward into a bullet-shaped head, prematurely bald. The man worked a toothpick slowly back and forth between strong teeth as he automatically dried a beer glass while he studied the youth in front of him. He pushed the toothpick to the corner of his mouth with his tongue, stepped over, and said with an amused look, "What'll you have, Jesse?"

"Huh," Colt grinned. "You got any sarsaparilla?"

The man set the glass and towel down in front of him, then leaned towards the cowboy with both hands spread out on the bar.

"A sarsaparilla?"

Colt nodded, feeling a little out of place. A sudden outburst of laughter from a couple of cowboys down the bar to his right caused him to look sideways in their direction. He grew even more uncomfortable when he recognized the two young toughs who had nearly run him down on the bridge.

The two cowboys appeared to be near his own age, perhaps a year or two older, and from their garb seemed to be working hands who were in town intent on blowing off some steam and maybe painting it a little red, too. The bigger of the two was loud and boisterous and pawing at a pretty, dark-haired girl, who stood laughing nervously at his jokes. The girl was heavily made up with dark eye shadow, garish rouge on her cheeks and bright red lipstick on her mouth. She was dressed in what could only have been described as a dance-hall girls' costume.

They were paying him no mind and Colt turned back to the bartender who stood with an amused grin on his face waiting.

"Sarsaparilla?" the man said again, not even trying to hide his disbelief.

Colt raised an eyebrow inquiringly, and cocked his head sideways, but said nothing, then turned back to watch the three down the bar.

"Okay, okay," the barman laughed, and turned to walk through a door behind the bar. He reappeared a moment latter, blowing the dust off a brown bottle, uncapped it and poured the dark amber liquid into a mug. Leaning on his elbows, he waited for the foam to stop fizzing before finishing filling the glass. Once the mug was filled with a nice head of foam on the top, he thumped the bottle down on the counter and slid the glass down the bar to where it bumped into Colt's arm. Colt looked up and turned back to take the mug handle and lift the frothing soda to his lips.

"Drink up, kid," the bartender said, then added with another glance at his sidearm, and a knowing wink, "I don't want any trouble in here."

Colt watched him move off and wondered why he had said that, he wasn't looking for trouble. He lifted the mug again and took another long swig, enjoying the sting of yeast and the way it prickled his nose. This stuff was good, he could get used to drinking it. Turning his back to the bar with the glass in hand, he leaned back against it, his elbows up, and surveyed the room.

It was a large room and full of patrons at this hour of the evening. It was Saturday night and several poker games were in progress at round tables, some with spectators nursing mugs of beer and watching the action. Colt noted that there were a number of ladies in revealing costumes circulating about, some dancing with cowboys or teamsters on a raised wood dance floor in one corner of the room. A homely fellow wearing a bowler hat and smoking a stubby cigar was pounding out a ballad on a tinny piano. With one hand, he occasionally took a sip of beer from a mug that danced on top of the piano, while he kept the music going with the other. Every now and then, Colt would see one of the couples leave the dance floor and climb a winding staircase situated to the right of the bar and disappear down a hallway that led away from an overlooking balcony. With a start, he realized where these couples were headed and felt his ears flush red. Feeling desperately out of place, he hurried to finish the sarsaparilla and leave, when a rude voice at his side addressed him.

"What kinda sissy drink you got here?"

He turned to see the cowboys from the bridge and the saloon girl, standing next to him. The bigger one had spoken and pushed to the front, while holding the near empty soda bottle in his hand and sniffing the contents. The fellow's demeanor and attitude was arrogant and belittling as he scoffed at Colt.

Twin pistols were slung low on the cowboy's hips, the handles protruding forwards in a cross-draw rigging. It was obvious the fellow fancied himself handy with a gun, maybe both of them. The man was sizing him up, a contemptuous sneer on his face, while his eyes lingered on Colt's new pearl-handled .44.

"Looks like a piss-ant drink for a piss-ant bucko to me boy, wha'da ya think?"

Colt's mouth depressed slightly into a tight line. He looked past the rude fellow to where his companion stood grinning like an ape, a glass beer mug in his hand and an arm carelessly slung about the dark-haired girl's shoulder. She stood ill-at-ease and looked as if she would like to be somewhere else about now.

Colt set his near empty glass down and pushed it a few inches, carefully towards the cowboy holding his soda bottle.

"Pour the rest of that in here," he said with a calmness that belied the quickening of his pulse and temper.

"Pour the rest of that in here," the snide cowboy said mockingly. He stared insolently into Colt's eyes, the open challenge, obvious.

Colt stared back, fixing his steady gaze, unblinkingly, on his adversary. He could see the fellow was intent on mischief and plainly seeking to impress his companion and the girl. He felt a little exasperated and even mildly amused. The enormity of stumbling out of the Mexican bad-lands and finally getting back to Texas, only to meet this gold-plated jackass was almost funny. After all he had been through, this was something of a marvel. He almost relished the chance to pin the fellow's ears back. After all he'd had to overcome in the past two years, it'd probably be like falling off a log, but still, the right thing to do was to ignore him, maybe he would go away. His strutting was actually kind of funny—perhaps he could appeal to the fellow's sense of humor.

"You ever piss on an ant?" he asked.

"What?" the cowboy said in surprise, then added with a smirk, "Pissed on 'em, stomped on 'em and kicked hell out of their ant hills. Wha'da ya think of that?"

"Uhm," Colt said with a dubious downturn of his mouth. "That ain't surprising. You ever notice how they just wait until all the pissin's over, then go on about minding their own business?"

The bartender had been standing back watching the whole thing and at Colt's last remark, he broke out into a loud guffaw. He was joined in his hilarity by the young tough's companion and the girl. Several onlookers at the bar had stopped their chatter to watch with interest the trouble brewing between the two, and also joined in the laughter.

It had been an inoffensive remark and, under ordinary circumstances, should have defused the situation, and, in fact, had largely put everyone at their ease. Everyone that is, but the cross draw cowboy. His ears turned red and he would have none of it. Seeing that he had lost face in front of the room and knowing that some sort of slight had just been handed him, but not understanding what the rest of the onlookers did—that he had just been politely told to mind his own business, he scrambled to regain the upper hand and put this smart-aleck kid in his place.

In a totally irrelevant response, he said with another sneer, "You mean like this?" and upending the bottle of Sarsaparilla, he deliberately poured the remaining contents onto the bar, purposefully missing the glass mug.

Colt took the slight in stride, an amused look on his face and waited, but with a growing sense of wariness. This fellow really was in need of having his tail feathers trimmed.

"Wha'da you think of that?" Cross draw said, and banged the empty soda bottle down on the bar, then turned to the onlookers with a loud laugh. He expected to find them approving of his actions, but found some of them looking at him with unfeigned disgust, others were shaking their heads and murmuring their disapproval. His partner had an *uh-oh*, look on his face and the pretty dark-haired girl said loud enough for all to hear, "That was pretty stupid, Latigo."

Nettled by the watching crowd that was waiting to see what would come next, and stung by the dancehall girl's remark, the man called Latigo turned angrily on the girl, and snaking a hand out, he caught the front of her low-cut bodice in a cruel grip and roughly jerked her back and forth several times.

Snarling at her, he said, "You can just shut your big yap, you dumb trollop, if I want any guff out of you, I'll knock it out of ya." He gave her a final shove, releasing his hold on the front of her costume to send her stumbling back into the arms of his friend. White-faced, she hurried to rearrange her clothing and conceal from the prying eyes of the crowd the immodest exposure his mistreatment had caused.

Colt grew angry and then quickly flashed cold. It was one thing to ignore the bully's boastful preening, it was another to see him assaulting this girl, so when Latigo turned back to face him with another contemptuous sneer, Colt slapped him hard with an open palm across his arrogant face.

At the loud smack, the room went silent and the startled Latigo stood in shocked disbelief with his mouth open and his nose smarting red. This sort of thing had never happened to him before.

"Why you. . ." he uttered in a strangled voice. His hand flashed to his side, but before he even touched leather, Colt's shiny new .44 appeared like magic in his face, settling under his stinging nose with the hammer cocked back.

"Wha. . .?" Latigo yelped, his hands hesitating on the handles of his own Colts.

In one fluid motion, Colt relaxed the cock on his gun and returned it to its holster, but the second Latigo made a move to draw, he slapped him again.

The crowd stared in stunned silence. Never had they seen anything like this and they were enjoying every moment of it.

The second slap galvanized the brazen cowboy into action, and with a curse and his best lightning-like cross draw, his hands went streaking towards his twin pistols, only to find lightning had already struck and both his holsters were empty. This time, his dark-clad adversary was holding two guns. Latigo was staring down both bores of his own twin Colts, while the taciturn stranger's thumbs held the hammers steadily back, in full cock.

In stunned unbelief, Latigo cried, "Lucky Dawg!" but his eyes followed with careful attention, as Colt returned his two pistols to their holsters. You could hear the big clock ticking on the wall as Latigo puzzled over what had happened. He fixed the younger cowboy with a hateful glare, his hands clutching futilely at the air.

Colt held Latigo's stare in an unwavering gaze, and the moment he saw the rude cowboy's eyes vacillate and his hands drop for his weapons, he popped him again with another stinging slap across his now throbbing nose.

Latigo was so surprised and so amazed and so enraged, that he literally jumped up and down, while bellowing like a sick calf on a short rope. Clasping his running nose with both hands and with his eyes teared up and smarting, he then heedlessly went for his guns again, only to find they were not there. Colt had easily snatched them first and stuck them in his face again.

What followed with dizzying speed, to the delight of the onlooking crowd, was a wonder to behold. Every time Latigo would lunge for his guns, Colt would draw them first, stick them in his face, return them to the holsters, and then smack the befuddled ruffian across the nose again.

Latigo spewed out invectives, tinged with unbelief, at the cowboy with the fancy black hat, but was always a half-second too late to gain the upper hand and stop the reign of terror to his stinging nose and face.

At one point, Colt saw Latigo's partner going for his own gun, and swift as a striking hawk, he allowed Latigo to palm his pair of pistols, but then grabbed both his wrists in syncopated orchestration, while the man was in his cross draw stance. As the guns came up, Colt forced them on around the sides of the tough, to where they discharged backwards. Colt directed the shots to shoot the other cowboy's gun from one hand and smash his beer mug in the other.

The friend let out a yowl and grabbed his throbbing hand to his mouth, after his gun went clattering across the floor, sending what spectators there were behind him scattering for cover. The dark-haired girl screamed when splattered with beer and glass from the shattered mug, then dove for cover behind a bar stool, where she continued peering out at this unbelievable spectacle.

For an instant, Colt stood face to face with his opponent while holding both his wrists in a vice-like grip. Behind him, the twin bores of Latigo's guns wavered about the room like relentless suppliers of justice, as if the divine eyes of retribution were seeking to avenge all wrong-doing ever done in this place. None of the shrinking patrons could know where the next shots would go.

A slow smile crossed Colt's face and he released his hold, but before the infuriated cowboy could bring his guns to bear on him, Colt stepped back, slapped him twice more then drew and cocked his own gun, poking it against Latigo's nose once again.

Bawling, the frustrated bully dropped his guns with a clatter to the floor and snatched his hands up to protect his smarting face. Tears were streaming from his eyes from the stinging blows and his teeth were grinding in fury.

Colt lowered his gun and holstered it once more. Through bleary eyes, Latigo lunged at him with his bare hands, only to be brought up short with another stinging slap and a gun barrel against his nose once more.

If it were not so pathetic, the whole thing would have been funny, but somehow the awe-struck occupants of T*he Jacks and Aces* could not help feeling humbled and a little bit sorry for poor Latigo. Twice more, Colt popped and drew on the hapless cowboy until finally Latigo sat down heavily on the floor and covered his streaming face with his hands, and sat there fuming and growling curses.

Colt holstered his gun, finished the last of his sarsaparilla and flipped a nickel onto the counter. With a cautious look at the bartender he held up his hands, palms outward, "No trouble. . . this piss-ant's going on about his own business."

Colt strode past Latigo, heading for the door. Nearly reaching it, he noticed in a mirror on the wall next to the swinging batwing entrance, that the deeply humiliated cowboy behind him was reaching for his two pistols still lying on the floor, with a malicious look in his eyes.

Without turning, Colt drew and aimed his own gun backwards under his left arm and snapped a couple of trick-shots, sending Latigo's pistols spinning out of reach and showering the luckless cowboy with splinters from the plank floor.

"Wha'da ya think of that?" he said calmly and holstered his .44, then walked out into the night.

As he stepped from the porch into the street, he heard the creak of the swinging saloon doors behind him. Whirling in a flash, his gun in hand, he came face to face with the pretty dark-haired girl, who had rushed from the saloon to follow him.

"Oh!" she cried, and came to a sudden halt when she saw the gun. "Are you going to shoot me?"

Colt noticed a certain cynicism mixed with fear in her startled voice. "No," he said, and relaxed the hammer, returning the gun to his hip. Without further comment, he turned and started back to his hotel. He could hear the girl step from the porch and begin to follow him without speaking. Feeling annoyed, he turned and said, "What do you want?"

"What do I want? How much time do you got?"

Again he detected her cynicism and felt it create a pessimism of his own.

"I'm turnin' in, it's getting' late."

"It's not that late," she said. "How about a cup of coffee, I'll buy?"

"No thanks," he said, barely civil. He had scarcely noticed this girl and the last thing he wanted was to get mixed up with her. He was totally absorbed in catching the stage on Monday and getting back to Suzanne. This dancehall girl was an interruption he had no time for.

"Can't you give me a few minutes? I would really like to talk to you."

They were passing in front of the little corner cafe he'd eaten supper in, and the girl stepped one foot up on the single step at its entrance and looked imploringly at him. "Please," she said, "I only want to talk."

Colt gave a sigh of resignation and turned to reach past her and twist the doorknob. Something about her tone of voice made him wonder if she was in some kind of trouble.

He followed her in and they took a table next to the window. Colt held out a chair, and then seated himself across from her without either of them speaking. A matronly waitress came over and they ordered coffee.

In the light of a kerosene lamp suspended over their table from the ceiling, Colt got his first good look at the girl. He could see a young woman, a girl really, near his own age, possibly even younger. Beneath the heavy makeup was a rounded face with a turned up nose, full mouth, high cheekbones and large sad eyes. Through the pancake of her makeup, faint lines of worry and desperation around her eyes were just beginning to show the ravages of a hard life. At his frank gaze Colt watched her drop her head nervously and start fiddling with a teaspoon.

"My name is Colt," he said, "Colton Saber."

The girl looked up at him through long lashes and replied, "I'm Trudy. . . Gertrude actually," she gave a self-conscious smile then went on, "Gertrude Borden, but no one calls me that anymore. Where are you going, Colt?"

"Home," he replied simply and felt a surge of longing and excitement wash over him that must have shown in his face, for he saw a glimmer of hope light up her own eyes for just a moment before it died out and the sadness return.

"Home?' she said gloomily. "Can anyone go home again?"

Colt looked up in surprise, but their coffee came just then.

"Not so's you would notice honey," the waitress said and set two cups of steaming coffee down with a clatter. "Will there be anything else?"

Both of them shook their heads no, and Colt turned to watch the waitress walk back towards the kitchen while Trudy stared at the bubbles on the fresh coffee in her cup.

"Never mind her," he said. "Why can't you go home again, Gertrude?"

The girl gave him a weak smile, "I like Trudy better, you sound like my father."

Colt smiled, "Trudy, then. Why can't you go home again, Trudy?

"There's nothing left for me there. Have you ever heard of burning bridges behind you?"

Colt nodded assent. He was wondering what this all had to do with him but decided to bide his time and let the girl speak her mind.

Trudy suddenly seemed flustered and fiddled with stirring sugar into her coffee while an awkward silence rose like a ground fog between them.

"I suppose you are wondering why I am bothering you with all my perturbations?" she said. "Maybe we should just forget it, finish our coffee and say goodnight."

Perturbations? What kind of word is that?"

The girl tucked her head in embarrassment, and said, "Bothers then."

Colt smiled, "What bridges have you burned?"

Trudy grimaced and shook her head. She took a drink and then set the cup back in its saucer and said, "Let's change the subject. Are you some kind of gunman?"

A broad smile broke out over Colt's face. "Naw," he scoffed, "I just bought these new duds and haven't had time to get them broke in good yet. You should a seen my old outfit, it had enough holes in it to get me arrested."

Trudy giggled and said impishly, "Maybe I should a."

"No, you shouldn't a. Why me?"

Trudy sobered, then said, "I watched you in there—in the saloon, and I don't know, somehow there seemed to be a goodness in the way you handled that situation. I've seen a number of tragic developments in my short and sordid career as a saloon gal, and let me tell you, Latigo doesn't know how lucky he is that he chose to pick on you. Most men would have shot him—or been shot by him and somebody would have ended up dead. What you did was decent—I've never seen anything like it before."

"Latigo is a hot-headed, big-mouth who thinks he's Billy the Kid or something and is used to pushin' folks around, if I'm any judge of character," Colt said. "But he didn't deserve to die."

"That is very generous of you, most cowboys would have rung his bell."

"I would have probably ignored him completely, if he hadn't started manhandling you."

There came a softening around Trudy's eyes. "That was another thing I noticed and I wanted to thank you for your gallantry."

Colt waved it off and took a sip of coffee. "Too bad some cowboys forget their manners when they fall into their cups."

"Tell me about it," Trudy murmured into her own cup. She had picked it up and was holding it in the palms of both hands, enjoying the heat.

"So what was a nice girl like you. . .?"

". . . doing in a place like that?" she finished.

Colt nodded and stared into her eyes while absently stirring a spoon in his coffee with no sugar.

"I was working there for a nickel a dance and Ruddy, the big guy behind the bar, said I was to show the cowboys a good time and encourage them to buy me drinks between dances. He said I didn't have to go upstairs with anyone if I didn't want to, and actually whacked a couple of guys with a bung bat he keeps behind the counter on two separate occasions, when they insisted on my doing so." Trudy paused and then seeing the unspoken question in Colton's eyes, said, "No, I haven't found anyone yet to go upstairs with."

Colt shrugged his shoulders and leaned back in his chair.

"I didn't ask," he said.

"Yeah, but you were thinking it, and by the way, the drinks Ruddy served me were cold tea. He sort of looks after me, for all the good it has done my reputation."

"If you don't like the life, why don't you leave?"

"And do what, go where?"

"Go home?" He put the statement to her as a question.

"Didn't you hear? You can't go home again."

"Who says?"

"That waitress over there," Trudy nodded towards the woman washing pots and pans in the back. "She knows, along with every other decent woman in the country."

"I don't understand," Colt said.

"I'm a dancehall girl, Colt, surely you can understand that a reputation like that's like a dead hen tied around a chicken-killin' dog's neck."

"Well, it doesn't sound to me like you killed any chickens," he said lamely.

"Doesn't matter," Trudy said. "Once you cross the threshold of those swinging doors you become a sidewalk-floozy, even if all you do is dance with the fellas and sip cold tea till you're in constant need of the privy."

Colt was skeptical, "C'mon Trudy, I saw Latigo pawin' you—the name of the game isn't exactly undeserved."

Trudy's eyes flashed dangerously, "You have no idea what it's like trying to hold down a job and keep your virtue intact. I live on nickels and nickels are all that stand between me and starvation—or the trip upstairs," she said meaningfully.

"So, I ask you again, why don't you quit?"

"Well," Trudy hesitated— "that's what I wanted to talk to you about."

"Me?" Colt was surprised, "What have I got to do with it?"

"I've been waiting for somebody to come along decent enough to help me and when I saw what you did tonight, well, I figured. . ."

"You figured I could take you away from all that."

"Something like that, yes."

"Huh," he scoffed and sat back again in bewilderment. After a moment he said, "Have you tried the church?"

"The church!" she exploded. "Are you kidding? All those frumpy, tightly wrapped, buns-in-the-hair old biddies? Have you any idea what would happen if I darkened a church door? Why the roof would probably fall in."

Colt chuckled, "Well, you would probably have to cover yourself up a little bit," he said and nodded towards her bare shoulders and low neckline, "but I've never seen the roof fall in yet of any church that I've ever been in and I've been in a number of them."

"You have?" she seemed surprised.

"Sure, I was practically raised in church. If you think you see any goodness in me you could probably chalk it up to that—better yet, give Jesus the credit, He's the one who's been working on me."

"I've never given much credence to some long-dead teacher hiding out in church," Trudy said. "If He's making folks good in there, most of them must be checking it at the door when they leave."

"That's just it, Trudy, the church ain't full of folks with harps and halos—it's more a place where beggars have found bread and are just trying to let other hungry folks know."

"That ain't what my Pa told me," Trudy said.

"Have you ever gone to church?"

"No, not much—maybe a time or two at Christmas and Easter when I was a kid—it was different."

"How do you mean?"

"All that standing and sitting and amens and halleluiahs. I didn't understand it much—the singing was nice though. Pa never went, he said they did all that just to get your money and the place was full of hypocrites. He said he didn't want no one telling him what to do."

"Hypocrites, huh? What better place for them then, than church?"

"What do you mean?" She seemed confused.

"You really ought to go once. If you think church is a comfortable place for hypocrites you really should try going."

"You think I am a hypocrite?" she asked in surprise.

"No, but you'd have to be smaller than one to hide behind 'em and not go to church."

"Oh, sure," Trudy said. "I could go looking like this," indicating her scanty costume. "Besides, I know I wouldn't feel comfortable there, you said so yourself."

"Are you admitting to hypocrisy then?" he said with a smile.

"No, but my life is a mess—I just know I'd end up being exposed and made a fool of."

"There is something you really ought to know about church and about Jesus, Trudy. He's not dead and his church is a place for the hurt and the lost and the lonely to be healed and found and befriended. Best of all, it is the place for the guilty to be forgiven and set free."

"Even a dancehall girl?" Trudy said. "It sounds too good to be true."

"Even a dancehall girl. Trudy, do you know who the first person was that Jesus revealed himself to after he rose from the dead?"

"No, but it must have been some real important, real good man."

"No, it was Mary Magdalene, a former prostitute from whom he had cast seven demons. He saw her first and he is waiting to do the same for you."

"You better listen to him, honey." The waitress had come over to refill their cups and leave the check on the table. Trudy looked up at her in surprise, unaware that she had been listening to their conversation.

After the waitress left, Trudy lowered her voice while watching the woman's back and said, "Do you think I have demons?" He could hear alarm in her voice.

"I think we all have the devil knock on the door of our hearts from time to time. I'm just glad when he does, I can send Jesus to answer it."

"My, I don't want any devils coming around me. Do you think I could get Jesus to answer my door?"

"Sure, actually Jesus is just outside the door of your heart knocking right now. All's you have to do is open it and invite him inside."

"Oh, I want to do that, can you help me?"

Colt seemed to hesitate. "Well, I could but I don't know if I should."

"Why not?" Trudy was puzzled. "I need him in there to chase the devil away if he comes around."

"I'll tell you what," Colt said. "I could help you say the words but I'm afraid I might only help you get just enough religion to keep you from getting a good dose of the real thing. If you are serious about meeting Jesus, you can go with me to church tomorrow. I kinda know the Baptist preacher and his wife here, and I know they recently built a new church. They are good people and would welcome you to their congregation."

Trudy looked doubtful. "I can't go looking like this," she said.

"Well," Colt paused, "You got anything else you can wear?"

"I suppose I could rummage up something. I just hate the thought of becoming some dowdy old church lady. Some of them look like death warmed over."

Colt nodded, "That's what happens when there's no beauty on the inside or the outside, and I agree, some of those old barns could stand a coat of paint, but you don't need any. Jesus has an inner beauty for you that's bound to make what's on the outside look even better."

"You think I'm pretty?" she asked without guile.

"Sure, anyone can see that, but you get fixed up on the inside, and after that you'll be surprised with what you find in the mirror."

"How do you know all this?" Trudy was amazed.

Smiling Colt said, "I've seen it before, some in church and some outside of church."

"Is there someone in particular you have in mind?" Trudy asked, probing curiously.

Colt just smiled and nodded slowly.

"Who, who is she?"

"My fiancée, Suzanne. . . Suzanne Kluesman. We have been separated for more than two years and I am on my way home to marry her."

"Separated for two years, how come?"

They talked until the waitress began to upend the chairs on the tables in preparation of closing. Colt told Trudy of his great love affair with the blacksmith's beautiful daughter and of all the hardships that had intervened.

Trudy listened in rapt silence and thought his story one of the most beautiful she had ever heard. There was a quiet tone of confident anticipation in his assertions of love and it brought the surprised girl to the certain knowledge that his was a hopeless devotion to whomever this Suzanne was. It also forever removed him from the possibility of anything more for her than her immediate rescuer, and it was with wonder and a little sadness that Gertrude Borden agreed to meet Colt Saber and go to church with him the next day.

Saying goodnight on the cafe steps they parted with Colton promising to pick her up at her boarding house at ten o'clock in the morning.

Colt and Trudy walked to the open door of the new church building while the church bell rang announcing the call to worship for the faithful and the not-so-faithful, too. They were greeted warmly at the door by a husky fellow in well-worn, but clean bib overalls. They found a seat on the polished wooden benches, three rows from the back, on the right side of the church and sat down. People were filing in and Trudy was nervously looking around to see if she recognized anyone, or more correctly if anyone recognized her.

Trudy elbowed Colt in the ribs and ducked her head. Colt looked to where she was inclining her head and saw that a woman on the other side of the church near the front was waving excitedly in their direction. He turned to see if she was waving at someone behind them but then Trudy said, "Oh no, here she comes."

Colt turned back to see the woman making her way back to greet them and recognized the waitress from the little cafe of the night before.

The woman was all smiles as she came up, holding both hands out to them. "I am Beatrice Watson, Bea. You're Trudy, right?"

Trudy nodded her head carefully, uncomfortable with her noisy greeting and the wondering stares of some of the congregants.

Bea beamed a smile and explained, "I remember you from the cafe." She turned to Colt, "I don't think I caught your name."

Colt stood and took the proffered hand she held out. "Colton Saber, Colt," he said and briefly shook her hand, then sat back down.

"I better get back to my seat," Bea said. "They are about to start, talk to you later."

Colt recognized the minister's wife seated at the piano and as she began to play, the congregation came to attention. A man stepped to the pulpit and announced a page number in the hymnal and Colt reached for a song book, found the page and holding the book for Trudy to see, began to sing heartily, *A Mighty Fortress.* Awkwardly, Trudy tried to follow the words and music as the opening hymn was sung.

The service proceeded pretty much normally. There was the opening song, opening prayer, two more songs, the announcements and offering, Pastoral prayer followed by a special song sung by some lady with a gray dress and her hair in a bun. She sang well though, and then Rev. Blankenship stepped into the pulpit and gave an impassioned message on the attitude of the heart, emphasizing Proverbs 4:23, that commands us: "*keep thy heart with all diligence, for out of it are the issues of life.*"

Colt settled back and began to mentally pitchfork everything the minister said, over onto Trudy. He was so thankful she was hearing this, thinking it was exactly what she needed to hear. He smiled smugly, recalling their conversation of the night before in which Jesus had been pictured as standing at the door of her heart knocking, and he was just waiting for the preacher to use that verse on her.

"Until you address honestly the motives of your heart, you will not begin to understand your own question. Who you are, what you are doing here, and where you are going." The preacher's words brought Colton up short. There it was again, the same stuff old Davilia had been talking about. He began to squirm a little on the inside. He had been so intent on Trudy hearing what she needed to hear, that this message of identity had somehow snuck up and hit him on his blind side, and he was left feeling a little disconcerted.

Colt began to take spiritual inventory. He was a believer, wasn't he? Yes, he knew Christ had taken his sins away. What about going into the saloon last night? Oh come on, he wasn't going to fall for that. Jesus ate and drank with sinners and he went where they were. Colt felt a minor irritation with those who would never darken a saloon door, in technical rule-keeping, but would turn around in a heartbeat, and assassinate somebody's character with gossip.

Oh, the motives of the heart, Colt thought. Why had he dressed down Latigo the way he did, last night? Was it because he was defending a saloon girl's tawdry honor, or was he just using that as an excuse to show off his own dangerous abilities? Would he have slapped him down and shot up the place like he did if there had been no audience to see? What about his gunman attire? Did he wear these clothes because he liked them, or because they made him look dangerous? And why was that? Did he want people to think he was dangerous so they would leave him alone? Was he afraid of people? He didn't think so but what lay behind it all?

The truth was, he felt dangerous and a little bit angry, too. Hadn't he just come through hell, the past couple of years? Hadn't he fought the likes of Hutch and L. T. Jones and his henchmen? Hadn't he killed a cougar with his bare hands. . .?

Or God killed it. That last thought came unbidden and it humbled him. Yes, he admitted to himself, what happened there was truly miraculous.

Maybe he should stand and testify to these good people and tell them how God had delivered him out of the mouth—or should he say paw—of the lion? Which would sound better, they both sounded so spiritual? He scoffed at himself. Why would he do that, there wasn't a testimony service going on? Did he truly want to bring glory to God or merely let folks know just how tough he was? What did God expect of him anyway? He hadn't shot the man.

"He hath shewed thee, oh man, what is good and what doth the Lord require of thee, but to do justly,

and to love mercy, and to walk humbly with thy God. Micah 6:8"

What was that? What had the preacher just said? Colt's thoughts were arrested with the scripture verse the preacher had just quoted. It came exactly at the point of his question and set him pondering on the clarity of its meaning. Do justly, love mercy, and walk humbly with God. It couldn't be any clearer than that.

Colt wrestled through the service as the preacher and the Holy Spirit shone a spotlight on his heart's motives and he came away with the notion that goodness, true goodness—goodness like Jesus' goodness—had no agenda, but sprang from a genuine desire for what was best. He also was reminded again that going to church was like finding out the preacher had been reading your mail, or so it seemed. He had missed church and visiting this little Baptist house of worship made him realize just how much. He had a lot of catching up to do.

A song of invitation was sung at the end of the message and it was with mixed feelings that Colt stepped back and watched Trudy slip past him and make her way down to the altar at the front of the church. There she knelt down and opened the door of her heart to Jesus. At least bringing her here was a good thing, he thought.

When the service was over, they accepted an invitation to dinner with the Watsons. Beatrice's husband, Zeb Watson, was a portly fellow and, compared to his wife, quiet and retiring, but seemed friendly enough. Colt and Trudy had agreed to meet them at their place in an hour, after Trudy took care of a few matters back at her boarding house, and Colt was walking her back when she stopped him with a hand on his arm.

"Thanks," she said. "Bea said she'll give me a job as a waitress, if I want it. Do you think I should take it?"

"You're welcome, and yeah, you should, at least until you figure out what it is you want to do. Do you know what you want to do?"

"Not really. Go home I guess."

"Would that be so terrible?"

"I left without telling Papa goodbye."

"Oh, the prodigal daughter, huh? I'll bet he'd be glad to see you. What about your mom?"

"She'll be glad, I'm not so sure about papa. What's a prodigal daughter?"

"The prodigal son in the Bible. Don't you know that story?"

"No, I'd like to hear it."

"Maybe we can read it at the Watsons. You got a Bible?"

"No."

"I'll see about getting you one before I leave."

"Well, if it ain't the slaphappy piss-ant." The mocking voice cut into their conversation and Colt looked up to see Latigo blocking the sidewalk in front of them.

Colt pushed Trudy against the side of the building they were passing. "Keep out of the way," he said tersely and stepped from the girl to confront the bully of the night before.

"I'm callin' ya out, piss-ant. Nobody slaps me around and gets away with it."

Colt carefully opened his coat revealing he was unarmed and said, "Sorry, I can't oblige you, I left my gun in my room, course if you step on over here I'd be happy to borrow one of yours again."

"What? You can go to and stay put, I ain't drunk now, and I'll wait. You got five minutes to fetch your hogleg and then, ready or not, I'm comin' gunnin' for ya.

"No bother, you can have me right now." Colt was a little surprised with himself. What was he thinking, he had no gun, but something about this fellow rankled him. He kept walking towards Latigo, who stood belligerently on the boardwalk, but as Colt approached he became increasingly agitated.

Funny how a free-wheeling Saturday night can turn into a slowed-down Sunday morning with the brakes on, Colt thought. He walked towards the man, and it occurred to him how shamelessly he had humiliated him the night before. Here the preacher's message was still echoing in his ears and he was ready to clean this fellow's plow again, or try. It might not be so easy with the man sober. This whole thing about motives had him a little boogered, too, if he'd admit it, so what was the best thing that could happen here? A part of him would have liked nothing better than to trim Latigo down a couple of notches and repeat last night's performance, provided he could get close enough, but that might not work so well, given the fellow's animosity towards him today.

Something in his demeanor must have telegraphed that to Latigo, for he began to backstep nervously, at Colton's approach. There was something else niggling in the back of Colt's mind, too. Something about being good to this man, and killing him or shaming him again wasn't it. Something about acting justly and being merciful and walking humbly.

"Now hold on," Latigo growled, a note of uncertainty rising in his voice. "I want you to get your shootin' iron and meet me in front of the *Jacks N' Aces*. You got five more minutes to prove you ain't the yellow-legged, four-flusher, I think you are."

Colt had nearly reached the man and said with a friendly smile, "No need for me to get my gun, I can prove that to you right now." He stuck out his hand to the fellow and watched as Latigo, reacting with surprise, stumbled backwards and quickly drew both his guns.

Ignoring the weapons leveled at him, Colt said, "Latigo, I would like to apologize for the way I humiliated you in front of everyone last night. I never should have done that and I am sorry."

Latigo's countenance clouded, a look of uncertainty coming into his eyes as he held the guns on Colt. Taking another step back he stared at the proffered hand.

"Let's just cut the funny business and get on with the draw."

"I shouldn't have slapped you and I'm sorry," Colt said again, his hand still out.

"No, you shouldn't a," Latigo said with a scowl and looked around to see who was watching. "What are you, some kind of sissy; slapping people like that?"

"No," Colt chuckled. He was relieved to see Latigo was calming down some.

"Me doing that was kinda sissified. I probably should a just plugged ya and got it over with."

"Huh!" Latigo flared back up. "If you think you can plug me, you're welcome to go ahead and

try. I ain't been lookin' at no redeye this morning."

"I know, I was just kiddin'. I can see you are a force to be reckoned with, what with your twin cannons there, and I am really sorry. I don't want to provoke you any further and besides, me and the lady here, have an invite to Sunday dinner in just a few minutes. Do you suppose we might dispense with the blood-letting? I'd hate to leak blood all over our host's front room carpet."

Latigo scratched the back of his head with the barrel of his left-hand gun, the other still pointed at Colt's brisket.

"Sunday dinner, huh? Wha'd you do, go off to Sunday School and get yourself invited over for fried chicken?"

Colt gave the perturbed cowboy a frank grin and said, "I sure did, you ought a try it sometime, it sure beats shootin' each others lights out—so how about it? You wanna plug me, or shake my hand?"

Latigo got this objective look on his face, then lowered his guns to their holsters. "I'll tell you what," he said, "I'll shake your hand. . ." he reached out and shook Colt's hand with a strong grip. . . "and I'll show you how to not hit like a sissy." With that he let go of Colt's right hand, and threw a well-aimed, left-cross, hitting him a solid blow to the chin.

There was a flash of light and the next thing Colt knew, he was sitting on his butt on the board-walk. In a daze, he looked at the hand the older cowboy was holding out to him. Slowly, he took it and allowed himself to be pulled to his feet.

"Now, that's called a left-cross and it ain't no girlie punch, whadaya think of that?"

Chapter Twenty-Three

Picking up the Pieces

Fall, 1870

School had started and Suzanne's days were filled with classroom assignments, lessons, correcting papers and students alike, and although she enjoyed the innocence and candidness of her younger students, she found that those in the upper grades, the boys in particular, would at times try her patience. She found it both interesting and annoying that the boys, when they first started noticing the girls, would invariably give negative attention to them. She frequently had complaints from the 5th and 6th grade girls that some boy or another had pulled their pigtails or stolen a ball from them on the playground. The capacity for devilment in the older boys was matched only by the open and honest devotion of the younger ones.

One little fellow, a third grader named Waldo, would bring her a shiny red apple each morning, rubbing it on his sleeve and presenting it to her before class. With a big smile and sparkling wide eyes he would just stand there expectantly waiting, following her every movement. The kids had nicknamed him Buck, for he had two large front teeth, his permanent top ones, with a wide gap in the middle. These had come in ahead of the rest of his permanent teeth and it gave him a comical look.

She would look up from her desk and say with a smile, “Thank you, Waldo.” Waldo would smile back, his face shining and nod his head, then just stand there while the rest of the kids took their seats.

“Is there anything else, Waldo?” she would say. Waldo would shake his head no, and keep right on standing there looking transfixed, his eyes never leaving her face.

“You may take your seat,” she would say and he’d just nod, smiling and stand there while the rest of the class watched, giggled, and snickered. It wasn’t until she would raise her eyebrows and say, “Now, Waldo,” that the lad would turn and go to his desk.

This routine went on for the first two or three weeks of school until one morning Waldo shyly whispered, “I love you,” and then turned and fled to his seat.

Suzanne was amazed. She was not unaware of the regard most of her students held for her, including the covert stares at her figure by the older boys, but this frank declaration of unfeigned love by one so young, gave her pause, and reminded her of the importance of her role in the lives of these sturdy, yet somewhat fragile, pioneer children. Many of them knew little of gentle affection or individualized attention, in the austere and hard life of the frontier.

Nor were her students the only ones who seemed to favor her. Since Colton’s death, not only had she garnered the attention of Sonny Saber and Clay Anderson, along with half the cowboys on the range, but both Al and Ron Trinidad had renewed their interests as well.

She spent many a Sunday afternoon with that family playing music, much to Sonny's dismay.

Of them all, Suzanne cherished her relationship with Sonny the most, for it was he who reminded her of Colt and even though she had tried to resign herself to Colton's death, there was a bittersweet connection to his memory in Sonny, a connection she knew she should let go, in that it was keeping Colt's memory far too much alive, and not being entirely fair to Sonny. He had made it perfectly clear that any relationship between the two of them would have to be on its own merit and not because of his brother's memory. But still, there were so many similarities between the two of them that Suzanne found it genuinely hard to let Colt's memory die and see Sonny in his own right. Besides, to be perfectly honest, she didn't even know if she wanted to. The ache in her heart to be loved like that—like Colt had loved her—had left her with such a sense of loss, that it seemed impossible for the dream to be fulfilled in any other.

So it was that her days that autumn were an odd mixture of work and play, of family and social functions and church life, of spending time with her would-be suitors at harvest parties and barn dances. Somehow she seemed to drift through it all as though she were only half there, more as a spectator than a participant, weighing it all against the happiness, joy and delight she had known with Colton. Most of it came up wanting in the balance.

Sonny was not oblivious to her moods and her lack of commitment—or was it indecisiveness—and it only served to more firmly entrench his desire for her to like him for himself and not because of Colt's memory. He finally opened his hand and let the bird of her affections fly to where it would, hoping that if it was to come back to him, it would be because it wanted to, not because it was compelled to.

He assumed more responsibility at the ranch, ramrodded the fall roundup, and with the moneys earned from the wild horse drive, he undertook the construction of a small, one-bedroom cottage at the far end of the alfalfa meadow, down near the creek. It was about a quarter mile from the main house. He moved into this, leaving to Tommy the upstairs room they had shared since Colt's death, although he still took his meals at his mother's table. There was speculation in some circles that he had marriage on his mind, although he never gave any indication that such was the case.

For awhile, after the time Suzanne caught Sonny in the pond and they had had that exchange, their relationship had seemed to improve. She actually sought out his company and they spent time together at church or the parties and barn dances, but when he'd driven fifty head of beef to Fort Stockton to fill an order for the Army and had missed the harvest party at the DeYoung's, Suzanne accepted an invitation to attend with Clay Anderson and the hopes Sonny held that he held a special place in her heart were dashed.

On impulse, he rode up the river to visit Margarita's place and took her for a long ride out on the prairie in the moonlight. No one knew what actually happened between them, but speculation ran high among her brothers and some others as well. By the time Suzanne got word of it, the incident was cast in the worst possible light. When next she saw him, she noticed his cool indifference to her and, feeling hurt, she responded in kind. Since then, they had seemed to drift apart.

It was then that Jessica Saber and Mabel Kluesman decided to lend a hand. They planned a picnic for the two families and a barbeque to celebrate the end of fall roundup, when they could be certain Sonny would be at the ranch.

Colt stared out the window of the stage as it rattled East, wishing that the horses could run faster even though the driver kept them in full gallop most of the time. His heart longed for Suzanne, to see her and hold her in his arms once more. *"If I ever get her there again,"* he thought, *"I will never let her go."* He'd boarded the Well Fargo couch the day after having reported to Colonel Lane at Fort Bliss. Colt gave the officer a full account of his experience in Mexico and of the illegal operation that had gone on there. The colonel took down his name and address and said they would be in touch, should they ever be able to mount an offensive against the Apache in Mexico. Now at last, Colt was on the final leg of his journey home and it seemed that the horses couldn't travel fast enough to suit his anxious heart.

The coach hit a bump and the jolt caused a stab of pain to Colt's sore jaw and he mused silently at the punch Latigo had given him. He supposed, in a way, it served him right and determined to be a little more circumspect in his meting out justice, mercy and the walk of humility—especially since the walk was with God looking over his shoulder.

He had last seen Trudy and Latigo in earnest conversation, their heads together over coffee cups. He'd said goodbye to them at Bea's Cafe and got up to leave with scarcely a farewell. Funny how things worked out, she now had a new job, a new start on life, and possibly a new beau, if Colt was any judge. He had grinned and headed for the door.

He only half listened to the idle chatter of the passengers talking of the Transcontinental Railroad that was soon to be completed and of the end of the stage line as the carrier for the U.S. Mail. One man in a brown bowler hat and shirt sleeve garters, declared, "The railroad will soon be the demise of the stage lines as a form of travel and good riddance, too." He blew dust from his prominent nose into a crumpled handkerchief to emphasize his point.

Much of the trip brought back memories of when Colt traveled this route previously and Colt thought again of Empress Carlotta and what might have become of her and of the woman's strange behavior, especially as it had concerned her jewelry. He felt sadness that he had not been able to return her crown to her, and thought of it moldering in the haunted bowels of Victorio's Peak. He wondered what other atrocities that fierce war chief had committed on the frontier since then. Maybe he should have killed him when he had the chance, although it was not for want of trying—Colt had succeeded in shooting two horses out from under the chief.

The discomforts of stage travel pressed upon him the miseries of dust and hard seats and the often unsavory character and unwashed bodies of his traveling companions. The plain fare and inconvenience of the swing and load stations, where food was gobbled in haste and passengers piled up at the facilities, was irksome, but it was still the fastest way to get home to Suzanne. Although uncomfortable and with little sleep afforded, the trip was largely without incident except for an attack by the Apache somewhere between the Van Horn's Well and the Deadman's Hole stations. Colt had climbed to the top of the racing coach with his rifle and assisted the shotgun guard in warding off the attack by successfully shooting several of the Apache off their horses. He was relieved to see the rest of the band fall back, raising their rifles and crying out in angry frustration at the deadly fire laid down by the hated white men. He couldn't swear to it, but one of them looked like Victorio, the Apache War Chief himself.

———

When Sonny rode in that Saturday afternoon, with the roundup behind him, it was to a festive occasion for all but the disgruntled cowboy and the distraught schoolteacher, for each went out of the way to avoid the other.

Sonny squatted on his heels, poking some baked beans around on his plate, aware of Suzanne sitting not far away at a homemade picnic table with her back to him. She and Becky were chatting until the later got up to refill coffee cups.

Suzanne said nothing but quietly went on eating, while Sonny shifted uncomfortably then broke the silence between them.

"How's school?' he said.

Suzanne turned halfway around, cocked her head and looked at him.

"Fine," she replied, then turned back to eating, saying no more.

"You got enough food?" he asked, feeling stupid and wondering if this conversation was even going to get off the starting line.

"Yes, thank you," Suzanne said.

Tommy was making a beeline for Suzanne when Jessica intercepted him and sent him off to the house for more dishes.

"Aw, Ma," he said, "I had something to tell Miss Kluesman."

"You never mind that," his mother said, "go and do what you are told." She caught the twinkle in Mabel Kluesman's eye, and her nod of approval.

Sonny absently watched his little brother trotting towards the house and then stood, stretched, and walked over to set his plate on the table.

"Nice seeing you again," he said to Suzanne then turned to walk off towards the barn.

"Is it?" she said.

Sonny stopped and looked back at her and saw the hurt expression on her face then scoffed, "Yeah, I know what you mean." He turned and walked off.

Mabel Kluesman was at her daughter's side before she even set down the cup she was sipping from while still watching the retreating form of the cowboy.

"Suzanne Kluesman you get up from there and go talk to that boy and don't you come back here until you get things settled between you two," her mother said.

Reluctantly, Suzanne got up and walked to the open barn door. It was dark and cooler in the barn compared to the outside, and she stopped for a moment in the open doorway, waiting for her eyes to adjust to the half light. Sonny was vigorously applying a brush to the back of a big dark stallion and didn't see her until she was nearly upon him.

"How come you walked off?' she said.

"How come you went out with Clay Anderson?" he answered

"How come you rode out on the prairie and spent the night in the moonlight with Margarita?' Her voice was heavy with hurt and accusation.

"I never spent the night on the prairie with Margarita," he said.

"Well, what did you do?' Suzanne questioned.

"Just talked," Sonny paused then added, "Wha'd you and Anderson do?"

"Just talked—talked and danced, why? I didn't know I couldn't accept his or anyone else's invitation—is there some prohibition against my doing that?"

Sonny looked at her long and hard and was about to say, *Apparently not,* but changed his mind when he saw the look of defiance on her face.

Slowly, in measured tones, he said, "If you want to be my girl, there is."

"And my beau won't go riding off into the moonlight with any pretty Mexican senoritas either," Suzanne said. "How come you did that, I thought you said you loved me?"

They stood then, staring at each other while a fly buzzed past.

"I did that because I was mad at you for going to the harvest party with Anderson—and to see whether or not you even cared what I did," he said.

"I cared—I cared a lot, especially since it was Margarita."

"Well, you've nothing to worry about on that account," he said. "She actually has a new beau from over Saint Gaul way."

"Oh!" Suzanne said. They stood looking at each other then and she knew he was expecting her to say more.

"Well?" he said.

"Well, what?" she said.

"Aw, never mind," he said in disgust and turned back to brushing Tornado. "If it ain't there, it just ain't there." Sonny turned back around and said, "Suzanne here," he held out his hand and opened it, palm up. "I set you free of any and all claims I may have ever made on you. Go and be whoever's girl you want—or not, I'm done with it."

Suzanne heard the bitterness in his voice and was overcome with a sense of sadness as well as anxiety, fearing that she had procrastinated to the point of driving away his love and devotion. She was saddened, too, that he chose to relinquish his claim on her heart. She didn't want that.

Suddenly she said, "I'll be your girl."

Sonny paused in his brushing but did not look at her.

"I don't care for your pity," he said and then resumed brushing the horse.

"No, really," Suzanne said. "I'll be your girl, Sonny, if you'll still have me."

Something in the tone of her voice arrested the cowboy and he paused to stare at her uncertainly.

"You will?" he said

"Uh hum," she said gently, and nodded to him while a slight smile tugged at the corners of her mouth. She watched his skepticism give way to wonder.

"Whooee," Sonny yelled. He stepped from the startled horse in the stall and caught Suzanne up in his arms. Lifting her off her feet, he planted a big kiss on her cheek. She patiently endured his excitement, a pleasant look on her face, as he whirled about with her in his arms.

The folks were all looking towards the barn door as they emerged from the big building. Sonny was still holding her clasped in his arms while her feet dangled a foot off the ground. Smiles and nods of approval were on every face and Becky and Tommy started to applaud as Sonny and Suzanne approached the gathering.

"Sonny, put me down, my dress is above my shoe tops," Suzanne said, feeling a little embarrassed at everyone watching.

Sonny set her on her feet and with a broad smile announced, “Folks, Suzanne just said she'll be my girl.”

There were happy congratulations and a knowing look and smile passed between Jessica and Mabel. With Suzanne blushing, Sonny led her over to the table where they sat down and Jessica gave them each a slice of apple pie, while Grant and Gunner came over and clapped the cowboy on the shoulder.

“It's about time,” his dad said.

“Now you're going to have somebody to stay with you in that sugarmoon cottage you built,” Tommy said, amidst everyone's laughter.

“That's honeymoon cottage, you goof,” Becky said with a laugh and slapped her little brother on the back.

“What's the difference?” he retorted and scowled back at her, “They're both sweet.”

“Tommy,” Jessica said, “you go to the house and bring back that jar of lemonade.” She shook her head watching the retreating form of her youngest child and said, “That boy,” then gave a reassuring look to Suzanne.

Suzanne turned to Sonny. “Well, how about it?” she said, “Are you going to show me your little place or not?”

Sonny wolfed down the last bite of his pie and then jumped up from the table. “Yes, ma'am,” he said, wiping his mouth on a sleeve and then offered her a hand to help her up.

Sonny showed her the house he had built and told her he intended to paint it white with blue shutters by the windows. He then led her out onto the west-facing porch, showed her the unfinished railings and where he would build a picket fence to keep out straying livestock.

While Suzanne was marveling at his workmanship, Sonny gently turned her towards him, pulled her into his arms and then bent to kiss her. She saw his eyes close and his face drawing near, then, for one startled moment just before Sonny's face blocked everything else from her sight, she glimpsed a figure standing in the brush staring at them.

When the stage reached the station at Comanche Springs, Colt went to the livery stable in the now-burgeoning town of Saint Gaul, a mile or so from Fort Stockton. Here, for eighty bucks, he purchased a three-year-old sorrel gelding, complete with rigging. Early the next morning, he rode out at a fast gallop on the road north towards Wade's Landing, with his heart beating faster. He had only thirty-five more miles to home and Suzanne, and just couldn't bring himself to wait for the afternoon stage. Finally, he slowed and held the stout cowpony to a ground-eating lope.

By noon, he rang the bell at Silas Wade's Ferry and paced nervously back and forth, impatient with the slow-moving flat-bottom barge. The gelding had regained his wind by the time he clattered off the gang-plank and up the bank to the staring old man, standing with his hand held out. "Hey," Silas called, "Thought you was dead."

"Not so's you'd notice," Colt hollered back as he flipped Wade a penny and a nickel.

Old Silas stared after him as he spurred his mount up the street through town. People stopped and stared as he galloped past them to Suzanne's house and bounded from the saddle. Flinging the reins over the gate post, he rushed up the pathway onto the porch and began to pound on the door.

"Suzanne, Suzanne, I'm back, Suzanne!"

Only silence greeted him, he rushed around back of the house and banged on the back door but there was still no answer.

"That's funny, nobody's here." A quick check of the barn revealed that both Suzanne's and her folk's buggies were missing. *It's Saturday*, he thought, *maybe they went out to the ranch.*

Colt ran back to his horse and swinging astride, he galloped towards home. Taking a short cut that intercepted the creek that flowed to the Pecos past their place, he found it slower going on this trail, for it twisted and wound along the bank, but it was a couple of miles shorter than going by the road.

He was almost sick from the anticipation of seeing her again, this girl he loved so. *How would he find her and would she be surprised? Of course she would, it had been nearly two, long, grueling years.* He couldn't wait, yet when he reached a spot on the creek, not far from the end of the alfalfa meadow at the home place, he reined up. He needed to wash some of the trail dust off before he saw her, and there was a small pool of clear water here.

Colt had just finished washing up and was about to mount up again, when he thought he heard voices coming from the direction of the meadow. *Somebody's over there,* he thought, *I wonder. . .* he left the horse tied to some willow and moved off towards the sound to investigate. He was surprised to see someone had built a little house on the edge of the meadow and then he found a pathway leading from the house to the creek. The building looked new and he emerged from the brush to step onto the path, and then stopped stock still.

Standing on the porch were Sonny and Suzanne. They had just emerged from the house and, to his utter amazement, he saw his brother enfold Suzanne in his arms while she lifted her face to him, and then Sonny kissed her full on the mouth.

For one terrible moment, time seemed to stop and Colt stood transfixed, his eyes riveted on the couple on the porch. *This was not possible, Sonny and Suzanne? There must be some mistake; he is kissing her like I used to do,* but no, that was the two of them alright. *Why would she be kissing Sonny—or let him kiss her at least, unless—*A sinking sensation coursed through his body like ice water in his veins. Something gave way inside of him with almost an audible sound.

They were together here at this little cottage—could it be that Suzanne had married Sonny in the time he had been gone? From deep in his soul, a desperate cry of denial began to arise in his throat as realization settled in. Sonny had taken Suzanne away from him—her cherished love, once promised to him—a love that had energized and sustained his very life, was now nestled there in the arms of his older brother. The ice water in his veins turned to a white-hot anger of rage at what could only be his brother's treachery and Suzanne's betrayal. In a long cry of desperation he screamed, "No!" and rushed towards the startled pair who turned to face him.

Sonny jumped protectively in front of Suzanne, and cried out, "My God, Colt, we thought you were dead!"

Unheeding his brother's cries, Colt stopped, his body numb and his mind in a whirl of confusion and despair. Desperately needing to blot out the vision of Suzanne, the one person who meant more than life itself to him, kissing Sonny, his hand flashed to his hip and the 44. appeared like magic in his grasp with the hammer eared back and his finger tightening on the trigger.

With a terrified cry, Suzanne screamed, "Colt, No!"

In less than a heartbeat, reason fled, and Colt fired the gun. In a benumbed fog, he saw the heavy bullet slam into his brother's chest and pass through his body to hit the girl behind him. The incredible blue azure of Suzanne's eyes registered shock just before her cry was cut short as Sonny's head snapped backward and hit her full in the face. Slowly, their lifeless bodies crumpled to the floor of the porch, blood staining the new, unpainted boards.

For one awful moment Colt stood mesmerized, shocked by the horrific deed he had done. His brother and Suzanne lay in a pool of blood before him, while his smoking gun hung from his nerveless fingers. He could hear someone shouting and running and turned in bewilderment, his mind trying to catch up with what had just happened. Rusty and Lance were running down the lane along the fence line, followed by Rebecca and Tommy.

In a daze, Colt stumbled a few steps toward the couple on the porch. Was Suzanne dead? Then, as the others drew near, he jammed his pistol into its holster and turned his back on the gruesome spectacle. Stumbling back down the path to where his horse was tied, he caught up the reins and swung into the saddle, then turned at a sound behind him. Becky was standing there, tears streaming down her face, her eyes wide in disbelief.

"Colton, why? What have you done?" she sobbed.

Totally devoid of any feeling or emotion as though all his life had just drained out of him and left him empty, he gave no answer, just turned in the saddle, spurred his horse, and rode away.

To be continued.

Excerpt from Part Four

The Kind of Western I'd Like to Read

I'd been riding for several days and time had sorta slipped by me, besides, it wasn't like my newly acquired "give-a-dash" was busted, it's just that the pony I was ridin' was lookin' side-ways back at me and I could tell he was wondering on whether or not to dump my sorry carcass and go find some grass, and that made me smile. I wondered if that smile might'a made my face crack 'cause there hadn't been anything to smile about for awhile, but the horse never paid no mind—he just snorted and stretched his neck to get me to let up on the reins.

"What's your problem?" I said, "you think filling your belly is the only thing that matters?"

The horse didn't answer, but I could tell what he was thinking and that got me to thinking, too. I hadn't eaten either, and my stomach was rubbing against my back-bone like a dead chinaberry branch against the house, tryin' to get my attention. So I started thinking about food, and of course bacon and eggs came to mind and

I could almost smell 'em. I'd left in quite a hurry and the way I had been feeling then crowded out any thoughts of food, as well as a lot of other things, for that matter, but it's funny how eatin' will catch up to you, eventually. I was sure hankerin' for some bacon and eggs.

I loosened my grip on the reins and let my horse drift towards a line of green off to my left a mile or so away. I figured maybe he smelled water, and since I wasn't really going anywheres in particular anyway, that direction seemed as good as any other and, who knows—maybe I might scare up a jackrabbit or something.

Some folks think the Llano Estacado is a barren high plains desert, devoid of life but it isn't. There's snakes and lizards and horn toads; a few miscellaneous birds, the occasional scrawny road runner or jackrabbit, with scruffy coyotes and flea-bit wolves to chase 'em. There used to be thousands of buffalo out here but they are fast disappearing, thanks to the buffalo hunters. I suppose there's still some antelope and an occasional whitetail or two hangin' round in some of the bottoms but you gotta be quieter than this clod-hopping nag I was ridin', if you're going to sneak up on one of them. Of course, it was a favorite haunt of the Comanche as well. With a menu like that, it was no wonder they were so danged mean.

I'm not sure why the Spaniards called this country the Llano Estacado, which means Staked Plains but I'd heard maybe it had to do with how they, or somebody, had tried to cross it and drove down stakes to mark the way to see how far they had come and maybe to find their way back, but I don't know if there's any truth to that or not. Personally, I suspect it got its name from the streaks of color in the cliffs and hills hereabouts, but it seems to me they'd a called it the "Streaked Plains" then, not the "Staked Plains." If it was up to me, they could a called it the "roof of hell," cause that was what it was like ridin' across it.

The horse picked its way down through a cut bank to a jumble of brush and willows that were making a gallant effort to look a little green and were fast losing the battle, then broke out into an old buffalo wallow that was several yards across and all growed up with prairie grass. From the green of it, water must have been somewhere nearby. The red horse near jerked the reins from my hand as he buried his nose in the grass. I let go, grabbed my empty canteen, swung a leg over the saddle horn and slid to the ground.

I'd no sooner hit the ground than my pony lifted his head, still chewing grass around the bit, and started for the other side of the wallow with the bridle reins tangled around his ears and hung up in his mane.

"Now hold on, hoss, you ain't fixin' to leave me afoot are ya?"

I hadn't had the horse too long and hadn't even come up with a handle for him yet, so I wasn't real certain if I could catch him should he get off to free-wheeling ways. The last thing I needed was to be left afoot out in this "no-man's land." I hurried after him, but he stopped after pressing through some buffalo berry brush and shoved his muzzle into a small pool of water. He was sucking it dry faster than the piddling little creek could fill it. He'd snort and blow through his nostrils and lift his dripping mug until another mouthful or two would flow in and then suck that up, too. I watched him until he finally had enough and turned to go back to the wallow to crop grass.

It t'wernt much of a creek, but this late in October it was a wonder it was running at all. Green scum ribboned the edges of the flow and some had dried on the exposed creek bed, while most of the mud underneath was cracked and dry from the hot sun. I walked over to the edge and found a smooth running place and stooped to fill my canteen and then took a long pull of the tepid water. I had tasted better—a lot better—and some worse. The bitter bite of alkali wasn't too bad, but there was a heavy taste of moss—or something like it. At least it was wet and there were no dried skeletons of dead critters around so I figured it was not poison.

I looked at the horse contentedly grazing and he was still on his feet so I took a couple more swallows of the water, shutting off my nose like you do so you can't taste, and had a good drink. Well—had a drink anyway, then listened to my stomach gurgle and growl and then renew its efforts on my backbone.

I refilled the canteen and started off up the little stream to see what was for supper and thought, if the Indians could hunt and gather, so could I. I decided right then and there against becoming a member of the local redskins' band, because all I could come up with was a couple of little leaf walnuts and a handful of buffalo berries, most of which I spit out as soon as I'd put 'em in when they turned to tasting like soap. They reminded me of the girl I'd fed a couple to a few years back, and since I didn't want to think about her, I chucked the rest of them into the brush and went looking for a rabbit or prairie chicken or anything with a little meat on its bones.

All I saw was a few little birds flitting about in the bushes and cheeping at me. I knew it was way past nesting season so there'd be no eggs, but I'd heard the Injuns would eat birds and remembered somewhere in the Bible it said something about a sparrow being sold for a farthing—whatever that was, and although I'd never thought about it before, what would they be buying sparrows for if it wasn't to eat them? I began to look at the little brown birds in a new light. After several unsuccessful attempts to bean one of the little critters with a rock, I gave up in frustration.

"Who wants to eat a dad-burned tweety bird anyway?" I grumbled, and continued making my way on up the creek bed.

I looked at the westering sun and thought, ma would be putting supper on the table about now and the idea of her cooking set "Mr. Stomach" to complaining again, but it was no use, I for sure was never going to stick my feet under that table again.

I suppose I would a gone hungry for another night if I hadn't near stepped on that rattler. It struck but, surprising myself, to say nothin' of scarin' the pea-waddin' out of me, I was even quicker and all's it got was a mouthful of dust before I smashed its head with a rock and stood watching the twisting writhing body until it lay still.

I hesitated. They say, "necessity is the mother of invention," but I'd never eaten rattler before. I'd heard it tasted like chicken. Pops used to say that. He was the grizzled old ranch hand that'd been on the place since before I was even born and he always sounded like he knew what he was talkin' about—he wouldn't steer me wrong and I like chicken. I picked up the snake, pulled my belt knife, and lopped off its head, then carried it back down to the spot where I'd left the horse.

The red horse lifted his head when he saw me and chuckled in his throat, then went back to cropping grass.

"Whadya think? I'd done, gone off and left ya?" I said. He just kept right on eating—like a horse and I figured, *that figures.* I skinned out the rattler, cleaned the carcass and cut the meat into several long pieces and washed them well in the creek. Finding some dry mesquite and a bunch of dead leaves, I soon kindled a little fire and waited impatiently while the meat broiled on green willow sticks that I had stuck in the ground around the blaze. I guess it was more black than golden-brown when I finally had them cooked to my satisfaction—I wanted to be sure it was done since you can't be to careful cooking up snake. I decided to think of it as chicken instead so it would be more appetizing. I took a skinny piece of "chicken" and gingerly bit it off the willow stick. It was hot and tasted mostly like—well—like burnt chicken with too much mesquite smoke on it. The next thing I knew, there was no more "skinny chicken" left and my stomach was smiling.

I stomped out the rest of the fire and splashed some water on the ashes, then walked over to where the red horse was and was just about to grab hold of the bridle when he head-shied and lunged away from me a few steps.

"What's the matter with you? Come here."

The horse dipped his nose to the grass snuffling while I walked over. Once again he moved off, trotting to the opposite side of the wallow.

"You jughead," I said, "I was just going to take that bridle off so you wouldn't have to eat with the bit in your mouth, but have it your way." I walked back to the stream looking for a shady spot and thinking about cooling off. "I wonder if there's a hole in this stream big enough to get wet in?" I said it out loud and the horse nickered back at me. "You never mind, I ain't talkin' to you."

I decided to explore up the creek a little farther, the country seemed a little flatter off that direction, and I suppose I traveled a half mile or so up the creek bottom before I found what I was looking for. As it turned out, I found a whole lot more than what I was lookin' for

First of all, I found a nice pool of water, mostly covered over with green scum. It was backed up behind a manmade rock and mud dam that was a couple of feet high with a stone lined spillway on one side. Someone had planted a couple of chinaberry trees near what had once been a little log cabin but now lay in a charred and weathering ruin with wild mistletoe and morning glory vines running all over. A few scraggly fruit trees struggled for life, the dry irrigation ditches at their base a mute testimony to their hardiness. I was delighted to find a few red and yellow apples hanging from some branches on a couple of them that were still alive. Hurrying over, I picked a big red one, rubbed it on the front of my shirt and bit into it.

"Lord, that's good," I said with a feeling of gratitude but no thought of a prayer, while the cool juice from the crunchy fruit ran down my throat. I had forgotten just how good an apple could be.

I walked around what had been the yard of the homestead and read the mute testimony of what had happened here. "I'll bet the Comanche found them and that was all she took. Too bad, they had a nice start here." Walking around to the upstream side of the place, I found just beyond the stunted fruit trees, what had been a garden area and nestled down in the grass was a whole patch of both watermelons and muskmelons. A tiny trickle of water still ran a course beside the vines before it eventually ran off and dried up in the sun-baked earth. Some of the melons appeared lush and ripe.

I hauled out my belt knife and hacked a big, long watermelon from off the vine and packed it over to a grassy spot in the shade of the chinaberry, sat down and then sliced it open. Now I like watermelon, and I particularly like watermelon on a hot, dry, dusty day like this one was. In fact I can't think of nothing more satisfying than a red, juicy, cold slice of melon on the best of days, let alone this one. It felt like the ultimate reward for trekking, Lord knows how long, across that ol' Llano and when I popped open that melon and carved out that juicy, red, heart, I practically foundered in the sweetness of it, and something revived in me a little and I decided maybe there were some good things left worth living for, even if people were no dashed good.

"Watermelon's good," I sighed, "it won't let you down." I scoffed then at my own cynicism—I'd been reduced to looking to watermelon for the meaning of life. 'Course I had thought at one time there was a whole lot more, but I'll be jiggered if I was going to let any of that stuff intrude now. This was just too good—too sweet. I squelched the rising ache in my gut and concentrated on the sparkling, pink drops of watermelon juice running down my arm and dripping from my elbow.

After a while, I stood to my feet and eyed a spot of clear water out in the middle of the pond and, shucking my clothes, I pushed aside the green scum and waded out to float in the water and rinse off the sticky watermelon juice. The water was cool and refreshing and I soaked for over an hour, just back-floating and watching clouds while occasionally squirting little geysers of water up in the air through my teeth and seeing 'em splash back down. I was probably a little colder than I wanted to be when I finally sloshed to shore and stared down with some embarrassment at the fancy tooled leather gun belt with it's silver studded holster and the pearl handled Colt. There was the matching silver concho belt, hatband and fancy silver spurs on my new black boots piled next to my black jeans and shirt, and they were all a reminder of the anticipation and impression I'd vainly hoped to make. I felt my ears burn and the sinking in my gut for the thousandth time, before I could shut it down and get back to recalling the merits of watermelon. Watermelon and a cool swimming hole. . . and red apples. Red apples and diamondback chicken. I scoffed at myself and turned to put on my duds.

End Notes

Chapter six:

1 Rocky Mountain News editorial, Dec. 30,1864.
2 Comanche for dog
3 Comanche for rabbit.
4 Comanche for pig.
5 Comanche for snout.

CPSIA information can be obtained
at www.ICGtesting.com
Printed in the USA
FSOW02n0905180917
38888FS